HUMAN REMAINS IN ARCHAEOLOGY

Human remains in archaeology

A handbook

Charlotte A Roberts

Practical Handbooks in Archaeology No 19
Council for British Archaeology 2009

First published in 2009 for the Council for British Archaeology
St Mary's House, 66 Bootham, York YO30 7BZ

British Library Cataloguing in Publication Data

A catalogue card for this book is available from the British Library

ISBN 978-1-902771-75-5

Typeset by Carnegie Book Production, Lancaster
Printing by Cambridge University Press

The publisher acknowledges with gratitude a grant from English Heritage towards the
cost of publication.

Front cover: Crouched Anglo-Saxon burial at Bamburgh Castle, Northumberland (with
permission of Sarah Groves and the Bamburgh Castle Project)
Back cover: top: periodontal disease (recession of the jaw bone and exposure of the
tooth roots) of the jaws of a medieval individual, reflecting underlying gum disease
(Charlotte Roberts)
middle: osteoarthritis (joint degeneration) of a hip joint in a medieval individual
(Charlotte Roberts)
bottom: retained deciduous tooth in the upper jaw of an early medieval individual
from Kent (Charlotte Roberts)

To Stewart, Joss and Cassie, with love

Contents

List of figures

List of tables

Acknowledgements

There are many people to thank in the production of this book; without them all, it could never have happened. However, any errors remain my own. The following are thanked:

Jane Thorniley-Walker and Catrina Appleby, both at the CBA, for all their help, guidance, and encouragement for writing this book.

Jacqueline McKinley (Wessex Archaeology), for reviewing the whole first draft of the book and providing me with an invaluable perspective from 'contract archaeology' (she was also was key to the sections on cremation and cremation burials).

Simon Mays (English Heritage), Myra Giesen (University of Newcastle), Anwen Caffell, Chris Caple, Rebecca Gowland, Tina Jakob, and Andrew Millard (Durham University), and Mary Lewis (University of Reading), for reading first drafts of chapters. Tina Jakob also provided me with help on various aspects of the logistics of writing the book. Chris Gerrard, Richard Hingley, Sarah Semple, Mark White, Pam Graves, and Tom Moore (Durham University), for guiding me to appropriate references for disposal of the dead in different time periods. Eileen Murphy (Belfast University), for guidance on Northern Ireland legislation. Keri Brown and Abigail Bouwman (Manchester University), for advice about sampling on site for ancient DNA analysis; Simon Mays (English Heritage), for opinions on sampling for ancient DNA on and off site; and Myra Giesen (Newcastle University), for information on NAGPRA. Dave Hunt (Smithsonian Institution, Washington DC) and Susan Pfeiffer (University of Toronto) provided useful guidance on the Terry and Grant Skeletal Collections, respectively. I would finally like to give special thanks to Bill White (Museum of London), for his unending patience with questions related to this book that I have asked and he has always answered.

Images and permissions for use were kindly provided by: Pia Bennike (University of Copenhagen), Rick Steckel (Ohio State University), Brian Ayres (Norfolk Museums and Archaeology Service), Stephen White, Sarah Macdonald, and Jay Jopling (White Cube), Richard Annis, Archaeological Services (Durham University) and Yvonne Beadnell, Alex Bentley, Anwen Caffell, Keith Dobney, Sarah Groves, Tina Jakob, Jaime Jennings, Jenny Jones, Bob Layton, Andrew Millard, Catherine Panter-Brick, Mike Richards, Chris Scarre, Jeff Veitch (all from Durham University), Dave Evans (Humber Archaeology Partnership), Don Brothwell (University of York), Simon Fowler, Bernardo Barriaza (Universidad de Tarapacá, Arica, Chile), Andrew Chamberlain, Patrick Mahoney, and Mike Parker Pearson (University of Sheffield), Abigail Bouwman, Terry and Keri Brown (University of Manchester), Tim Sutherland, Alan Boyde (Barts and the

London School of Medicine and Dentistry, Queen Mary, University of London), Megan Brickley and Martin Smith (University of Birmingham), George Maat (University of Leiden), Anne Stone (Arizona State University), Albert Zink (EURAC Research), Andreas Nerlich (University of Munich), Jacqueline McKinley (Wessex Archaeology), Carole Rawcliffe (University of East Anglia), Margaret Cox and Roland Wessling (Inforce, Cranfield University), Robin Daniels and Rachel Grahame (Tees Archaeology), Susan Ward, Bill White and Nikki Braunton (Museum of London), Andy Chopping (Museum of London Archaeological Services), Richard Hall (York Archaeological Trust), Amanda Forster (Birmingham Archaeology), Cathy Patrick (CgMs Consulting, Birmingham), Rosalie David and Malcolm Chapman (University of Manchester), Victor Mair (Pennsylvania State University), Kim Dung and Lorna Tilley (Australian National University), Mary Lewis (University of Reading), Dave Lucy (University of Lancaster), Frank Ruhli (University of Zurich), Chris Knüsel (University of Exeter), Alan Lupton and Louise Loe (Oxford Archaeology), Jane Hughes (Hunterian Museum), Rod MacKey (University of Hull), Jenny Glazebrook (East Anglian Archaeology), Anna Smith (Wellcome Trust Medical Photographic Library), Luigi Capasso (University of Chieti), Mario Castro (University of Chile, Santiago) and Stewart Gardner.

Also thanked for permissions are: BABAO, Norfolk Historic Environment, Norfolk Museums and Archaeological Services, Cambridge University Press, American Journal of Physical Anthropology and Wiley, White Cube (London), Oxford Archaeology, Humber Archaeology Partnership, Biological Anthropology Research Centre (Archaeological Sciences, Bradford University), Trustees of the Hunterian Museum at the Royal College of Surgeons, Bamburgh Castle Research Project, Tees Archaeology, Picture Library at the Museum of London, Museum of London Archaeological Services, York Archaeological Trust, CgMs Consulting, Birmingham, The Manchester Museum (University of Manchester), Towton Battlefield Archaeological Survey Project, Wellcome Trust Library, Elsevier, and Birmingham Archaeology.

I am much obliged to Sebastian Payne of English Heritage for guidance on the recent changes to the law and burials in England and Wales.

I offer especial thanks to the populations of East Witton and Finghall, North Yorkshire, for making my sabbatical years so enjoyable and providing me with a change from sitting in front of a PC! Stewart as ever gave tremendous support, and Joss and Cassie reminded me sometimes that taking them for walks or runs was more important than writing books.

Preface by Don Brothwell

At the age of ten years, I was shown a collection of human bones dredged up at a gravel quarry on the River Trent, near Nottingham. After that, I was hooked. Over the years, the enthusiasm for skeletal studies shown by hundreds of archaeology students and field archaeologists has demonstrated to me that there is a universal interest in such remains from the past. Indeed, if the many undergraduate skeletal dissertations and postgraduate PhDs are anything to go by, then calcified tissue is a potent but quite harmless drug. Addiction is pleasant but mild, and there are no serious side effects, unless it is the lifelong enthusiasm to study such remains.

In Britain, the excavations of barrows and cemeteries by the mid-19th century had stimulated a specialist interest in human skeletal material, and indeed by 1865, Drs J Davis and J Thurnam had published a large and impressive volume on the early British, from the Neolithic to Saxon times. By the turn of the century, the statistician Karl Pearson at University College London, had established something of a centre for the study of human remains, especially skulls, from all over the world, but principally from British and Egyptian sites (numerous analyses appearing in the journal *Biometrika*). At this time also, Sir Grafton Elliot Smith and colleagues were consolidating the field of palaeopathology, particularly by reference to large Egyptian cemeteries and mummies. Yet surprisingly, there were very few academic positions that allowed such work to be done, and those who were active were usually employed in biology or medicine, not archaeology. In fact, it is only in my lifetime that there has been a shift of this research into mainstream archaeology, and the creation of teaching and research positions in this discipline.

The focus of this book is the analysis and interpretation of human remains, and in this respect, Charlotte Roberts has more experience than most of us. In this handbook for archaeologists in Britain and beyond, she provides a broad review of information related to the analysis of ancient skeletons. It is well illustrated, up-to-date, and ideal as a compact reference work. It will be of value in the field or laboratory, and will help to make sure that studies on our human past are biologically complete. Fifty years ago, reporting on human remains consisted of some measurement, including stature, and brief comments on the health status of each individual. But now we see that far more detail can be provided, and that the more complete it is, the more we can get an intimate feel for the lives of our ancestors. Has physique changed through time? Did earlier groups suffer from environmental stress, dietary, or otherwise? Was cancer a problem in the past to the extent that it is today? Buried house foundations or pottery have provided information on material culture, but the bones and teeth have revealed hard evidence of the total biocultural impact on people, and the extent to which they survived.

A few decades ago, the scientific study of human remains was generally far more respected as revealing information of value in reconstructing the lives of earlier populations. But the situation is changing, I believe for the worse, as regards our freedom to study and curate peoples of the past. Politics and poorly discussed matters of repatriation are taking excavated human remains out of the scholarly jurisdiction of archaeology and placing them in the hands of representatives of groups who sometimes have far less understanding of the long-term value of these ancient dead. None of us objects to the handing over of human remains with direct links to living families, but where there is no clear ancestral link, then it would seem preferable to include archaeological specialists with other interested parties to make considered decisions that can secure the preservation and study of human remains, whilst also being mindful of the respectful treatment of those ancient people. Respectful preservation and curation are very reasonable alternatives to 'repatriation' and destruction or reburial. The more the archaeological community, and people at large, know of the great range of valuable bioarchaeological information to be derived from these studies, the more a sensible compromise might eventually be achieved with various repatriation groups and national legal rulings on reburial.

This handbook is, without doubt, a contribution to understanding why the ancient dead, whilst deserving our respect, can nevertheless help to bring the past to life. It is therefore with pleasure that I recommend this book to the archaeological community and general reader.

Don Brothwell, 2008

CHAPTER ONE

Why study human remains from archaeological sites?

Interest in human remains has probably never been so great as at present
(Waldron 2001, 10)

1.1 Introduction and scope

Why is it that human remains from archaeological sites so fascinate us? Why are programmes on television concerned with archaeological and forensic finds of human remains so alluring? Why do people flock to look at human remains being excavated if they get the chance? Why do courses that instruct about the study of human remains in our universities attract so many interested students, and why are displays of human remains so popular in museums? It is probably because we, as humans ourselves, can relate better to a skeleton or mummy than to a pot that has been excavated from an archaeological site. We all possess a skeleton and we appear to want to know more about it.

This book is aimed at a very wide audience: students studying the archaeological evidence for human remains in universities, at colleges and in schools, or even at day, evening, and summer schools; field archaeologists; academics; students from other disciplines such as history; and the interested public. By its very nature it is a 'handbook' and covers a wide range of information, but it does not aim to cover everything you ever wanted to know about the study of human remains but was afraid to ask – at relevant points you are directed to other, more detailed sources for further insights. This book will give you a flavour of the subject and will touch upon all relevant areas; while its focus is on Britain, there are also sections that delve into other parts of the world where a comparative approach is seen as appropriate and helpful in discussing certain subjects.

1.2 Structure of the book

This handbook is divided into eight chapters. Chapter 1 provides a context from which the other chapters develop. It describes how our discipline fits into the study of archaeology (and anthropology) as a whole, how its study has progressed through time, and the main influences on its development. Additionally, it provides an overview of the major projects currently being undertaken and their value to our understanding of our ancestors; it tackles the main problems that practising bioarchaeologists encounter; and finally it looks at how a bioarchaeological approach is needed to enable us to appreciate the evidence we record in human remains within its social context in the past.

Chapter 2 focuses on ethical concerns and the study of human remains. While not as much of a concern in Britain, in other parts of the world the repatriation and reburial of human remains are more common. Beyond this international perspective, the main focus of the chapter is on the following: the circumstances in which human remains are excavated; how ethical concerns are projected to the excavation, laboratory, and museum situation; how religious feelings about the subject differ; and whether media and museum use of human remains is useful and appropriate.

Chapter 3 discusses the various ways that the dead have been disposed of in the past and the different funerary contexts we see in Britain from prehistory to the post-medieval period. The methods of disposal employed are also analysed from the perspective of archaeological survival and ultimate research value. The chapter also looks at the different preservation environments in which human remains have been found and the factors that might affect survival to excavation and analysis – dry and hot, dry and cold, tropical and wet environments are discussed, along with special disposals such as in caves and shell middens. Chapter 4 focuses on how human remains are excavated, processed following excavation (cleaning, drying, marking, packaging), and how they may be conserved and curated.

Chapter 5 is the first of three chapters looking at the analysis of the human remains (skeletal remains rather than preserved bodies): here we consider the structure of human bones and teeth; how to identify different bones and teeth; how to tell the difference between human and non-human bones and teeth; how to assess the sex and age of an adult and non-adult skeleton; how to look at the demography of a sample population; how measurements and non-metric traits help us to look at variation between people and populations; and how we might analyse all the data. Chapter 6 deals with how disease is recognised in the skeleton, as well as what other sources of evidence might be used to reconstruct the history of disease. It explores some of the limitations of study and goes on to give examples of themes that may be explored in palaeopathology. Chapter 7 considers other methods beyond just 'looking' at the skeleton. Histological, radiographic, stable isotope and ancient DNA (aDNA) analyses, and dating techniques are considered as methods for answering specific questions about the past.

Finally, Chapter 8 looks at the future and what that might hold for the excavation and study of human remains from archaeological sites. It also suggests some of the subjects with most potential for further research and exploration.

1.3 Archaeology, anthropology, and human remains

If a journey around the world was made to establish how the study of human remains fits into archaeological/anthropological establishments such as university departments, contract archaeology, and museums, it is likely that a different picture would emerge from each country. This obviously impacts on how common and popular the discipline is within that country and how much money is focused on this sort of work. For example, in the United States where archaeology is a sub-discipline of anthropology (the study of humans, past to present) along with physical anthropology, studying archaeological human remains can be reasonably common as most departments of anthropology employ a physical anthropologist. In Britain, where archaeology departments are the norm in universities, there are far fewer people employed as physical anthropologists within those departments, and thus undergraduate and postgraduate students do not necessarily have the chance to study human remains during their archaeology and archaeological science courses; this has implications for those archaeology graduates who may end up excavating a cemetery site not having the requisite skills and knowledge. Likewise, the few anthropology departments we do have (relative to archaeology) in Britain all have physical anthropologists employed but they rarely teach about archaeologically derived human remains analysis, focusing more on early hominid remains, questions of human evolution, and non-human primates.

Thus, in North America (United States and Canada), the discipline is more developed and interdisciplinary than it is in Britain, for example, although times are changing. There are more physical anthropologists employed in universities and in contract archaeology now, even though skeletal remains have been excavated for a long time in the latter. However, in the museum environment, this situation is not as commonly replicated (Bill White pers comm, June 2007). In Britain, therefore, there is a wide variety of organisations who employ people to study human remains; these include universities, contract archaeology units, museums, and charity organisations such as the National Trust, along with other archaeological organisations such as English Heritage. There are also many different groups of people who might work on human remains and these include undergraduate, masters, and PhD students at universities (practical sessions during their course, and for dissertations), academic teaching and research staff (using skeletal remains for teaching and for producing research papers and books), bioarchaeologists working in contract archaeology (producing skeletal reports), museum staff (producing skeletal reports and placing human remains on display), and interested amateurs who might be involved in excavating cemetery sites and processing the skeletal material.

Working to represent these many people and organisations are official professional bodies such as the American Association of Physical Anthropologists (http://www.phys.anth.org/), the British Association for Biological Anthropology and Osteoarchaeology (BABAO: Figure 1) (http://www.babao.org.uk/), the European Anthropological Association (http://eaa.elte.hu/), and the Paleopathology Association (http://www.paleopathology.org); these bodies bring together members for meetings and provide guidance documents. They also act as a focus for extending knowledge through publications and conferences, along with dealing with particular issues that arise.

At the same time, there are some very large and ambitious projects being carried out on extensive samples of human remains in order to answer specific questions. These projects likewise bring together many people globally. A project entitled the Global History of Health, based at Ohio State University in the United States (http://global.sbs.ohio-state.edu/), is aiming to make a comparative analysis of health through time between European countries based on thousands of skeletons. It is very much an interdisciplinary project where a variety of people from different specialisms, apart from physical anthropology, are involved, ranging from geography, through history, to archaeology. This project follows that of the Western Hemisphere Health Project, where a similar, although less detailed, study revealed that health declined through time in all parts of the Americas, ie as social complexity developed (Steckel and Rose 2002: Figure 2). Two projects based at the Museum of London's Centre for Human Bioarchaeology (www.museumoflondon.org.uk/English/Collections/OnlineResources/), now ending after several years, have focused on creating a database of all the museum's skeletal remains as a base for future researchers, and also analysing the several thousand skeletons from the late medieval site of Spitalfields Market. Collective studies of large samples of skeletons appear now to be increasing in Britain and we can see the results of some of these studies (eg Roberts and Cox 2003). There are also recent excavations of hundreds of skeletons in places like Leicester and Hereford, as well as in London, generating wonderful samples from which large amounts of data can be collected. The Spitalfields Market in London alone has generated 10,516 skeletons (Bill White pers comm, June 2007), and will provide a very important (and likely unique) skeletal dataset which may not be seen again in my lifetime (Connell *et al* in press).

Of importance too for the discipline is the availability of relatively modern collections of skeletons which were assembled early in the 20th century for research purposes and have associated documentation; these exist in different parts of the world. The sex of the individual, age at death, height, ethnicity, and cause of death are recorded for each skeleton. While recognising that 20th-century people in North America and Portugal, for example, are far removed from the average Romano-British person in terms of their diet and lifestyle, these collections are particularly key to developing methods of analysis for archaeologically derived skeletons where no personal documentation exists. In North America there exist three main collections that are regularly used: that of the Hamann Todd in the Natural History Museum, Cleveland, Ohio (http://www.cmnh.org/); the Robert J Terry Collection in the National Museum of Natural History, Smithsonian Institution, Washington DC (Hunt and Albanese 2005; http://www.nmnh.si.edu/anthro/cm/phys_intro.htm); and the Grant Collection in the Department of Anthropology, University of Toronto (http://www.chass.utoronto.ca/anthropology/). There are other collections, less well known but

Figure 1: The logo of the British Association of Biological Anthropology and Osteoarchaeology (with permission of BABAO)

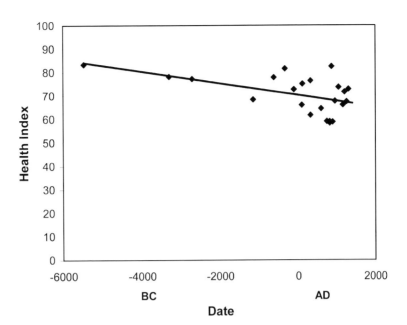

Figure 2: The Western Hemisphere Health Project Health Index showing the decline in health through time in the Americas (from Steckel and Rose 2002, and with permission of Rick Steckel and Cambridge University Press)

equally useful at the Forensic Anthropology Center, University of Tennessee in the US (http://www.web.utk.edu/~anthrop/FACResources.html): the William M Bass Forensic Skeletal Collection and the William M Bass Donated Skeletal Collection, along with the W Montagne Cobb Collection at Howard University, Washington DC (http://www.coas.howard.edu). Likewise, in Portugal there exists the Coimbra Identified Collection curated in the Department of Anthropology, Coimbra University (http://www.uc.pt/en/cia), and the Luis Lopez Collection at the Museo Bocage in Lisbon (Cardoso 2006a). It is rare to have available archaeological collections of skeletons with associated information but one such does exist in Britain and is currently curated in the Department of Palaeontology at the Natural History Museum in London. The crypt at Christ Church, Spitalfields in London was excavated in the 1980s and contained over 900 individuals in varying states of preservation. Many were buried in coffins, and 383 individuals were identified by plates on their coffins which contained information on name, age at death, and date of death. Additionally a lot of individuals could be traced in historical documentation associated with the population buried there (Molleson and Cox 1993). It is therefore possible using collections of skeletons, like those described, to test methods of analysis such as those used for adult age at death estimation to see if researchers are achieving an accurate assessment.

1.4 Definitions

There have been many terms used to describe those who study human remains from archaeological sites, and definitions vary around the world. In fact, there have often been heated debates about what term should be used, especially in Britain! Here are some of the titles used: physical or biological anthropologist (these terms come from anthropology and refer to the study of humans past to present, so from the earliest hominids to living people, witness the long-running American Association of Physical Anthropologists – see later); palaeopathologist (strictly refers to one who studies only disease in human remains – witness the United States-based Paleopathology Association – this term is often used incorrectly in Britain to refer to someone who studies human remains in general); osteoarchaeologist (could be applied to one who studies human and/or non-human remains in their archaeological context, as seen in contributions to the journal *International Journal of Osteoarchaeology*); osteologist (somebody who studies bones per se); human skeletal biologist; and bioarchaeologist – in North America bioarchaeology would refer to the study of human remains only, but in Britain would usually encompass the study of any biological remains, again in their archaeological context – plants, animals, and humans. In Britain there is also the Association of Environmental Archaeologists (http://www.envarch. net) whose members work on archaeologically derived biological materials, but generally speaking there is not much of a focus on archaeological human remains within this Association. There is also a tendency for people working with human remains to be addressed as a forensic 'scientist' or 'archaeologist' even though they are not dealing with forensic contexts! One can imagine the confusion; in fact our national organisation in Britain is actually called the British Association of Biological Anthropology and Osteoarchaeology because the membership felt that one term could not be used to describe all the disciplines of its members.

In this book these terms will be used interchangeably, as appropriate, but the author currently prefers the term *bioarchaeology*. This reflects the aim of ultimately studying human remains from archaeological sites, that of approaching it from a multidisciplinary perspective, and integrating the biological data from the human remains with archaeological and other data, as appropriate, in order to understand our ancestors' lives. While the term bioarchaeology arose independently in North America and Britain during the 1970s, it has always had different meanings. Originally in Britain, Clark used it to refer to animal remains (1972) but, as we have seen, it can now encompass all biological evidence from archaeological sites (Buikstra 2006a). In the United States the term arose in 1976, and was coined at the Southern Anthropological Society Annual Meeting (Buikstra 1977). Here it was reserved only for the study of human remains but the emphasis was on a multidisciplinary approach and problem solving rather than descriptive studies.

1.5 History of study of human remains from archaeological sites

While the United States has recently documented in detail the history of the study of bioarchaeology (Buikstra and Beck 2006), such a recent volume has not appeared in Europe, or indeed Britain. Nevertheless it is possible to summarise how the study of human remains has developed in Europe, but more specifically in Britain. By the second half of the 19th century the field of physical anthropology had been recognised in Europe (Shapiro 1959), with a surgeon in France called Paul Broca (1873), and a physician and anatomist in Germany, Rudolph Virchow (1872), advancing research on human remains. The study of disease in bones had already been established by Esper (1774) when he identified a cancerous bone in a cave bear, but it was not until the early 20th century that a French/German physician called Marc Armand Ruffer (1859–1917) coined the term 'palaeopathology', along with making the first studies of palaeoepidemiology, or looking at the relationship of various factors determining the frequency and distribution of diseases in a population – ie trying to understand why specific diseases appear (1921). The late 19th century, however, also fixed the stereotype of the physical anthropologist frequently measuring skulls, probably one that remains with many today, especially with the added image of the white coat.

In Britain early work in physical anthropology concentrated on measuring bones, including skulls. Karl Pearson and Geoffrey Morant contributed research on the evolutionary significance of Neanderthals and the origin of modern humans during the late 19th and first half of the 20th century. A considerable interest in the study of skulls in particular developed over the course of the 19th century (eg Davis and Thurman 1865). As early as 1800, British scientists put forward the theory that there was a single human biological species, united by a common humanity (Stepan 1982). However another school of thought called 'polygenism' felt that human 'races' were separated from each other by mental, moral, and physical differences – ie species. In an increasingly imperial age, theories about humankind's origins did not remain objective and became associated with beliefs about the superiority of 'whites' over 'non-whites'. During the 19th century, data were collected on different 'races' and by the century's close 'race' was firmly established in popular opinion and science in Britain, although quite largely as a concept to justify political stances. Between 1900 and 1925 the eugenics movement took 'race science' theories to their most extreme culmination – aiming to 'improve' the quality of the human population by selective breeding for desired characteristics. The movement became a worldwide and frightening phenomenon that ultimately provided pseudo-scientific justifications for aggressive militarism and racial 'cleansing'.

Despite the dangerous direction taken by much of the work on skulls, there were some very real advances. Karl Pearson took a statistical approach, examining large samples of skulls, and explored the belief that evolution progressed by small and continuous variations (Stepan 1982). He criticised some research because of the use of small sample sizes (his work on stature and on the characteristics of the bones of the English skeleton reflects the large samples he worked on: Pearson 1899; Pearson and Bell 1919). He also attacked the non-standardisation of contemporary methods of analysis, and he highlighted how the environment could affect the measurements recorded (all issues remaining today in the study of human remains from archaeological sites, and not always being tackled). Pearson (fortunately) decided that there was no 'typical' Englishman, there being much variation in people's appearances, but his ideas were not taken seriously.

Keith (1924) published on a range of subjects based on his study of human remains from archaeological sites, for example, early cave deposits, and Parsons and Box (1905) looked at a method of ageing adult remains using cranial suture closure, or what happens to the joints between the bones of the skull as a person ages. Cave looked at various subject matters, including trepanation (the surgical production of a hole in the skull: Cave 1940), and the anatomist Dawson worked on mummified remains from Egypt (1927), along with another anatomist, Wood-Jones (Elliott-Smith and Wood-Jones 1910), who studied skeletons from Egypt. Oakley was involved with the famous work on the dating of the Piltdown skull found in Sussex in 1912. The supposed earliest human in western Europe was accepted by people such as Elliott-Smith, but later, through fluorine-dating in the 1950s, was found to be found a hoax and very recent in date. Oakley also studied ancient brain tissues and trepanation (Oakley *et al* 1959). In the 1960s Berry and Berry, anatomists, developed methods for studying normal variation in the skeleton from their studies of mice (1967); the features or traits identified are not abnormal or pathological, but may be present in some people and not others. At that time it was believed that they were all inherited through families but now they are considered to be the result of a mix of inheritance and environmental factors such as physical activity. Clearly, during the 19th and early 20th century in Britain (and Europe) there was a strong focus on looking at features that classified people into groups.

The late 20th century saw some important developments in Europe whereby more population-based innovative work became increasingly common. For example, Vilhelm Møller-Christensen, a doctor in Denmark, excavated and analysed some large cemeteries, including a medieval leprosy hospital, and contributed much to bioarchaeology (Møller-Christensen 1958; Bennike 2002: Figure 3). Likewise, in Sweden, Gejvall analysed in detail a medieval cemetery from a churchyard at Westerhus (1960). In Britain two key people advanced the study of human remains from archaeological sites, Calvin Wells (1908–78), a doctor from Norfolk with an interest in archaeology, and Don Brothwell (b 1933) who combined expertise in archaeology and anthropology with knowledge of both geology and zoology. Although they would both have been unaware of the term bioarchaeology in their early years of working with human remains, both did take a bioarchaeological approach, and Don Brothwell continues to do so (see Roberts 2006 for more details of these two key people; Dobney and O'Connor 2002 for a tribute to Brothwell's work; and Hart 1983 for a full list of Wells' publications). The breadth of their work is considerable although neither had careers and training akin to the majority of people working in the field today in Britain. Comparing their contributions, Brothwell clearly published on a much wider range of biological materials than Wells (detailed in Roberts 2006), including human (Brothwell 1981) and non-human remains (Baker and Brothwell 1980) and bodies such as that of Lindow Man, the bog body from Cheshire (Brothwell 1986).

In their early years Brothwell and Wells both produced reports on human remains from archaeological sites (eg Brothwell 1967; Wells 1982) and made specific studies on individual skeletons (eg Brothwell 1961; Wells 1965). The latter

Figure 3: A view of the late medieval Naestved cemetery in Denmark (a), and of Vilhelm Møller-Christensen (b) excavating (with permission of Pia Bennike)

type of study has been prominent ever since in Britain, as seen in Mays' (1997a) review of the study of palaeopathology in Britain. Unlike in North America, population-based contextual studies which answer specific questions about our ancestors were slow to develop in Britain, and a recent review by the author shows that since Mays' paper in 1997 (a), little has changed. Nevertheless, Calvin Wells, particularly, did attempt to interpret his data with reference to archaeological context, even though some of his 'stories' took his data well beyond what it could support! One could argue that many television programmes featuring skeletons from archaeological sites have also failed to recognise the scientific limitations of the data in the desire to produce an exciting scenario! However, Wells 'put flesh on the bones' and made 'his' skeletons come alive. One could argue that this is what the study of archaeology should be about – people!

Keith Manchester, another doctor (Bradford, West Yorkshire), followed in the same vein as Calvin Wells and published many works including skeletal reports for archaeologists on excavated cemeteries (eg 1978), and papers focusing on individual skeletons with interesting diseases (eg 1980), and on infectious diseases (eg 1984). His book on the 'Archaeology of Disease' (1983) is now in its third edition (Roberts and Manchester 2005), and his research on the bioarchaeology of leprosy has been globally very influential. Tony Waldron (University College, London) and the late Juliet Rogers (University of Bristol) have also made a significant contribution to the archaeological study of human remains in Britain, particularly with their work on the recording, diagnosis, and interpretation of the joint diseases found in skeletal remains such as osteoarthritis (Rogers and Waldron 1995). Both scholars also came from a medical background. Waldron has produced an excellent book on understanding how to deal with data collected on human remains (1994), and reminded us that inferring occupation from bone changes in the skeleton is not an easy task, even though there is much interest and work on the subject (Waldron and Cox 1989). Simon Hillson (University College, London) has made a large impact on the study of both human and non-human teeth from archaeological sites through his books (1986, 1996 a and b); Andrew Chamberlain (University of Sheffield) has advanced the field of palaeodemography in particular (2006); the late Trevor Anderson (Canterbury Archaeological Trust) published on a wide range of subjects (eg 2000); and Simon Mays' (English Heritage) contribution to bioarchaeological studies has been considerable (eg Mays *et al* 2003; Mays and Faerman 2001). Britain has also been at the forefront of biomolecular studies of human remains, a development over the last fifteen years or so. For example, analyses of chemical constituents of teeth and bones have provided a window on the type of diet people were eating (Richards *et al* 1998), where they were born and raised (Montgomery *et al* 2005), and the diseases from which they suffered (Taylor *et al* 2000; Bouwman and Brown 2005).

Buikstra (2006a,133) has illustrated that the role of women in the development of North American bioarchaeology has until now remained invisible, even though 'there are numerous women who have contributed significantly to our scholarly heritage as bioarchaeologists'. In Britain there have also been a number of key women in bioarchaeology, but many of them appeared in the second half of the 20th century. They include: Juliet Rogers, discussed above; Theya Molleson (Natural History Museum, London), with publications on a wide range of subject areas (eg Molleson and Cohen 1990); Dorothy Lunt's extensive work on the analysis of dental remains (eg 1974); Ann Stirland, famous for her work on the skeletons of the Tudor warship the *Mary Rose* (Stirland 2000); and Jacqueline McKinley (Wessex Archaeology) whose research on cremated remains from archaeological sites has been pivotal in the development of the study of cremated remains – arguably in a global context (eg 1994a). More recently, Margaret Cox (Bournemouth University) has made her mark on the study of post-medieval skeletal analysis and interpretation (eg 1996); Mary Lewis (Reading University) has highlighted the value of studying children from archaeological sites (2007); Louise Humphrey (Natural History Museum, London) has contributed to our knowledge of growth rates in non-adult remains (2000); Megan Brickley (Birmingham University) has made some key contributions to the diagnosis of metabolic diseases such as scurvy and rickets in skeletal remains (eg Brickley *et al* 2006); Sonia Zakrzewski (Southampton University) has enlightened us about population affinities and diversity in Egypt, Britain, and southern Iberia (eg 2007); and Rebecca Gowland has focused on ageing skeletal remains as well as social identity (eg Gowland and Knüsel 2006). It seems that women are now tending to dominate studies of human remains from archaeological sites at academic and contract archaeology levels in Britain and are contributing considerably to the development of bioarchaeology, and its recognition globally.

Overall, bioarchaeological studies in Britain are increasingly dominating the literature, are focusing on question-driven studies using large samples of skeletons, and are placing the data in an archaeological context. However, it will be a long time before Britain can produce a volume equivalent to Buikstra and Beck (2006). Studies in Britain today include an emphasis on the integration of biological data from skeletal remains with mortuary analysis, concentrating on the social implications of skeletal data, and the use of stable isotope analysis to answer fundamental questions about past diet and economy, and also the movement of people in the past. While North America has led the way in most of these developments, in Britain we are fast catching up! This has been in part because of the development of Masters courses in universities on the study of human remains in archaeology since the 1980s (see Chapter 8), and also due to the rise in developer-funded excavations concentrating on cemeteries. However, there are some problems that need addressing to allow further development. For example, there currently exists no database which documents all skeletal collections and where they are curated; this makes finding the right samples to address specific questions extremely difficult.

Some issues

While bioarchaeological studies of human remains are becoming more common in academic circles, there is also much work in this vein in contract archaeology via the 'skeletal report'. Most skeletal reports undertaken by bioarchaeologists are prepared for contract archaeologists who win contracts for archaeological work from developers of land in Britain. Clearly, prior to this situation, and the 1990 Planning Policy Guidance Note 16 (Department of the Environment 1990), availability of funding for the preparation of skeletal (and other specialist) reports could be poor. However, since 1990, funding has vastly improved (Jacqueline McKinley pers comm, November 2007). In effect, money is available now to do very thorough skeletal reports. Unfortunately, however, many skeletal reports have tended not to reach publication, thus contributing to the burgeoning 'grey' literature in archaeology, but this situation is slowly improving. Non-publication is often the case for pre-PPG 16 backlog sites and finding funds to bring these sites to publication is very difficult (Jacqueline McKinley pers comm, November 2007). For example, Roberts and Cox's (2003) study which considered health data from over 300 cemetery sites found over one third of reports were unpublished, thus making much skeletal data unavailable. Without knowledge of where the temporal and geographical gaps in data are, how can we develop the discipline and focus on those gaps? Furthermore, if published, it is sometimes not possible to publish a report in the detail needed, or at the right level, for the intended audience, although with microfiche, compact discs, and internet archiving, this problem can to a certain extent now be alleviated.

A further problem highlighted has been the lack of standardisation of methods used for recording skeletons from archaeological sites. The development of standard methods for recording human remains has dominated the last twenty years or so in an effort to enable people ultimately to compare their data with other sites in the same country and the same or different period of time – but also with sites in other parts of the world. This particular issue was noted in North America when the threat from repatriation and reburial of Native American skeletal remains arose in the late 1980s and early 1990s (Rose *et al* 1996); the response was the production of a 'how to record' volume that was essential to ensure that all data collected from skeletons prior to reburial would be standardised, and thus comparable (Buikstra and Ubelaker 1994). This has been followed, albeit ten years later, by a volume produced in Britain (Brickley and McKinley 2004), specifically addressing the standardisation of recording of skeletal data here. This resulted from research that had identified problems in collating data on health from published and unpublished skeletal reports (Roberts and Cox 2003). In Britain, there has also been a development recently in providing guidance for bioarchaeologists when they are writing assessment reports on human remains and also the final human skeletal report (English Heritage 2004), discussed in more detail in Chapter 5. Of even more recent date is the *Global History of Health Project* (http://global.sbs.ohio-state.edu/) which has used standard recording methods based largely on Buikstra and Ubelaker (1994). Ultimately, it will be possible to compare data from thousands of skeletons dated from the Palaeolithic to the Early Modern period, all recorded using the same methods. These data will also be integrated with other types of data (eg archaeological, ecological, historical) in order to generate a well-informed perspective of global health through time. This is a major ambitious advance in bioarchaeology.

It is hoped that the quality of future skeletal reports will continue to improve, in addition to there being more integration of skeletal, archaeological, and historical data. As a country, we have moved from being physical anthropologists who were interested in studying skeletal remains for their own sake, with little attempt to contextualise data, to a proliferation of people, now called bioarchaeologists, who wish to make their data truly matter in the understanding of our ancestors.

1.6 Skeletal collections

In order to conduct research and teach students the rudimentaries of how to study human remains from archaeological sites, as well as interpret the data collected utilising a bioarchaeological approach, collections of skeletons from archaeological sites are necessary. Our archaeological museums hold the majority of skeletal samples in Britain, but in the 18th and 19th centuries, as a result of collecting activities principally by medical doctors and anatomists, more medically oriented collections developed. The Royal College of Surgeons Museum of Edinburgh holds one of the largest and most historic collections of surgical pathology in Europe (http://www.rcsed.ac.uk), while the two Hunterian

Museums in Glasgow (http://www.hunterian.gla.ac.uk) and London (http://www.
rcseng.ac.uk/museums) are probably the most famous. The Hunterian Museum
and Art Gallery in Scotland was established in 1783 in Glasgow as a result of
the bequeathment of specimens resulting from the anatomical and pathological
collecting activities of William Hunter (1718–83). The Hunterian Museum in
the Royal College of Surgeons, London, was established in 1799 as a result of
the acquisition of the collections of John Hunter (1728–93), brother to William
and a surgeon and anatomist. By the end of the 19th century there were 65,000
specimens, including anatomical, pathological, and physiological examples. In
1941 during the bombing of London two-thirds of the collection was destroyed,
but in recent years the museum has been reorganised and refurbished, and it has
become very much an educational establishment for a variety of users (Figure 4).
These anatomical and pathological museums of (relatively modern) wet and dry
specimens of parts of the body are particularly useful for learning about normal
variation in the human body, and the effects of different diseases on the body
parts, and especially bones. Medical students and people working with human
remains from archaeological sites benefit much from these collections. However,
of more relevance to people working on archaeological human remains are the
large collections of skeletons in the Duckworth Collection at Cambridge University

(http://www.human-evol.cam.ac.uk/Duckworth/duckworth.htm), named after the anatomist William Duckworth. The collection has been assembled over the last 150 years and now there are over 17,000 human and non-human primate skeletal 'items' (Foley 1990). Many museums also curate skeletal remains from archaeological sites for educational and research purposes and, unlike museums in North America and elsewhere, those human remains placed on display in Britain are presented respectfully, hopefully in their correct archaeological context, and for clear educational reasons.

1.7 Key organisations

Like any profession, there exist a number of organisations to which people working with human remains belong, both within Britain but also elsewhere. The American Association of Physical Anthropologists was founded in 1930 (http://www.physanth.org), has annual meetings and a monthly journal (*American Journal of Physical Anthropology*); it has around 1700 members. The British equivalent, the British Association for Biological Anthropology and Osteoarchaeology, founded in 1998 (http://www.babao.org.uk), and currently with 200 members, also has annual meetings, and an Annual Review which summarises members' work of the previous year. The European Anthropological Association, with 600 members and founded in the early 1970s (http://eaa.elte. hu/), represents European physical anthropological interests, while the Dental Anthropology Association (http://anthropology.osu.edu/DAA/index.htm) has members interested in the study of teeth, past and present. The Paleopathology Association, another United States-based organisation founded in 1973 (http:// www.paleopathology.org), has 500 members and promotes the study of health and disease in archaeological human remains, including mummified bodies. Members of these organisations have been instrumental in promoting the study of bioarchaeology and developing standards for recording and reporting data.

1.8 Summary

The study of human remains from archaeological sites has developed over a long period of time. It has changed considerably in its outlook, especially in Britain where, until recently, the emphasis was on studying human remains 'for their own sake', with little reference to where the remains derived from, how the people lived, what they ate, or what they did for a living; with very few exceptions interpretations of data were limited. When this approach changed, essentially from 1990, with the advent of training courses (one year taught Masters) designed for archaeology and anthropology graduates, Britain started to follow more closely the American-based bioarchaeological standpoint with studies becoming more question and hypothesis driven. Thematic studies are now more common in Britain, as they are globally. People are interested in studying human remains to understand migration patterns (Budd *et al* 2004); how economy and politics influenced past diet and health (Cohen and Crane-Kramer 2007); the effects of conflict (Larsen and Milner 1994), air quality (Roberts 2007) and climate (Lukacs and Walimbe 1998) on population health and welfare; the origin and evolution of specific diseases (Roberts and Buikstra 2003) or treatments (Arnott *et al* 2003); whether occupation can be recognised in the skeleton (Jurmain 1999); and the specifics of particular groups of people such as males and females (Grauer and Stuart-Macadam 1998) and children (Lewis 2007), in addition to the impact of social status on health and welfare (Robb *et al* 2001). There has also been a large interest in the study of historically documented collections of skeletal remains in Britain and elsewhere around the world, mainly because of the opportunity, through excavation of these cemeteries in advance of modern development, to study the human remains excavated (eg Molleson and Cox 1993; Grauer 1995; Saunders and Herring 1995; Boyle and Keevil 1998; Scheuer 1998). This has allowed methods of analysis of human remains to develop, such as for determining stature, age at death, especially in adult skeletons, and identifying changes in the skeleton associated with specific diseases.

1.9 Key learning points

- the study of human remains is popular
- bioarchaeological study in Britain has been affected by developments in higher education, museums, and contract archaeology
- training is very common at Masters level in British universities (seven run courses)
- more ambitious and larger bioarchaeological projects are being carried out with themes being considered and key questions being asked
- there is an emphasis on multidisciplinary/cross disciplinary approaches to bioarchaeology
- archaeological and relatively modern skeletal collections are important to the discipline
- terms applied to people who work on human remains vary considerably but the author favours *bioarchaeology*
- a database of curated skeletal remains in Britain is badly needed
- standardisation of recording of human remains needs to be consolidated
- more integration of biological and archaeological data is needed, as are more population-based studies
- there are a number of key organisations that promote the study of human remains from archaeological sites

CHAPTER TWO

Ethical concerns and human remains

Human remains are not just another artefact; they have potency, they are charged with political, evidentiary, and emotional meanings ...

(Cassman *et al* 2006a, 1)

2.1 Introduction

The respectful treatment of human remains varies considerably in different parts of the world, reflecting socio-cultural values and opinions, including religious beliefs. Within countries, variations also occur on a regional and local scale. The excavation, study, and curation of archaeological 'materials' in their broadest sense are subject to serious thinking about the ethical issues surrounding the nature of archaeology as a whole (Zimmerman *et al* 2003), and the ethics of studying human remains from archaeological sites have been the focus of many studies (eg Walker 2000; Fforde *et al* 2002; Scarre 2006; Tarlow 2006).

Is it ethical to excavate and study human remains excavated from archaeological sites, and then keep them in a museum or other curating institution for further study? This is not as straightforward a question as it might seem because the answer will depend on many factors. However, it is generally agreed that it is a privilege and not a right to excavate and study human remains, rights being inherent, and privileges being granted on stated conditions that create responsibilities (Joyce 2002, 102). Nevertheless, it should be remembered that in Britain the majority of human remains are excavated as a result of modern 'building', in its broadest sense (Figure 5).

Of note for Britain was a session held within the annual Institute of Field Archaeologists (IFA) conference in 1991 to discuss the excavation of human remains (Stirland 1991), where it was identified that there was a need to develop policies for the excavation of human remains. At this point, it is worth considering the study which was the stimulus for the session. In 1990 a questionnaire on the nature of excavation of human remains in Britain was sent to 123 (then) archaeological units, museums, and university departments; it gained 44 responses (McKinley 1991). On average 26% of respondents had excavated more than one cemetery site per year over the preceding ten years, and 40% of those had excavated sites with over 100 inhumations, the majority being unexpected finds and of medieval or post-medieval date. Over 80% had done excavations for 'rescue' purposes only, which included land planned for quarrying, new houses and roads, and church alterations – at the request of local councils, developers, and the church. The majority of organisations had never had to rebury any human bone but, in 27 cases, reburial (following analysis) had occurred because the site contained Christian burials; nevertheless, <50% of reburials had been at the request of the church. Following this meeting, over ten years then went by before clear policies and guidance developed (see below).

Even as recently as 2003, when there seemed to be signs of action on the part of relevant organisations such as the Department of Culture, Media and Sport (DCMS), Roberts and Cox (2003, 385) asserted that, 'the archaeological and anthropological community have failed to engage (in this issue), as have most of our key archaeological organisations' and that, 'given the situation that has developed within the US, Australia, New Zealand, and Israel, such complacency is at best naïve and at worst arguably negligent'. At that time they emphasised that all those parties with a legitimate interest in the fate of the dead should come together to discuss the issues. Indeed, there have been debates and suggestions by professionals in archaeology about how human remains should be treated in Britain for some time (eg Locock 1998; Reeve 1998 – the latter of which includes aspects of assessment of potential, screening during excavation, basic

Figure 5: Removal of a burial from a post-medieval cemetery by contractors in advance of modern development (with permission of Margaret Cox and Roland Wessling)

recording, a statement of objectives, sampling, disseminating results, taking photographs, display, and reinterment). By late 2007 the BABAO sought to draw up a Code of Ethics to provide guidance on the study of human remains, although there had already been some attempts to do this (Parker Pearson 1995, 1999a). BABAO's website now also has a page devoted to reburial and repatriation (http://www.babao.org.uk/index/reburialissues). Thus, Britain is seeing more focus and consideration now of how the dead from archaeological sites are treated, but there is much more work to do.

The way we view the remains of the dead and how they should be treated is complex and bound up with our belief systems, our life experiences, and many other conscious and subconscious feelings. For example, more recent burials may evoke, in some, much more of a sense of identity with the dead, and relatives of the deceased may even still be alive (as with the Christ Church, Spitalfields, London crypt excavation: Molleson and Cox 1993) – so that even if the remains have to be excavated then there is a strong desire for reburial. Burials that are much older and perhaps felt to be more distant may, to many, possess anonymity, which for some makes excavating, studying, and curating them more acceptable. In fact,

Jones and Harris (1998, 258) feel that 'if no links can be established with a direct descendant or a group of descendants, then the remains should be available for reputable scientific investigation, since the findings will, in the broadest terms, be applicable to all humanity'. Where the cemetery contains indigenous remains which may be proved to be the (albeit, usually distant) ancestors of the living population, as in the case of Native American or Australian aboriginal groups, then excavation and analysis may not be desirable and, if carried out, reburial of the human remains would be required, with or without analysis. There are also people around the world, who may or may not hold religious beliefs, who feel extremely strongly about the fate of their bodies and those of their relatives when they pass away; in this respect they may be concerned for the rights of all the dead from time immemorial until the present day. Clearly, religious faiths not only determine how a body is disposed of today (Green and Green 1992), but also any beliefs in an afterlife. These beliefs will also affect whether it is thought acceptable to disturb a body (and ultimately display it in a museum). Of course, this is also relevant to the past where, for some periods of time, we are familiar with religious beliefs whereas for other periods we cannot be sure; again this affects how we should, and do, treat the dead.

As Hubert and Fforde (2002, 1) have stated, because of an increasing outward indication of people's sense of identity with their past, some are now 'contesting the ownership of human remains housed in museums and other institutions', and demanding the remains be repatriated and/or reburied according to cultural beliefs associated with the dead. This is in addition to them requiring museums to disclose the human remains they curate, and to remove any on display. As long ago as 1989, the 1st World Archaeological Congress held in South Dakota, USA, drew up what is termed the Vermillion Accord on Human Remains (http://www. worldarchaeologicalcongress.org/site/about_ethi.php), which was adopted by the World Archaeological Congress Council in 1990. The agreement concerned respect for the mortal remains of the dead, irrespective of origin, race, religion, nationality, custom, and tradition, and for the wishes of the local community and relatives of the dead, as well as respect for the scientific research value of human remains; it stressed cooperation between archaeologists and indigenous people, and stipulated that agreement on the disposal of human remains should be reached by negotiation. Later, in 1991, the World Archaeological Congress then outlined a range of ethical principles for studying human remains. More recently, in 2006, the World Archaeological Congress Council adopted the Tamaki Makau-rau Accord on the Display of Human Remains and Sacred Objects (http://www. worldarchaeologicalcongress.org/site/about_ethi.php).

In certain cases, although there are no genealogical descendants or cultural communities to 'claim' their ancestors officially, groups asserting descent from, or having the best interests of, the human remains do exist. These groups are often marginalised in contemporary Western society (Brooks and Rumsey 2006), and tend to be referred to as 'special interest' groups. For example, recently modern pagan groups in Britain, such as those of Druidry, Wicca, Witchcraft, and Shamanic traditions, have become united into an organisation represented by 'Honouring the Ancient Dead' (HAD) (http://www.honour.org.uk/?q=node). They wish, and aim, to be involved with consultation and decision-making processes regarding the excavation, analysis, and care thereafter of human remains dating from prehistory to AD 600. Although HAD has declared that reburial is not the only option, it feels it is a key area of focus. HAD asserts that its members have legitimate claims to human remains in Britain, but are not identifiable descendants of them. Bienkowski (2007) notes also that local communities other than pagan groups feel that they have a right to contribute to decisions about the fate of human remains in their areas.

Naturally, those excavating, studying, and curating human remains may not all have the same views on the treatment of human remains as do genealogical descendants and affiliated communities around the world. Indeed, those who advocate reburial are not, as Hubert and Fforde (2002, 5) state, 'an homogenized, undifferentiated whole, in which all share the same views'. Different cultures view and manage death differently. On a radio programme in the 1970s, for example, Sir Mortimer Wheeler, a prominent archaeologist, was heard to say regarding burials in the archaeological record, 'we do no harm to those poor chaps. When I'm dead you can dig me up ten times for all I care' (Bahn 1984, 214), while the inscription on William Shakespeare's gravestone in Stratford-upon-Avon, England quite clearly indicates that he does not want his body to be disturbed (Figure 6).

Figure 6: Shakespeare's gravestone, Stratford-upon-Avon, Warwickshire, England (with permission of Susan Ward)

In summary, as Tarlow (2006) says, archaeologists overall have an ethical responsibility to present-day groups of people, including the public at large. There is clearly an increasing awareness of the treatment and ethical consideration of human remains around the world, and of course we have a responsibility to both past and living people. The question is: what does it mean to show respect for the wishes of the dead (Scarre 2006); respect, after all, is constituted in different countries, by differing cultures, and by people within any one culture. Perhaps the treatment of human remains can only be deemed unethical if living people are harmed by this act (Tarlow 2006). Any work on human remains must contribute to human knowledge, and in bioarchaeology there are constant examples of contributions to knowledge (see later chapters). Furthermore, one could argue that 'since archaeologists spend so much time, energy, and imagination on knowing past people, they are in a better position to represent past people than most' (Tarlow 2006, 209).

As archaeologists, bioarchaeologists, and museum curators know, the excavation and study of people brings in many visitors to museums, sells books and builds careers; we therefore have a responsibility to look after our dead ancestors (Tarlow 2006). It is important, however, to maintain a balanced view between value judgements and human rights, which this chapter hopes to do, although as Lackey (2006, 162) says, 'There is no magical formula for adjudicating the requirements of religion, art and science'. Nevertheless Buikstra (2006b, 408), while admitting there is no global solution to the issues raised, emphasises that 'The need for openness for communication, for mutual respect, and for initiatives that are of interest to all collaborating parties *is* global'. It is disappointing then that some 'scientists' see scientific value to be more important than the cultural beliefs of living populations (Hubert 1989), especially with respect to some countries outside Britain.

2.2 Justification for the retention of human remains

If the view is that it is ethical to excavate, analyse, and curate human remains from archaeological sites, bearing in mind that in Britain the excavation of human remains is usually required because of modern development, then how is this justified? Clearly if remains are reburied this is a 'loss to science of a unique source of information about the past' (Hubert and Fforde 2002, 3), but it is also a loss ultimately to the public who has an immense interest in human remains from archaeological sites. A recent survey of the public in England by Cambridgeshire Archaeology Historic Environment Record found that 80% of the 220 responses felt that human skeletal remains should not be reburied or only reburied when there were no further research uses (Carroll 2005). Furthermore, 88% of the respondents thought that human remains could aid future scientific study and that it was appropriate to curate them. Perhaps 'this is a vote of confidence in the professionals, with the public trusting us to do the right thing with human remains ...' (*ibid*, 11). It should, however, be pointed out that the survey was playing to an active audience and not the wider public; therefore a more widespread survey is probably appropriate now. Carroll (*ibid*) suggested that it is time for a national debate about the issues. Such a debate has started with a limited number of interested parties engaged in discussion. Apart from the recently passed legislation (see below), few events have provided opportunities for discussion across all interested groups – for example there have only been two recent conferences in London (in 2004 and 2007), and one in Manchester (in 2006), which focused on the treatment of human remains. There is certainly room for wider consultation in the public sphere across a full range of socio-economic and religious backgrounds, and ages. However, it is not only in museums that the public have expressed their support for the retention, study, and display of human remains. Recent TV programmes such as BBC2's *Meet the Ancestors* have attracted large viewing figures that also pleased the broadcasters.

Human remains from archaeological sites are the primary evidence for people in the past; we can study their pottery, houses, and food waste but it has to be remembered that without humans none of these would exist. To understand the past, which has been created by our ancestors, we need, through studying their physical remains, to appreciate how they managed to adapt to their living environment. As we have already seen, it is essential to study the human remains in context in order to generate a bioarchaeological perspective of the past, and this might include the study of associated settlement or historical data. Furthermore, as techniques of analysis develop, it is possible to do much more detailed and explorative work than was possible twenty or even ten years ago. For example, the extraction and analysis of ancient DNA of disease-causing organisms to diagnose health problems in human remains had not been achieved before 1993. If human remains are removed from curation and passed for repatriation and/or reburial then new and informative data about the past would not be possible using these new techniques. If, as we believe, the world's population has a strong interest in its heritage then this alone is a justification for the retention and study of human remains.

Further justification for the retention of human remains has been shown in a survey of published papers (Buikstra and Gordon 1981). The authors reviewed 310 papers published between 1950 and 1980 in three major journals to assess whether any papers were re-studies of skeletal collections and if new methods had been used. Some 724 skeletal collections were described in the papers, of which 32% were re-studies, and 63% tackled new research problems. Of the 37% that looked at old research problems, in 62% of papers the conclusions were altered. In the re-studies, 48% of papers used new techniques of analysis, with 55% looking at old problems; of those, conclusions were altered in 74% of studies. Many studies were re-studies of curated skeletal collections, and the majority of studies got new data using new methods of analysis, thus in this study justifying the retention of curated human remains.

It is suggested here that, of all types of archaeological sites, burials and their contents require particularly careful attention and respect during excavation and in subsequent analysis, curation, and display of the remains. Nevertheless, there can be a tendency for many archaeologists and bioarchaeologists to focus on the benefits of excavating and analysing human remains, often neglecting to consider any perceived spiritual harm that may be done to the dead or to the living; one must not forget that the remains are both biological and cultural in value (Joyce 2002).

2.3 Guidance and legal requirements for the excavation of human remains by archaeologists in Britain

Of relevance to discussions concerning ethics and the study of human remains are the laws surrounding the removal of remains. It is of course unlawful to disturb human remains without good reason and without appropriate authority (see below, Table 1), ie without the necessary legalities in place. Furthermore, human remains should always be treated with respect and care, and relevant directions, licences, and *Faculties* provide guidance in this area for archaeologists and bioarchaeologists.

In England and Wales, Scotland, and Northern Ireland, laws relating to the excavation of human remains differ. Furthermore, of note, in June 2007, the interpretation and application of burial laws in England and Wales changed (see below). Additional to this, the affairs of the Department for Constitutional Affairs (http://www.dca.gov.uk/corbur/buriafr.htm), which dealt with applications for exhumation, were transferred to the new Ministry of Justice (MoJ) in May 2007 (http://www.justice.gov.uk/whatwedo/burials.htm). The MoJ now makes decisions on exhumation licences, regulates the removal of human remains from disused burial grounds, and considers applications for the closure of graveyards.

The majority of the laws relating to human remains reflect a concern with matters relating to public health, emphasising and maintaining public decency and respect, and the interests of relatives, in addition to highlighting the responsibilities of the Church and other bodies responsible for burial places. Most of the relevant laws are fairly old, some going back to the mid-19th century. When they were established, archaeological investigation was not a consideration, and thus they are not always clear in relation to archaeological excavation.

This outline sets out to summarise an understanding of the current position (May 2008) in relation to the excavation and study of human remains by archaeologists; this is following changes in interpretation and practice by the MoJ in May 2007 and April 2008. It is anticipated and expected that further changes will be forthcoming, especially in relation to reburial, and therefore it is sensible for archaeologists excavating human remains to check the current position with the MoJ or the Church of England, as appropriate.

Prior to describing the relevant legislation, it should be noted that over the years there have been a number of publications that have provided recommendations and guidance on dealing with human remains from archaeological sites, from excavation to curation, including legal aspects. These include documents for:

- human remains buried in Christian burial grounds in England since AD 597 (English Heritage and the Church of England 2005 – http://www. english-heritage.org.uk/upload/pdf/16602_HumanRemains1.pdf, although some of this is out of date now),
- human remains curated in museums and other institutions in England and Wales (DCMS, 2005 – http://www.culture.gov.uk/Reference_library/ Publications/Archive_2005/guidance_chr.htm, although again some of this is out of date now),
- human remains buried in Scotland (Historic Scotland, 1997 – http:// www.Historic-Scotland.gov.uk/human remains.pdf), and
- human remains buried in Ireland (O'Sullivan *et al* 2002; and O'Sullivan and Killgore 2003 for Eire – http://www.heritagecouncil.ie/publications/ human_remains/index.html; and Buckley *et al* 2004 and the Institute of Archaeologists of Ireland generally for Ireland 2006 – http://iai.ie/index. html).

The following sections summarise the laws pertaining to England, Wales, Scotland, and Northern Ireland (United Kingdom).

(i) England and Wales

As Garratt-Frost (1992) states, in England and Wales there is no property in a corpse so it cannot be stolen, but it is however an offence to disinter a body without lawful authority. In Britain, the government began to pass laws regarding inhumation and cremation burials, and their exhumation, in the 19th century. As has been noted above, these are now seen as inappropriate for archaeological disturbance of human remains. When human remains are, or have been accidentally, disturbed in an archaeological context, consultation with the relevant authority is necessary, the relevant body being determined mainly by the context in which the remains are located (see Table 1). If an excavator expects to find human remains, a licence, *Faculty* (authorisation by the Church under ecclesiastical law), and/or directions should be sought, as required, and obtained before starting to excavate. If remains are found unexpectedly, work should stop until the necessary authorisation is obtained – when necessary, authorisation is usually obtained within a couple of days. If the remains are believed to be less than 100 years old or are interred in a recognised burial ground, then the local coroner and police have to be informed (English Heritage and Church of England 2005).

As Table 1 shows, the *Burial Act* of 1857 is the 'default' legislation for archaeological excavations of human remains. Where it applies, excavators have to apply to the Ministry of Justice for a Section 25 licence. In the past, where appropriate, Section 25 licences allowed for the retention/curation of human remains in museums and other suitable places, such as universities, for later study. However, following the most recent MoJ interpretation of current laws, all licences issued after April 2008 have to set a date for reburial of excavated human remains. For example, as the situation stands today, a reburial date would have to be agreed for any new early hominid remains discovered at the Palaeolithic site of Boxgrove, Sussex (Roberts and Parfitt 1999). Normally two years is allowed for study unless longer is requested and can be justified; deadlines can be subsequently extended if necessary and reasonable by a further application to the MoJ (Ministry of Justice 2008), although an application must be made before the set date has expired. It should be noted that the MoJ recognises that it is desirable to retain older and more important archaeological human remains for future research. The MoJ takes the view that current legislation requires a reburial date to be set, but they are working on ways to address this potential obstacle to the full study of excavated human remains (and indeed the retention of remains in the long term). Earlier licences which permit retention in museums and other suitable places remain valid.

The *Disused Burial Grounds (Amendment) Act 1981*, and similar legislation, applies instead of the *Burial Act 1857*, where a disused burial ground which has not passed into different use is developed, and especially when it is compulsorily purchased. Where one of these Acts applies, excavators should apply as soon as possible to the MoJ for 'directions'. These Acts apply most frequently to relatively recent burial grounds, and therefore 'directions' include requirements to advertise in order to give any relatives an opportunity to exhume and rebury the remains of family members; there may also be requirements that relate to public health concerns. A reburial date again has to be set, and relatively rapid reburial is expected, although a reasonable time will be allowed for study which can, again, be extended if necessary, as under the *Burial Act 1857*.

Ecclesiastical law (Faculty) applies to human remains located in Church of England churches, churchyards, and burial grounds – and in these cases an application for a Faculty should be made to the Church of England. Again, Faculties normally require reburial dates and these can be extended, if necessary. The *Burial Act 1857* does not apply if burials are disturbed by the normal management of CoE burial places, but it does apply if archaeologists remove human remains from CoE burial places in order to move and examine them elsewhere, in which case archaeologists need to apply for a Faculty and a Section 25 licence.

Other Acts that are, and may be, important include the *Human Rights Act* of 1988 (http://www.opsi.gov.uk/acts/acts1998/ukpga_19980042_en_1), and the *Human Tissue Act* of 2004 (http://www.opsi.gov.uk/acts/acts 2004/ukpga_ 20040042_en_1); of relevance too is the Human Tissue Authority (http://www. hta.gov.uk) that regulates the removal, storage, use, and disposal of human bodies, organs, and tissues from the living and deceased. The *Human Tissue Act* governs remains less than 100 years old in museums and other institutions. It is worth noting that the *Human Rights Act* defines human rights abuse as only applicable to the living, so it cannot be invoked for perceived harm or wrong done to human remains from archaeological sites. However, remains could technically be covered by Common Law regarding respectful treatment of the dead (McKinley pers comm, November 2007). Certainly there are some who argue that the treatment of human remains should be viewed within a broader human rights perspective and that this would be a better way of protecting the dead from disrespectful treatment. The *Human Tissue Act* stemmed from a realisation that in some British hospitals organs and body parts had been removed and retained from deceased patients following post-mortem examinations, along with stillbirths and foetuses, without the knowledge or consent of relatives (Department of Health 2000, in Hubert and Fforde 2002).

During 2008 and 2009, a second stage of reform of burial laws for England and Wales is expected to consider amendments to existing burial ground legislation, with the aim of 'allow(ing) otherwise lawful and legitimate activities, such as the archaeological examination of human remains, to proceed without the constraints of legislation not designed to deal with such issues, and with retrospective effect as far as possible' (Ministry of Justice 2008). It will also look at the circumstances for the retention of human remains from archaeological sites in museums and other institutions. At this stage (Ministry of Justice 2008), 'it is intended that this should be possible, subject to appropriate conditions and safeguards, if acceptable and justified by circumstances'.

Situation	Authority	Relevant legislation	Action	Comment
In a burial ground in the care of the Church of England	Church of England (Ministry of Justice)	Church Law (Burial Act 1857)	Faculty required (Section 25 licence also required if the remains are going to be taken some-where else for study)	
In an active burial ground in other care	Ministry of Justice	Burial Act 1857	Section 25 licence required	
In a disused bur-ial ground which has not passed into other use	Ministry of Justice	Usually Disused Burial Grounds (Amendment) Act 1981 or similar	Directions should be applied for	Various Acts can apply depending on circumstances; consult MoJ as soon as possible
On land which has passed into other use includ-ing pasture, arable, industrial, recreational, or built over	Ministry of Justice	Burial Act 1857	Section 25 licence required	

Table 1: Laws pertaining to different situations where human remains may be found in England and Wales, and the relevant authorities

(ii) Scotland

In Scotland, the previous acts do not apply (Logie 1992; Historic Scotland 1997), but Civil and Criminal Law provides for dealing with disinterment of human remains. As for England and Wales, in Scotland there is no property in a corpse. Furthermore, Logie (1992, 12) states that, 'The basic premise … is that human remains are sacred whenever they are interred, and that graves and tombs are not to be disturbed. This protection is not necessarily absolute'. All human remains have the 'right of sepulchre' (Historic Scotland 1997, 3). However, there are three exceptions to the rule that human remains must not be disturbed and, if disinterment cannot be effected through these exceptions, then it is illegal:

- if those managing a public burial ground are compelled to disturb graves,
- if the burial was in ground where there was no right of burial or,
- where a warrant has been obtained from the Sheriff Court to disinter a body – usually if relatives wish reburial elsewhere or if necessary work has to be done in the graveyard or associated buildings; there is no report of a warrant being granted for archaeological, educational, or scientific reasons (Logie 1992).

If human remains are disinterred and reinterred, they are expected to be treated with decency and respect. The same rules apply to bodies buried outside of recognised burial grounds, but 'there are considerable complexities and areas of doubt in this particular branch of Scots law' (Logie 1992, 14).

(iii) Northern Ireland

The Environment and Heritage Service of Northern Ireland (EHSNI) provides guidance for archaeological excavations in general. All archaeologists excavating a site have to apply for an Excavation Licence, and the current legislation covering monuments and objects is the Historic Monuments and Archaeological Objects (Northern Ireland) Order for 1995 (http://www.opsi.gov.uk/si/si1995/uksi_19951625_en_1.htm), although there has been protection for monuments since 1869. A licence has to be applied for to the EHSNI at least fifteen working days prior to the start of fieldwork on the site, except if remains are found accidentally.

The legal requirements for the excavation of human remains are outlined in Buckley *et al* (2004). If human remains are discovered accidentally then the Police Service of Northern Ireland (PSNI, formerly the Royal Ulster Constabulary, or RUC) have to be contacted. If the remains are considered >50 years old then the EHSNI need to be informed. The landowner of the site has to be identified, and the 'status' of the land. If the burial ground belongs to a District Council, the Burial Grounds Regulations (Northern Ireland) 1992 has to be complied with, subject to Section II (4) of the Coronerís Act (Northern Ireland) 1959. If the burial ground belongs to the Church of Ireland then it may be necessary to obtain a *Faculty* from the church authorities.

2.4 Excavation, analysis, and curation of human remains in Britain

As we have already seen, in Britain today the vast majority of archaeological excavation is undertaken by contract archaeologists following successful tenders for work in areas where modern development will disturb archaeological deposits, including human remains. Therefore, those who feel human remains should not be disturbed need to be aware that 'it is rarely the archaeologist who seeks their disinterment' (White and Ganiaris 1998, 19) but rather, disturbance occurs due to the desire for property development. British planning law can also lead to professional cemetery clearances (and controlled excavations), often with immediate reburial, especially if the burials are post-1500 AD. Furthermore, as Scarre (2006, 183) states, 'Human remains probably receive, on the whole, more sensitive treatment from archaeologists than they do from developers who ... are not professionally interested in re-creating former lives'. In general, Britain does not face looting of graves, as seen in some parts of the world (Figure 7) but, in circumstances such as this, rapid excavation is necessary to prevent loss of heritage information and to try to alleviate what is seen as a lack of respect for the dead.

Figure 7: Exposed and robbed (archaeological) graves, Jordan (Charlotte Roberts)

There are many thousands of human remains from British archaeological sites curated in our museums, academic institutions, and research laboratories ranging in date from the Palaeolithic (*c* 10,500–8,000 BC), or prehistory, to the post-medieval/Early Modern period (*c* AD 1550–1850). Remains are curated to enable research to continue beyond the skeletal report produced at excavation stage. Indeed, recently there has been a move, unique to Britain, to curate human remains in other places. For example, the skeletal remains from the church of St Peter's, Barton-on-Humber, Lincolnshire, have been returned to the church and are being curated in the consecrated area, with availability for further study. In 2005, English Heritage and the Church of England agreed that depositions of archaeological human remains such as this in consecrated redundant, or partly redundant, churches were acceptable (Mays 2007), termed Church Archives of Human Remains (CAHR).

Curation of human remains allows them to be used for education and research. Ultimately, if human remains are retained then they really *must be* utilised for these purposes. Otherwise, one has to question why the remains are being retained, especially if claims for repatriation and/or reburial exist. The curation of human remains for specific purposes of course has to be justified but, as Jones and Harris (1998, 262) remind us, 'We cannot justify a situation whereby thousands of skeletal remains from the recent past linger unstudied in universities and museums for years on end because … ongoing … scientific work is essential to justify their maintenance'. Of course one of the main arguments for retaining human remains for study is that the development of new methods of analysis will produce new data and interpretations of our ancestors that were not possible before. However, one could also argue that, 'The expectation that one day someone may want to work on them is not sufficient reason for keeping them' (*ibid*, 262). Even so, as we have already seen, studies have shown that re-study of human remains using new methods produces new data.

The maintaining of adequate curation facilities is essential for long-term storage, research and display and, increasingly, guidance on the proper care of human remains is being published for museums (Alfonso and Powell 2006; Cassman *et al* 2006b; Lohman and Goodnow 2006); it is appropriate here to say that other institutions that curate human remains such as universities and research laboratories should also be thinking of adopting this guidance. Clearly, cultural, spiritual, scientific, and educational values and sensitivities must be respected, while ensuring information is shared with a wide range of interested parties. It should also be noted and stressed that 'learning with real skeletal remains' is essential in a university context because plastic skeletons do not preserve the detail that is necessary to understand human variation. Related to this is the worrying, and increasing, move away from using real human bodies in medical schools to learn about the anatomy of the human body in favour of computer software programmes.

Bearing all this in mind, one should also remember that in countries that were colonised in the past, cultural heritage, including burials, was plundered in the name of 'collecting' and 'science' (Hubert and Fforde 2002), and back in the 19th century grave robbers stole bodies for anatomists and surgeons. Jones and Harris (1998, 261) feel that if human remains were obtained unethically in this way in the past, it is inappropriate to accuse people wishing to work on those human remains today of the 'grave robbing' that took place 80–120 years ago: '... we can find no moral connection between killing and grave robbing of 100 years ago and work undertaken today'. Simpson (2002) nevertheless notes that there has been an increasing focus on the repatriation of museum collections of human remains and other cultural objects in Britain and elsewhere, and that this reflects the broader concern with trade in illicitly exported works of art, and indigenous claims for the repatriation of human remains removed from colonies during the colonial era by the British (most common at the end of World War One in 1918).

Whatever is felt about the way human remains were acquired for museum collections, methods of acquisition do need close scrutiny. With this in mind, the curation of human remains from other countries has recently attracted attention and discussion, resulting in a guidance document for England, Wales and Northern Ireland (DCMS 2005) following a House of Commons Select Committee on cultural property being established in 1999 (Simpson 2002). It was felt that human remains should be considered as an issue distinct from the broader issues of repatriation of ancient property, and they recommended the DCMS should look at the subject. In 2001, the DCMS established a Working Group on human remains, leading to a publication by the DCMS (2005); separate guidance for Scottish institutions is under consideration and development, and of course the *Human Tissue Act 2004* governs remains dating from the past 100 years that are curated in institutions.

As Walker (2000, 25) emphasises, 'our reconstructions of what happened in the past are refined and corrected through re-examination of collections using new analytical techniques and theoretical perspectives', while Simpson states that 'what is important is the rationale for the proposed contemporary scientific work, the quality of this work, and its potential value to the human community (including the descendants of those whose bones are to be studied)' (Simpson 2002, 261). Of course, museums need to be familiar with developments in the study of human remains and be reliably informed particularly about the potential for destructive analyses. These methods are so much more common today where there is a desire to know more about diet (stable isotope analysis), relationships between people (ancient mitochondrial DNA analysis), and disease evolution and presence (ancient pathogen nuclear DNA analysis). Moreover, funding bodies in Britain are more likely to support these types of analyses, but they can be expensive and are by no means routine in Britain. Of note also is the apparent rise in papers being published in these fields of study in recent years (Stojanowski and Buikstra 2005). Clearly too, the public feels that it is appropriate to curate skeletons for future scientific work, as seen above (Carroll 2005).

2.5 Displaying human remains and using them on television

The question of whether it is acceptable to display human remains in museums is contentious, and in some parts of the world it is prohibited, for example in Australia and the United States; clearly 'the display of dead bodies is an increasingly contested issue' (Brooks and Rumsey 2006), and questions have been raised recently on whether the movement of human remains from one country to another can even be justified for display purposes (Cook 2007).

In Britain, there does nevertheless appear to be a strong desire on the part of the general public to visit museums and view human remains, whether skeletons, bog bodies, mummies, body parts, or more recent bodies such as Jeremy Bentham, the philosopher and jurist (1748–1832), whose dissected skeleton was padded out and clothed, and has been on display at University College, London since 1850 (Fuller 1998, in Brooks and Rumsey 2006). Bentham was adamant that religion should not be a hindrance to medical research and that his body should be publicly displayed after his death. Perhaps this indicates the need of the public to have a strong link with the past through the actual remains of their 'ancestors'. The real question concerns who gives consent to the display of human remains. Bentham obviously did wish his body to be used for medical research and eventual display, but what of human remains from prehistoric burials in museums?

In 2004, during National Archaeology Week, the Museum of London surveyed visitors to the museum about the display of human remains. Eighty-eight of 99 people said they would like to see human remains on display and 98 of the 99 felt it appropriate for the museum to curate and research human skeletons from London's excavations (Bill White, Museum of London, pers comm, January 2008). As a further example of public attitudes to the display of human

Figure 8: Display of human remains at the *London Bodies* exhibition at the Museum of London (with permission of the Picture Library, Museum of London and Nikki Braunton)

remains, Carroll (2005) found that 79% of 220 survey respondents in Cambridgeshire felt that human skeletons should be on display and 73% felt it was appropriate. Similar findings are noted by Rumsey (2001) who surveyed 51 people mainly aged from 30 to 50 years, with equal representation of male and female, and from five religions. In a more recent similar survey in 2007 (Bill White, Museum of London, pers comm, January 2008), 53% of respondents expected to see human remains on display in museums, and 92% approved of display in museum galleries. When asked if they would still approve if the human remains were deemed anonymous Christians, 92% said yes, although 22% said they would disapprove if the remains were of known identity. A convincing 95% said that display should be the ultimate fate of human remains.

Simpson (2002) also reports that, in the mid-1990s, the Museums Association surveyed museums and sought information about human remains in their collections (Simpson 1994). Twenty-four respondents had or once had human remains in their collections, and nineteen still had some on display, but none showed Native American, Australian aboriginal, or Maori materials of human origin. Nevertheless, seventeen of the nineteen had removed remains from display in the past and almost half attributed this to changes in staff attitudes. One has to ask why museum curators appear to be speaking for the public in this, often overly, politically correct world in which we live? This could ultimately affect how the public learn and expand their knowledge about the past, and alter the role and purpose of museums today. However, one must consider how different 'types' of human remains may be treated for display; consider cremated remains, fragmentary skeletal remains, complete skeletons, complete bodies such as Egyptian mummies and those from bogs, parts of bodies such as hair and skin, children's remains, foetal remains, people who suffered gruesome deaths, and more recent specimens of body parts (diseased or not) in pathological museums. Should they be displayed differently and does this affect the public's acceptance of the display?

There have been notably large audiences in recent years for displays of human remains of all ages and types in museums. Take, for example, the *London Bodies* (Figure 8) exhibition at the Museum of London in 1998–99, which attracted a

Figure 9: Display of humans: Antony Gormley, *Domain Field*, 2003 – 287 Domain sculptures, various sizes, derived from moulds of local inhabitants of Newcastle/ Gateshead aged 2.5 years to 84 years; stainless steel bars 4.76 x 4.76mm (copyright: the artist; photo: Stephen White; courtesy: Jay Jopling/White Cube, London)

record number of visitors (Museum of London 1998; Swain 1998; Ganiaris 2001), as did the *Body Worlds* anatomical exhibition of human bodies in London in 2003 (Discover the mysteries under your skin, Exhibition catalogue 2002) – 3200 people per day visited this exhibition, and 14 million visited the exhibit that went around the world (Brooks and Rumsey 2006). Ganiaris (2001) describes in detail how the *London Bodies* exhibition was developed and implemented, including the formation of an 'ethics statement' (Museum of London 1997). The *London Bodies* exhibition attracted nearly 70,000 people (Ganiaris 2001), and surveys of visitors' reactions to how material was presented and attitudes to the display were generally positive. It was the skeletons of a child with rickets and a mother and foetus which disturbed people most. The *Body Worlds* exhibition was more a display of how beautiful human bodies can be (Brooks and Rumsey 2006), but also stressed the educational value of them. There are of course questions as to whether the dramatic poses used for many of the bodies was respectful and if using slogans to describe exhibits was appropriate, although the suggestion that this display was 'a cross between a medical, art, and freak show' cannot be supported (*ibid*, 278). Both exhibitions were developed for specific reasons: *London Bodies* to increase visitor numbers, and *Body Worlds* to generate income; both were successful in achieving their aim. Related to these two very successful exhibitions where both historic and relatively recent bodies were on display was Anthony Gormley's *Domain Field* exhibition at the Baltic in Gateshead, Tyne and Wear, in 2003. Here, the local public were encouraged to become part of the exhibition as volunteers.

They had their bodies moulded and the resulting casts were then filled with a matrix of thin steel bars by a welder. The result was a room full of steel matrix figures of different sizes and shapes, representing a range of ages, both sexes, and different builds with which visitors could engage (Leader 2003: Figure 9). Likewise, at the same place in 2006, Spencer Tunick produced a photographic exhibition of naked bodies of 1700 volunteers who posed for photographs early one July morning in 2005 (Fabrizi and Ley 2006). Both exhibitions were very successful.

As demonstrated above, the public are incredibly interested in the human body, both past and present, probably because they can relate directly and closely to the fact that they also have a body and skeleton. It may also be because few people come into contact with dead bodies and therefore, as Chamberlain and Parker Pearson (2001) suggest, the living rarely see the dead. By way of contrast to Britain, in many parts of the world today, death is very much part of life, and is celebrated as such – for example the annual Mexican Day of the Dead (the Christian feast of All Saints and All Souls) from 31 October to 2 November (Figure 10). This private family feast is seen as a reunion of the living and the dead, where food and drink offerings are made to the dead, and graves are tended and decorated (Carmichael and Sayer 1991).

Figure 10: Display at the Mexican Day of the Dead (Charlotte Roberts)

This fascination with the dead can also be seen in the success of programmes on British television that depict the study and interpretation of human remains; these include the BBC2 series *Meet the Ancestors* (J Richards 1999), Channel 4's *Secrets of the Dead* and *To the ends of the earth*, and some of the programmes in Channel 4's *Time Team* and BBC2's *Timewatch*. The question to be asked is, even if museum displays and TV programmes about human remains are very popular, does this justify them? Again, the issue of whether this is acceptable to people will depend on many factors, including their religious attitudes. Furthermore, if human remains are displayed, should there be ethical guidelines to say how they should be displayed? For example, the frozen and preserved body of Ötzi (see Chapter 3) has attracted a wide audience since his discovery, and continues to do so through the display of his remains in a temperature- and humidity-controlled chamber in the South Tyrol Museum of Archaeology, Bolzano, Italy – but is the display sensitive and respectful? Recently, staff at the Pitt Rivers Museum in Oxford have reported being increasingly uncomfortable with the display of shrunken heads there, despite the exhibit being the Museum's most famous and popular exhibit (www. spiked-online.com/index.php?/site/article/3017/).

Many museums would state that one of their missions is to be aware of viewer sensitivity when displaying archaeological finds (Tyson 1995, in Aufderheide 2000). If this is done then the public should be given the opportunity to view human remains, whether they be bodies or skeletons, as long as the display contributes to a wider display and understanding of a particular place and/or time period; visitors should also be warned that human remains are on display before they encounter them in the museum (as was done for the *London Bodies* exhibition). Displaying human remains purely for curiosity's sake is unacceptable, and of course codes of practice have been developed to deal with this problem (DCMS 2005, 20; Museum Ethnographers Group 1994; Museums Association – http// www.museumsassociation.org/ma/10934; World Archaeological Congress 2006 – http://www.worldarchaeologicalcongress.org/site/about_ethi.php; International Council of Museums – http://icom.museum/ethics.html (section 4.3)). There is, however, still some way to go in providing detailed ethical and moral guidance for those staging displays.

2.6 The United States: a case study

While New Zealand and Australia, in particular, have seen laws passed to prevent excavation of human remains, and/or immediate repatriation and/or reburial of remains excavated (see Jones and Harris 1998), developments in the United States will be detailed here from the perspective of providing a comparative example from outside Britain to illustrate how human remains have been treated elsewhere. It should be emphasised that considerations regarding human remains in other parts of the world are very different to the experience in Britain.

In the United States in the late 20th century there was an increased concern by Native Americans about the excavation of their ancestors' burial sites and the storage of human remains and associated funerary artefacts in museums and other institutions (Buikstra 2006b). This was supported by the public in later years which resulted in legislation being passed in 1989 and 1990. Discussions prior to the passing of legislation were presented as a conflict between ethics and science (Lackey 2006) and the legislation was described as 'an earthquake that transformed perception and memory' (*ibid*, 147). Some argue that the legislation was created to right wrongs, pay debts to the dead, establish and maintain justice, and return what belonged to Native Americans.

The National Museum of the American Indian Act (NMAIA) was passed in 1989, while the *Native American Graves Protection and Repatriation Act* was passed in 1990 (NAGPRA), with its accompanying regulations appearing in 1995. Additionally, within each of the States, laws can differ regarding

Native American human remains and artefacts that fall outside the umbrella of NAGPRA (Ubelaker and Guttenplan Grant 1989). Of course, the excavation of human remains and funerary objects in the name of 'science' has seen a long history in the United States, and the collection of human remains and associated materials started long ago. In 1862 the Army Medical Museum was founded as a repository for thousands of skeletal specimens, photographs, and other medical records obtained during the treatment and autopsy of military casualties of the Civil War of 1861–65 (Walker 2000); Native American crania and artefacts were also collected by army doctors from battlefields as well as cemeteries. During the 20th century, collections of human skeletal remains of Native Americans grew in American museums, and included the curation of skeletal collections with associated records such as age at death, sex, ethnicity, stature, and cause of death. However, it was not until the late 20th century that Native Americans found that their voice had been heard. Many tribal members feel linked spiritually to all or many other Native American people, living and/or dead, and believe they have a responsibility for the spiritual well being of their ancestors. Retention of their ancestors' remains in museums therefore interferes (and interfered) with the afterlife and separates the spirits of the dead from the living (*ibid*).

NAGPRA (http://www.cr.nps.gov/nagpra/) has two principal objectives (Myra Giesen pers comm, June 2007). The first is to deal with existing collections of Native American cultural items (human remains, funerary objects etc) by producing summary inventories – the collections are those made before the passage of the Act. The second is to protect Native American graves and other cultural sites still within archaeological sites on federal and tribal lands. The former objective is satisfied by the Act's provision of a mechanism for museums or federal agency officials to consult with Native Americans, and upon request repatriate human remains to lineal descendants or culturally affiliated Native American organisations. The latter objective is provided for by a system for federal land managers to consult with those organisations to determine the proper disposition of cultural items accidentally discovered or deliberately excavated on federal or tribal lands. Therefore, all federally funded public and private museums that curate cultural items are subject to this law, except the Smithsonian Institution in Washington DC, which is governed by the NMAIA; both Acts cover materials dated to AD 1492 or later.

All institutions were required to identify cultural items in their collections subject to NAGPRA and prepare an inventory of the items. They then had to consult with lineal descendants, Native American tribes, and Hawaiian organisations regarding identification and cultural affiliation of the items, and then inform them that these cultural items could be repatriated. For new discoveries of archaeological sites, only federal and tribal lands are included in the Act. As of November 2006 nearly 32,000 individual sets of human remains, nearly 700,000 associated funerary objects, 118,000 unassociated funerary objects, and 3584 sacred objects have been identified in Federal Register notices as being determined to have lineal descendants and/or cultural affiliation (http://

www.cr.nps.gov/nagpra/FAQ/INDEX.HTM); it is unknown what proportion of these items has undergone repatriation (Myra Giesen pers comm, June 2007). Naturally, there are many cultural items that cannot be assigned an affiliation because there is inadequate evidence. As of the end of December 2006 the number of non-identifiable human remains stood at 118,400 and 627 associated funerary objects (http://www.cr.nps.gov/nagpra/ONLINEDB/INDEX.HTM).

The National Museum of Natural History set up a Repatriation Office in 1991 in response to the NMAIA to inventory and assess the cultural origins of skeletal remains potentially affiliated to Native American, Native Hawaiian, and Native Alaskan people (http:/www.nmnh.si.edu/anthro/repatriation/). As of the end of May 2006, 89,848 funerary objects and the human remains of a minimum of 3585 individuals had been repatriated. At the end of September 2006, 65 Notices of Intended Disposition had been received by National NAGPRA, identifying 207 individual sets of human remains, 851 funerary objects, 25 unassociated funerary objects, and four objects of cultural patrimony recovered from federal lands (http://www.nps.gov/history/nagpra/NOTICES/NID.pdf).

In addition to the two laws, several professional bodies in the United States have also provided ethical guidelines for dealing with human remains, for example the American Association of Physical Anthropologists (http://www.physanth.org/positions/ethicsmain.htm), the American Anthropological Association (http://www.aaanet.org/committees/ethics/ethcode.htm), the Society of American Archaeology (http://www.saa.org/repatriation/repat_policy.html), and the Advisory Council on Historic Preservation (http://www.achp.gov/docs/hrpolicy0207.pdf); see Watkins *et al* (1995) for a summary of the policies.

Many bioarchaeologists in North America would say that NAGPRA has benefited anthropology as a whole, and bioarchaeology in particular (Ousley *et al* 2005), including more comprehensive analyses of human remains – filling gaps in knowledge of the human past, increasing study of human remains overall, allowing new analytical techniques to be used on old skeletal collections, and improving curation facilities for human remains that are not repatriated and/or reburied. Lackey (2006, 162), a professor of philosophy in New York, also describes the NAGPRA experience as 'positive on the whole'. It has improved relationships and increased collaboration between archaeologists, bioarchaeologists, and native groups (Rose *et al* 1996), although not always (Buikstra 2006b, 412–13), and stimulated the production of standards for recording human skeletal remains (Buikstra and Ubelaker 1994). For example, Philip Walker at Santa Barbara University in California has worked profitably with the Chumash for over 25 years and, through discussions and consultations with their leaders, has had an ossuary built on his university's campus to hold Chumash human remains for research (Buikstra 2006b).

Clearly, in the United States the push by indigenous people to have their ancestors' remains treated with respect, repatriated and/or reburied, has led to legal developments that have required archaeologists and anthropologists to look closely at how they treat human remains within a cultural context. It has also been beneficial to the discipline of bioarchaeology as much more descriptive and analytical work has now been done, inventories have been made of skeletal samples, and new research agendas developed, leading to cooperation and collaboration between archaeologists, bioarchaeologists and Native American groups.

2.7 Summary

The excavation, study, and curation of human remains from archaeological sites can be controversial. Opinions about whether this work can be justified vary considerably and depend on a variety of factors. It would appear that a more balanced view has now developed about what is acceptable and unacceptable, and there is much more dialogue between interested parties, particularly in some parts of the world such as the United States. As for Britain, there is some way to go to enable all those with a vested interest in the dead and their possessions to have their say. However, unlike in some other parts of the world, we can *all* claim a common ancestry with our forebears, and we can *all* have opinions about how human remains from archaeological sites should be treated.

2.8 Key learning points

- the study of human remains is a privilege and not a right
- repatriation and reburial of remains occurs at varying intensities around the world
- opinions about the treatment of human remains varies geographically, culturally and temporally, and will vary within countries, locally, regionally and nationally
- all interested parties should have equal rights to engage in debates about the treatment of human remains
- in some parts of the world human remains have not been treated with respect at all times (often relating to associated injustices to minority groups)
- the value of the study of human remains in contributing to our knowledge of the past is undoubted
- more debates about the issues are needed for British-derived human remains
- laws and guidelines regarding the ethical and legal treatment of human remains in Britain exist but, as a result of a recent review of aspects of burial legislation, archaeologists and bioarchaeologists remain in limbo regarding best practice
- the public in Britain are generally favourable to the excavation, analysis, curation, and display of human remains
- retention of human remains must be justified
- people have a fascination with human remains, past and present

CHAPTER THREE

Disposal and preservation of the dead

3.1 Introduction

The focus of this book is the analysis and interpretation of human remains from archaeological sites. Two of the most important factors that will determine the type and quality of the remains analysed are how the dead were disposed of and what happened to the body after death, before it was excavated. The first section of this chapter briefly describes and summarises methods of disposal through time from the Palaeolithic to the Early Modern period, with a focus on Britain, although it should be appreciated that people around the world have treated and do treat their dead in very many different ways (eg see Barley 1995; Parker Pearson 1999a).

In Britain today the majority of the dead are cremated rather than inhumed; this is because cremation is generally cheaper, is perceived as 'cleaner', and graveyards are filling up fast in our overcrowded country. However, as McKinley (2006, 81) has emphasised, modern cremations are 'stripped of "ritual" and reduced to a utilitarian means of disposing of the dead': this is very different from what we see in the past. Cremation was legalised in Britain in 1884, and the building of crematoria was most intense between 1950 and 1969 (Davies 1995, 2005). People are, of course, also using more novel methods of disposing of the dead, for example dispersing cremation ashes in fireworks (http://www.heavensabovefireworks.com), and many are opting for natural 'green' burials in coffins of traditional materials (http://www.somersetwillow.co.uk), often in rural areas that are considered to be more 'wildlife friendly' than conventional burial grounds (http://www.naturaldeath.org.uk). In effect, people are taking greater control over what happens to them following death, and hopefully embracing death as a part of life, as we see in other countries of the world (Carmichael and Sayer 1991). Prior to the Roman period, which was characterised by an expansion of formal cemeteries, there was greater diversity in the treatment of the dead, including a leaning towards more 'natural' disposals similar to those currently gaining in popularity.

3.2 Disposal of the dead

The provision of a final resting place for someone's mortal remains is generally a carefully thought through procedure which may have taken days, months or even years to plan and execute. Burial is thus a deeply significant act imbued with meaning

(Parker Pearson 1999a, 5)

(i) Introduction

Societies through time have disposed of their dead to show respect, for health reasons, and to fulfil religious obligations (Iserson 1994); the word 'burial' comes from the Anglo-Saxon word 'birgan' which means to conceal, and the dead have been buried in a wide variety of ways over the long time span for which we have evidence for human occupation (Figure 11). Archaeologists have also, since time immemorial, had a strong interest in excavating human remains from funerary contexts. Unfortunately that interest has not always been driven by a desire to discover information about the people themselves through their remains, and we have seen, and still see, many instances where associated grave goods have been the target of investigations. Thankfully, in Britain (at least now) we have systematic and scientific approaches to, and an interest in, the excavation of the whole of the funerary context, ultimately providing an integrated understanding of how people lived and died. The study of the mortuary context is not without its challenges in archaeology. Scholars over the years have suggested that archaeologists will never understand mortuary practices as they were so complex (Tarlow 1999), and studies of methods of disposal of the dead in traditional societies have further supported this concern (Ucko 1969). 'The simple equation of practice with belief, and the existence of cross-cultural regularities or of stable and conservative rituals and traditions cannot be taken at face value' (Parker Pearson 1999a, 44). Nevertheless, study of disposal of the dead in archaeology is alive and well! We will now look at the most common methods of disposal in Britain from the early prehistoric to post-medieval periods.

Figure 11: Burial from the late Neolithic site of Man Bac in Ninh Province, North Vietnam (1500–1000 BC) (with permission of Lorna Tilley, Australian National University)

(ii) Prehistory

Finding the dead who were buried in the past can be a challenge and all those that were buried in Britain from prehistory to the Early Modern period have certainly not yet been discovered and excavated, and never will be. This might be because the areas in which they were buried have not seen archaeological attention yet, perhaps because they are in rural areas that are not under threat of modern building development, or because the places in which they were buried do not preserve human remains (eg acidic soils of Scotland and Wales and parts of south-east England). However, it could equally be because their burial sites are just not visible. There have been extensive debates about when humans first developed an awareness of death, but it is generally agreed that it occurred within the last 100,000 years (Middle/Upper Palaeolithic) and possibly around 25,000–20,000 BP. It is also accepted by many that Neanderthal burials from the Middle Palaeolithic were likely deliberate, such as Burial 4 in Shanidar Cave, Iraq where it appears that flowers had been placed on the grave indicating that the burial had occurred during the summer (Leroi-Gourhan 1989). Prior to discussing the disposal of the dead in prehistory, a note on the dates used for specific sites should be provided. Based on Scarre (2005), for the Paleolithic period dates will be given in 'years ago' (years before present [BP]) and the other dates have been provided in calendar years (BC/AD).

In Britain there are few human remains that have been excavated for the Palaeolithic in general. This could be due to the fact that population density would have been very low at that time, the available areas for occupation would have been restricted to the south-west of England and Wales (free of ice), and at that time there was no recognised funerary practice. The burial environment and, to a certain extent, how long a body has been buried, affect the survival of human remains, making discovery and subsequent excavation rare. Thus, for the Palaeolithic, these factors probably contribute to the lack of evidence. Most of the evidence for human remains comes from cave sites in the south-west of England and Wales, for example the Lower Palaeolithic site of Pontnewydd Cave in Wales dated to c 225,000 BP (Cook et al 1982). While the oldest remains of humans have been found at Boxgrove in Sussex dated to the Lower Palaeolithic at 500,000 BP (Roberts and Parfitt 1999), and Barnfield Pit, Swanscombe in Kent (c 400,000 BP: Stringer and Hublin 1999), the oldest known formal 'ceremonial' site where human remains are deposited is at Paviland Cave in Wales, dated to c 24,000 BP, or the Upper Palaeolithic (Aldhouse-Green and Pettitt 1998). Here a male was buried with walrus ivory bracelets and perforated seashells, and covered with red ochre. A recent find of a humerus from Eel Point on Caldey Island, south Wales, dated to 24,470±110 BP (Gravettian or Mid-Upper Palaeolithic) is suggested possibly to have come from a cave and it becomes the third oldest anatomically modern human remain from Britain (Schulting et al 2005). There have been also human remains of Late Upper Palaeolithic date, mainly skull fragments, found in Gough's Cave (11,820±120 BP–12,380±110 BP), and in Sun Hole Cave (12,210±160 BP), Cheddar in Somerset (Currant et al 1989; Barton 1999). At the latter site there is clear evidence for deliberate deposition of adults and children.

Figure 12: Neolithic chambered tomb at Camster, Caithness, Scotland (with permission of Chris Scarre)

In the Mesolithic (8000–4000 BC), which commenced just after the end of the last Ice Age, Britain became an island as sea levels rose (Mithen 1999). Again the discovery of human remains from this period in Britain is rare. Some skeletal material from Gough's Cave in Somerset has been dated to the Mesolithic (*c* 5100 BC: Newell *et al* 1979) and there are other cave sites that have produced human remains of this date. For example, Aveline's Hole in the Mendip hills, Somerset, is the earliest scientifically dated cemetery, which was in use *c* 8200 BC (Keith 1924; Schulting 2005). It was discovered and excavated in the late 18th and early 19th centuries and 50–100 skeletons were found articulated on the cave floor. Unfortunately, the remains were 'lost' before analysis (http//:capra.group. shef.ac.uk/5/avelineshole.html), but between 1914 and 1933 the University of Bristol Spelaeological Society excavated the fragmentary remains of around twenty individuals. Recent research has found evidence of childhood stress in the teeth and bones, and toothpick grooves on the teeth (Jacobi 1987; Schulting and Wysocki 2002; Schulting 2005). Microwear analysis on the teeth suggests that plant foods probably played an important part in the diet, more than would be expected for a hunter-gatherer group, but stable isotope data suggests high consumption of animal protein. At cave sites in Derbyshire and Wales, for example Caldey Island (Schulting and Richards 2002), fragmentary skeletal remains have been excavated, while in Scotland excavations of shell middens have revealed some evidence for the disposal of human remains, usually in the form of bone fragments and teeth (for example, those excavated on the island of Oronsay, Orkney: Mellars 1987). These Palaeolithic and Mesolithic people were hunter-gatherers and often on the move searching for wild animals and plants; consequently, one would not normally expect to find formal cemeteries. However, in some areas of Europe such as Scandinavia formal cemeteries of these periods *are* found.

It is not until the Neolithic and the first agricultural communities in Britain (4000–2500 BC) that a plethora of very visible burial monuments appears. This includes earthen long barrows and stone cairns (Figure 12), with or without internal chambers for the placing of the dead, for example Belas Knap in Gloucestershire, Wayland's Smithy in Berkshire (Atkinson 1965) and West Kennet in Wiltshire (Piggott 1962). Usually the skeletal remains are found disarticulated, meaning the skeleton is not anatomically positioned. Thus, the deposit may contain the bones of many people mixed together, representing successive disposals of the dead, possibly following other treatment such as exposure of the body and/or 'curation' of remains. At West Kennet around 50 unburnt inhumed individuals were excavated from the central chambers; most of the disarticulated remains and finger bones had been placed in gaps in the stone walling of the chambers. At some sites, there appears to be 'zoning' of the burial chambers into areas for males and females and different age groups, including at West Kennet (Whittle 1999). Formal resting places for the dead also included passage graves (eg in Ireland – Newgrange, County Meath: O'Kelly 1973, and the north of Scotland – eg Maes Howe on Orkney; Henshall 1963 and 1972), the ditches of causewayed enclosures (eg Hambledon Hill, Dorset), henges, round barrows (north-east England), and latterly in the Neolithic, houses. From the middle Neolithic onwards individual burials are also found under cairns or in small enclosures (eg Radley, Oxfordshire: Bradley 1992; Whittle 1999). At Hambledon Hill there appears also to have been a mixture of mortuary treatments, including exposure, excarnation, and probable defleshing (McKinley pers comm, November 2007). Clearly the range of different disposal sites and methods used for the dead is impressive and illustrates how important these monuments were in society at

Figure 13: Bronze Age barrows at Lambourn, Berkshire (with permission of Chris Scarre)

that time, how it would have needed many people to construct them, and also how significant the treatment of the dead had become.

During the Bronze Age (2600–800 BC) both cremation and inhumation were practised. McKinley (1997) provides a very good overview of funerary rites and rituals of cremation in Bronze Age contexts, and has also described what cremation pyres consisted of (McKinley 1998, 18), although the few pyre sites that have been found that are of Bronze Age date have been covered by a barrow. Crouched individual burials were made in graves beneath round barrows (Figure 13) in southern England (eg Crichel Down, Dorset) or in stone-lined graves (cists) sealed beneath cairns in northern England and Scotland; this was a change from the Neolithic where collective burial was the norm. However, in the 'Beaker' period (see below), there appears to be growing evidence for collective graves (McKinley pers comm, November 2007). By the middle Bronze Age cremation was universal (Parker Pearson 1999b), and from this point on burial appears to have been more closely associated with settlements (Ray 1999). At certain points in the Bronze Age, characteristic grave goods such as 'Beaker' pottery (c 2000–1600 BC), and rich items (c 1700–1500 BC), appear and have been utilised to signify 'Beaker' people/culture and 'Wessex' people/culture (for example, West Overton G6b: Smith and Simpson 1966; and Bush Barrow, Wiltshire, respectively). At Bush Barrow, the male burial was accompanied by a range of rich grave goods, including three metal daggers and an axe, a probable helmet, a lozenge-shaped plate of sheet gold, and a macehead (Megaw and Simpson 1979). In the Wessex culture, barrows were clustered together and different forms are noted: 'bell', 'bowl', 'disc', and 'pond'. In the later Bronze Age, there is little evidence for burials and it is likely that disposal of the dead took place in locations that are essentially the most invisible to the archaeologist, such as in water. However, while cremation appears to have been most common, there is evidence for other disposal methods, such as formal inhumation burial.

Disposal of many of the dead in Britain in the Iron Age (late 800 BC–AD 100) was likely by excarnation or the scattering of cremated remains, and there appears to have been some interest in disposal at watery places such as rivers (Darvill 1987; Bradley 1998). Cunliffe (2005) defines three stages of mortuary behaviour in Iron Age Britain. The 8th to 6th centuries BC saw the preference for cremation

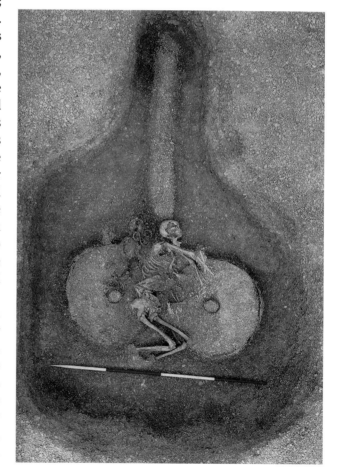

Figure 14: Iron Age chariot burial from Wetwang Slack, Yorkshire (with permission of Oxford Archaeology)

coming to an end, but inhumations were still very rare. In the 5th to 1st centuries BC (middle Iron Age) inhumation and excarnation were practised, and regular cemeteries with crouched burials are also seen. Bodies and redeposited disarticulated and decomposed human remains were also disposed of in pits and ditches on settlement sites, for example at Maiden Castle in Dorset (Goodman and Morant 1940). It is clear from the remains excavated that excarnation was practised, where the dead body was initially exposed to the elements, but also excarnation without exposure. There was a particular interest in the head, as seen on some settlement sites where remains of skulls are more common than other parts of the body (Cunliffe 2005). Burials with grave goods were not common in southern England until the late Iron Age (100 BC–AD 43) and river finds also increase at this time (Bradley 1998). In specific regions of the country we see different burial traditions (Stead 1979; Haselgrove 1999): for example, in north and east Yorkshire, the Arras tradition is characterised by the grouping together of small barrows in large cemeteries (eg at Burton Fleming), rich vehicle burials (eg at Wetwang Slack, Figure 14), and individual barrows surrounded by rectangular ditched enclosures (Cunliffe 2005). In south-west England disarticulated unburnt remains are seen on settlement sites and in hillforts (Darvill 1987), and there are individual crouched burials in cist graves set in rows (eg at Harlyn Bay, Cornwall where 130 inhumations were found). In the late Iron Age, cremation was reintroduced to the south-east of England, but there was also, from the late 2nd century BC until the Roman invasion, a group of elite individuals that were buried with weapons or mirrors, depending on the sex of the person (Cunliffe 2005); most are found in Yorkshire. We must not of course forget the famous bog body, that of Lindow Man from Cheshire (Brothwell 1986), also dated to the Iron Age and illustrating a more unusual method of disposal for this period.

Compared to previous periods, there are few burials apparent, which can perhaps be explained by unconventional (and invisible) disposal; indeed, over large parts of Britain there is no evidence of burial. In the 1st century BC, not only do more formal cemeteries appear (Hill 1995), but cremation reappears, as seen, for example, in the burials from the Aylesford cemeteries in Kent. By the Roman conquest in AD 43 cremation burial in an urn was a very common method of disposal, although inhumation continued even after the Roman Conquest (Whimster 1981).

(iii) The Roman period

Burial practice in Roman Britain was 'dynamic and regionally varied' (Philpott 1981, 1). When the Romans conquered Britain in AD 43 both inhumation and cremation were practised, although inhumation was rare in some regions. At the Roman Conquest the predominant burial rite in the south and east of England was cremation, and this did continue (*ibid*). However, from the middle of the 2nd century AD there was a clear switch to inhumation, reflecting changes in Italy and the Western provinces which had occurred earlier in the century.

Inhumation burials are found in a number of urban and rural contexts from the mid-2nd century onwards: major towns, small towns, forts and vici, and villas, and also as isolated burials in and around buildings (Esmonde Cleary 2000); from the mid-3rd century inhumation burial was common in all the Roman provinces and was maintained until the end of the Roman era in Britain (Philpott 1981). In major towns such as at Winchester, Hampshire (Clarke 1979), Cirencester, Gloucestershire (McWhirr *et al* 1982), and Colchester in Essex (Crummy *et al* 1993), cemeteries were usually placed next to roads; in the Roman Empire burial within the boundary of a town was forbidden (because of sanitary precautions and the fear of defilement: Toynbee 1971). In effect, 'the dead were the first of a town's citizens to be encountered on entering the town, and the last to be left behind on quitting it' (Esmonde Clearly 2000, 136). Very few burials have been excavated from forts and vici (but see Cool 2004), such that Esmonde Cleary (2000, 129) states that, 'the study of burial at military sites can hardly even be described as being in its infancy'. Similarly, burials at villa sites are rare (eg Lullingstone, Kent: Meates 1979; Rudston, east Yorkshire: Stead 1980), although not for infant burials (Rebecca Gowland pers comm, November 2007). Nevertheless, other contexts for Roman burials include the reuse of prehistoric monuments, disposal in wet places (wells, shafts, pits), and particular body parts have even been found at some sites, for example skulls at the mid 2nd-century AD site of Walbrook, London, where younger males were identified (Bradley 1998; Bradley and Gordon 1988). Infants (up to 18 months old) tended to be treated separately and are rarely found in adult cemeteries until the 4th century AD (Philpott 1991). They were disposed of in shallow 'scoops' under floors, in pits and ditches, in enclosures, and occasionally in discrete infant cemeteries. Grave goods are rare (coins and pottery).

Inhumed bodies were placed supine (on their backs) in an extended position with varied positioning of the arms, hands, legs and head, usually in an earth-cut grave (*ibid*). In some rural areas, even as late as the 3rd century AD, the late Iron Age crouched burial tradition continued (but this was more common in the early Roman period). Also, the evidence for decapitated burials in the Roman period (eg at Driffield Terrace, The Mount, York: Hunter-Mann 2006; Figure 15) shows some continuity with the Celtic veneration of the human head, but prone and/or decapitated individuals are relatively rare and are mostly found in the 3rd and 4th centuries AD. The skulls of decapitated individuals may be missing or buried separately nearby, replaced on the neck area in the correct anatomical position, or placed elsewhere in the grave (Philpott 1991).

The poor were placed directly in simple marked graves, or occasionally in wooden coffins, while the rich were buried in elaborately decorated stone or lead coffins (Toynbee 1971). Sometimes the grave was lined with stone slabs or ceramic tiles and some bodies were shrouded, had coverings of gypsum plaster or lime, or were embalmed (Philpott 1991). By the 3rd and 4th centuries AD, the majority of burials were simple and unfurnished. Grave goods to honour the dead and make them feel comfortable in the afterlife included pottery and glass vessels, food for the journey to the underworld, coins in the mouth, armour and

Figure 15: Burial with grave goods from the Roman cemetery of Driffield Terrace, York (with permission of York Archaeological Trust)

weapons, cooking implements, gaming counters, and children's toys (Toynbee 1971). Women were often accompanied by toilet boxes with mirrors, tweezers and cosmetics, and also jewellery. With the adoption of Christianity in the 4th century AD, there is a decline in grave goods, the most common inclusions being hob nails from boots. Orientation of the body with the head to the west, facing east, is a feature often associated with Christianity.

By the middle of the 3rd century, cremation was rare (Wacher 1980), but some rural areas and small towns continued the tradition, and even in London there is evidence for cremation in a late Roman context (Barber and Bowsher 2000). In fact, evidence now suggests that cremation was actually more common than has been believed, especially in northern frontier areas (eg Cool 2004) and in towns such as Winchester and London (McKinley pers comm, November 2007). During the mid-1st to 3rd centuries the majority of cremations took place on pyres away from the final burial site, but in close proximity, and the cremated bone was collected and placed (mainly) into pottery jars (Philpott 1991). The container was then placed in an earth-dug pit which may have been lined with wood, stone slabs or tiles; occasionally brick chambers were constructed. Less common was cremation in situ. Many cremation burials were accompanied by grave goods, especially pottery vessels, but also non-ceramic items such as vegetable food remains (Barber and Bowsher 2000). At the late Romano-British site of Brougham in Cumbria, McKinley (2004a) excavated and analysed 322 contexts and sub-contexts containing cremated bone. There were urned, unurned, and otherwise 'contained' cremation burials with or without associated pyre debris in the grave fills, along with accessory burials (related to the main burial, urned, or unurned), discrete formal pyre debris deposits, and cenotaphs (very small quantities of bone buried outside the confines of the cemetery). Pyre debris consists of 'all the material remaining at the pyre site after the bone and pyre goods intended for "formal" burial have been removed' (McKinley 2004a, 284). Redeposited pyre debris often contains cremated bone and fuel ash (charcoal), pyre goods, and possibly burnt flint/clay/soil and fuel ash slag; pyre debris has been found for most periods in Britain where cremation has been practised (eg at Brougham and also at the Eastern Cemetery in Roman London: Barber and Bowsher 2000); it signifies that there has been a 'formal' burial close by (McKinley 2000a, 2004a).

(iv) The early medieval period

Inhumation and cremation (urned or unurned remains) were both practised in the early medieval period (c AD 410–c 1050), but only inhumation is seen in the later part of the period. Cremation was certainly predominant in East Anglia and Yorkshire but not in the south and south-east of England. The vast majority of East Anglian and Yorkshire cremation burials were urned (Figure 16), as were most in the south of England, but rites varied (McKinley pers comm, November 2007). Certainly by AD 600 in southern Britain cremation had been superseded everywhere by inhumation (Hills 1999). Both rites included the provision of pyre/ grave goods and grave goods, respectively, although by the 7th and 8th centuries those provisions had diminished. By the 8th century, high-status graves have also disappeared and more simple inhumation graves with no grave goods are found. This illustrates a major shift away from the religious beliefs of the late Roman period (Lucy 2000). Unique evidence for burial at this time is represented by a special mound burial dated to the 7th century AD at Sutton Hoo in Suffolk (Carver 1998). Here, a richly furnished grave, which included Christian artefacts, illustrates the strong and extensive links that England had with the east, including Scandinavia, Egypt and eastern Europe (Lucy and Reynolds 2002).

In the 5th to 6th centuries the position of the body tended to be supine and extended, with the arms by the sides and legs straight or slightly bent (Figure 17, and Daniell and Thompson 1999); the head was usually at the west end of the grave. However, prone (laid on the front, and possibly seen as punishment) and crouched burials (foetal position) have been noted (Figure 18), along with burials made on their sides. As we have seen for the Roman period, large inhumation cemeteries are seen, for example at Castledyke South, Barton-on-Humber, east Yorkshire (late 5th/early 6th to late 7th century AD) (Drinkhall and Foreman 1998), and at Edix Hill, Barrington, Cambridgeshire (6th–7th century AD) (Malim and Hines 1998), along with occasional large cremation cemeteries such as at Spong Hill in Norfolk, the largest cremation cemetery excavation to date (6th century AD) (McKinley 1994a). Between the late 8th century and the 11th century, Viking settlement spread across much of England but the evidence for (pagan) burial is sparse (Daniell and Thompson 1999). Two sites in Derbyshire,

Figure 16 (right): Cremation urns at Anglo-Saxon Spong Hill, Norfolk (Number 1665: Urn numbers 2192 and 2193 of two older adult cremations; copyright: Norfolk Historic Environment, Norfolk Museums and Archaeology Service)

Figure 17 (below left): Extended Anglo-Saxon burial at Bamburgh Castle, Northumberland (with permission of Sarah Groves and the Bamburgh Castle Project)

Figure 18 (below right): Crouched Anglo-Saxon burial at Bamburgh Castle, Northumberland (with permission of Sarah Groves and the Bamburgh Castle Project)

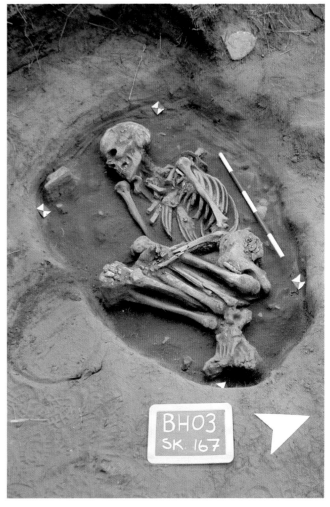

however, do illustrate how different the disposal of the dead could be at that time, even when the sites were in close proximity (4km) (J D Richards 1999): at Ingleby (9th–10th century AD), cremations were found and the remains reburied following excavation (McKinley pers comm, November 2007), while at Repton there were individual inhumation burials and a mass grave (9th century AD. Christian burials are also seen in churchyards later in the period, for example at the 10th- to 11th-century cemetery at Raunds in Northamptonshire (Boddington 1996).

(v) The late medieval period

During the late medieval period (*c* AD 1050–1550) Christianity, as advocated by the Catholic Church, prevailed and burial for the majority was by inhumation of the unburnt corpse in graveyards associated with parish churches (eg at St Helen-on-the-Walls, York: Dawes and Magilton 1980). There are other 'contexts' too that have produced human remains from formal cemeteries, for example leprosy hospitals (eg that of St James and St Mary Magdalene, Chichester, Sussex: Magilton *et al* 2008); non-leprosy hospitals (eg St Bartholomew's, Bristol: Price and Ponsford 1998); monasteries (eg St Andrew, Fishergate, York: Stroud and Kemp 1993); mass graves (eg victims of the battle at Towton, Yorkshire: Fiorato *et al* 2007; and victims of the 14th-century plague at East Smithfield, London: Hawkins 1990; Margerison and Knüsel 2002; Figure 19); and charnel houses (eg at Rothwell Church, Northamptonshire: Roberts 1984; Garland *et al* 1988).

Figure 19: Part of the 14th-century Black Death cemetery at East Smithfield, London (with permission of the Picture Library, Museum of London and Andy Chopping)

The majority of people were buried in an east–west orientation, with the head to the west, supine and in an extended position (Figure 20). Higher-status burials were afforded coffins of wood, lead or stone (Roberts and Cox 2003), but for the vast majority, a simple shroud was used (Daniell 1997). Some graves were lined with stone, tile, metal, or brick and in some cases head supports in the form of stones or pillows were placed in the grave or coffin (Gilchrist and Sloane 2005). Grave goods were rare but can be seen early in the period, just after the Norman Conquest. For example, at St Nicholas Shambles, London, pebbles had been placed in

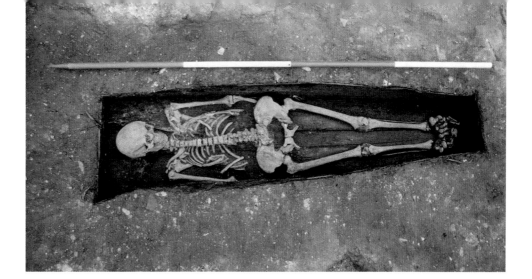

the mouths of four people, and priests could be buried with a chalice and/or paten, as at St Giles, Brompton Bridge, North Yorkshire (Cardwell 1995). Late medieval cemeteries, like many of their early medieval counterparts, can be very large and most are associated with urban contexts, although rural cemeteries have also been discovered and excavated (for example a large part of the cemetery at Wharram Percy, North Yorkshire: Beresford and Hurst 1990; Mays *et al* 2007).

(vi) The post-medieval (Early Modern) period

From around AD 1550–1850 (the post-medieval or Early Modern period), a different and more diverse burial practice is seen, although inhumation dominated until the end of the 19th century. The Reformation in the 16th century placed emphasis on the resurrection of corporeal remains which led to the desire that mortal remains should not be disturbed (Roberts and Cox 2003). Of course, with very overcrowded cemeteries it was not always possible to avoid disturbance as new burials disturbed old, the exception being the privileged in society who could pay to be buried inside the church and so got some protection. The Reformation opened the way for a number of changes in religious practice that impacted on burial, with the later nonconformist movement also developing distinctive styles of burial ground such as those of the Quakers (Stock 1998). People also invested in new civic cemeteries. Large urban cemeteries with individual discrete graves are also evident at this time, for example at Cross Bones burial ground, Southwark in London (Brickley *et al* 1999), St Martin's in Birmingham (Brickley *et al* 2006), and the high-status crypt at Christ Church, Spitalfields, London (Adams and Reeve 1993; Molleson and Cox 1993). At St Martin's (Figure 21), a total of 857 burials were recorded at excavation, 86% of which were in simple earth-cut graves. Within the earth-cut graves the most common burial was in a wooden coffin with metal fittings, although brick-lined graves, chambered vaults and family vaults were also noted. In general, however, post-medieval burials are less commonly excavated and analysed (but see Cox 1998), and it is only in recent years that an increase in excavation of these sites has been noticeable due to modern development in British urban contexts.

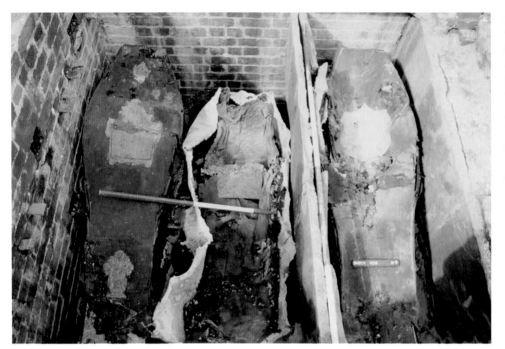

Figure 21: Burial vault of the Warden family at the post-medieval site of St Martin's-in-the-Bull Ring, Birmingham (with permission of CgMs Consulting, Birmingham; supplied by Amanda Forster, Birmingham Archaeology)

(vii) A note on cremated burials

Cremations are found in all periods from the Bronze Age to the early medieval, and it is clear that cremation burial played a significant role in the lives of our ancestors. As McKinley (1994c, 132) states 'A cremation is more than simple collections of human bone', and, 'cremated bones represent not only the physical remains of one or more individuals, but also the production of a series of ritual acts that comprise the disposal of the dead by the mortuary rite of cremation' (McKinley 2000b, 403).

Cremation will dehydrate and oxidise the organic parts of the body – an appropriate temperature, a specified time, and enough oxygen are necessary prerequisites for a 'successful' cremation. In modern circumstances it takes from around one to one and a half hours to cremate a body at a temperature of between 700 and 1000°C (McKinley 2000b). In the past, of course, open pyre cremation would have been the norm, as seen in some pictorial and documentary sources, and still practised in some parts of the world today such as India and Nepal. Layers of timber set in a rectangle and infilled with brushwood (on a flat surface or over a pit) allow circulation of oxygen, support the body and pyre goods, and provide a fuel source for the cremation to take place (McKinley 2000b). Experimental cremations indicate that temperatures >1000°C are achievable in a pyre. Climate is an important consideration as wet conditions present problems, which may lead to temporary burial (this may also be done to allow time for the family to prepare for the funeral). In the case of the Roman upper classes, the body lay in state for seven days, although most Romans were cremated and buried shortly after death (McKinley 2006).

Cremation burials have a particularly special place in archaeology because, until very recently, they have been relatively ignored by the bioarchaeologist as being particularly time consuming to analyse and not generating useful information. However, McKinley (2000b, 2000c, 2006) has highlighted well the immense possibilities for understanding many aspects of our ancestors' lives through studying their cremated remains. In particular, she has pointed out the previous lack of attention paid to excavating and analysing the 'whole' cremation deposit, which allows us to explore the ritual act of cremation in the past. In that deposit may be found cremated human bone, fuel ash from the pyre, pyre goods (ie burnt with the body) and grave goods (only incorporated at the time of the burial). Most pyre goods are found with urned burials, and are most common in Anglo-Saxon cremations (McKinley 1994c). Personal items, food remains, gifts, animals representing joints of meat or just pets, and worked bone and antler are also found in cremated remains (eg see Bond and Worley 2006 on animal remains). It may also be possible to learn about aspects of the cremation ritual, for example the position of the body on the pyre, and pyre technology, by analysing the presence of staining of pyre goods on bones or even adherence of the same.

Important in the analysis of cremation deposits is to look at the physical and stratigraphic relationships between the components of the cremation, and record pre-excavation bone fragment size as there is a tendency for the bones to fragment even more following excavation (McKinley 1994b, 2006). Additionally, the deposit is examined for charred plant remains (flotation) and also wet sieved down to 1mm in order to retrieve the smallest fragments of bone and other inclusions. The position of the corpse on the pyre during cremation may be inferred, along with the efficiency of the cremation (colour of the bone and appearance of the pyre 'goods' and debris). A range of colour is often seen in the bone fragments from any one cremation, from brown/black, through blue, to buff/white, and there is a relationship between temperature and colour (lighter bone indicates that there was sufficient oxygen available to enable the cremation process to proceed – oxidation). A shortfall of oxygen or a poor fuel supply can lead to incomplete cremation. For example, clothing, the position of the head, arms or legs, collapse of the pyre or insufficient fuel may affect oxygen supply (McKinley 2004b); in fact, the body is not a good conductor of heat (*ibid*). The weight of the cremated bone analysed will also suggest how efficiently it was collected following the cremation process – relatives, friends, or professional collectors would have gathered the remains and the time taken to do this may reflect how 'important or popular' the person was. McKinley (2000b) also emphasises the importance of distinguishing between multiple cremations (corpses cremated on the same pyre), multiple burials of cremated remains (one vessel/grave for remains from a few separate cremations), and multiple graves (remains from separate cremations and burials in one grave).

Thus, the act of cremating a body and disposing of it creates a very special archaeological context which necessitates very detailed analysis of the cremated bone, and the remains of fuel, pyre and grave goods in order to reconstruct the series of ritual acts which lead to such contexts on archaeological sites.

3.3 The effect of funerary context on study

From this brief survey of methods of disposal of the dead through time in Britain, it is easy to see that the ways in which people buried their dead will have a great impact on, firstly, whether they are identified in the archaeological record, secondly how they are excavated and, thirdly, the quality of the information that it is possible to record from the skeletal remains. A recent survey of health through time (Roberts and Cox 2003) identified many more skeletal remains from the Roman period onwards. The prehistoric samples, being smaller, cannot be used as representative of the populations living at the time. The analysis of isolated fragments of bones in a shell midden of the Mesolithic period will generate much less information about the people they represent than multiple discrete individual skeletons from a late medieval urban cemetery. Likewise, as the majority of Roman burials are from urban civilian contexts, we can learn very little about rural populations or military personnel at that time. Nevertheless, the wealth and variety of funerary contexts have produced much useful data from the human remains analysed but the data has to be considered with respect to the limitations outlined.

3.4 Summary

In prehistory it is not until we reach the Neolithic period that the evidence for burials increases, with inhumations in a variety of funerary monuments, and also at ritual sites such as causewayed enclosures. In the Bronze Age, both inhumation and cremation burials were made under barrows and cairns, while in the Iron Age both cremation and inhumation of the corpse continue, although the evidence of burial is scarce and probably reflects the nature of some methods of disposal of human remains. In the Roman period a lot of our evidence comes from urban inhumation cemeteries, but also some very large cremation cemeteries. The early medieval period sees, initially, cremation and inhumation, but later a move towards inhumation only; this practice continues into the late and post-medieval periods.

3.5 Key learning points
- the history and development of funerary practice in Britain has great variety
- funerary monuments are particularly striking in the prehistoric period
- as social complexity develops through time, disposal of the dead becomes much more formalised
- funerary practice through time illustrates how the corpse was treated and some of the influencing factors
- disposal methods affect visibility of the buried dead, and the amount and quality of information obtainable from skeletal remains
- many more skeletal remains have been excavated and analysed from the Roman period onwards

3.6 Preservation

Golden lads and girls must,
As chimney-sweepers, come to dust.
(Shakespeare, *Cymbeline*, **IV, ii**)

(i) Introduction

The information that can be generated by the study of human remains from archaeological sites can vary enormously and depends on many factors inherent in the survival of the remains through to examination; Waldron nicely illustrates factors affecting survival (1987, figure 6.1). It does not take much thought to realise that a preserved body potentially will contain far more information about that person than a skeleton, or indeed the remains of a cremated body. Likewise, if a bioarchaeologist is studying several hundred well-preserved skeletons from a late medieval cemetery, this will produce a more realistic perspective on the life of the population from which those people derived than examining a few fragmentary and poorly preserved skeletal remains from a Bronze Age barrow. In this chapter the different ways in which human remains are preserved into the archaeological record, and ultimately into the laboratory situation, are explored.

(ii) Decay of the body

The body decays through two processes (Mays 1998). Firstly, autolysis occurs whereby there is destruction of the body tissues by enzymes released after death (proteins which increase the rate of biochemical reactions), and secondly there is putrefaction (decomposition) whereby the soft tissues decay because of the presence of micro-organisms. When a person dies the bacteria which are present normally in the intestines invade the body tissues, along with micro-organisms from the grave environment, such as the soil. As a result of putrefaction, the soft tissues become liquid and gas is produced, which swells the body. If there is a lot of protein in some tissues then decay will be slower (eg hair – see Wilson 2001 on the survival of hair in archaeology; Figure 22). The chemical processes that occur during putrefaction of the body's fat, protein, and carbohydrate are complex and can influence the decay of bone (Garland and Janaway 1989). Following the decay of the soft tissues of the body, the bones (composed of protein – mainly collagen; and mineral – mainly hydroxyapatite) will decay; their protein-mineral bond will alter according to physical, chemical, and biological factors (see below). Mann *et al* (1990) suggest that it takes about ten to twelve years for the body of an adult to decompose to a skeleton, and half that time for a child, but it very much depends on the many factors discussed below. Once a body has decayed to a skeleton, the decay of bones and teeth proceeds in a complex way (Millard 2001). Although a fair amount is known about the deterioration of cortical bone, there is much we need to know about the enamel and dentine of the teeth, different types of bone such as immature lamellar bone, and the microscopic structures within bone

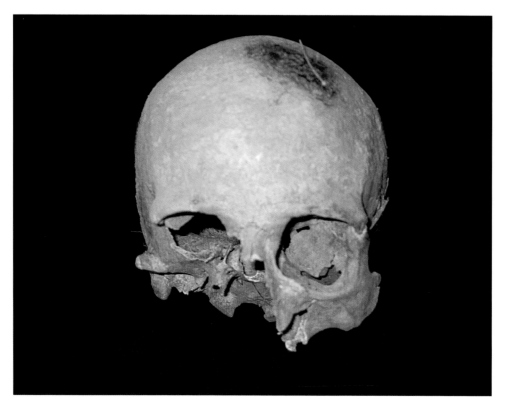

Figure 22: Hair and hair pin preserved on a post-medieval skull from Matterdale, Cumbria (with permission of Jaime Jennings)

such as osteons (*ibid*). Data also suggest that the external appearance of bone may belie how well-preserved the bone is throughout its structure (Garland 1987; Bell 1990). Ultimately, all these factors affect the deterioration or preservation of bones and teeth and so influence the quality of the human remains that are discovered, excavated, and analysed.

(iii) Environments of preservation

Taphonomy is the field that describes this scientific study of the processes that happen to a body after death, and the many interlinked factors that are involved can be divided into intrinsic and extrinsic; these factors may accelerate or delay the decay of bodies. It should be noted, however, that even if conditions appear to be the same for different buried bodies, they may decay at different rates. For example, Mant (1987) describes two people being killed at the same time, being buried in the same graveyard in adjacent graves, and decaying at different rates. In his study of forensic contexts such as mass graves, he noted emaciated people being skeletonised earlier, bodies buried in coffins decaying faster because of poor drainage of decomposition products, and clothing giving better preservation to a body than a coffin.

If one considers briefly the world in which we live today, a great range of environments exists with different mean temperatures and humidity, and indeed potential for survival of human remains. For example, in the Arctic and

Antarctic freezing temperatures and dry air create an environment which can preserve buried bodies very well; the excavation in the 1970s of 15th-century AD Greenland mummies from Qilakitsoq, 450km north of the Arctic circle on the west coast of Greenland, saw the preservation of six women and two children, along with their clothing (Hart Hansen *et al* 1991). A more unusual mode of preservation of a body in the cooler, damp climate of a north European context can be seen in the remains of a woman at St Bees, Cumbria, England, dated to AD 1300. Here the body had been covered in embalming wax/resin, wrapped in a shroud of linen, placed on a lead sheet and then in a wooden coffin, and the space between the lead-sheeted body and the coffin packed with clay. It is likely that the lack of oxygen inside the coffin preserved the body well, although there has been a suggestion that the person had been embalmed abroad and then transported to Cumbria for burial (Chamberlain and Parker Pearson 2001). It is clear that many different factors may contribute to the decay or preservation of a body.

Experiments on the preservation of bodies have been, and are being, done at the 'Body Farm' in Knoxville, Tennessee, made famous through Patricia Cornwell's novel (Bass and Jefferson 2003). These experiments started in 1981 and involve donated bodies being disposed of in different ways in an enclosed compound. For example, bodies have been deposited in shade, in full sun, in woodland, in the boots of cars and on back seats, on the ground, in graves, and in water. These experiments provide invaluable data for understanding the decay rate of human remains both in archaeological and forensic contexts; in the latter case it is particularly important to be able to assess time since death as this might help to solve the crime. As Bass, in Bass and Jefferson (2003, 275) states, 'My goal for the data was simple. Anytime a real-life murder victim was found, under virtually any circumstances or at any stage of decomposition, I wanted to be able to tell police – with scientific certainty – when that person was killed'. There have also been similar experiments in Europe but mainly using pig remains; these are apparently good analogues for human bodies as the decomposition process and rate are similar (Morton and Lord 2002).

(a) Intrinsic factors

Intrinsic factors refer to those characteristics inherent in the body, including the bones, at the time of disposal that may affect whether, and how well, the body or derivatives of it survive. Some of these are described below to show their impact on the survival of human remains.

Size, shape, density, and bone mineral content

As Millard (2001, 637) states, 'Bone is popularly regarded as a dry, inanimate, uncomplicated and robust material'. This could be no further from the truth as many factors can influence how well preserved it is. Generally speaking, children's bones are smaller, less dense, and have less mineral in them than adult skeletons; they thus have less chance of survival into the archaeological record. However, the adult skeleton contains small bones too and those of the hands and feet are often partly absent once the skeleton has been excavated; compare, for example the size of the femur to one of the wrist bones. Waldron (1987) found in his study of the skeletons from a Romano-British cemetery at West Tenter Street, London, that the densest and relatively heavier bones of the skeleton (eg the top part of the femur and one of the forearm bones, or ulna, along with parts of the lower jaw or mandible) survived better than less dense and lighter bones. Some parts of the bones are also much more porous than others and have a larger surface area, and are therefore are more likely to decay, for example the spongy bone of the vertebrae of the spine and the top and bottom ends of the long bones of the arms and legs. Nevertheless, the external, or cortical, layer of the long bones does tend to survive well purely because in adult skeletons that layer is very dense. For example, Willey *et al* (1997) documented the mineral density of bones against survival of different parts of the skeleton at an AD 1350 massacre site in south-central Dakota, USA. They found that density had a strong impact on survival of bones and fragments, ultimately affecting calculations of the minimum number of individuals represented. The teeth of course are the best survivors of burial, the outer white enamel being hard and very resistant to decay; this explains why early hominid remains thousands and even millions of years old are often represented by just teeth or fragments of them.

Age and sex

The bodies of infants (birth to end of first year) and children (two years to puberty) are much smaller than those of adults and therefore will 'disappear' from the archaeological record more quickly. Once the body is represented by a skeleton, the bones, being smaller and more fragile, may also decay faster than those of an adult. Therefore, age at death may inherently affect how fast a body decays, and the younger the person is the faster it will potentially decay. However, older people with osteoporosis (loss of bone mass) will also be more susceptible to faster decay. Generally speaking most cemetery sites have fewer non-adult skeletons than those of adults, non-adult meaning ones whose bones and teeth have not fully developed; this is surprising considering historical sources which suggest there was high infant mortality in the past. For example, the London Bills of Mortality from 1728 to 1850 show that in the period up to 1800 over 30% of deaths were in children in the first two years of their life (Roberts and Cox 2003), and the figure rose to 40% for children aged five or less. This was, of course, because of high levels of childhood disease and the traumatic effects of weaning.

Although infant and child skeletons in cemeteries make up a smaller proportion than the figures quoted here, this is not to say that archaeologists do not find and excavate the remains of non-adult bones, just that they are less frequent than adult skeletons (see table 2.1 in Lewis 2007). This may be because they are often buried in shallower graves and this affects survival (McKinley pers comm, November 2007). However, they may also survive better at some sites because they are found in burial environments which aid preservation. Some archaeological sites in Britain have revealed large proportions of non-adult skeletons which indicate that, if the conditions are right, there is an equal chance of the survival of child and infant skeletons. For example, of over 1000 burials at the Romano-British camp at Poundbury, Dorset, 374 skeletons were non-adults (Farwell and Molleson 1993), and at the early medieval site of Raunds Furnells in Northamptonshire with over 360 burials, 208 were non-adults (Powell 1996). It may be that differential burial practices, and perhaps infanticide in some cultures, along with excavation techniques (including whether soil is sieved or not to find the smaller bones) also greatly influence the number of sub-adults in an archaeological sample of skeletons. However, as described above, the bones of infants and children have low amounts of mineral in them, which makes them 'softer' and more likely to suffer from crushing in the soil matrix and be subject to decay in acidic soils (Guy *et al* 1997).

The bodies and skeletons of males are generally speaking more robust than those of females and therefore one would expect the former to be better represented within the archaeological record than the latter (as seen by Lieverse *et al* 2006), although this is not always the case. Women are also more susceptible to osteoporosis (especially post-menopause, and with increasing age), and therefore if the bones are less dense and ultimately more fragile then they will decay faster in the ground. A study of a Siberian cemetery in the Lake Baikal region dated to 5000–3700 BP showed that adolescents and young to middle-aged adults (12–20 years, 20–35 years, and 35–50 years at death) were much better preserved than infants, children, and older adults (Lieverse *et al* 2006). An obese person will also decay much faster into a skeleton after death than one who is thin because of the large amounts of flesh available to feed micro-organisms and maggots (Bass and Jefferson 2003).

Disease

If a person had a health problem when they died then it is likely that the disease process will speed up decomposition, for example if a person had an infection of the blood (septicaemia). Likewise, if a person had an open wound or wounds at death, this enables decomposition to occur faster than normal because micro-organisms can enter the body more easily. When it comes to the skeleton, most diseased bones are inherently more fragile; the bones of a person with a bone tumour, osteoporosis, or an infectious disease will often deteriorate faster in the ground than the bones of a person without any disease. The contents of the gut, including micro-organisms, can also accelerate the deterioration of the body, along with (certainly today) medicinal drugs in the body.

(b) Extrinsic factors

Perhaps of more complexity are the many extrinsic factors that can slow down or speed up decay processes, and they should be considered as factors that act in combination (along with intrinsic factors). These can be usefully divided into the environmental features of a cemetery site, the flora and fauna, and the activities of humans (Henderson 1987). Space does not allow a full description of all these factors.

Disposal methods

How the body is disposed of can also influence survival to excavation as we have seen above. Is the body buried or cremated? Lieverse *et al* (2006) found that skeletal remains that had been charred and calcined were less complex and more fragmented than those unaffected by fire at the prehistoric site of Khuzhir-Nuge XIV in Siberia. How was the person buried? For example, burial in clothing or in a shroud, or with decompositional matter such as straw or wood shavings in coffins, may attract insects, thus hastening decay, while burial in a coffin might produce an anaerobic environment (lack of oxygen) which will be good for preservation. Obviously the material of the coffin is of fundamental relevance – a lead coffin is most likely to have an anaerobic environment, and so preserve bodies well, while a wooden coffin can attract insects, is less airtight, and may increase decay of the body. If a body is left exposed to the elements before final burial (excarnated), then scavengers and the effects of the environment, such as climatic factors, will take their toll on its survival (see Duday 2006 for more details). If a body has been deliberately embalmed then it may survive longer as an intact body. While embalming, which leads to artificial mummification and slows the decay processes, has been practised since around 3000 BC in Egypt (Snape 1996; Chamberlain and Parker Pearson 2001), its success in preserving the body varies. Embalming today, using chemicals, is primarily for public health reasons and for presenting the body acceptably for public viewing; it is also suggested that the process preserves the body for longer than would be the case if it was not embalmed, ie until it is buried (Iserson 1994), although there appears to be some dissent here amongst some people because it is not often done very thoroughly. Cryogenic suspension is another technique that has been introduced in recent times whereby the dead body is frozen and maintained at a very low temperature. The idea is that the body can be resuscitated if, for example, there are medical developments which can be used to treat a previously untreatable disease (Iserson 1994).

In addition to the factor of place of burial – eg in a cemetery grave, in a chambered tomb, or in a watery place or crypt – the time between death and burial as well as burial and excavation will certainly have some impact on survival of the remains. The people buried in the Christ Church, Spitalfields, London, crypt and dated to the 18th and 19th centuries were exposed to several factors that preserved bodies and skeletons well, for example coffins, an internal burial space, and a short time between burial and excavation (Molleson and Cox

1993). Whether a burial site is disturbed by human or non-human intervention following disposal of the dead will also affect preservation. A shallow grave, for example, could potentially be disturbed by ploughing activities (see Haglund *et al* 2002 for a discussion of the effect of cultivation on buried human remains).

Burial environment following disposal

The soil microbiology and chemistry, together, will of course have a significant impact on the survival or decay of body tissues, including bones. Microbial attack, for example, can increase the porosity of the bone (Jans *et al* 2004), while the water content of the grave can aid decay of the body or, if the grave is very waterlogged and thus anaerobic, microbial activity will be inhibited and the body tissues may be preserved (such as with bodies buried in peat bogs in northern Europe: Turner and Scaife 1995). The impact of water on the survival of a body or skeleton relates to relative humidity, mean annual rainfall, and whether there is any drainage (Henderson 1987). The presence or absence of oxygen also plays a crucial role in the rapidity of the body's decay.

An alkaline (or higher pH) burial environment/soil will preserve a body better than an acidic soil but, in the case of bog bodies, a lack of oxygen and an acidic environment combined can generate very well-preserved bodies. Acidic solutions will, however, dissolve the mineral part of the bone and an acidic sandy soil will accelerate decay, as in the famous sand bodies or stains of Sutton Hoo, Suffolk, England (Bethell and Carver 1987; Carver 1998). A lower temperature and humidity will be better for preservation, along with burial at a reasonable depth; bodies buried close to the surface suffer possible later disturbance by humans and other animals, and are subject to exposure to more oxygen, which hastens decay. The decay rate doubles, generally speaking, with a 10°C rise in temperature, and micro-organisms are more active in warmer soils. Of course, the significance of the location of the burial (latitude and longitude), and in what season it was buried, will relate to the standard temperature in that location and season.

Interference in the grave by animals such as rodents (including gnawing of bones), and insects, along with the infiltration of plant roots and rootlets can cause much disturbance to the body (and bones). These processes may accelerate decay, and even the pressure of the soil can damage bones. Roots of plants secrete acids and these can etch the surface of bones but the etched areas are lighter in colour than the rest of the bone and hence are identifiable as post-mortem damage (White and Folkens 2005). If a body is buried close to the surface then scavenging larger mammals may take parts of the body away (eg a polar bear: Merbs 1997), and weathering of the bones may occur, thus compromising preservation.

(iv) Extremes of heat, cold, wetness and dryness, and their effect on survival of human remains

Generally speaking, if conditions are very hot, very cold, very wet, or very dry, the body may be preserved extremely well and the potential information that can be derived ultimately increases. In Britain, however, these extremes are rarely present and skeletal remains largely conform to the norms outlined above – except for the occasional bog body, and preserved bodies in post-medieval sealed coffins. A broader geographical perspective is therefore useful in this section, in order to outline the possibilities for extraordinary preservation of bodies. The reader is directed to Aufderheide (2000), a magnificent work on the scientific study of mummies around the world, and also Lynnerup (2007); these are key places to find out everything you need to know about mummified bodies in the archaeological record!

(a) Dry and hot places

We have already seen that if a burial area is dry and hot then human remains will potentially survive very well; the dryness and low humidity decreases or stops decomposition resulting from insect activity. It is in these environments that the term 'mummification' is particularly appropriate, where the soft tissues are preserved in a dehydrated state (Chamberlain and Parker Pearson 2001, 82); here we might have spontaneous or natural mummification (accidental), intentional natural mummification (deliberately disposed of in a place where natural mummification occurs), or artificial mummification (where there is direct human intervention to prevent decay, eg the use of embalming).

Figure 23: Mummy of Asru, Temple of Kamak, Thebes, Egypt (Late Period, c 900 BC) (with permission of The Manchester Museum, University of Manchester)

Egyptian mummification (Figure 23)

In Egypt, prior to deliberate mummification, natural mummification occurred in the dry desert environment during the pre-Dynastic period (c 4500–3000 BC). Deliberate mummification started around 3500 BC, the method consisting of wrapping the bodies in linen and using resin and linen padding (Chamberlain and Parker Pearson 2001). By about 2500 BC (4th Dynasty) the removal of the organs of the body was recognised as a method for inhibiting decomposition, but it was not until the beginning of the Middle Kingdom (2025–1700 BC) that natron (a mineral containing hydrated sodium carbonate found in salt deposits and lakes) was used to dry out muscle before resin and wrappings were applied to the body. These Middle Kingdom bodies appear to have been mummified by removing the internal organs through the abdomen, and the brain through the nose. The organs were soaked in natron. As the body was being bandaged ointments were poured onto the body; individual limbs and digits were bandaged separately, incorporating small artefacts, and then the whole body bandaged (*ibid*). Later, in the New Kingdom (1550–1069 BC), a wider variety of oils was used, along with more resin. Clearly, mummification in Egypt, whether artificial or natural (through dessication), allowed exceptional preservation of the body, including rare examples of parts of the body (eg a placenta with a female mummy dated to 1550–1080 BC: Mekota *et al* 2005).

The Chinchorro mummies of Chile (Figure 24)

The first evidence of artificially prepared mummies comes from the arid coastal Atacama Desert of northern Chile and southern Peru dated to as early as 7000 years old (Bahn 2002). The mummies, usually buried in cemetery groups, were generally wrapped tightly for natural mummification to occur but others were covered with clay and black or red pigment, and some had clay masks. A further type of mummification involved removal of the skin, soft tissues and organs, and then the wrapping of the bones and tying of sticks to them for reinforcement. The body cavities were filled with vegetable matter, the skin replaced, and the whole body covered with clay. Grave goods included textiles, bags, skins, bone and stone artefacts, and fishing implements such as hooks and nets. It is suggested that these people were mainly exploiting the sea as hunter-gatherers for their food but that they also ate plants and animals from the land. Studies of these mummies are providing much information about the life of these hunter-gatherer people, including evidence that they were fairly healthy, and there is continued surprise that these early people practised such complex funerary procedures.

Figure 24: Chinchorro child mummy with artificial mummification, red style (*c* 2000 BC) (with permission of Bernardo Arriaza)

The mummies of the Taklimakan Desert, north-west China (Figure 25)

In one of the world's most arid areas, the Taklimakan Desert in Xinjiang Province, China, the country's oldest spontaneously mummified bodies were first reported in 1994 (Barber 1999; Mallory and Mair 2000). A truly remarkable find, some of these mummies date back to 4000 years ago, and are extremely well-preserved, with colourful clothing. The question that has always surrounded the mummies is where these people came from, because they appeared to have Indo-European facial features, and associated archaeological and historical data support this suggestion. The answer lies in the Silk Road, and particularly the part that goes through the Tarim Basin, along which the mummies have been found. The Silk Road stretched thousands of miles from the west all the way to eastern China, and for several thousand years it was a very important trade route. Amongst the finds of mummies, one dated to 1200 BC, of a young female from Loulan, was dressed in furs. She has been very well studied and was discovered to have suffered anthracosis of the lungs and head lice, and had blood group O (Aufderheide 2000). Another from Cherchen was that of a man dated to around 1000 BC; he had light brown hair and wore deerskin boots, trousers, and a shirt, along with felt leggings (Kamberi 1994, in Aufderheide 2000). Some of the weave patterns on the clothing were likened to a Celtic design (Barber 1999). There have also been finds of paintings of people with blue and green eyes in the area, Celtic-style tattoos on some of the mummies, and even ancient DNA data, that all suggest biological links between Europeans and the mummies (Francalacci 1995). This collection of mummies has much potential, following more scientific investigation, to provide us with a detailed picture of the characteristics of the people in this area of China and the outside influences that had an impact on the population.

Figure 25: Male mummy covered in arrows, from Small River Cemetery #5, Xingjian, China (dated to *c* 1800 BC) (with permission of Victor H Mair)

(b) Dry and cold places

Cold, freezing temperatures and a lack of humidity also delay the decay of bodies, and some have been discovered from the coldest parts of our world. While freezing temperatures do preserve soft tissues, the action of freeze-thaw cycles can affect their ultimate preservation (Micozzi 1997).

The Iceman of Italy

In 1991, a male body around 5000 years old was found in ice on the Austrian/Italian border. He was excavated and then extensively studied (Bahn 2002). Not only was an array of artefacts found with the body – including a bow and arrows, a copper axe, a backpack made of wood and leather, birch bark containers, and a net of grass twine – but there was also a set of clothing consisting of a cap, coat, leggings, belt, loincloth, shoes, and a cloak (made of goat hide, bearskin, deer-hide, and calf skin). The body was very well-preserved, even revealing over 50 tattoos and clues to how he died (Spindler 1994). A CT scan (computed tomography – a sophisticated X-ray technique, which shows 'slices' of the body), revealed a flint arrowhead in his shoulder, and wounds to his wrist and hand which might be defence wounds, but

it is probable that he died between the ages of 40 and 53 years through exposure to high altitude weather.

Inca sacrificial victims, north-west Argentina (Figure 26)

High up in the Andes, on the border of Chile and Argentina, archaeologists found the frozen bodies of three children at the summit of Llullaillaco volcano. At 6723m, this is even higher than where the Iceman described above was discovered. The bodies were of two girls (six and fifteen years of age) and one boy (seven years old) dated to around 500 years ago (Bahn 2002). It is suggested that these children were sacrificial victims of the Inca, chosen for their beauty and made to take large amounts of coca and narcotics before being sacrificed on top of a mountain. They were buried in separate tombs below a stone platform. Their soft tissues, and even blood vessels filled with blood, were preserved, and the hair of one of the girls was seen to have evidence of narcotics in its structure. Along with remarkable body preservation, wonderfully brightly coloured clothing was recovered together with fabulous artefacts such as jewellery, figurines, and pottery.

Figure 26: The head of a boy mummy from Cerro El Plomo, Chile (dated to between AD 1480 and 1540) (with permission of Mario Castro)

The mummies of Greenland

In the 1970s two Inuit graves dated to around AD 1475 were found by two brothers on a hunting trip at Qilakitsoq on the west coast of Greenland, under a protective natural rock overhang. In grave I a six-month-old baby, a four-year-old boy, and three women aged around 25, 30, and 45 years old were found. In Grave II, three women were found, two aged 50 years and one aged 18 to 22 years (Hart Hansen *et al* 1991). Skin and fur clothing were also preserved on the bodies. They had been preserved by the action of cold dry air circulating through the stones over the grave. The remarkable preservation allowed the visualisation of tattoos on the women's foreheads, and even signs of smoke inhalation into the lungs, probably from burning sea mammal fat for light, heat, and cooking. By analysing tissue type it was possible to establish that in Grave I was a grandmother, two daughters and one or two grandchildren, and in Grave II two adult sisters could have been present, along with a younger woman.

(c) Wet places

Nearly three-quarters of the earth's surface is covered with water, including the sea, rivers, and lakes, and bodies may be disposed of in any of these contexts (eg see Figure 27). Each one of those watery contexts will hold specific characteristics which may delay or accelerate decay of either accidentally or deliberately deposited bodies. For a detailed account of the decay of bodies in watery environments, see Haglund and Sorg (2002), but for the purposes of this section a few examples will be helpful.

Bodies in bogs of northern Europe (Figure 28)

Probably as famous as Egyptian mummies are the many peat bog bodies of northern Europe (Ireland, Britain, the Netherlands, Germany, and Denmark). Peat is comprised of the accumulation of partly decomposed plants in water (Aufderheide 2000), and there are different types of peat according to the plants contained in it. In northern Europe sphagnum moss occurs in raised peat bogs where some of the plant's components are converted to an acid called sphagnan when it dies, and then humic acid, a sphagnan product. These chemicals reduce the growth

Figure 27: Burial in a rice paddy in Hanoi, Vietnam (with permission of Simon Fowler)

of micro-organisms and tan collagen fibres (Chamberlain and Parker Pearson 2001), thus preserving soft tissues. In these anaerobic acidic peat bogs, while the mineral of the bones dissolves, the hair, skin, ligaments and tendons survive well. There are several factors that lead to good preservation of the bodies, including a lack of oxygen and no scavengers, and an inherent low temperature. It is in these raised peat bogs that nearly all the 700+ bog bodies with preserved soft tissues have been found (Aufderheide 2000).

Probably the most famous group of bog bodies comes from Denmark, and more recently Britain. In Denmark, Glob (1969) described the remarkable body of Tollund Man, dated to 220 BC, found in 1950 with a cap and belt on his body, and a noose around his neck. Study of his intestinal contents revealed that he probably died during the winter because of the plants present, and also that he had suffered from intestinal worms. More recently, in Cheshire, England, Lindow Man was found in 1984 (Brothwell 1986); he was in his mid-20s and 1.68cm (5ft 6in) tall (Stead 1986). He had a skull fracture, fracture-dislocation of the neck, and a laceration to the neck, likely contributing to his death; there was also evidence of osteoarthritis in his joints. His gut contents were analysed and illustrated that his last meal was likely an unleavened bread made of wheat, oats, and barley, with no indication that this was a 'special' meal (Holden 1986).

Many of these people died in the Iron Age and Roman periods (800 BC–AD 500) and sometimes, but not as frequently as thought, of what appears to have been a gruesome death by murder. Evidence for stab wounds, asphyxiation (choking or hanging), and unhealed wounds to the body, including the head, have all been noted. However, bogs could have been used traditionally for burial by some communities, and people could have accidentally drowned while crossing them, or been mugged and deliberately pushed into the bog; indeed, attempts to rescue people who ended up in the bog, it is suggested, may have led to wounds to the body that have been misinterpreted (Briggs 1986). Most of the bodies were of young adults or non-adult individuals, with no differentiation or selection between the sexes, but there were some who showed health problems that likely affected their lives, and many were possibly of high status (because of their undamaged hands and fingernails: Chamberlain and Parker Pearson 2001). Why in these periods were people placed in bogs? It may well be that they were places with some religious or ritual significance; we know for example that in the Iron Age water was certainly a special place for activities such as votive offerings.

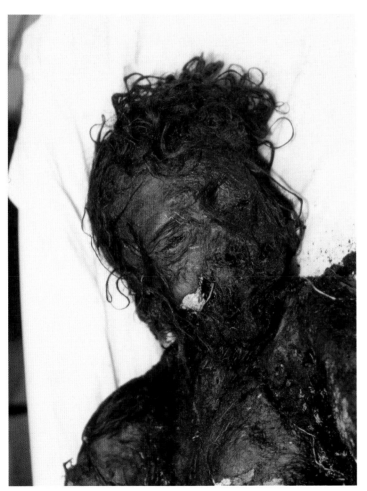

Figure 28: Female bog body from Meenybraddan, County Donegal (dated to 730±90 BP) (described in Delaney and Ó Floinn, 1995; reproduced with permission of Don Brothwell)

Bodies in the Florida Swamps, United States

In Windover, central Florida, one of the earliest cemeteries in the US was found dating to 7000–6000 BC; it served people who hunted and gathered (Chamberlain and Parker Pearson 2001). These people were buried originally in waterlogged peat; now the site is covered by a seasonal lake and the chemical constituents of that lake appear to have preserved the bodies extremely well. This situation did not particularly preserve whole bodies, as the remains were mainly skeletons, but parts of the brain were present inside some of the skulls; microscopic study illustrated that some of the original brain cells had survived. It was possible to extract and amplify ancient DNA from some of this tissue (Doran *et al* 1986). Brain tissue has survived in other burial contexts and it is suggested that this is because it contains lots of fats, which can convert into fatty acids, leading to the formation of the waxy compound of adipocere, usually in anaerobic environments (Chamberlain and Parker Pearson 2001).

The sailors of the Mary Rose, *England*

Detailed consideration of how bodies decompose in the sea is given by Sorg *et al* (1997), but generally speaking bodies buried in the sea decompose about four times faster than those buried on land, and even faster if the water is warm (Iserson 1994). However, even though the vast majority of the crew of Henry VIII's warship, the *Mary Rose*, drowned in July 1545 when the ship sank, their skeletons were very well preserved (Stirland 2000). The sinking occurred very rapidly and, after the ship came to rest on the sea floor in clay just off the south coast of England, four tides a day provided strong currents, flowing east–west and north-east–south-west, which deposited silts in the ship. The anaerobic nature of this environment arrested decomposition of the organic materials, including the skeletal remains of the sailors. Ninety-two individuals were reconstructed from the deposit of disarticulated bones found, although the minimum number of individuals was calculated as 179, based on the number of skulls and lower jaws; this represents 43% of the 415 crew known to have been on board when the ship set sail. Through analysis of the skeletal remains, it was possible to infer that they were all strong robust males, and that within the crew there was a group of specialist war bowmen, supported by the presence of preserved bows and arrows in the ship.

(d) Other unusual preservation of human remains

Death by volcanic eruption (Figure 29)

In AD 79 Vesuvius erupted in southern Italy and volcanic ash and lava covered large areas, including the settlements of Pompeii and Herculaneum, around the Bay of Naples. It was estimated that around 15cm of ash fell per hour. People who took cover in their houses were killed as buildings collapsed from the weight of ash on roofs (Bahn 2002) and many of those who tried to escape were either buried by the heavy ash fall or asphyxiated by volcanic gases. The buried settlements were only excavated in the 20th century, and amongst the astonishing remains of Pompeii were found the perfect shapes of bodies imprinted in the solidified ash; these were filled with plaster of Paris to create a cast, and thus some of the bodies could be reconstructed. Many had their knees flexed, the forearms raised, and hands clenched, which indicate the person was probably crouching to protect themselves and that they were exposed to a high temperature which leads to shortened muscle fibres (Chamberlain and Parker

Figure 29: Cast of the body of a victim of the volcanic eruption in AD 79 at Pompeii, Italy (with permission of Luigi Capasso)

Pearson 2001). At Herculaneum people fled the town to the sea shore and into boat huts where their bodies were found represented as skeletons; their deaths were probably the result of inhalation of volcanic ash and suffocation. This example illustrates that even though human remains may not be found at a site, bodies may be reconstructed using other means (which can be likened to the 'bodies' recreated by Anthony Gormley, described in Chapter 2).

The Fenghuangshan Tomb 168 in China

In the 1970s the body of a high district official called Sui Xiaoyuan was found in Siyang, China. He was buried in a wooden tomb chamber which contained four rooms (Bahn 2002). The body was placed in two coffins, inner and outer, and the coffins sealed with an airtight and waterproof seal. This preserved the body extremely well, including skin, the inner organs, and the brain, and detailed microscopic examination revealed the microstructure of the cartilage and muscles. The man had died at aged 60 years, was 1.68m (5ft 6½in) tall and weighed 52.5kg (c 8st 3lb), and the blood group AB was identified (Bahn 2002). It was even possible to suggest what health problems he had: inflammation of the gall bladder, a gastric ulcer, tapeworms, whipworms, liver fluke, and disease of the arteries. Preservation of the body was determined to have occurred because of the 'perfect geological, hydrological and climatic environment provided by the [burial] context' (Bahn 2002, 63).

The mummies of Cladh Hallan, South Uist, Western Isles of Scotland (Figure 30)

In recent years excavations at Cladh Hallan on the island of South Uist have revealed late Bronze Age/Iron Age roundhouses (Parker Pearson *et al* 2005) with dates ranging from 2200 to 700 BC. In these roundhouses the burials of three children, a male, and a female were found. Four of the burials had been placed in the ground a long time after death but before the peaty sand floors of the houses had been constructed. The nature of the burials are suggested to represent prior mummification and post-mortem manipulation of body parts. The male and female skeletons were buried in a tightly flexed position. Two of the female's teeth had been placed in her hand and the male skeleton appeared to have been comprised of the bones of three different people; there was no evidence that there had been disturbance of the grave once formed. As a result of studying the burials using microstructural, contextual, and dating methods, it is suggested that a local method of mummification was practised, perhaps to secure 'these select dead people a place in the afterworld' but also that they were 'the past personified, the ancestors in embodied form, the guardians of ancient traditions' (*ibid*, 543). This remarkable find has extended discussions about the extent of mummification in the ancient world and taken the subject beyond the famous mummies of Egypt, South America, and the Arctic into a part of the world where one would not expect to find evidence of mummification.

Figure 30: Late Bronze Age burial from Cladh Hallan, South Uist, Outer Hebrides, Scotland (with permission of Mike Parker Pearson)

3.7 The effect of preservation on study

Clearly there are many advantages to studying bodies compared to skeletal remains. Soft tissues are preserved, potentially containing important health information and also cultural influences such as tattoos. It may also be possible to determine the blood group of the person and look, through ancient DNA analysis, at relationships between people and also the occurrence of disease that does not reveal itself in the skeleton. The gastrointestinal contents of bodies may display the constituents of the person's last meal, and hair might provide information on hairstyles and the care of hair, while a study of the nails might suggest whether a person worked or not, and indeed whether they cared for their nails. Clothing is also often preserved with bodies and can illustrate cultural aspects of the population such as 'fashion' styles or status, and also what materials were being exploited. However, it should be appreciated that preserved bodies are often isolated individuals and therefore any interpretations can be biased and not representative of the population from which the person derived; they may also be 'special' people whose disposal and preservation was specific to their 'social group'. Nevertheless, because all the tissues are preserved, a body can be subject to a wider range of techniques of analysis than would be possible for skeletal remains.

3.8 Summary

There have been some remarkably well-preserved human remains found around the world, ranging from skeletons to mummies, but clearly the environment of deposition is very influential in determining how much of a body survives to be excavated and studied. In Britain, the vast majority of the human remains that bioarchaeologists study are skeletal remains, principally unburnt, but sometimes cremated, with very few preserved bodies (usually in exceptional circumstances). Although we are familiar with the main factors that are advantageous to the preservation of human remains, it is usually impossible to disentangle the multitude of factors that lead to preservation and/or decay in any one funerary context.

3.9 Key learning points

- the processes of decay of all parts of the body should be considered even though it is skeletal remains that are usually studied; survival of the skeleton can also be influenced by soft tissue decay
- decay of bodies ultimately affects the evidence available for research purposes
- external preservation appearance of bone can be deceptive as internal preservation may be very different
- experimental 'burials' allow us to understand how bodies decay and are useful for archaeology and forensic situations

- intrinsic (internal to the body) and extrinsic factors affect decay rates, but in Britain the burial environment is the major factor
- extremes of heat and cold, along with dryness and wetness, can preserve bodies well

CHAPTER FOUR

Before analysis: excavation, processing, conservation, and curation

Excavation and analysis are complicated by the heterogeneous circumstances in which human remains are encountered and the diversity of mortuary customs around the world

(Ubelaker 1989, 1)

4.1 Introduction

The previous chapter outlined the main factors that can affect whether human remains survive in the ground to be discovered and excavated. This chapter focuses on how human remains are excavated; how they are processed following excavation; what can be done to conserve skeletal remains; and how they should be curated. Because in Britain the majority of human remains found are inhumed or cremated, the emphasis is on skeletal remains. However, it should be noted that, even though each excavation that involves human remains has different conditions, there are still general principles that should be followed.

Obviously, in this chapter, we are getting closer to analysing the human remains in a laboratory situation. However, it is not only methods of disposal of the dead, and what happens to bodies when they are disposed of, that affect the quantity and quality of what is left of a body to analyse. We have to consider the measures by which the remains were excavated and handled in post-excavation. Methods of conservation of human remains and their ultimate curation will also affect how much information is potentially present to record, although in most British excavations human remains are not subject to conservation measures except in rare circumstances when a museum wishes to put the remains on display (McKinley pers comm, November 2007). Human remains are a non-renewable resource. Therefore, a body may be very well preserved in the ground but inappropriate methods of recovery of that body may compromise its integrity; likewise, the human remains may be very well excavated but poorly handled in post-excavation processing. Finally, a skeleton may have been well excavated and processed but it could have been curated in poor-quality storage, with a lack of temperature and humidity control, thus leading to deterioration of the remains.

4.2 Excavation of human remains

(i) How are remains excavated?

First and foremost, all personnel on a cemetery site should be advised to treat human remains respectfully. Once a 'grave' is identified and, for example, a grave cut recognised (by a contrast in soil colour), it should be remembered that the excavation of human remains is a very delicate and time-consuming process taking one to two days. This depends on the depth of the grave and if grave goods or coffin furniture are present (McKinley pers comm, November 2007). The delicacy of 'the process' also depends on the burial context, including the soil matrix. For example, in a light sandy soil, remains will be uncovered more rapidly, and will be less likely to be damaged than remains in a heavy wet clay soil, which will take longer to excavate. Ideally, the remains should be excavated as completely as possible, with the aim of enabling the bioarchaeologist to collect the maximum amount of data.

Excavation of human remains should always involve experts who are familiar with the study and interpretation of those remains, so bioarchaeologists should be employed for any burial excavation from the start of the project. If this is not done then a great deal of data may be lost and the potential of the cemetery, or other context, will not be realised. If a bioarchaeologist is employed for the excavation then they should advise and familiarise other site personnel with what to expect. As McKinley and Roberts (1993) state, the fact that all the excavators have their own skeletons does not mean they know how their skeleton is constructed, ie what bones to expect! Understanding the difference between animal and human bones, and adult and non-adult bones, is also essential so that confusion does not arise later. It is useful to have available, at the very least, a basic diagram of the skeleton for site personnel to consult (eg the photographic manual of the skeleton: Abrahams *et al* 2008), but a plastic (disarticulated) skeleton would be even better. This may not be possible, however, due to expense and on-site conditions (McKinley pers comm, November 2007).

(a) Inhumation burials

Remember that the skeleton is three-dimensional and, even though you may know which bones of the skeleton should be there, they may not always be found where they are expected (McKinley and Roberts 1993). For example, the body may be laid face down (prone) and therefore the spine will be uppermost, while the sternum (breastbone) will be underneath the spine, ie opposite to that found with a body that has been buried supine (on the back). Later disturbance of a burial can also move the bones around from their normal anatomical position and some may even 'disappear'! To provide protection for the public, the excavation area is shielded from public view with screens. Once the top of the skeleton has been reached, excavation is undertaken using very delicate tools such as paintbrushes, teaspoons, dental instruments, and plasterers' leaves. The aim is to excavate the soil around the bones so that eventually the skeleton is

Figure 31: Excavating a skeleton at Bamburgh Castle, Northumberland, England (with permission of Sarah Groves and the Bamburgh Research Project)

exposed and visible, and then the bones can be lifted following recording (Figure 31). The bones should be shaded from strong sunlight so that they do not dry out and crack (a light spray of water may help to keep them damp), but excavating the skeleton all in one day will avoid damage from unnecessary exposure to the elements, and vandalism (or cover with plastic sheeting overnight to keep it from

Figure 32: The AD 1461 burial pit at Towton, North Yorkshire (with permission of Tim Sutherland and the Towton Battlefield Archaeological Survey Project)

Figure 33: Individual with scoliosis of the spine from the cemetery of Hemingford Grey, St Ives, Cambridgeshire (with permission of Oxford Archaeology)

drying out). Skeletal material should be left exposed to the elements for as short a time as possible (Spriggs 1989). Particular care should be taken to ensure: all the teeth are recovered, all the hand and foot bones are excavated (particularly useful for identifying joint diseases affecting the hands and feet), that the pubic symphysis of the pelvis is excavated with care as this is needed for age estimation of adults, that the ends of the ribs that meet the sternum are carefully recovered as they are useful for a particular adult ageing technique, that non-adult remains of children and adolescents are recovered as completely as possible, and the excavator is aware of the possibility of gall (see Figure 86), bladder, and kidney stones being present (and where they are most likely to be seen in relation to the skeleton), along with sesamoid bones in the hands and feet, calcified cartilages in the neck (thyroid, cricoid, arytenoid) and on the ribs, and also the neck's hyoid bone. It is also possible that foetal bones may be identified in the abdominal area of female skeletons.

Following exposure of the burial, the bones are drawn (planned at a scale of 1:10) using a planning frame over the grave. Planning a full skeleton takes about one hour by an experienced archaeologist using a ½ or ¼ frame for ease of access and to reduce parallax by placing it as close to the skeleton as possible (McKinley pers comm, November 2007). Both manual and digital photographs (with scales and magnetic north arrows) are advised, in case digital ones are lost. Three-dimensional recording on excavations is performed using an electronic distance meter (EDM); digital information describing the position of the skeleton, and key points on the skeleton, can be recorded very quickly and accurately using the latter. For example, Sutherland (2000) describes the use of the EDM to record sixteen key places on each skeleton buried in the 15th-century mass grave at Towton, North Yorkshire (Figure 32); the EDM can measure data points to an accuracy of 1mm and of course record the data on a computer for later interpretation. At Towton this allowed each individual skeleton to be located within the grave and in relation to the other bodies; without this method of recording it would not have been possible to see accurately the stratigraphic relationships within the grave. Any interesting features of graves should also be photographed such as grave goods, coffin furniture, and unusual pathological conditions (Figure 33), including disease that has led to fragile bones which might disintegrate once they are lifted.

A 'Skeleton Record Sheet' (Figure 34) is completed for each burial. However, each skeleton is classed as a 'context' because it is often the only surviving remains of the burial, ie part of the formation process (McKinley pers comm, November 2007). This sheet should be kept as simple as possible so that it is more likely to be completed properly (McKinley and Roberts 1993). The aim of the sheet is to record which bones are present for each skeleton (on a skeleton diagram), bearing in mind that the excavators should know how many bones to expect for an adult (206) and non-adult (many more), and that a person can have extra vertebrae or ribs. Additionally, contextual data should be recorded which includes: whether the skeleton is articulated (in the right anatomical alignment) or not; which direction the burial was oriented (in terms of compass direction);

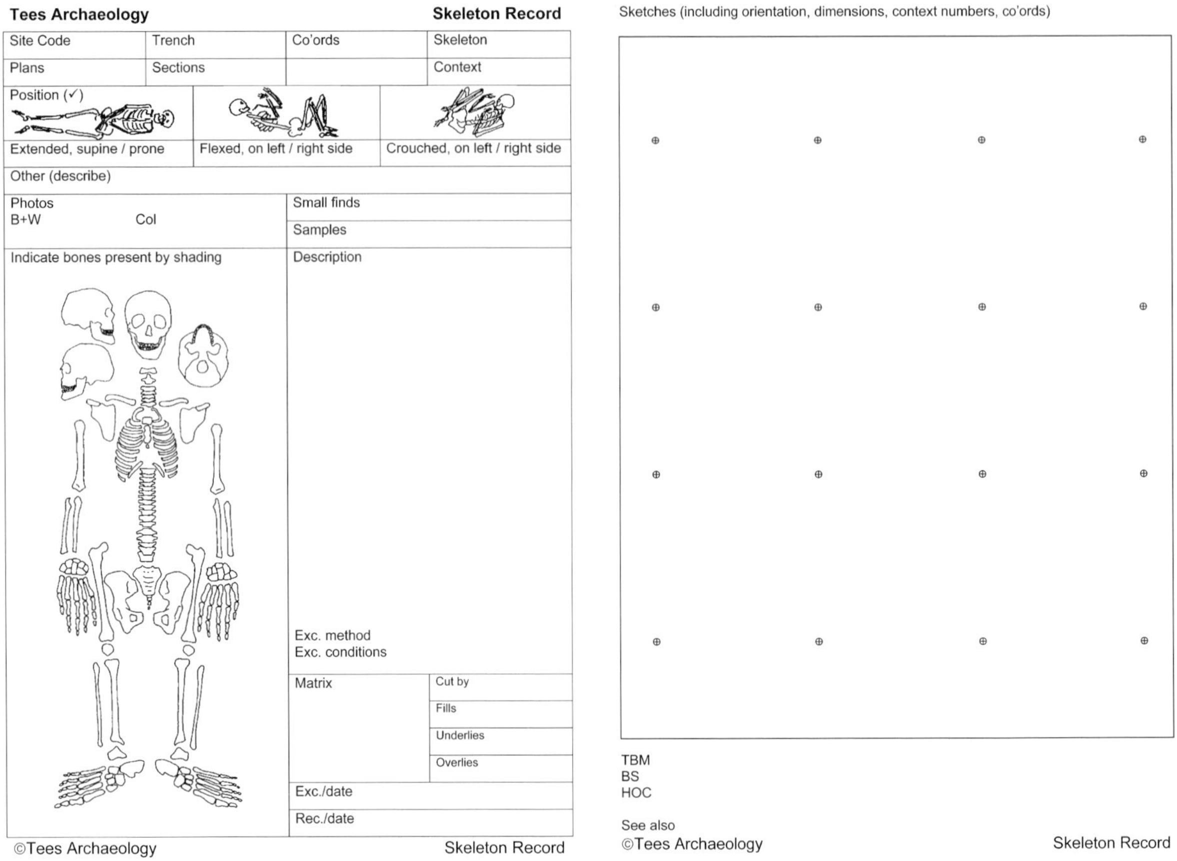

Tees Archaeology **Skeleton Record**

Sketches (including orientation, dimensions, context numbers, co'ords)

Site Code	Trench	Co'ords	Skeleton
Plans	Sections		Context

Position (✓)

Extended, supine / prone | Flexed, on left / right side | Crouched, on left / right side

Other (describe)

| Photos B+W   Col | Small finds |
| | Samples |

Indicate bones present by shading | Description

Exc. method
Exc. conditions

Matrix	Cut by
	Fills
	Underlies
	Overlies
Exc./date	
Rec./date	

©Tees Archaeology   Skeleton Record

TBM
BS
HOC

See also

©Tees Archaeology   Skeleton Record

in what position it was placed in the grave (supine or on the back; prone or on the front; on either side; extended or body straight out; crouched or the body, legs, and arms curled up); the position of the arms and legs (flexed or bent, semi-flexed, arms crossed over the chest or pelvis, or extended straight beside the body); and the head (facing left, right, forward, or upwards); whether there are any grave goods or grave furniture such as a coffin or coffin nails, and any association of the burial with others.

Bones should not be lifted until they are totally exposed and free from the soil matrix. As the bones are lifted they should be placed in plastic bags. To avoid mould growth before the bones are washed, the bags may be left open slightly, or the bags pierced, to allow the contents to breathe. Separate labelled bags should be used for: the cranium, mandible, maxilla, the sternum, left ribs, right ribs, spine, left upper limb, including the clavicle, right upper limb, including the clavicle, left hand, right hand, pelvic girdle, left lower limb, right lower limb, left foot, and right foot. Waterproof labels resistant to damage should also be placed inside each bag. Label writing should be as durable as the label itself and therefore a permanent marker pen should be used. It is recommended that, following lifting of all the obvious bones, the layer of soil below the skeleton

Figure 34: Basic skeleton record sheet (with permission of Robin Daniels, Tees Archaeology, and Richard Annis)

is collected and sieved (1–2mm mesh) to ensure no small bones or teeth, or fragments, have been missed (McKinley and Roberts 1993).

Sampling of soil may be undertaken in a number of areas of the skeleton for a variety of purposes, for example at the head, neck, chest and abdomen regions. Firstly, the soil is sieved, usually through a 2mm mesh to ensure that tiny bones such as those of the hands and feet, those associated with non-adult skeletons such as small unfused epiphyses, and bones such as the sesamoids of the hand and foot, and ear bones, and ossified tissues such as cartilage are retrieved (along with teeth). Secondly, sieving will also allow the extraction of gall, bladder, and kidney stones which provide evidence of disease in those organs of the body; Steinbock (1989a and b, 1990) provides an excellent guide to the variety of appearances of these 'stones'. Thirdly, samples may also be sieved to retrieve small artefacts such as beads, plant remains, small animal bones, insects, and parasites, much of which, if from the gut area of the body, might reflect consumption of particular foods, or indicate disease. In acidic waterlogged environments insects, pollen, seeds, and parasite eggs can be particularly well-preserved, providing information about not only diet consumed, but plants being grown, plants and trees in the environment, and climate. Finally, sampling of soils is usually undertaken when biomolecular analyses of bones and/or teeth are done, for example to check that there have been no post-mortem changes in the bones and teeth that have been influenced by the surrounding soils which may affect biomolecular data.

In addition to soil sampling, bones and teeth can be sampled for future analyses at this stage of the investigation so that there is some control on the possibility of future contamination. However, sampling should only be undertaken (at excavation or post-excavation stage) when there are clear reasons for the procedure, and sampling should be as unobtrusive as possible (Richards 2004). Usually, however, sampling takes place following skeletal analysis, ie in the post-excavation analysis of the skeleton. It also takes place commonly during curation of skeletal collections in the museum environment; here, ideally, the history of the curation of the skeletal samples should be known, including the use of any consolidants and adhesives etc (Richards 2004). The most common biochemical analyses performed currently on samples of bones and teeth from archaeologically derived skeletons are those for stable isotope and ancient DNA. For carbon and nitrogen analyses, bone or tooth dentine is needed, and for strontium, oxygen, and lead it is tooth enamel; for aDNA analyses it is bones and teeth. These analyses potentially provide data on diet, movement of people, relationships between people and populations, and the diagnosis of disease. It should be emphasised that before samples are finally taken for analysis, the bone/tooth should have been fully recorded, including the use of photographs and radiographs, where appropriate.

Sampling for stable isotope analysis is reasonably straightforward (Richards 2004). For carbon and nitrogen analysis, there is little risk of contamination as the pre-treatment of the bone or dentine samples (a few milligrams) involves removing most of the mineral. As Richards (2004, 44) states, 'if possible samples should be taken from the same bone element from different individuals'; this is usually thick cortical bone (eg femur), but also rib shafts. For oxygen, lead, and strontium analyses less than 100mg of tooth enamel is needed. Sampling for ancient DNA analysis is described by Brown and Brown (1992) and Brown (1998); detailed guidance is provided on sampling of bones and teeth for ancient DNA analysis at the excavation level in order to avoid contamination of samples with modern DNA from the excavators and other DNA in the environment. The key points to note are not to touch or breathe on the bones/teeth, so wearing a face mask and gloves are required, and areas of bare skin should be covered. Wearing a forensic-style white suit is not always needed, but a common sense approach is (Keri Brown pers comm, January 2008). Implements for taking samples must be clean, and cleaned between samples from different skeletons. Sterile clearly labelled airtight containers/ziplock bags should be used for the samples and placed in a cool bag until they can be transferred to a freezer (at -20ºC). The sample should be taken as soon as possible after the skeleton is first exposed to ensure contamination is kept to a minimum. The procedure used to amplify ancient DNA (polymerase chain reaction or PCR) preferentially amplifies well-preserved DNA molecules and these are more likely to be modern contaminants (White and Folkens 2005). The sample eventually used for aDNA analysis is usually around three grams in weight and/or the dentine of one tooth; this also allows enough of the sample to be analysed in another laboratory for independent replication, which is essential to ensure results are genuine. However, a sample from another skeleton in the same skeletal collection is also needed for comparative purposes. There does, however, appear to be some debate about the sampling method used for aDNA analysis, and when sampling should take place. The key point to make in relation to any destructive sampling is that full recording of bones or teeth must have taken place before the sampling occurs. Furthermore, much aDNA analysis has successfully been accomplished on bone and tooth samples taken from curated human remains.

Histological analysis of sections of bones and teeth is also increasingly being used to determine adult age at death and diagnose disease (see later chapters). For radiocarbon dating, often necessary to determine the time period for the burials, about 500mg of bone is needed, subsequently dated using accelerator mass spectrometry. For all these sampling procedures, wherever the samples are to be analysed, it is advisable to contact the laboratory to establish the sampling procedure required; laboratories may differ in those requirements and will need specific information about the samples – including their excavation, post-excavation, and storage history (Richards 2004). Furthermore, the bones and teeth used for these analyses must have been recorded prior to sampling, as for the other methods described above.

(b) Cremation burials

Cremation burials were very common at some periods of time in Britain, and were made both in urns, or unurned (McKinley and Roberts 1993). However, the burial is not the only deposit that is potentially excavated; in situ pyre debris and redeposited pyre debris may also be present (McKinley 1998). The physical and stratigraphical relationship between these features helps an understanding of the context as a whole and detailed recording is essential to understand the funerary rite (*ibid*).

Possible pyre sites with in situ pyre debris are subject to whole-earth recovery, with the entire contents being wet sieved at a 1mm fraction and floated for botanical evidence (McKinley 1998, 2000a). If the site has been disturbed the stratigraphic relationships may not survive and the fill is recovered in total. Undisturbed or slightly disturbed contexts are excavated in equal-sized blocks and spits – the size being dependent on the feature size and depth, but blocks of equal size being vital (a minimum 2m x 1m area should be excavated in half-metre blocks of 50–100mm depth spits: McKinley 1998, 2000b, c). Initially the deposit should be half sectioned or quadranted to look at the distribution of the archaeological components of the soil matrix. The bioarchaeologist can then look at the vertical and horizontal distribution/spread of bone fragments. Recording of the distribution in plan and section is needed.

Beyond the cremation burial itself, cremated bone may also be found in pyre debris. Redeposited pyre debris may be found in backfills of graves, over cremation graves or dumped in earlier features (McKinley 1998). It can contain a mixture of fuel ash slag, charcoal, burnt flint, stone and clay, pyre goods, including food offerings, and may be identified from cremation grave fills. Excavation of the whole of the context should be undertaken, full recovery being essential to assess the number of cremations represented and viewed which materials were 'discardable' (*ibid*). The deposit should be recorded on a context sheet, showing how much and where the debris occurred in relation to any cremation burials (McKinley and Roberts 1993). Contexts should be half sectioned or quadranted to look at the relationship of the archaeological components, and large areas of material should be divided into blocks of equal size, as above, using spits of 50–100mm depth (McKinley 1998).

Recording of the maximum size of cremated bone fragments before lifting is important. This allows an assessment of how much fragmentation has occurred during and following lifting. A complete undisturbed urned burial should be lifted whole after crepe bandaging the urn for support. The burial may have been made with the urn inverted and, if this is the case, then any bone that has slipped out of the urn should be retrieved. If the urn has been broken then it and its contents will have to be excavated on site. Following lifting, the urn's contents should be excavated, preferably by a bioarchaeologist, using 20mm spits to examine the formation process (McKinley 1998). If the burial was made unurned, whole-earth recovery is necessary as soon as bone or pyre debris is noted (*ibid*). If disturbed, then the context should be bagged as a whole, but if undisturbed then it is advisable to excavate in quadrants and spits of *c* 100–150mm of deposit, if the deposit is >150mm deep, bagging the spits separately and labelling them clearly. This allows a 3D examination of the distribution of the archaeological components.

(c) Other types of burials

Different burial contexts, especially those that are rare, require different approaches, and different questions will be asked of each of them, for example crypts (Cox 2001), and there is no time or space within the aims of this book to describe each situation in depth. For this reason, the reader is referred to two examples of funerary contexts that required adaptation and development of excavation and recording procedures: that of the excavation of the crypt at Christ Church, Spitalfields (Adams and Reeve 1993) and the mass grave at Towton, North Yorkshire (Sutherland 2001), a mass grave being defined as 'one which contains a number of individuals within a single grave cut' (*ibid*, 36) but usually one that has many individuals in it.

(ii) Health and safety

As for any archaeological site excavation, a high standard of health and safety is a priority for excavators. This is no less important for cemetery excavations, and an outline of the work and risk assessment needs to be made before commencing excavation (Kneller 1998). In this section, the focus is on the possible health hazards of excavating human remains, or potential associated microbiological risks. It should be stressed that each excavation environment will be different and carry its own special health and safety risks, along with the general risks of excavation.

Obviously, the excavation of skeletal, as opposed to mummified, remains will produce different potential health risks. The majority of excavations of human remains are from contexts that are hundreds and even thousands of years old, and micro-organisms that might cause harm to humans are extremely unlikely to survive beyond about 100 years (EH and CoE 2005, 45). Potentially, if organisms were viable, this could affect anybody coming into contact with the human remains, for example excavators, bioarchaeologists, and museum curators. It is probably the more recent burials of post-medieval date in Britain that could be hazardous to health; they may be in sealed lead coffins, for example. However, it is advisable that any worries whatsoever about hazards relating to the excavation, analysis, or curation of human remains should be discussed with the Health and Safety Executive (HSE) prior to excavation.

The possible risks of contracting disease from excavated human remains are highly negligible, but could include the virus smallpox, the spore producing the conditions of tetanus and anthrax, the bacterial infection leptospirosis, and the fungal diseases called mycoses (often a problem in dry dusty soils and in crypts), but it is probably only from more recent burials where there are risks. Tetanus and leptospirosis are also risks for any excavation involving soil, archaeological or not. Certainly excavators should be up to date with their tetanus inoculations. So far, no living ancient organisms have been isolated from archaeological contexts (Arriaza and Pfister 2006), and those organisms that might be found are more than likely to derive from post-mortem contamination. Anthrax may be contracted from a person who had died from the disease, but also any materials from animals used for coffin pads, pillows or coffin packing (Kneller 1998). Kneller (1998) also lists Lyme Disease, histoplasmosis (one of the fungal diseases), and ornithosis as possible specific hazards on archaeological excavations, but one would not necessarily expect to encounter all these risks in Britain. Lyme Disease is a tick-borne bacterial disease which is found in Europe (Leff 1993), histoplasmosis is an infection caused by a soil fungus and is a hazard for people working in environments where bird or bat faeces have accumulated, for example caves or in wooded areas, but it is rare in Europe (Davies 1993), and ornithosis is a disease of birds and domestic fowl which can be transmitted to humans and includes psittacosis (Novak 1995). Arriaza and Pfister (2006) also note that the hantaviruses and the bubonic plague may also pose a problem on excavations in some parts of the world, for example the USA. These conditions, passed from rodents to humans, are commonly transmitted via inhaled aerosolised faeces, saliva or urine, but contraction can occur via inhaled dried materials contaminated by the excreta, through broken skin, and via ingestion of food and drink; they can cause haemorrhagic fever and hantavirus pulmonary syndrome. The bubonic plague is a bacterial disease that affects rodents, but fleas can pass the bacteria to humans from rodents via bites. Unlike in 14th- and 17th-century Britain when thousands of people died from the plague, this disease is now treatable with antibiotics.

Zuckerman (1984) suggests that the smallpox virus becomes inactive in skin lesions within a couple of years. However, Baxter *et al* (1988) stress that in dry or permafrost conditions preserved bodies may contain viable smallpox viruses. This was suggested by Fornaciari and Marchetti (1986) in a 16th-century Italian mummy, although Marennikova *et al* (1990, in Arriaza and Pfister 2006) do not support this; good structural preservation of the virus was found, but its viability to cause disease or reproduce in the laboratory had been lost. Young (1998) provides a very useful review of smallpox and its possible viability at archaeological sites. If conditions of storage of human remains promotes the growth of moulds on the remains (high humidity and temperature) then it is possible, although rare, that people working with the material could contract pneumonitis, or allergic alveolitis (inflammation of the air sacs of the lungs due to mould allergy) (Arriaza and Pfister 2006). There have been comments that prions, protein infectious particles that cause diseases like Creutzfeldt-Jakob disease and bovine spongiform encephalopathy ('mad cow disease'), are very resistant to decay (Rutala and Weber 2001, in Arriaza and Pfister 2006). Psychological stress can be another health problem that may be associated with excavating cemeteries (Thompson 1998), along with lead poisoning arising from high levels in the atmosphere generated by lead coffins in more recent burial contexts (Needleman 2004, in Arriaza and Pfister 2006). Normal hygiene measures such as washing hands before eating should be observed, and wearing masks or gloves as appropriate, for example in dusty situations, or if soft tissue survives (EH and CoE 2005, 45). Dusty environments at excavation sites, both within buildings and in the open air, may be common in Britain. This could increase the risks of chronic obstructive pulmonary disease (COPD, including chronic bronchitis and ephysema: Pauwels and Rabel 2004, in Arriaza and Pfister 2006).

As an example of dealing with possible health hazards, for one year before the excavation of the post-medieval crypt at Christ Church, Spitalfields, consultation was undertaken with various bodies to develop a health and safety code (Adams and Reeve 1993). Although not initially realised, the crypt environment had little air movement, high dust levels, poor visibility, restricted work areas, and heavy coffins to move (*ibid*, 17); this led to low morale at times. The main worry was possible viability of the spores of the smallpox virus, although this never became a reality. What did become a problem were high blood lead levels, which rose in excavators when sealed lead coffins began to be excavated (see figure 2.1, in Adams and Reeve 1993); this led to some excavators with levels over the safe limit not being allowed on site until their levels dropped. Following the establishment of a procedure for protecting excavators, which involved clean and dirty work areas, all people involved in the excavation were surveyed medically by an Environmental Health Officer throughout the excavation. Hard hats, overalls, steel-toe-capped Wellington boots and surgical gloves were to be worn at all times, along with protective respiratory masks. Showers were available for emergencies, first aid facilities set up, and heavily soiled clothing was burnt at an HSE-approved site (*ibid*). This clearly shows how complex a health risk 'cemetery' excavation can be, but it should be noted that the type of environment described here is not the normal experience for most archaeologists in Britain.

4.3 Processing of human remains once excavated

As for excavation, great care must be taken in cleaning, processing, and packaging skeletal remains prior to analysis, or valuable information may be lost.

(i) Cleaning, drying, and marking of skeletal remains

(a) Inhumation burials

Cleaning of skeletal remains is essential if they are to be recorded fully later but the amount of cleaning, and the methods used, must be applicable to the remains excavated. It is advisable to let the remains dry a little before washing them; this appears to consolidate the bone (McKinley pers comm, November 2007). One skeleton should be cleaned at a time. If the soil is very lightly adhering to the bone, dry brushing may be sufficient to clean the remains. If dry brushing is not possible because of heavier adherent soils then it is best to use a bowl of tepid or cold water (no detergents) and a brush such as a soft or medium toothbrush or nailbrush; small dental tools or wooden picks are useful too. If the remains are fragile, the worst of the soil should be taken off manually. Some could then be washed carefully and left to dry naturally; some skeletal remains, however, will be too fragile to risk washing in water.

The levels of hardness in water are relevant. Beware of, for example, hard water; this contains large amounts of magnesium and calcium and can add dissolved

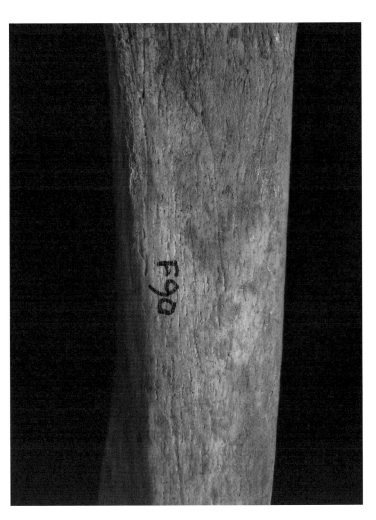

Figure 35: Example
of marking a bone
(Charlotte Roberts)

minerals and other substances to bone (Odegaard and Cassman 2006). Soft water can alter the salt and acid content of the bone. The water should be changed frequently as dirty water will produce dirty bones (Stroud 1989), and using a 1mm mesh sieve in the bowl will prevent loss of bone fragments and teeth with the soil that is being washed away. The residue in the sieve should be checked following cleaning of each skeleton.

Bones should never be fully immersed in water because this could lead to disintegration, especially with fragile bones (McKinley and Roberts 1993). Small bones can be placed in a 1mm sieve to remove soil. Bones should never be scrubbed to remove the soil as this will ultimately damage them. Care should be taken with bones that are broken, for example the ends of the long bones where more fragile cancellous tissue will not withstand vigorous washing and brushing, and with (inherently) fragile pathological bones. Do not clean stains made by artefacts from the bones. Ear orifices should be left packed with soil so that ear bones can be 'excavated' in the laboratory (three in each ear would be expected). Care should also be taken with teeth that have plaque (calculus) deposits on them as this can easily be dislodged during cleaning. Particularly fragile areas of the skeleton include the facial part of the skull, the ribs and scapulae, the vertebrae, the pelvis, and of course pathological bones. If an intact skull has soil impacted inside it then it is advisable to remove that soil before transport of the skeleton for analysis; if this is not done then, once the soil hardens inside the skull, it will damage it. Once washed, bones and teeth should be allowed to dry naturally away from direct sunlight, and artificial drying devices should never be used.

Once dry (and importantly *clean*), each bone and tooth, and fragments of bone, should ideally be marked (Figure 35) with its unique identification number (site code and skeleton number) in permanent waterproof (Indian) black ink; with very small fragments where it is not possible to mark the bone, there is no alternative but to leave them. Marking bones is necessary because it helps to prevent mixing of bones and teeth between skeletons, and makes it possible to separate bones and teeth that have been mixed together, but belong to different individuals (Caffell 2005). However, it is appreciated by the author that the cost and time involved in marking all bones cannot be justified in contract archaeology, and would be in addition to the work contract bioarchaeologists do to fulfil the client's obligations (McKinley pers comm, November 2007). Nevertheless, for disarticulated bones from prehistoric contexts marking bones is always essential.

In the case of skeletal collections that are being used a lot for teaching and/ or research purposes by many different people, it is absolutely essential that marking of the skeletons has been done as the potential for mixing of different individuals is much higher. The marking should be clear, legible, neat, and unobtrusive (eg on the posterior surfaces of bones, and not on joint surfaces and pathological parts of bones). It is a good idea to practice on pieces of paper before trying to write on bones, especially if pen and Indian ink has never been used before. Marking is extremely time consuming, and it is better to take a bit longer and do it neatly and legibly than to rush – the benefits can far outweigh the time costs. However it should be noted that areas of bones with ink on them should not be used for sampling, unless the composition of the ink is known, as the ink may affect subsequent analyses (Richards 2004).

(b) Cremated remains

Cremated remains must be wet sieved using a stack of 10, 5, 2, and 1mm mesh sieve sizes (McKinley and Roberts 1993). Care must be taken to minimise further fragmentation, and the removal of stones, if present, will help. Once dry, post-depositional materials are removed, including pyre debris (which must be recorded and analysed by relevant personnel depending on the material). Marking of cremated bone is not practical because the fragments are usually very small, the bone fragment surfaces not very smooth, the marking would mask too much of the surface, and it serves no useful purpose (McKinley pers comm, November 2007).

(ii) Packing skeletal remains

Bones and teeth must be totally dry before being placed into bags and boxes. Boxes must be large enough to accommodate the largest bones of the skeleton (Figure 36). Most skeletal remains are placed in plastic bags in cardboard or plastic boxes. Each skeleton may be packed in one or more boxes, the skull often being kept in a separate, smaller box. The number of boxes used will depend on the individual organisation or institution and the size of boxes available.

Within the boxes, bones are usually packaged into labelled plastic bags, the former being more durable and transparent, and thus making it is easier to see the contents. Ideally, if standard boxes are used, the bones should be put into plastic bags with specific parts of the body being placed into separate bags, and labelled with the site code, skeleton number, and its content; a label should also be placed inside each bag. Bags are needed for the skull, jaws, the clavicles,

Figure 36: Example of bones being too long for the storage box (Charlotte Roberts)

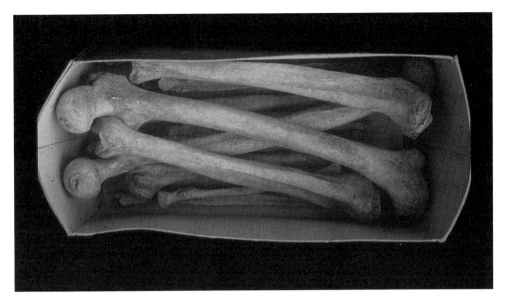

scapulae and sternum, the long bones of the upper limb (left and right in separate bags), a bag for each of the hands, the left ribs, the right ribs, the spine, the pelvic girdle, the long bones of the lower limb (left and right in separate bags), and a bag for each of the feet. Some parts of the skeleton, eg the jaws, may benefit from extra packaging with acid-free tissue paper; 'nests' or 'pillows' of acid-free tissue paper should be created to support the bones and prevent or minimise bone to bone contact (Chris Caple pers comm, November 2007). Wrapping each and every bone is a waste of resources, and frequent unwrapping and wrapping is potentially damaging. For people working on the skeletal material, it is frustrating (McKinley and Roberts 1993), and it may ultimately lead to breaking of skeletal elements.

The (acid-free) box(es) should be packed carefully and not too much should be placed in any one box such that damage to the bones occurs. Lewis (nd) produced a useful diagram of guidance for packing a skeleton into a single box which consisted of placing the heavier and more robust bones in the bottom while the lighter and more fragile bones were put at the top (Figure 37). Lining the base of the box with crumpled newspaper helps protect/cushion the skeleton, but bones must be in bags in this instance because newspaper is acidic and will damage bones in direct contact, whilst the ink will stain the bone surface (Caple pers comm, November 2007). Accurate marking of the boxes with the correct site and skeleton number is essential and, if more than one box is used, they should be marked '1 of 2', '2 of 2', for example. The marking of the boxes (at their ends, which will show on the shelves) should reflect exactly what is in them. The problem with the standard method of storing skeletons, ie in one cardboard box, is that there is too much potential for damage to occur to the bones during use. Take, for instance, a situation where a researcher is interested in measuring the leg bones of each skeleton in a cemetery; if the box has been packed according to Lewis's guidance then the rest of the skeleton has to be removed from the

HOW TO PACK A SKELETON

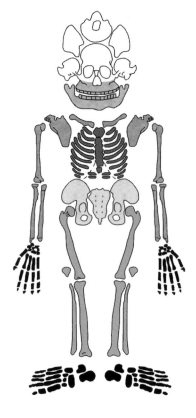

Figure 37: How to 'pack' a skeleton into a box (with permission and after Mary Lewis)

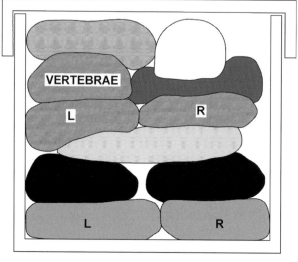

NEVER pack the skull, maxilla and mandible at the bottom of the box. Heavy bones go first.

Loose teeth, maxillae and mandibles should be bagged separately and not with the heavier cranial vault.

Pathological bones and fragile maxillae should be wrapped in acid-free tissue paper.

If you unwrap pathological bones you MUST make sure that they are re-wrapped in their tissue paper and bubble wrap when you have finished with them.

Please handle skeletons with the utmost care and respect. Thank you.

Seal the bag!

SITE:	CH86
No. :	C-283
BONE:	R.Foot

box to access the lower limb bones. Some people will be careful and remove all the uppermost bags to reach the leg bones, but others might not; the potential for damage to the skeleton is considerable. Equally important, too little skeletal material should not be placed in boxes; the bones should remain stationary when the box is moved (Caple pers comm, November 2007).

A recent development in box design solves this problem (despite creating some of its own). A study of the impact of use of skeletal collections found that continued use of curated skeletal remains for teaching and research compromised their integrity considerably (Caffell *et al* 2001). This led to the design of a new boxing system for skeletal remains which protected remains from damage and preserved them for future generations of scholars (Bowron 2003). The box was designed as 'boxes within a box' so that individual parts of the skeleton could be stored separately (Figure 38). It also allowed researchers, teachers, and students to select specific bones as needed without disturbing/damaging the rest of the skeleton. The box design was first used by Field Archaeology Specialists and Mike Griffiths and Associates for the late medieval skeletal remains from Fishergate House in York. The box is larger than normal which makes handling difficult, and it is more expensive than a normal box; this also means that it does not fit conventional-size museum/university storage shelves. However, its use at Durham University to curate the Fishergate House skeletal sample is showing considerable promise in preventing damage to this collection.

Cremated bone is usually packed in marked re-sealable polythene bags, with a label inside the bag, and placed in plastic sealed boxes. Care must be taken not to overpack boxes or place heavy weights on top of the bags of cremated bone; this prevents further fragmentation of already brittle bone (McKinley pers comm, January 2008).

Figure 38: The 'Emma Bowron Box' (Charlotte Roberts)

4.4 Conservation of human remains

Odegaard and Cassman (2006) are keen to emphasise that invasive treatments of human remains in the past have at times compromised future research, and that *extreme thought* must be applied to the question of whether active invasive conservation should be undertaken. The success of biochemical analyses for ancient DNA and stable isotopes, and radiocarbon dating, can all be affected by the use of consolidants. Richards (2004) also cautions the use of consolidants and preservatives on human remains, emphasising that it is an outdated procedure, is rarely practised, and the problems it causes far outweigh the benefits. While Millard (2001) indicates that consolidants have a destructive effect on ancient DNA survival, he suggests that if conservation treatments have to be used then surface treatments are to be preferred over penetrating treatments, although treatments in general are not commonly used. It may even be sensible in the future to use different consolidants on different bones from one site so that different classes of biochemical information may be preserved for analysis (Millard 2001).

'Invasive conservation' includes cleaning, consolidation, adhesive repairs, the use of fixed reconstructive materials such as filling and pigments, and the use of pesticides (*ibid*). Treatments applied to human remains should be avoided if one follows the concept of minimum intervention (Watkinson and Neal 1998; DCMS 2005), but, as Millard (2001) indicates, 'treatments' are often chosen by archaeologists, not conservators. Conservation work should only be done when absolutely necessary and under strict protocols. The work should be undertaken by a trained conservator used to dealing with biological materials, overseen by a bioarchaeologist. Records of treatments should always be kept (eg what was used, how and when), and preferably some bone/teeth should be left untreated and stored for future analysis.

(i) In the ground prior to excavation

As indicated in *Management of Archaeological Projects 2* (Andrews 1991), there must be clear guidance on calculating the scale of on-site conservation needed during excavation, but the following is based on guidance outlined in Watkinson and Neal (1998). There are three options for on-site conservation needs: have an on-site conservator if the excavation warrants it, have a conservator make regular site visits, or have a conservator on call to answer queries. In general, Watkinson and Neal recommend 'a policy of non-intervention on-site', with the general premise that conservation on-site 'aims to prevent objects deteriorating both chemically and physically, using correct recovery, packaging and storage procedures' (*ibid*, 2–3).

Choosing when to intervene to conserve human remains, and what with, is a complex procedure, and a balance has to be struck between ensuring that the scientific potential of the remains can be realised and that the material does not deteriorate, thus ultimately compromising its potential. Some studies have documented the effects of the use of conservation materials to provide structural

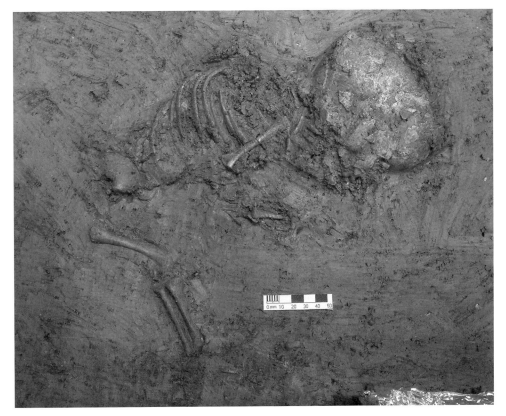

Figure 39: A neonatal skeleton block-lifted from the Roman site of Stretton Grandison, Herefordshire (with permission of Archaeological Services Durham University)

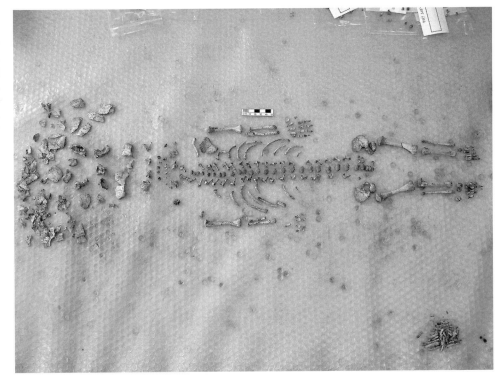

Figure 40: The remains of the neonate in Figure 39, once excavated from the block (with permission of Archaeological Services Durham University)

stability to fragile bones and teeth and how that may impact on further analysis (eg Moore *et al* 1989), but there is much more work needed. However, as Johnson (2001) illustrates, there is no 'silver bullet' as to what to choose to do.

If remains are very fragile there may be a case for lifting the bones with their surrounding soil matrix. Bandaging and block-lifting techniques are described in Watkinson and Neal (1998). For example, see Figures 39 and 40; here a neonatal skeleton was block-lifted in heavy clay and subsequently excavated in a laboratory situation over 2.5 days. The skeleton was almost 100% completely recovered, and cremated remains and potsherds were also retrieved from the block (Anwen Caffell pers comm, January 2008). Other methods are also described, such as the use of solid CO_2 pellets to freeze the ground to allow the lifting of a Bronze Age skeleton and associated artefacts (Jones 2001; and Figures 41 and 42). However, the commonest method involves consolidating the bones with a consolidant (polymeric material) before lifting them, but this must be done only as a last resort and thought through very carefully. As is indicated (*ibid*, 80), 'It is impossible to remove all traces of even a highly reversible resin from a porous object'. There are two types of consolidant used: aqueous emulsifiers/dispersions (particles of the consolidant are made compatible with water) and synthetic resin solutions (individual molecules of resin are dissolved in an organic solvent such as acetone). The concentration of the consolidant influences the amount of polymer entering the bone. Therefore, lower concentrations are better, preferably 5–10% of the weight of the polymer/volume of solution (Watkinson and Neal 1998).

The aqueous emulsifers need acetone to dissolve them, have a limited shelf life, and thus they do not have long-term stability (*ibid*). They are applied to bone using a brush, a syringe, or by a spray. PVA, Primal WS-24 and Revacryl are recommended. PVA is acetone soluble, but it does not penetrate into bone well, has high permeability to water, and may be difficult to remove (*ibid*); it can also end up ranging from soft and sticky to hard and brittle at normal room temperature (Johnson 2001). Primal WS-24 has a very small molecule size and is believed to penetrate bone more effectively than other consolidants. Additionally, because it is applied to bone by carriage in water, conservators are tending to choose this consolidant over others because it is less toxic (*ibid*). The synthetic resins are dissolved in a solvent such as acetone; this carries the resin molecules into the bone and then the solvent evaporates. Synthetic resins are incompatible with water and therefore can only be used on dry bone. Paraloid B72 is considered a standard treatment in conservation (*ibid*), and is normally applied in solvents such as toluene and acetone (Caple pers comm, November 2007). It is applied in 2–10% concentrations with either a brush or syringe (Watkinson and Neal 1998). The absolute minimum amount of an appropriate consolidant needed should be used (Spriggs 1989), and Johnson (2001) provides detailed guidelines on their use. However, only experienced conservators should undertake this work and they need to take measures to avoid inhaling solvent fumes; the bones should also be free of soil so the two are not glued together with the consolidant. Resins are brushed, dropped, or sprayed onto the bone, possibly in several layers, with each layer being left to dry before the

Figure 41: Poorly preserved burial which was lifted using solid CO_2 pellets to freeze the ground (from Jones 2001; reproduced with permission of Jenny Jones)

Figure 42: Part of the burial partially excavated from its soil block, with sand bag support (from Jones 2001; reproduced with permission of Jenny Jones)

next is applied. Strict records of what has been used are essential so that if, in the future, any chemical analyses are proposed then the consolidant type can be accounted for (Spriggs 1989; McKinley and Roberts 1993). As has already been discussed, the use of consolidants may interfere with future analyses and, if it is anticipated that chemical analyses will be performed on the skeletal remains in the future, and consolidation *has to take place*, a sample should be taken before consolidation. Once the bone is strong enough to be lifted it can be placed inverted in a suitable plastic tray, and once off-site the untreated side of the bone can be dealt with by cleaning and consolidation. Spriggs (1989) recommends that if some support is still required for lifting the bone then strong heavy duty aluminium foil can be used. Where bone is recovered from waterlogged contexts and has lost mineral content, consolidation with PVA or a similar polymer is inappropriate – wet storage and conservation treatment with methods similar to those used for wet wood may be more applicable (Caple pers comm, November 2007).

(ii) Following cleaning

As Panagiaris (2001, 95) states: 'The change in environment, which occurs when human remains are excavated, can result in significant changes that may ultimately lead to deterioration'. Therefore, skeletal remains may deteriorate during analysis and curation. Once skeletal materials are out of the ground the environment is richer in oxygen, there is an abundant supply of water in the form of water vapour, it is warmer than the burial environment, there are temperature fluctuations and higher light levels, packing and handling can be physically damaging, and the environment is richer in bacteria, fungal spores, and chemical and biochemical contaminants (Watkinson and Neal 1998). For example, a higher moisture environment can encourage micro-organisms to attack the bone, and low or fluctuating moisture in the atmosphere can lead to drying out of the bone.

Many recommend reconstruction of fragmentary bones (eg White and Folkens 2005), but this should only be done by a bioarchaeologist with anatomical expertise, if at all. The colour and texture of the fragments, and of course anatomical expertise, will help join the right fragments together. However, often the adhesives used are unsuitable (Janaway *et al* 2001). If adhesive is used it ideally should not be stronger than the bone it is used on or it may lead to further post-mortem breaks, as Caffell *et al* (2001) found. It must also be reversible in a solvent that does not damage bone, it must not adversely affect bone, and if future biochemical analyses are done on the bone treated then it should be assumed that the adhesive may affect the results. HMG Paraloid B72 adhesive is recommended by conservators because it is long-term, stable, and always reversible. The use of Blu-tack® should be strictly avoided, not least because it leaves a mark on the bones and teeth and is radio-opaque. Some bioarchaeologists use masking tape to join fragments together, for example for measuring; this is regarded as a very temporary measure and the tape should be removed immediately following measurement. When left in place for longer, if it is then removed, it can take away the outer cortex of the bone (possibly losing important evidence of disease). Teeth should never be glued back into the tooth sockets because this prevents access to check the tooth roots for disease, for example. If reconstruction is to be done then the fragmented bone edges must be totally clean and the reconstruction done accurately, or distortion may result; a sand box may be used to support bones that have been glued together. Filling in the gaps where parts of, for example, the skull are absent is recommended by some (White and Folkens 2005), but this can be a very subjective process.

This author is sceptical about reconstructing bones in order that measurements can be taken and other features recorded; if reconstruction is done and is not performed well then the ultimate measurements taken will not be accurate. Furthermore, use of adhesives may increase the measurement of the bone taken. Odegaard and Cassman (2006, 87) emphasise also that during sticking bone fragments together 'hands are generally used to hold two pieces together in a fashion that "looks about right"'. The reconstruction of human remains is frequently subjective and can be influenced by factors such as: adhesive selection, stability and reversibility, and also the competence of the person who is undertaking the reconstruction. However, there are instances where careful glueing of skull fragments back together can provide information that was previously not possible to access, for example the head injury patterns of people buried at the battlefield of Towton, North Yorkshire (Fiorato *et al* 2007). What are the alternatives? To measure complete bones that have been fragmented may be possible by temporarily holding the fragments together with masking tape *briefly*, as has been described above. Parafilm M is also suggested as a material that could be used for holding bones together temporarily (this is a wax-like material that self-seals and clings around shapes and surfaces, is mouldable and flexible (Odegaard and Cassman 2006)), along with microcrystalline wax sticks placed on cranial fragments, front and back, to bridge the break. Once the reason for the reconstruction has been achieved then these materials should be removed. None of these methods introduces a layer of material between the fragments, and therefore measurements are not affected.

(iii) For display

A noted methodological advance, although rare, has been the reconstruction of faces (Wilkinson and Neave 2003), and heads affected by abnormal change such as disease (Kustár 1999; also see Prag and Neave 1997), often for display purposes. It has proved of use to see the person's face as they were when living, particularly for the public. Of course, much facial reconstruction in archaeology is for museum purposes to bring back to life the person whose skull has been reconstructed; it is also sometimes used in forensic situations to 'jog' the memories of people for identification purposes. However, media attention on the study of human remains from archaeological sites has also been considerable over the last ten years, and facial reconstructions have been popularly received (eg *Meet the Ancestors* on BBC 2).

4.5 Storage and curation of human remains

The long-term curation of human remains enables further research to be done on those remains beyond the initial, and often basic, skeletal report. Britain is one of the world leaders in the study and interpretation of human remains from archaeological sites (English Heritage and Church of England 2005) and, apart from research, retention also allows for an educational use of the remains in teaching, as long as ethical guidelines are provided to those both teaching and being taught. Naturally, any human remains that are curated and utilised by researchers must be treated with respect and their use not taken for granted.

A recent book (Cassman *et al* 2006b) has addressed the many issues surrounding the curation of skeletal remains including guidance on best practice. Suffice it to say, human remains, like any other material curated in institutions, are not a renewable resource, and a code of ethics for the treatment of these human remains should guide all involved with their care, as recommended and described by Alfonso and Powell (2006). Their suggestions guide bioarchaeologists in areas including ethical obligations to the remains, science and the community, the publication process, and the teaching and supervision of students. There are also numerous professional organisations which have their own codes of ethics and standards of practice (*ibid*) for archaeology and anthropology in general, but there is currently very little particularly focusing on human remains (Cassman *et al* 2006c). Furthermore, appropriate mission statements (institution/ organisation/department goals) are not provided for many university skeletal teaching collections, and the same can be said of policies for the management of human remains collections in many institutions, although these are increasing in Britain. Cassman *et al* (2006c) recommend that the following considerations should be included in a 'human remains policy', some of which some institutions describe: the purpose of the institution curating the collections; how they were and are acquired; how they may leave the collection (de-accessioning); how remains are accessed; storage requirements; care and handling for remains; dealing with applications for sampling and destructive analysis; photography/radiography and the use of images for research; whether exhibition is allowed; associated artefact disposition and care; associated archives and records disposition; allowance for making of casts of bones and teeth.

Many arguments for curation of skeletal remains, rather than reburial, have been made, and the scientific value of opportunities for long-term study and re-interpretation, and the use of newly developed techniques, still stand (eg see Buikstra and Gordon 1981 above). However, if human remains are to be retained then adequate storage conditions and controlled access must be in place, and it is accepted that some collections will have more scientific value than others. For example, that value may be assessed on the basis of the size of the collection, the type of the collection (urban, rural, rich, poor, monastic, hospital), its preservation, dating, and particular special value (eg coffin plates identifying individuals) – these are all factors that will influence its worth as a study collection. Most importantly, institutions should recognise the need to employ a person (or persons, depending on the size of the collections) to care for the material to ensure minimisation of damage through use of the collections for teaching and research. A range of institutions store skeletal collections, including universities, museums, archaeological contractors and research bodies; these places are responsible for storage and access. Furthermore, the number of skeletal remains curated in British institutions runs into thousands, although a much-needed database that centralises that information has yet to be created (see comments in Roberts and Cox 2003, 401–02).

(i) Storage areas

Following cleaning, skeletal remains need to be properly packaged in boxes, as we have seen, but preferably a baseline *Condition Assessment* should be made to enable skeletal condition to be monitored later in order to prevent deterioration whilst being curated (Janaway *et al* 2001); for many bioarchaeologists this is done for their skeletal report. While museums that curate archaeological and anthropological materials have sometimes tracked the condition of artefacts, there does not appear to be a similar procedure for human remains (Cassman and Odegaard 2006a). Having this initial condition assessment of human remains when first curated will allow monitoring of condition, which will in turn allow changes to be made to access, handling and conservation policies. However, the condition assessment must be written using vocabulary that everybody is familiar with, including the meaning of particular (non-subjective) words; for example, poor, good and excellent as terms to describe the 'condition' of a skeleton can be extremely misleading and be interpreted in many ways. Both descriptive and photographic records are essential, with dates of both made clear, and descriptive terms must be used consistently between skeletons, including the 'anatomical' position of damage. Any past 'treatments' of the skeleton, including adhesives, reconstruction, consolidants etc, should also be recorded.

Skeletal remains (cremated and unburnt) are stored in a variety of ways and much depends on the time, money and space available to package and box the skeletons. Ideally, human remains should be stored in dedicated secure areas away from public view, not mixed with other archaeological materials, and not exposed to sunlight (which will lead to ultraviolet light damage). They should be regularly inspected to ensure the highest standards of care are being implemented (DCMS 2005), including checking temperature and humidity, damage from pests, mould growth, cracking and flaking of bones. All written records associated with the skeletal collection should be held at the curating institution, and original recording forms (hard copies/electronic) should be retained as information available for people accessing the remains in the future. There does not, however, appear to be any specific agreement on the ideal store for human remains.

Storage of skeletal remains should be in a cool dry place, protected from frost, at an ambient relative humidity of about 55%. This can have a ± 5% fluctuation but, if left to go above 65%, mould growth can occur (eg see Garland *et al* 1988), and if left to go below 45% it can then be too dry and lead to cracking and flaking of the bone (Watkinson and Neal 1998). An ambient temperature of 18°C (range 10°–25°C) is recommended (Janaway *et al* 2001). The temperature and humidity of the storage area should be monitored. Skeletal material inside a box will experience a far lower level temperature and relative humidity than the room it is in (Caple pers comm, November 2007). Boxes should be on shelves of metal and the bottom shelves should be at least 10cm off the ground (Cassman and Odegaard 2006b) to avoid low temperatures, high relative humidity, rodent and flood damage. Compact storage is desirable to create more space; shelf units move on a track to provide aisle space for the relevant shelf when access is needed. There should be enough space between the shelves to allow access and removal of the remains. Boxes should not be piled on top of each other such that the bottom boxes and their contents suffer crushing. Boxes should be shelved in order by number of the skeleton, which makes access for researchers (who often have limited time to make their observations) easier and more efficient.

If a storage area has not been used for skeletal remains before then it should be monitored for temperature and humidity for several days, and it should be noted that temperature and relative humidity may vary during seasons of the year (Caple pers comm, November 2007). There is an increasing need to understand how bones deteriorate in storage as new methods of analysis develop. For example, ancient DNA analyses of curated skeletal collections rely on the survival of the DNA, but also the absence of contamination with modern DNA from a variety of sources. The older the remains are, and the warmer the storage area is, the less likely it may be that the remains will contain ancient DNA (Odegaard and Cassman 2006). It is also possible that invasive treatments of skeletal remains will affect DNA survival, including the use of consolidants and adhesives, and materials that might act as PCR (polymerase chain reaction) inhibitors (eg see Nicholson *et al* 2002). Therefore, before destructive sampling is undertaken, consideration should be given as to whether it is likely that ancient DNA will survive in the skeleton to be sampled should ideally be made.

(ii) Access by researchers, including university students

Access to work on human skeletal remains should, in the first instance, be controlled by the holding institution, and secondly by the completion of an appropriately developed *Access Form* (Figure 43) guided by an *Access Policy*. Thirdly, all people who access the remains should be *bona fide* and in good standing, and fourthly, good reason for access should be given, including justification for loans of skeletal material and/or destructive sampling (histological, isotope and aDNA analyses, and radiocarbon dating). Access applications should be assessed by a competent committee or a qualified individual (English Heritage and Church of England 2005). With regard to destructive analyses, the question that should be asked is: can the information be accessed without destructive sampling of the skeleton? If destructive sampling is undertaken then ideally no sampling should be allowed from pathological parts of bones, unless the analysis concerns specifically diseased bone, and

Application to utilise skeletal remains held in the Human Osteology Laboratory, Department of Archaeology, University of Durham

Name: ....

Position (e.g. research assistant, research student, undergraduate/masters student) ....

Institutional Affiliation: ....

Supervisor (and email address); please also provide a supporting letter from your supervisor ....

....

Address: ....

....

Email: ....

Fax: ....

Telephone: ....

Short outline of research project, including title ....

....

....

....

....

Undergraduate/ Masters/ M.Phil/ PhD Thesis? ....

Or is this part of a research project supported by a research grant? ....

Which skeletal collection are you wishing to access? ....

How many skeletons do you wish to examine, and are there any particular groups of skeletons or specific individual skeletons you wish to look at? ....

Is there any other documentation you wish to see for the skeletons? ....

For how long (days, weeks, months)? ....

When (please give approximate dates; three possible choices please)?

1. ....

2. ....

3. ....

What types of analysis are you intending to use? (e.g. macroscopic, radiographic, photography, sampling) ....

Could any of these be destructive to the skeletal material? ....

Do you need access to any equipment or are you supplying your own? ....

Are you intending to publish any of the data you collect? ....

Signature of applicant: .... Date: ....

(By signing this form I the applicant fully understand the agreement outlined below and agree to be bound by its conditions)

Signature of supervisor (where appropriate): ....

As the supervisor of the above named student I support the request for access to the skeletal and/or other material requested. I also acknowledge that I am responsible ultimately for the student's conduct

Signed: .... Date: ....

By signing this form the applicant will undertake to:

1. Read the guidelines of the Durham Human Osteology Laboratory on handling of skeletal remains

2. Take extreme care with the skeletal remains handled, and preserve the skeletal collection to the best of their ability.

3. Replace the correct bones into their respective boxes, refrain from mixing skeletal elements from different skeletons, repackage skeletal remains as they were found

4. Provide a list of skeletal and other material studied

5. Provide a copy of any papers/books/photographs/radiographs etc. resulting from the study of the skeletal material

6. Acknowledge the Department of Archaeology, University of Durham and the appropriate excavator of the site in all publications resulting from the analysis of the skeletal collection

For Office Use

Application form received (date): ....

Application considered (date): ....

Permission given or denied (with date): ....

Any further conditions on access? ....

the sampling can be justified adequately. A detailed descriptive/photographic/ radiographic record, as appropriate, of the bone or tooth used for sampling should be acquired before the sample is taken and, in some circumstances, repair of the damage may be needed to reinstate the integrity of the bone or a cast of the part destroyed made. The Arizona State Museum Destructive Testing Policy (Cassman and Odegaard 2006b) has useful principles of how to assess the value of destructive sampling. This includes considering the potential knowledge to be gained by the proposed analysis, whether the methodology is sound, if the researcher is competent, the extent of loss, damage, or disfigurement of the specimen versus its uniqueness, and the possible cultural sensitivity of the material being requested.

Along with a *Mission Statement*, each institution should have an *Access Policy* for the treatment of the human remains it holds and ensure that those who use the remains adhere to that policy. This should include (Cassman and Odegaard 2006b): where access happens; who is responsible for time and space allocation; what instruments/equipment can be used; whether visitors should wear gloves and other protective clothing; whether photography, radiography and /or destructive sampling are allowed; what happens with respect to publications – for example if copies go to the curating institution and who is acknowledged in them; and whether copies of data collected and photographs/radiographs taken are given to the institution.

Guidelines for treatment of the remains should be provided to each worker (based on a *Code of Ethics* – see Alfonso and Powell 2006 for suggestions), and facilities should be available to work on the remains. It is recommended that laboratory coats and gloves should be used to protect both researcher/ student and the skeleton. Additionally, mental and personal preparations should be made (Cassman and Odegaard 2006b) and human remains should only be handled and analysed with a specific reason in mind. Remains should be handled carefully, as described in Cassman and Odegaard (2006b). The absence of a code of ethics in bioarchaeology in general has been described as 'shocking' (Alfonso and Powell 2006, 7), and the author is inclined to agree, although some institutions and organisations in Britain have indeed developed one (eg see http://babao.org.uk/index/ethics-and-standards) or endorsed and supported others (eg see http://www.dur.ac.uk/archaeology/research/ethics/). A code might include an outline of acceptable behaviour, standards of practice, and a framework for professional behaviour and responsibilities (as defined by MacDonald 2000, cited in Alfonso and Powell 2006). Clearly, bioarchaeologists have a duty towards a range of people whom that code has to address – these include the scientific community, the public (and in some countries indigenous communities), and maybe grant-giving bodies, students and their institutions, governments, and the 'objects' under study (in this case the human remains). However, if a code is developed by institutions that curate skeletal remains then this would help to evaluate best practice and reassure the public, if there is any doubt, that those who study human remains will be treating the remains with respect.

It is advisable too that people working with the remains note and report any apparent deterioration in the condition of the remains (English Heritage and Church of England 2005), and an *Access Log*, is a good way of monitoring this (Janaway *et al* 2001). The use of an access log along with the original condition assessment (see above) to monitor 'use damage' to collections will allow access arrangements to be suitably modified to specific skeletal collections. If regular condition assessments of skeletal collections are made, and publicised, this should also encourage those who handle the remains to take great care. This is particularly important as recent research has shown the impact of the use of skeletal collections on their condition (Caffell *et al* 2001); a survey of adult skeletons from two different archaeological sites showed damage since acquisition into the institution's collections. Forty skeletons from the two sites were selected on the basis of 'heavy' and 'light' use, with a small proportion 'unused' (five). Analysis was based on comparison of the condition of bones at the time of study with photographs taken at acquisition, or shortly afterwards. Damage included bone element loss (and gain!), post-mortem fractures to bones, and surface erosion. The most heavily used skeletons naturally suffered most damage and loss, with hand and foot bones and teeth being lost the most. It was also found that the glue used to repair bones had often failed and on occasions it was suggested that the glueing of some bones had led to new breaks in the material. Recommendations were made for a condition assessment to be conducted, preferably immediately following excavation by the bioarchaeologist, but certainly when skeletal remains are acquired by curating institutions (Janaway *et al* 2001); it is unknown whether these are being implemented routinely during analysis or in curating institutions. Certainly, in the author's experience of utilising skeletal collections from a variety of institutions, what you might expect to find in a skeleton box could be very different to reality.

4.6 Summary

The efficient and proper excavation, post-excavation, conservation, and curation of human remains is vital for research and teaching in bioarchaeology, ultimately providing us all with a detailed knowledge of the lives of our ancestors. While guidelines are suggested, it is essentially the responsibility of excavators, bioarchaeologists, conservators, and curators to implement these suggestions as far as possible. Implementation frequently depends on the availability of time and money, which can be limited. In Britain's current culture of contract archaeology, responsibility for funding matters related to future research on skeletal material, such as the marking of bones, cannot routinely be placed on developers. Nevertheless, the cost in time and money can be well justified by the bioarchaeological research already done. As bioarchaeology is a key part to our understanding of the past, if remains are not ultimately handled correctly then the data derived from them will be compromised.

4.7 Key learning points

- excavation and recording of inhumed and cremated remains are time-consuming and delicate
- excavation teams should include people familiar with the skeleton and its analysis
- there may be health hazards associated with specific burial contexts but these are rare in Britain
- processing of human remains needs to be done with great care to preserve integrity and avoid damage to valuable information
- following analysis and before curation, a condition assessment for each skeleton is recommended in order to monitor condition during curation
- conservation treatments can be damaging and affect future scientific analyses and should be done only when absolutely necessary, and by a trained conservator
- reconstruction of remains should be done with care, if at all, and only by a conservator or bioarchaeologist
- curation environments should be temperature and humidity controlled, and the condition of the human remains monitored frequently
- a code of ethics, an access procedure and log, and a policy for the use of human remains collections are recommended for institutions that curate human remains
- curating institutions should employ people specifically to curate human remains, monitor their condition and control access

CHAPTER FIVE

Recording and analysis of data I: basic information

Human remains are the most tangible and direct form of evidence for understanding how people lived in the past ... (they) must rank as one of the (if not the) most information-rich sources of archaeological evidence

(Gowland and Knüsel 2006, ix)

5.1 Introduction

Prior to starting to discuss the methods of analysis of human remains and the types of information it is possible to record, a discussion of the working environment in which data collection takes place is necessary.

5.2 Working in a laboratory environment

As has been repeatedly said in previous chapters, working with human remains from archaeological sites is a privilege and not a right, and guidelines for laboratory work should be provided by institutions that curate human remains. The following are some general recommendations.

(i) The laboratory layout

The recording and analysis of human remains needs to take place in a dedicated 'laboratory', or more often termed 'workroom', where remains can be left out, as necessary, but preferably for the shortest possible time (Figure 44). The laboratory should not generally be accessible and/or on view to all, but only to those working in it, unless for example it is used for open days in universities. It should be secure at all times, and no food or drink should be allowed. Benches should be present in the laboratory that are large enough to accommodate the laying out of a fully articulated skeleton, and shelving should be available to hold boxes of human skeletal material (see Chapter 4). Further shelving may be needed for anatomical plastic skeletons and models, comparative radiographs, and books, and filing cabinets may be needed to hold papers etc. A step ladder should be available to reach shelving safely, and bone and hand washing facilities are essential, with sieves, washing up bowls, and soft brushes being available. However, for the purposes of contract archaeology work, bones and teeth have usually been washed before being sent to the bioarchaeologist for analysis. Efficient lighting to enable effective observation of the remains, in the form of general overhead lighting and

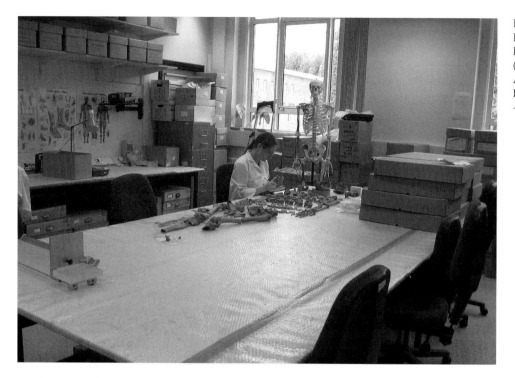

Figure 44: Typical
Human Osteology
Laboratory
(Department of
Archaeology,
Durham University
– Charlotte Roberts)

angle poise lamps with magnifiers, is also needed. Radiographic viewing
boxes, preferably wall mounted, are necessary to view and analyse/interpret
radiographs.

(ii) Laboratory 'clothing'

The wearing of laboratory coats and gloves protects the remains and the
bioarchaeologist from 'contamination' by each other. Handling human remains
using disposable gloves can be the norm for some institutions now to ensure
safety for the handler, respect for the remains, and also to prevent contamination
for future analyses (Cassman and Odegaard 2006b). However, for students who
are learning the nuances of the anatomical points of bones of the skeleton direct
handling is necessary, and for the most part in Britain this is the case. Sometimes
masks may be necessary if remains are dusty or have soil adhering to them to
prevent irritation of the respiratory tract.

(iii) Handling remains

Human remains should be analysed over a bench surface padded with inert
material such as textiles or microfoam so that no damage can occur to the
skeleton (see table 5.1 in Cassman and Odegaard 2006b). While all remains
should be handled with great care, the larger bones such as the long bones and
skull should always be handled using two hands, and the facial skeleton can be
extremely fragile. A cork ring or a bean bag, masking tape rolls, or even bubble

wrap rings are helpful to prevent undamaged skulls rolling around on the bench or even falling off. Care should also be taken with ensuring the smaller bones, and teeth, are not overlooked such that they are lost. Large and small plastic trays, again with protective material on their bases, can be useful for keeping together fragmentary skeletons or parts of skeletons, and also hand and foot bones; they can also help with moving skeletal materials around the laboratory. Putting the two or more bones of a joint together to make them 'move' is not advised since this can cause surface damage to parts of the joint (Cassman and Odegaard 2006b), and plastic joints are available anyway for teaching the movements of the joints. Only one skeleton at a time should be analysed so that mixing of remains does not occur, and it should be set out in normal anatomical position as if the 'person' was laid down on their back on the bench.

(iv) Equipment

There are a number of basic pieces of equipment that are used for analysis of human remains, once the skeleton is laid out on the bench. The first concerns measuring equipment. While there are sophisticated laser scanning methods for measuring bones and teeth in three dimensions using particular computer software (O'Higgins 2000), most people working with human remains use conventional measuring techniques and instruments. Sliding and spreading callipers are generally used for measuring lengths and diameters on bones and teeth but care must be taken to ensure that the (often) sharp pointed ends do not damage the remains. Osteometric boards can also be 'hard' on bones when measuring their lengths, as can mandibulometers (for measuring parts of the mandible), but measuring tapes (preferably cloth) are 'kind' to the integrity of bones and are usually used to measure circumferences. Casts of known age and sex pubic symphyses and sternal ends of the ribs are necessary as comparators for the skeletal remains to determine adult age, as are the 'Arizona' dental casts to record dental non-metric traits (see later). Relevant publications which provide comparative data/methods/illustrations for age and sex estimation of skeletal remains, definitions of measurements, and skeletal and dental non-metric traits, provide baselines for analysis.

An endoscope, with a diameter as small as 2mm, may be used for exploring interior areas of the skeleton such as inside complete skulls, and sinuses and the ears. In clinical situations endoscopes are used a lot for visualising the body internally. This is a powerful fibre optic lens system which provides light and visualisation (Cassman and Odegaard 2006b), and can be attached to a camera or video recorder. Photographic equipment to produce conventional photographs in black and white or colour or, more commonly today, digitally, should be available either within the laboratory or in facilities close by. Photographs should be taken with an appropriate scale, against a dark background. Of course, with the advent of digital photographs, bioarchaeologists have the facilities now to send images to other people for opinions, and publishers usually expect digital format photographs (high resolution: minimum 350dpi).

Facilities for plain film radiography, again, should be available and accessible, including the radiography machine, the radiography film, technical support, and processing facilities. Nevertheless, most bioarchaeologists working in contract archaeology do not, and could not be expected to, have radiography facilities 'in house'. Some institutions may also have access to more sophisticated radiographic equipment, such as digital radiography and computed tomography (CT), where 'slices' of the body/bones can be radiographed. While many bioarchaeologists have previously used hospital services to obtain radiographs, hospital services should be used for the living and not the dead, unless facilities are used out of normal hospital working hours and the costs paid for in full. Portable radiography machines are available for use in the 'field', although again are not widely purchased because of the expense. Finally, magnifying glasses and low power microscopes are often available in bioarchaeology laboratories purely to take a closer look at detailed features on bones and teeth. This might be to distinguish post-mortem from perimortem injuries or to look for dental enamel defects on teeth, for example. If more complex histological analysis is undertaken, such as examining sections of bone to determine age at death or looking at features in pathological bones for diagnosis of disease, then more sophisticated microscopic facilities may be needed such as scanning electron microscopy, including technical support. However, again, use of these analytical techniques depends on access availability and real need; in contract archaeology it would not normally be considered as necessary to fulfil the requirements of the developer funding the production of a skeletal report. Nevertheless, in Britain in the future, provision of access to facilities for radiography and histology would be very helpful for contract bioarchaeologists.

(v) Standardisation of recording human remains, recording forms, spreadsheets, and databases

Prior to detailing methods of analysis, an outline of recording methods should be given. In Britain, in the commercial world of contract archaeology, prior to full recording of skeletal remains, assessment reports are made to evaluate the potential of the human remains, and other finds, along with estimating costs (English Heritage 2004). This follows the planning and fieldwork and comes before the analysis and dissemination of the data. English Heritage (2004) provides detailed guidance about the desired contents of an assessment report (quantity of human remains, condition, ratio of adults to non-adults, proportion showing disease, potential of the assemblage, cost, time needed, curation provision), and also a full human bone report. The reader is directed towards that reference for information.

Until the publication of Buikstra and Ubelaker (1994), bioarchaeologists in Britain used Brothwell (1981) and Bass (originally 1987, but now 2005) for general guidance on recording, and generally did not appear to be concerned with using standard methods of collecting their data; for example, different methods would be used to age a skeleton or measure bones. Since the establishment of 'standards

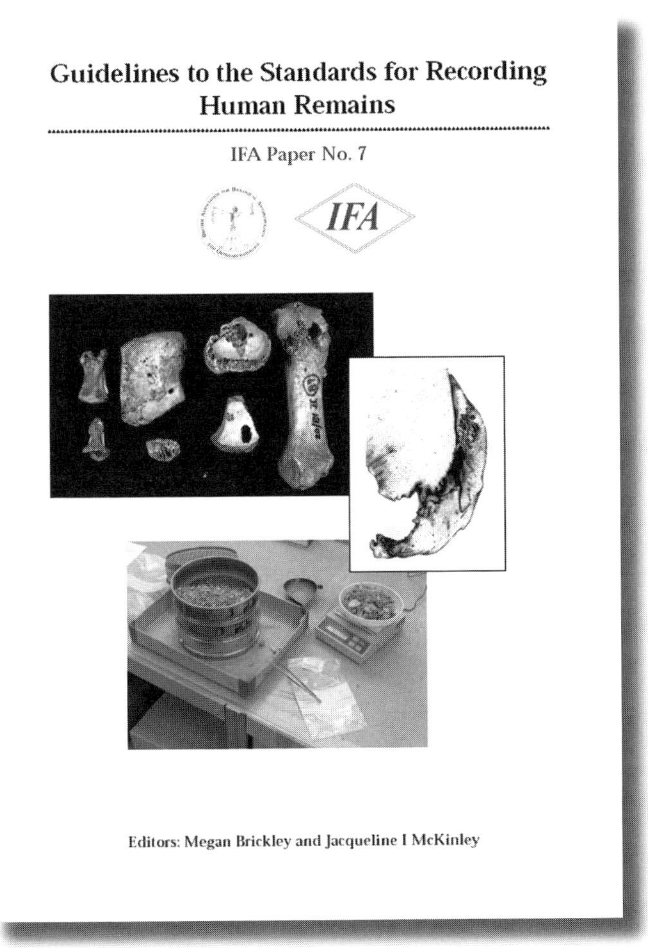

Guidelines to the Standards for Recording Human Remains

IFA Paper No. 7

IFA

Editors: Megan Brickley and Jacqueline I McKinley

Figure 45: British Association of Biological Anthropology and Osteoarchaeology Standards for Recording Human Remains cover (with permission of BABAO)

for data collection' more people have begun to recognise that recording the data using the same methods provides a base for realistic comparison of skeletons within the same and different geographic contexts and time periods. Unless bioarchaeologists have the time and money to record all the data they wish to use themselves (unlikely), they have to rely on published data and need to be assured that it has been recorded in the same way (and correctly). Buikstra and Ubelaker (1994) was followed by Brickley and McKinley (2004) which referred to the former as a base, but additionally produced a set of advisory 'Guidelines to the Standards for Recording Human Remains' with British skeletal material in mind (Figure 45). Furthermore, the Ohio State University-initiated 'Global History of Health Project' (see Chapter 1) has established a 'coding format', which documents what should be recorded for each skeleton that will be part of this ambitious project. It is with this project that finally a large dataset illustrating health through time will be created from many countries of the world, data that will be sound enough to enable comparative work.

Alongside developing standards for data collection, people have also developed their own 'hard copy' recording forms, spreadsheets, and databases, with further (now more complex) analysis and archiving in mind. There is not the time and space to provide an assessment of these forms and databases; suffice it to say, if the guidelines above are followed and appropriate forms and/or databases are created, with room for additions where appropriate, for example if particular research questions demand a specific observation or measurement that are not included in the 'standards', then the result will be the adequate recording of human remains.

5.3 The skeletal structure (macroscopic and microscopic) and its function

Prior to discussing the identification of the component parts of a skeleton, it is worth documenting the skeletal structure, both outside and inside and at both macroscopic and microscopic levels.

(i) What are the functions of the skeleton (Figure 46)?

The skeleton has a number of functions. It is a supporting framework such that if we did not have one, we would not be able to stand, sit, walk, run, or do anything. It protects the delicate organs of the body, for example the lungs are surrounded by the ribs, sternum, and spine, whilst the skull encloses the brain. Its surfaces provide attachments for muscles, tendons, and ligaments, thus allowing the body to move. It also forms blood cells, and stores calcium, phosphorus, and red and yellow bone marrow. The teeth allow us to chew a normal diet and they may also be used for particular tasks. Thus if the skeleton is disrupted in any way then any of these functions may be affected.

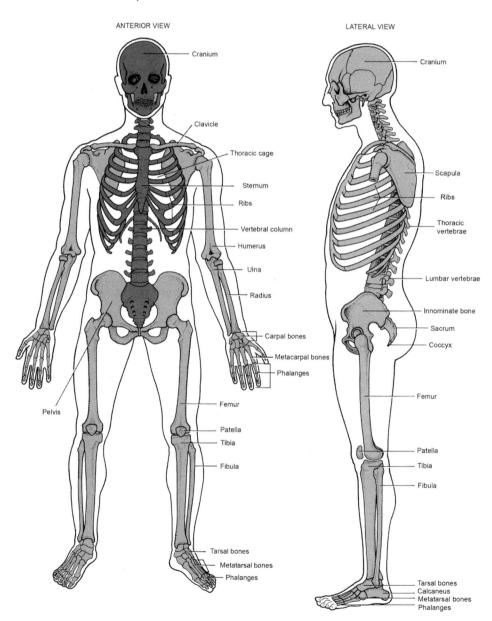

Figure 46: Skeleton with the bones named (redrawn by Yvonne Beadnell, after Wilson 1995). Darker areas = axial skeleton; lighter areas = appendicular skeleton

(ii) What are bones and teeth comprised of?

Bone is composed of one of the hardest tissues in the body, connective tissue, which in dead archaeological bone comprises 'material' that is 40% organic (ie living) and 60% inorganic (ie without 'living' characteristics). However, in a living bone, 20% of the structure is taken up with water, with the remainder being made up of 30–40% organic, and 40–50% inorganic material (Wilson 1995). The organic part is 90% collagen, a protein which provides resilience, and the inorganic component, mainly bone mineral crystals of a form of calcium phosphate embedded into the collagen fibre matrix, giving the bone strength and rigidity. When a person dies, the organic part of the bone also dies and the bones become very 'brittle'.

(iii) Types and structure of bones, joints, and teeth

(a) Bone

There are five different types of bone that make up the skeleton: long (eg femur, or thigh bone); short (eg bones of the wrist and ankle); irregular (eg the vertebrae of the spine); flat (eg the scapula, or shoulder blade, and the skull vault or 'braincase'); and sesamoid (eg the knee cap or patella) (Figure 47). Long bones have a shaft or diaphysis and two ends, called epiphyses. These different bones make up the axial (skull, spine, including the sacrum at the end, the sternum or breast bone, and ribs), and the appendicular (upper limb, and lower

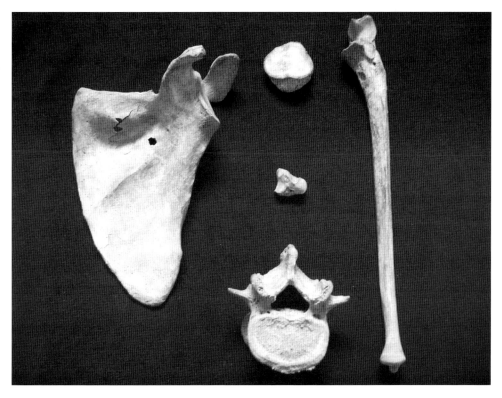

Figure 47: Examples of short, long, sesamoid, irregular, and flat bones (with permission of Stewart Gardner)

limb, including the innominate bones of the pelvis) skeleton. In an adult skeleton there are normally 206 bones in total, although people can have extra ribs in the neck and lumbar regions (cervical and lumbar ribs) and vertebrae in the spine (usually at the lower end), or there may even be a lack of some bones through congenital absence (ie the person is born lacking a particular bone).

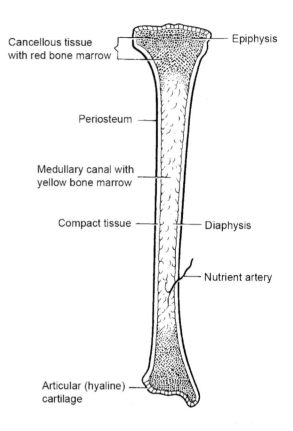

A typical long bone has a number of different 'layers' (Figure 48). The outer layer in the living is called the periosteum, a fibrous membrane. This protects the bone, provides attachment for muscles and tendons, and has a very good blood supply. The periosteum is not found on synovial joints, which are covered by cartilage, or on the inside of the skull, which is covered by the dura mater, the outer of the three membranes between the skull and the brain, and between the vertebrae and spinal cord. Underneath the periosteum is the cortical or compact bone which is very dense. Inside the compact layer in the centre of the bone is the medullary canal, which contains the yellow (fatty) bone marrow. At the ends of the bone is cancellous/trabecular/spongy bone; this bone has a large surface area and its spaces are filled with red bone marrow where red blood cells are formed. Different bones have differing amounts of cortical and cancellous bone; for example the vertebrae have a lot of cancellous bone and a thin cortex, while the femur has a thicker cortex and proportionately less cancellous bone.

Figure 48: Typical long bone showing cross section (redrawn by Yvonne Beadnell, after Wilson 1995)

Microscopic structure

Within the cortical bone lie microscopic structures called Haversian systems (Figure 49). Each 'system' or osteon contains a central Haversian canal which encloses nerves and vessels containing blood and lymph. The lymphatic system is a subsidiary of the circulatory system (Wilson 1995). The lymph vessels take away waste materials, noxious substances, and micro-organisms from the body tissues via the lymph to be deposited eventually in the lymph nodes (many of varying sizes situated throughout the body); following drainage into the nodes and loss of the waste materials, the lymph then returns to the blood. The Haversian canal is surrounded by layers (lamellae) of bone and between the layers there are spaces (lacunae) which contain lymph and osteocytes (mature bone cells). Canaliculi (small 'canals') link the lacunae with the lymph vessels in the Haversian canal, and the osteocytes (bone cells) get nutrients from the lymph. Between each Haversian system are more layers of bone (interstitial lamellae) and the Haversian canals are linked together by Volkmann's canals.

Bone cells

There are three types of bone cell, the osteoblast, the osteoclast, and the osteocyte. As we have seen, the osteocytes reside in Haversian systems; they are involved with final mineralisation of bone, regulating the flow of calcium and phosphorus in and out of bone, and ultimately maintaining the bone structure. The osteoblast is found in the periosteum and where immature new bone is being formed; they have a six-month lifespan and form bone (eventually around 10–15% become osteocytes). The bone formed is initially osteoid, ie unmineralised at that stage. The osteoclast resorbs or destroys bone at bone surfaces, under the periosteum, and around the walls of the medullary canal; they sit in small depressions called Howship's lacunae. The proportion of osteoblasts and osteoclasts (active throughout life) is usually balanced in health but not in disease. For example, in osteoporosis, more bone is destroyed than is made so that the net effect is loss of bone mass, which ultimately can lead to fractures. When bone is first formed it is called woven bone, for example when the bones of a foetus are formed, when a fracture is healing, or as the first response in disease, but eventually it is replaced with mature lamellar bone. Woven bone is filled with many holes (porous) and its structure is disorganised. Lamellar bone is stronger than woven bone, is more organised in structure, and is much less porous.

Figure 49: Microscopic image of bone (redrawn by Yvonne Beadnell, after Wilson 1995)

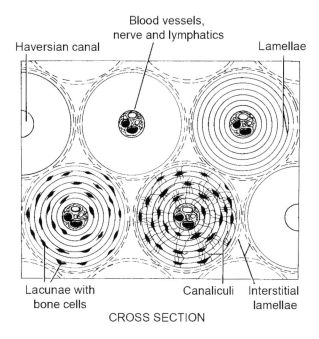

Blood vessels, nerve and lymphatics

Haversian canal

Lamellae

Lacunae with bone cells

Canaliculi

Interstitial lamellae

CROSS SECTION

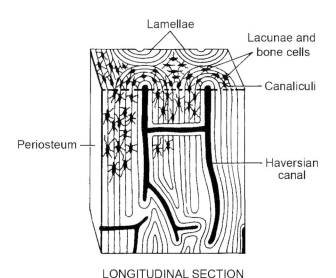

Lamellae

Lacunae and bone cells

Canaliculi

Periosteum

Haversian canal

LONGITUDINAL SECTION

Joints

The bones of the skeleton 'articulate', ie they fit together, via joints, of which there are three types with typical structures (described in detail in Wilson 1995: Figure 50). Firstly, synovial joints move freely and can be subclassified by range of movement or the shape of the parts of the joint into ball and socket (eg hip), hinge (eg elbow), gliding (eg carpal and tarsal bones of the hand and foot), pivot (between the two top vertebrae, or the atlas and the axis), and saddle (eg the base of the thumb, and the temporo-mandibular, or the joint between

(A)

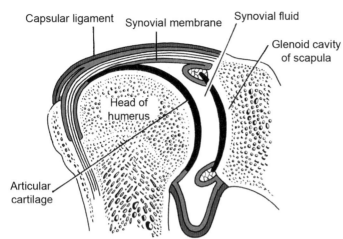

Capsular ligament Synovial membrane Synovial fluid

Glenoid cavity
of scapula

Head of
humerus

Articular
cartilage

Figure 50: Examples of different joints:
(A) synovial; (B) fibrous; (C) cartilaginous
(redrawn by Yvonne Beadnell, after Wilson
1995)

(B)

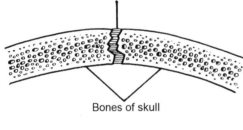

Fibrous joint

Bones of skull

Figure 51: Example of bones of the
forearm and hand with muscle
markings: red = origin of muscle;
blue = insertion of muscle
(Charlotte Roberts)

(C)

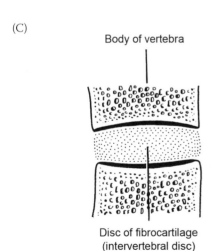

Body of vertebra

Disc of fibrocartilage
(intervertebral disc)

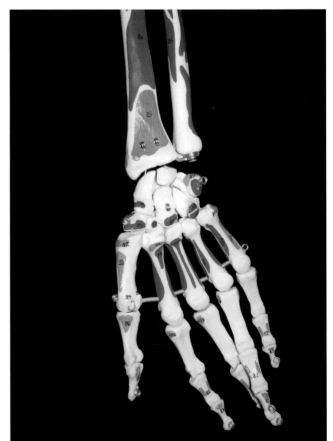

the lower jaw and rest of the skull). Secondly, fibrous or fixed joints are immovable, for example between the bones of the skull (sutures) and the teeth and jaws. Finally, the cartilaginous or slightly moveable joints include the joints between the vertebral bodies and the 'front' joint of the pelvis (pubic symphysis).

The joint surfaces are covered with cartilage, also a connective tissue, which contains chondroblasts, chondroclasts, and chondrocytes, with the same functions as their equivalents in bone. Hyaline cartilage covers the ends of bones in joints and the vertebral bodies, and fibrocartilage comprises part of the intervertebral discs between the vertebrae (Wilson 1995). Fibrous tissue forms the muscle sheaths which extend beyond the muscles of bones to become the tendon, and ligaments are made of fibrocartilage and link bones together (eg the lower leg bones, tibia and fibula). Muscles that serve the skeleton are classed as voluntary or striated, voluntary because their contraction and relaxation is under conscious control (see details of the different skeletal muscles, which bones they are associated with, and how they work in Stone and Stone 1990). While the soft tissues of the body need a skeleton to enable the person to stand and sit upright, the body could not move without the presence and combination of joints, muscles, tendons and ligaments (Figure 51). There is often a tendency in bioarchaeology to forget that 'our' skeleton was once living and breathing, was 'clothed' in flesh, and moved; appreciating this is essential in understanding how things can go wrong in disease.

Blood and nerve supply

The arterial and venous blood supply to bone is extremely good and there are numerous vessels serving all areas of the typical bone; the entry and exit of these vessels into bones can be seen as small holes in specific places, for example on the posterior (back) upper part of the lower leg bone (tibia). Once into the bone the supplying blood vessels branch off into smaller arterioles and capillaries, and the veins and venules transport blood out of the bones and eventually back to the heart. The nerves accompany the blood vessels into the bones and are more numerous in the joints, flat bones, and vertebrae.

Directional terms

There are a number of directional terms with which anybody working with human remains should be familiar. They include: proximal (nearest the centre); distal (farthest from centre); anterior (in front); posterior (behind); cranial (towards the head); dorsal (back); external (outside); internal (inside); inferior (lower); superior (upper); lateral (to the side, away from the midline); medial (to the side, towards the midline); ventral (in front); ectocranial (outside of the skull); endocranial (inside of the skull).

(b) Teeth

Types

There are four types of teeth normally found in the alveolar bone of the jaws: the incisors, canines, premolars, and molars (Figure 52), although the milk (or deciduous) teeth do not include premolars. The incisors cut food, the canines tear food, and the premolars and molars crush and grind. There are normally twenty milk or deciduous teeth, ten in each jaw, comprising of two incisors, one canine and two molars for each half jaw. In the permanent adult dentition, which replaces the milk teeth, there are normally 32 teeth (sixteen in each jaw), comprising two incisors, one canine, two premolars, and three molars. However, sometimes there may be extra teeth or missing teeth, for example the 3rd molars (wisdom teeth) can often be absent today, and the milk teeth can be retained once the permanent teeth are in position.

Structure

The basic tooth structure consists of the crown and the root, and there may be one or more roots depending on which type of tooth is being considered (Figure 53). The outer enamel covers the dentine inside, within which resides the pulp cavity containing blood vessels and nerves. Cementum and the periodontal ligament keep the tooth fixed in place in the jaw bone. The enamel is almost entirely inorganic (96–97%: Hillson 1986), has enamel cells (ameloblasts), and is made up

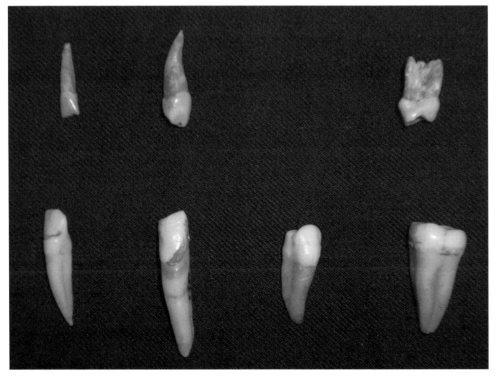

Figure 52: Examples of different types of teeth: top – deciduous teeth (left to right: incisor, canine, and molar); bottom – permanent teeth (left to right: incisor, canine, premolar, and molar (with permission of Tina Jakob)

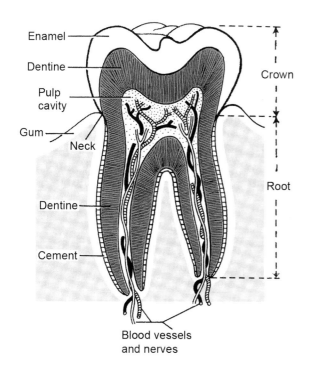

Enamel

Dentine

Pulp cavity

Gum

Neck

Dentine

Cement

Crown

Root

Blood vessels and nerves

Figure 53: Typical tooth section (redrawn by Yvonne Beadnell, after Wilson 1995)

of microscopic structures called prisms; it also has incremental structures in it which can be used to assess age at death and indicate 'stress'. The underlying dentine is mainly inorganic, with a small organic (*c* 18%) component, principally collagen. Dentine cells (odontoblasts) and microscopic structures called dentinal tubules, along with incremental structures, are encompassed in the dentine structure. Cement is also composed of around two-thirds inorganic components and contains cement cells called cementoblasts and incremental structures.

Directional terms

As for the bones, there are directional terms that are used for the teeth. They include: labial (side towards the lips – canines and incisors); buccal (side towards the cheek – premolars and molars); lingual (towards the tongue); mesial (towards the median line, or front); distal (away from the median, or back); occlusal (the biting surface); crown (above the gum and covered with enamel); neck (the constricted portion just below the crown and the area known as the cemento-enamel junction or CEJ); and the root (part of tooth below the crown and neck enclosed in the tooth socket and covered in cementum).

5.4 Starting to analyse a skeleton: identification of human bones and teeth (including fragmentary material)

A bioarchaeologist aims to collect specific information regarding the sex and age at death of the individual, and record features indicating normal variation in the appearance of the bones and teeth, through the taking of certain measurements and observation of non-metric features, along with identifying evidence for disease. However, the first task is to identify the human bones and teeth from each burial, and lay the skeleton out in anatomical position in the laboratory. An anatomical reference skeleton should be available to allow this to be undertaken, and also a good text with anatomical detail such as that by Abrahams *et al* (2002), White and Folkens (2000, 2005), Bass (2005) and, for non-adult skeletal remains, Scheuer and Black (2000a), along with Van Beek (1983), and Hillson (1986, 1996a) for teeth. The bone elements and teeth should be identified and also whether they are left or right (and in the case of teeth whether they are upper or lower). Of course, some bones and teeth are easier to identify and side than others, and fragmentary bones can be hard to identify at times, but knowing what the cross sections of teeth and bones look like can help (Figures 54 and 55).

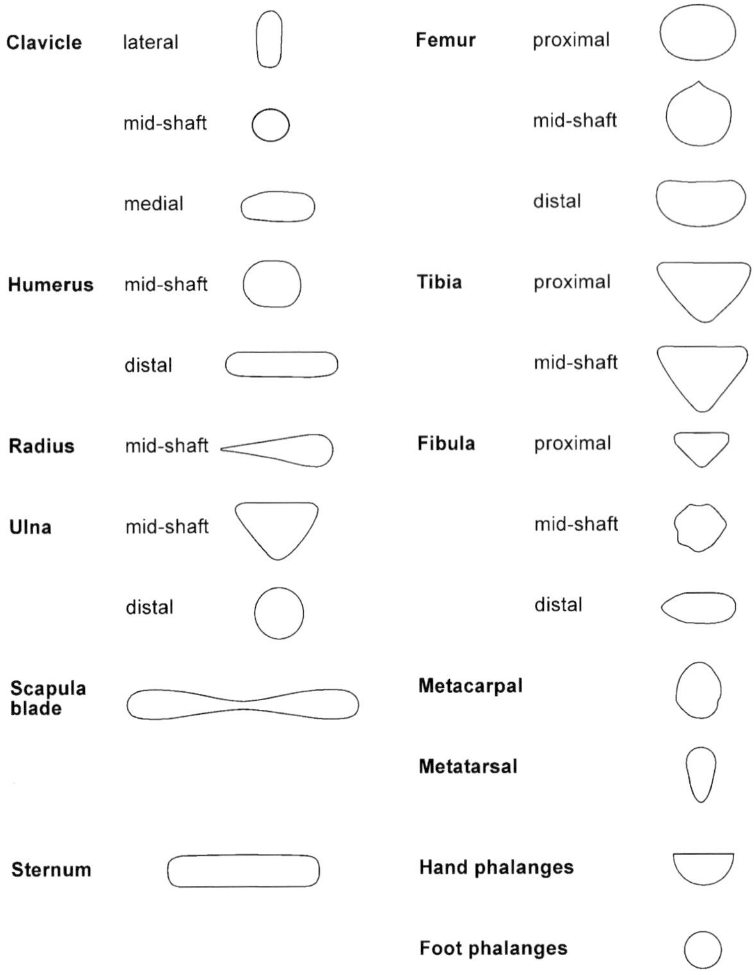

Clavicle	lateral		**Femur**	proximal		
	mid-shaft			mid-shaft		
	medial			distal		
Humerus	mid-shaft		**Tibia**	proximal		
	distal			mid-shaft		
Radius	mid-shaft		**Fibula**	proximal		
Ulna	mid-shaft			mid-shaft		
	distal			distal		
Scapula blade			**Metacarpal**			
			Metatarsal			
Sternum			**Hand phalanges**			
			Foot phalanges			

Figure 54 (left): Cross-section profiles of bone elements and regions of bones to aid in identification of fragments (redrawn by Yvonne Beadnell, after Charlotte Roberts)

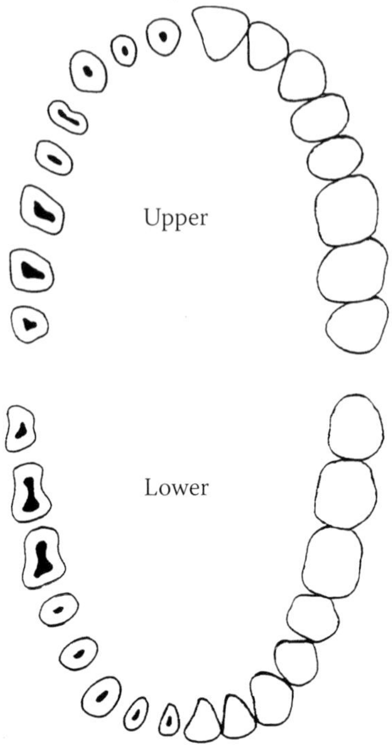

Upper

Lower

Figure 55 (above): Cross-section profiles of the different teeth to aid in identification of worn teeth (redrawn by Yvonne Beadnell, after Van Beek 1983)

There are a number of questions that should be asked when identifying bones:

- Is it human or not?
- What type of bone is it?
- Which bone element is it?
- Which side is it?

Looking for identifying anatomical features such as blood vessel or nerve holes (Figure 56), muscle markings or other 'lumps' or 'bumps' specific to a particular bone or tooth is important.

Figure 56: Recognition of a fragmentary bone by muscle marking, blood vessel/nerve hole (proximal tibia) (Charlotte Roberts)

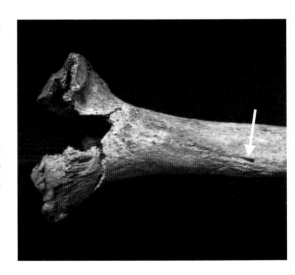

For teeth key questions are:

- Is the tooth human or not?
- Is it a deciduous or permanent tooth?
- What type of tooth is it?
- Is it lower or upper?
- If an incisor, premolar, or molar – which one is it, and from which side?

In the case of cremated human bone, the remains are usually very fragmentary (Figures 57 and 58), and perhaps this explains why, until recently as McKinley (2006) indicates, the study of cremated remains was the poor relation of inhumed remains. However, as a result of McKinley's extensive work on cremated remains, bioarchaeologists do not seem as 'fearful' of tackling the analysis of this challenging material! The size of fragments in a cremated burial do vary and are determined by the cremation process, how the remains were collected and buried following cremation, how they were excavated, and what happened to them post-excavation (McKinley 1994b); essentially the fragments the bioarchaeologist examines are the result of 'post-mortem' activities and they do not necessarily represent the fragment size immediately following deposition. Identifying cremated bone fragments is therefore challenging, although the smaller bones of the skeleton often survive complete (eg phalanges). McKinley (2000b) suggests that, on average, 50% or less of the bone remaining after cremation was buried in the past; of that only 30–50% of the remains may be identified to tooth or bone element. Additionally, the weight of the cremated bone may indicate how much of the original body, following cremation, is represented. McKinley (2000b) highlights that between 57g and 3000g may be recovered for single adult cremation burials, based on the analysis of c 5000 multi-period cremation burials in Britain, and multiple burials of two adults would be expected to produce a weight of >2000g, but many double burials have far less. If the weight is >3000g then there is probably more than one person, but some of that weight may be taken up by animal bone. Thus, weight is generally not a good guide to the number of people represented (McKinley pers comm, November 2007). The quantity of the bone may also actually relate to the time devoted to collecting it following cremation, which in turn may accord to the person's status and popularity (McKinley 2006).

Sometimes animal bones may be incorporated into unburnt and burnt human remains and being able to distinguish them from the human bones is essential. With good human anatomical knowledge it is relatively straightforward but fragmentary animal remains may prove more difficult, and access to an animal bone reference collection and/or manuals for identification of animal bone are essential (eg Schmid 1972; Cohen and Serjeantson 1996; Hillson 1996b). There have also been a number of methods described for distinguishing the differences both histologically and radiographically (eg Owsley *et al* 1985; Chilvarquer *et al* 1991; Harsányi 1993; Hillier and Bell 2007). While the morphology (shape) of the individual bones of the human and non-human skeleton are basically similar, the proportions of each part of each bone will differ depending on to which animal

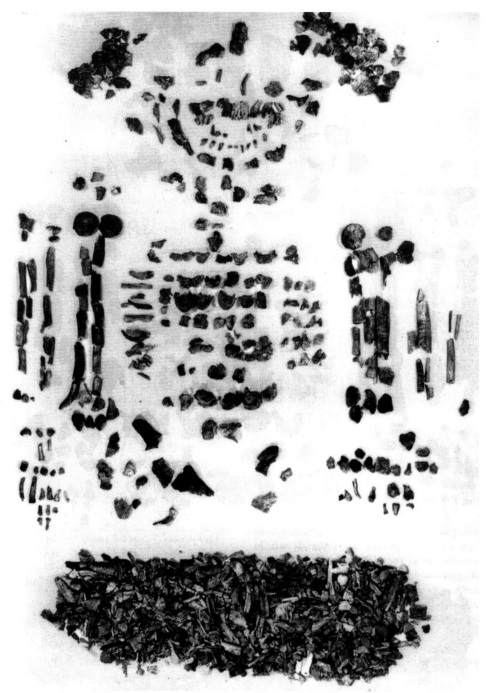

Figure 57: Cremated remains: Spong Hill Anglo-Saxon cremation cemetery, Norfolk (Number 1665: younger mature female; unidentified bone at the bottom of picture) (copyright: Norfolk Historic Environment, Norfolk Museums and Archaeology Service)

the bones belong (Figure 59). Features that may be considered for identification purposes include: different cross-section shapes for human versus non-human bones and teeth; the cortex of non-human bone is usually more dense and less porous; the microstructure of the cortical bone is different for humans

Figure 58: Example
of cremated burial
(fragments) (with
permission of Tina
Jakob)

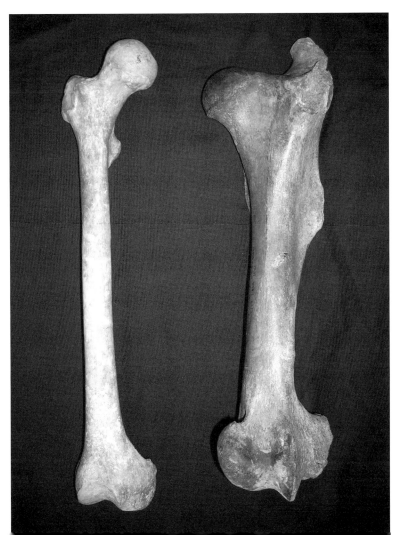

Figure 59: The
femur of a human
(left) and horse
(right) compared
(Charlotte Roberts)

119

and non-humans (for example the diameter of Haversian canals); and radiographic features will be different, for example the trabecular bone pattern. Common mistaken identifications in bioarchaeology include human foetal remains as immature pig, rabbit or dog skeletons, and human hands or feet as bear paws/pig and sheep phalanges. Even more than with archaeological remains, this is a problem for forensic identification where it is imperative that human and non-human remains are correctly identified. Correct identification is also very important for cremated remains as it reflects part of the mortuary rite – animal remains could be part of the pyre goods (McKinley pers comm, November 2007).

The bones present for each skeleton are usually shaded in on a diagram of the skeleton, and the teeth recorded onto a chart with relevant notations (see Figure 60). An inventory of the bones and teeth that are present for each skeleton should be made; guidance on inventories for bone, teeth, cremated human bone, and for skeletal contexts that preserve disarticulated or commingled remains (eg ossuaries, pits) is provided by Brickley (2004a), Connell (2004), and McKinley (2004b and c), with a useful chapter by Ubelaker (2002) on methods for analysing commingled remains (where there are multiple bones of the same type and side, for example). Once an inventory is produced, it is possible to determine the minimum number of individuals (MNI). This is based on counting the bone elements and teeth represented and identifying the highest count. The following variables must be considered in coming to a final MNI count: the age at death represented by the bone (adult or non-adult?), the biological sex (if possible to determine), bone size and type, whether it is left or right, and presence of disease, for example bones making up joints may be identified from the same individual if there is presence of similar amounts of osteoarthritis. As an easy example of determination of the MNI, if there are 50 complete left femurs and 55 right femurs from a cemetery site then there is a minimum number of 55 people represented. Of course, when fragmentary bones are being assessed, the process is rather more complex because several fragments of a femur, for example, may actually represent only one complete femur. It is important not to have anatomical duplication, and not to use the fragment count to represent more than the number of originally complete bones.

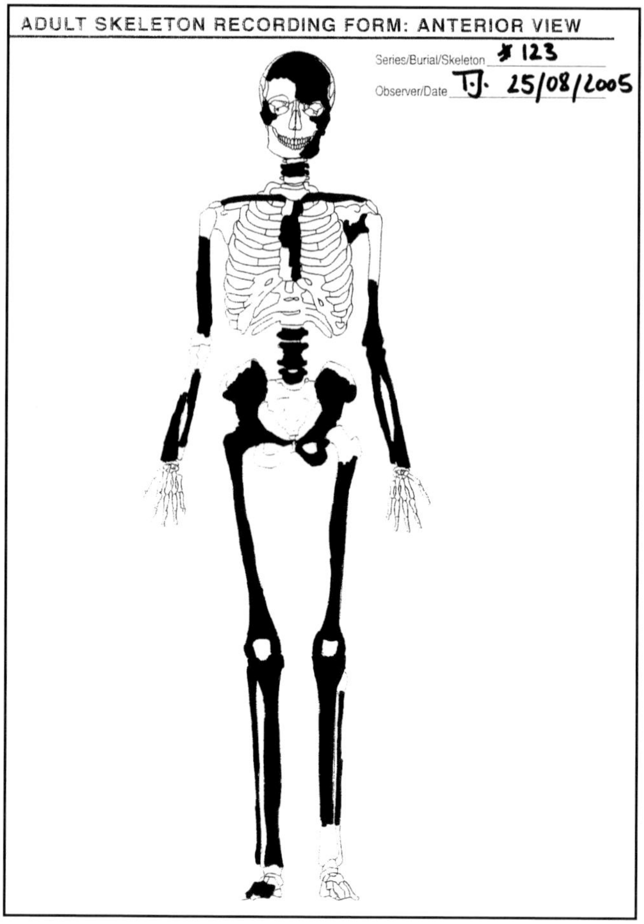

ADULT SKELETON RECORDING FORM: ANTERIOR VIEW

Series/Burial/Skeleton *123*
Observer/Date T.J. 25/08/2005

Figure 60: Example of a skeleton diagram partially completed (with permission of Tina Jakob)

5.5 Sex estimation

Probably the main characteristics that are noticed in a person on first acquaintance are: whether they are male or female; how old they are; and how tall they are. These are the basic first things bioarchaeologists would like to know when they analyse any one skeleton.

(i) What can it tell us?

Usually the first information needed is what the skeletal remains tells us about their biological sex. This is the initial step in creating a palaeodemographic profile for the sample population (along with age at death). Methods for assessment of sex have developed, and are still developing, to improve accuracy, and provide specific recording methods for particular populations. Large amounts of data have been collected, and methods created, using skeletal collections where the sex and age of the individual is known through associated documentary records. The collections most used are those of Robert J Terry (Smithsonian Institution, Washington DC, USA), Hamann Todd (Cleveland Museum of Natural History, Ohio, USA), the Coimbra Identified Skeletal Collection (Department of Anthropology, University of Coimbra, Coimbra, Portugal), and the Luis Lopez Collection (Natural History Museum, Lisbon, Portugal), all early 20th-century collected skeletons (see Chapter 1 for references), and the Christ Church, Spitalfields 18th/19th-century skeletal sample in London (Molleson and Cox 1993). In order to utilise such data on archaeological skeletons, one has to assume that the expression of the features used to assess sex (and age at death) have not changed through time, and that diet, activities, and the environment of the population was the same as today. It is clear that this is not always the case, with Milner *et al* (2000, 477) stressing that the collections are 'highly selected samples'; for example, people's diets have changed over time and therefore growth rates in the past may differ considerably. As these are the only data available to assess sex (and age at death) in archaeological skeletons, there is no choice, but nevertheless, these problems must be considered.

Knowing the sex of skeletons in the 'sample' allows us to utilise the many methods of adult ageing (see below), as some methods depend on knowing the sex of the skeleton. The sex of a skeleton is needed to determine stature or height. It also provides tools for interpreting health patterns in a sample and for exploring the differences in disease frequency between males and females (Grauer and Stuart-Macadam 1998). Females have a stronger immune system generally (Stinson 1985; Ortner 1998), and therefore can fend off disease better than males, and of course the occupations of men and women in the past may have differed such that they were differentially exposed to risks associated with occupation, and the environment in which they operated (eg see Larsen 1998; Roberts 2007). The components of their diets may also have varied and, since quality of diet is related to the strength of the immune system, this could have affected their propensity to contract specific diseases (eg see modern study by Dufour *et al* 1997). Frequently studies of living populations have documented the many lifestyle and disease differences between the sexes (eg see Pollard and Hyatt 1999a; Lane and Cybulla 2000). Furthermore, women in western society today are living on average longer than males, and there is evidence that men do not visit their doctor as much as women (Courtenay 2000). These living population data are highly relevant for interpretation of disease in the past.

The sex of a person is established when they are conceived. It can be defined as: 'the specific genetic and hormonal make-up of individuals and their subsequent development of secondary physical characteristics which places them into the category "female"... or "male"...' (Pollard and Hyatt 1999b, 2). People with two X chromosomes (XX) are female and people with one X and one Y chromosome (XY) are male. However, there are many variations on this theme, with people having atypical chromosomal patterns, and experiencing transexualism and intersexuality. For males, testosterone, secreted by the testes, is mainly responsible for the development of male characteristics, including in the skeleton, and general robusticity. In females oestrogen does not affect development so if the chromosomes say XX, the person will be female and develop as such. Differentiation between the sexes is determined by testosterone because this promotes masculinisation; if this is not present then the cells in the developing foetus will develop along female (ovarian) lines (Saunders 2000).

The expression of the traits, or features, in the skeleton for both adult and non-adult skeletons may vary according to age, lifestyle, and environment, and they may change through time. For example, the skeleton of a young adult male often has more female-looking traits and that of an older female may appear more male (Walker 1995). Furthermore, in some contexts where there are only a few (or even one) skeletons, especially if incomplete, one has to be careful not to misinterpret the features seen; for a specific small sample, what might be assumed to be male features may, for that group of people, represent female. If there are large numbers of skeletons, this problem can be alleviated because they can be 'seriated'. This means that skeletons that have definitely male or female features are at either end of the spectrum, with skeletons having less clear features in the middle, but probably more identifiable to one sex, if they are either side of the midline. The expression of normally accepted features in the skeleton that indicate biological sex may be affected in people with atypical chromosomal patterns, or with transexualism or intersexuality (Sofaer 2006), although this has not been studied with any degree of rigour in bioarchaeology.

There are basically six categories of biological sex that a skeleton may be assigned to: non-adult and therefore not sexable using macroscopic methods; ?sex or an adult that cannot be sexed; male; ?male or one where the features are more male than female; female; and ?female or one where there are more female features than male. When analysing the resulting data bioarchaeologists sometimes pool the male and ?male, and female and ?female data so that the sample size for analysis is reasonable.

(ii) Sex or gender?

At this point it should be noted that there is a difference in definition between the terms sex (biological) and gender, the latter a term that has crept into modern 'speak' to refer to biological sex. Sex refers to the *biological differences* between the sexes, and gender refers to the *socio-cultural differences* placed on those biological differences throughout life. Usually a biological female or male will be 'gendered' female/male, ie they will behave as a female or male is expected to in their society, but of course we know that there can be exceptions to this pattern. Sometimes a person may be a specific biological sex but feel and behave more like the opposite sex. In bioarchaeology it has been stressed that the two terms must remain separate because they refer to two different aspects of a person (Walker and Cook 1998; also see recent review by Sofaer 2006). There have been some studies in bioarchaeology correlating biological sex and gender through the study of skeletal remains and grave goods, respectively, in graves (eg females and jewellery; males and weapons). Some studies have revealed differences between the two pieces of evidence (eg see Effros 2000), although we must be careful of our interpretation of what grave goods actually mean, as emphasised so long ago by Ucko (1969).

(iii) Non-adult

The assessment of the biological sex of the skeleton of individuals who have not attained adulthood, ie around 18 years of age, is very difficult, if not impossible, and not recommended (Saunders 2000; Scheuer and Black 2000a). This is because it is not until puberty that the changes in the skeleton which define males and females start to occur. However, for skeletons in the late teenage years (16–18 years) it may be possible to assign a probable sex. There have been a number of papers published on the use of specific features of the skeletons of non-adults for sex estimation, for example the pelvis (Holcomb and Konigsberg 1995) and the skull (Molleson and Cruse 1998; Loth and Henneberg 2001), although many bioarchaeologists will not attempt to sex non-adult skeletons.

In humans, measuring the crowns of the teeth may also provide an indication of sex; the canine teeth are considered the most useful (Hillson 1996a), although a recent paper suggests that relative measures of crown size are better for looking at sexual dimorphism in permanent teeth than absolute measures (Saunders *et al* 2007). The presence of the Y chromosome promotes enamel and dentine growth, while the presence of the X chromosome promotes only the growth of the enamel (Mays and Cox 2000). There appears to be a range of success rates for correctly assigning male or female to teeth from known sexed non-adult individuals (see De Vito and Saunders 1990, as an example); size differences between male and female teeth are in fact very small (Hillson 1996a) and around a mean of <1mm in adults and less in non-adults. As taking measurements of teeth (and bones) can involve intra- and inter-observer error, determining sex on the basis of tooth size may be compounded by this problem. Nevertheless, new methods of measuring the skeleton using 3D morphometric analysis may help in this regard (see DeLeon 2007). In summary, a solution to sex estimation of non-adult skeletons might be to take specific measurements and plot them to see if two groups emerge – it might be that these illustrate the males and females (Mays and Cox 2000). Furthermore, it may be possible to compare adult crown sizes with developing crowns in non-adults as a way to sex a non-adult skeleton, but there are very few modern reference collections or documented archaeological ones of non-adult skeletons where deciduous tooth sizes have been measured (and using those measurements as a baseline for archaeological skeletons would be inappropriate). One further problem with using measurements of the teeth for sex estimation is that the size of the teeth may be affected by a number of factors that have influenced growth, for example nutritional status. Therefore, the teeth of a poorly nourished child will not necessarily grow at the normal rate for their age. Taking measurements on their teeth will therefore be erroneous.

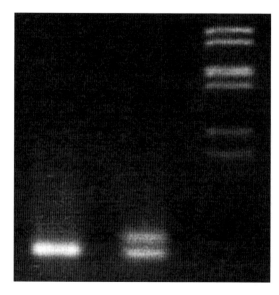

Figure 61: Experimental study to amplify DNA from amelogenin genes on the X and Y chromosomes: two bands = male, and one band = female (with permission of Keri Brown; see detailed caption in Brown 2000, figure 5)

The method that is proving to be increasingly very useful for sex estimation of non-adult skeletons in recent years is ancient DNA analysis; it has also been used for sex estimation of fragmentary adult remains and cremated bones where it has not been possible to determine sex by any other method. The method works by detecting X and Y chromosome-specific sequences within the amelogenin gene which is present on the X and Y chromosomes (Stone *et al* 1996). Brown (2000) describes how the DNA can be amplified, with the 'picture' showing sex-specific size differences through two bands of different lengths (male) or just one band (female) – see Figure 61. Cunha *et al* (2000) have used the method to sex a child (boy) at a medieval convent cemetery in Portugal, and Mays and Faerman (2001) and Faerman *et al* (1998) have determined sex of some purported infanticide victims from Roman Britain and Israel, respectively. There are of course many problems associated with the analysis of ancient DNA from skeletal remains (Brown 2000) such as non-survival of ancient DNA, contamination with other DNA, expense, and access to facilities but, if overcome, using this method of analysis helps to put the non-adults into the demographic profile of a cemetery and allows us to look at sex differences in the health of past children.

(iv) Adult

We can sex the adult skeleton more easily than the non-adult because all the bones of the skeleton have matured and passed through puberty. The skull and the pelvis are normally used to assess sex of an adult skeleton (Figures 62 and 63). The pelvis takes priority over the skull because of the clear differences in shape and features in the female, which reflect adaptation to childbearing and childbirth.

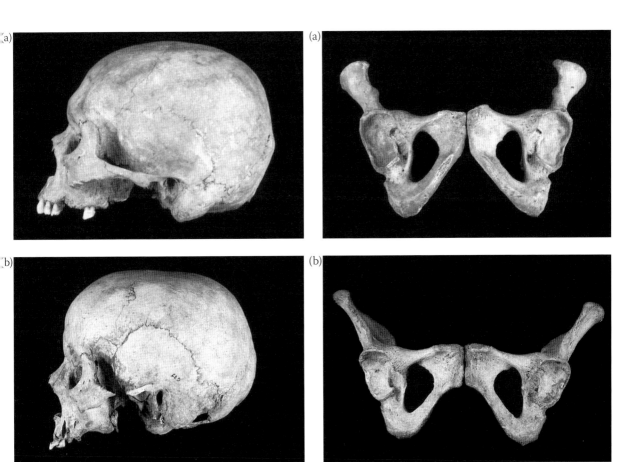

(a)

(a)

(b)

(b)

Figure 62 (above left): Male (a) and female (b) skulls (Charlotte Roberts)

Figure 63 (above right): Male (a) and female (b) pelves (Charlotte Roberts)

The details of what features are recorded in the pelvis and skull are described in Mays and Cox (2000), Brickley (2004b), Buikstra and Ubelaker (1994) and Bass (2005); note that the use and analysis of 'parturition scars' is not recommended (Cox 2000a). In general the female pelvis is more capacious than the male with wider angles, providing the opportunity for successful delivery of a child. The pubic bones, at the front of the pelvis, are the bones most observed to assess biological sex but they are often the parts of the pelvis that get damaged whilst buried. In the skull the larger features observed reflect general increased robusticity of the male due to more muscle mass; the features also reflect the diet being eaten, a coarser diet needing more chewing, thus increasing the use of the chewing muscles. Likewise, male skeletons tend to be larger and more robust, and thus if their bones are measured then they will be larger than those of females from the same population (although there may be exceptions). To determine the sex of a skeleton, therefore, certain measurements can be taken, such as the femur head diameter. This may help to determine sex in fragmentary skeletons or confirm what is seen in the pelvis and skull (see Bass 2005 for some of these measurements). However, the measurement ranges for males and females, determined again on known 'modern' sexed skeletons, may be inappropriate for archaeological skeletons because of differences in lifestyle and diet affecting growth and ultimate size. Other ways of using measurements involve discriminant function analysis, which uses multiple measurements that are then put into a computer programme; this generates a probable sex for the individual (eg Giles 1963, obtained an 84% accuracy for eight measurements on the skull; and Schulter-Ellis *et al* 1985, obtained a 95–97% accuracy using the pelvis). Using the skull and/or measurements alone is not advised when assessing the sex of a skeleton; if the pelvis is not present and relatively complete, then a definite sex should not be assigned. It should be noted also that the pelvis may show a different assigned sex when compared to the skull. For cremated human bone, the pelvic bones do not often survive to be used for sex estimation and therefore the skull (which does) is usually used. However, it will only be possible to assess sex on a small proportion of the adults at any one site; for example, at Spong Hill, Norfolk only 38.4% of the adults were assigned a sex (McKinley 1994a). Using measurements of the bones for sex estimation is also problematic because the cremation process tends to lead to variable shrinkage of bone elements.

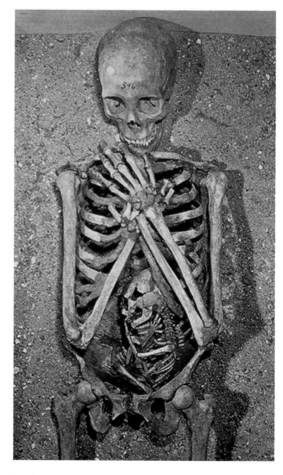

Figure 64: Child in abdomen of female skeleton: late medieval, Abelholt, Denmark (with permission of Pia Bennike)

There may be other indicators of biological sex that could, indirectly, help sex the skeleton. For example, if clothing is present on the body, cultural convention for the time period could indicate male or female. Grave goods may suggest biological sex, even though they may have been placed there to reflect gender (see above), a foetus or child may have been buried with a female body (see Figure 64; but sometimes this occurs with males), mummified bodies may preserve the external genitalia that allow sex estimation to be made, and the presence of specific sex-related diseases may point to male or female (for example, rheumatoid arthritis is found more in females). A coffin plate may identify the person, and finally the funerary context could reflect whether the burials are more likely male or female, for example in religious (males in monasteries and females in convents) and conflict (males) contexts – but beware that assumptions cannot always be made.

5.6 Age at death assessment

(i) What can it tell us?

Bioarchaeologists have strived for decades to attain accurate assessments of age at death when analysing human remains. However, when analysing skeletal remains, we are looking at biological age at death rather than chronological age, and we should remember that, biologically, people age at different rates. Nevertheless, even though we aim to age skeletons, we can never be sure what specific age meant to people in the past (see Gowland 2006 for a survey of age as an aspect of identity in the past). Specific age was probably more related to important biological or cultural events such as attaining puberty, or starting work, and our western view of the importance of age, in its numerical sense, may be inappropriate for the past.

If a skeleton is relatively complete, and fairly young, it will allow us to attain a more accurate age. Skeletons that are non-adult are much easier to age (up to around 18 years of age) than those in the adult years. This is perhaps reflected in the number of methods of age estimation that have been developed for adult remains compared to those for non-adult remains. It is useful to know how old people were when they died to interpret patterns of disease, and we know that some diseases affect different age groups more than others. For example, osteoporosis tends to affect older women, while diseases like measles and whooping cough affect children. Along with the sex of individual skeletons, age at death data allow us to reconstruct a demographic profile for the sample of skeletons (see below).

(ii) Factors affecting growth

There are many factors that can affect normal growth, but quality of diet and exposure to infectious disease are probably the main variables that will enhance or retard growth. These are inevitably related to 'events' in people's lives. Changes in subsistence and technology which might affect how food is produced and processed, political unrest which could lead to pressures on food supplies and the diet that is eaten, environmental degradation such as clearance of forests affecting general health and well-being, and natural disasters such as drought and floods, can all directly or indirectly affect growth of individuals within different populations. For example, today males in the Netherlands are the tallest people in the world, which is mainly due to an increase in wealth and an improvement in their diet (Maat 2005). There are also diseases that may lead to abnormal growth such as those affecting the pituitary and thyroid (endocrine) glands. For example, a person could be abnormally tall (gigantism) if the epiphyses at the ends of the long bones do not fuse when they should (caused by an endocrine gland problem). Furthermore, people may have a genetic predisposition to be small or large, for example the small pygmy populations in equatorial Africa.

(iii) Non-adult

There are many terms attributable to skeletal remains that are not fully adult in appearance; these include juvenile, immature, sub-adult, and non-adult. For the purposes of this section the term 'non-adult' will be used.

For cremated human bone, there are fewer options for assessing age at death, compared to skeletal material from inhumations, because of the nature of the material; this includes incomplete recovery of remains for inclusion in the burial from pyre sites and the level of fragmentation (McKinley pers comm, November 2007). For non-adult remains, unerupted tooth crowns held in the jaws survive cremation, and it is possible to see the development and fusion of bone growth centres; both may be used for assessing age at death (McKinley 2000b). However, at the Anglo-Saxon cremation cemetery at Spong Hill, Norfolk, McKinley (1994a) was able to age, within limits, nearly all the cremation deposits (eg young infant, infant, older infant, young juvenile, juvenile, older juvenile etc).

(a) Bone growth and development

Non-adult skeletal remains are aged according to their dental development and eruption, and their bone development, growth, and maturation. Bone development occurs in either membrane (the calvarium or upper part of the roof of the skull, and the face), cartilage (the base of the skull, spine, and bones of the limbs and shoulder and pelvic girdles) or a mixture of the two (the clavicle or collar bone, and some sutural areas – joints – of the skull). These two types of bone formation are called intramembranous and endochrondral ossification. The sesamoid bones (eg the patella) form in tendons. Eventually the original membrane/cartilage 'model' is replaced by osteoid or immature bone, formed by osteoblasts. There are a total of 806 ossification centres originally in the foetus, at birth 450, and eventually these fuse together to become the 206 bones of the (normal) adult skeleton.

A normal long bone has a primary centre of ossification (ie bone formation), which develops before birth and forms the diaphysis or shaft of the bone, with secondary centres (epiphyses) developing mostly after birth at the ends of the bone or other places on the bone. There are no secondary centres in the wrist bones or the skull. However, in archaeological contexts, even if newly formed centres of ossification were located and excavated, it would not be possible to identify them in isolation (Scheuer and Black 2000b). Nevertheless, if mummified remains of non-adults were radiographed then these 'centres' would be identifiable because they would be held in place by soft tissue. The epiphyses are separated from the diaphysis by an epiphyseal (growth) plate; this allows the bone to grow in length, but eventually the epiphyses fuse to the diaphysis at certain times for each bone. This is also when the epiphyseal plate ossifies. The metaphysis is the area of the diaphysis of the long bone adjacent to the growth plate; this is where growth in length takes place. The bones also grow in width by the addition of bone (osteoblast activity).

Each bone of the skeleton has a main primary ossification centre that appears in a certain age range, with accompanying epiphyses that appear and fuse also in certain age ranges. These age ranges are documented fully in Scheuer and Black (2000a). Data are, however, mainly from relatively modern populations, and development in populations past and present around the world may differ (eg see recent study by Nyati et al 2006). As an example of the ossification centres, see

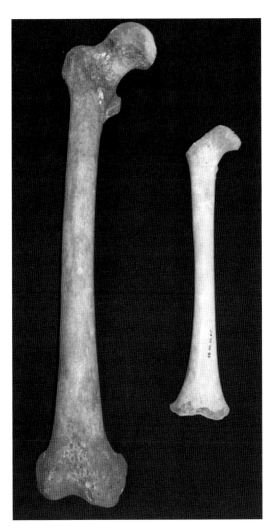

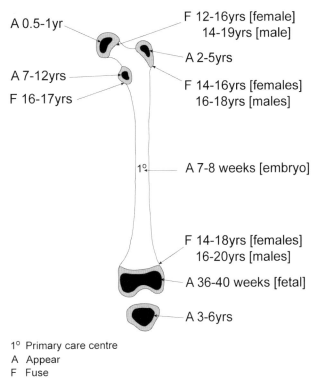

A 0.5-1yr

F 12-16yrs [female]
14-19yrs [male]

A 2-5yrs

A 7-12yrs

F 14-16yrs [females]
16-18yrs [males]

F 16-17yrs

1º ——— A 7-8 weeks [embryo]

F 14-18yrs [females]
16-20yrs [males]

A 36-40 weeks [fetal]

A 3-6yrs

1º Primary care centre
A Appear
F Fuse

Figure 66 (above): Example of epiphyseal fusion sequence for the femur (redrawn by Yvonne Beadnell, after Scheuer and Black 2000a)

Figure 65 (left): Adult and non-adult femurs compared; non-adult (right) shows no epiphyseal fusion (with permission of Tina Jakob)

the diagram of adult and non-adult femurs, and the times of appearance of the ossification centres in a femur for males and females (Figures 65 and 66). Epiphyseal fusion in the skeleton starts around 11–12 years of age (elbow) and ends with fusion at the knee between 17 and 19 years of age (Lewis 2007). Fusion data are obtained from observations of radiographs of known aged people and also dry bones, but it should be noted that the timing of development obtained from these two sources of data may vary because of the way the data have been recorded. Female epiphyses fuse one to two years earlier than those of males, and bone development in general may be delayed if certain factors, discussed above, affect normal growth. Not only can we look at the appearance and fusion of ossification centres of bones, but also the size of the bones themselves. The length of long bones without their epiphyses, for example, can also provide an insight into age at death of non-adults (Humphrey 2000); the lengths of the diaphyses of the long bones are particularly used for estimating the age of foetal skeletons.

By comparing the state of development of the bones of the skeleton with data from observations of skeletal development in documented samples, it is possible to suggest an age at death for the skeleton under observation (eg see some growth studies of medieval English populations by Hoppa 1992 and Ribot and Roberts 1996; an Iron Age population from South Africa by Steyn and Henneberg 1996; and a 19th-century Canadian sample by Saunders *et al* 1993a). Many bioarchaeological studies show that children in the past were shorter than their modern peers (eg Humphrey 2000). However, studies correlating growth (bone length) with indicators of stress in the skeleton, such as enamel defects, have also found no correlation, suggesting that children who suffered stress during growth effectively 'caught up' later on when they recovered; in these circumstances the growth rate can increase three-fold compared to normal (Tanner 1981, in Lewis 2007). Nevertheless, it should be remembered that 'documented' samples are often derived from relatively modern populations, from a variety of geographic locations and gene pools, and from populations that have different diets and lifestyles when compared to our bioarchaeological samples (and for some parts of the world we have no data even for living populations that we can use). Thus, when ageing a skeleton, the data used should ideally derive from a sample that has a similar 'background'. The reader is directed to Humphrey (2000), Saunders (2000), and Scheuer and Black (2000b), for specific references for data on bone growth and development in a number of modern and archaeological samples.

(b) Dental development

Older children and adolescent non-adult skeletons are usually aged not only on diaphyseal lengths and the appearance and fusion of the epiphyses, but also on dental development. However, as the epiphyses start to fuse, long bone diaphyseal measurements are no longer used for ageing. Dental development is a more accurate method of ageing non-adult skeletons because the teeth are not as affected by 'environmental influences' such as poor diet or disease during growth (see the recent study of a documented non-adult Portuguese sample in Cardoso 2006b). They also survive better than bone in the ground, and growth occurs from the embryonic period into late adolescence and early adulthood (Scheuer and Black 2000b, 13), unlike bone which develops in 'punctuated fits and starts'.

Data about the development of the teeth come most commonly from dental radiographs of living people, and less commonly from studies of skeletons of children of known age. There are ages for initiation of tooth development in the jaws (mineralisation), completion of formation of the crowns of the teeth, completion of the roots and closure of their ends, and eruption (eg see Figure 67). It is generally accepted that the ages for completion of formation of the various parts of the teeth are more accurate than those for eruption, the latter potentially being affected by environmental influences. Data on the timing and sequence of dental eruption are usually based on emergence through the gums. An additional factor to be borne in mind is that timings for tooth eruption will be based on radiographs and observation of living people, and as a result the emergence of

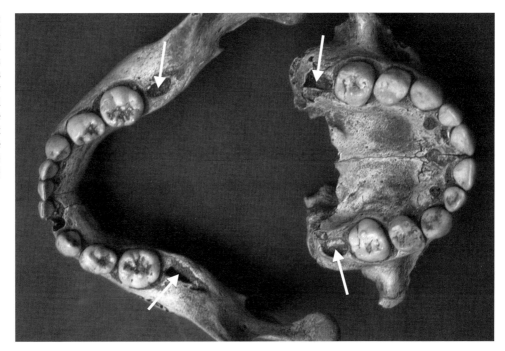

Figure 67: Example of dental development in a non-adult skeleton; the ten deciduous teeth in each jaw have erupted, and the crypts for the four first permanent molars are visible (arrowed) (Charlotte Roberts)

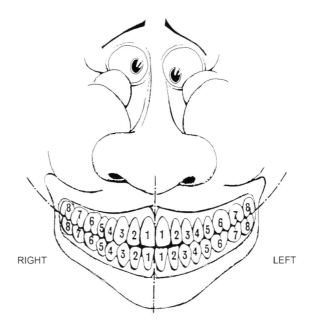

Figure 68: Diagram of permanent teeth in the jaws: 1 and 2 = incisors; 3 = canine; 4 and 5 = premolars; 6, 7 and 8 = molars (redrawn by Yvonne Beadnell, after Van Beek 1983)

RIGHT   LEFT

the tooth through and into the jaw and/or emergence through the gum will not directly correlate with what is noted in an 'archaeological' jaw.

As we have seen, a human has two sets of teeth, the first being the deciduous or milk teeth (numbering 20), which are then replaced by the permanent teeth (numbering 32); at some stage in development there will of course be people who have both deciduous and permanent teeth. The teeth mostly develop inside the jaw bones, before erupting into the jaws, followed by root formation and closure of the ends of the roots. The first part of the tooth to be formed is the tip of enamel which eventually forms the crown, with the underlying dentine developing later (also making up the roots). The deciduous teeth start to form about 14–16 weeks following fertilisation, in utero (Hillson 1996a), and are completed by 3–4 years of age. The permanent teeth start developing around 3–4 months after birth (incisors, except upper 2nd), with the 1st molar crowns being completed by 3 years, incisors at 4–5 years, canines and 1st premolars at 6 years, and 2nd premolars and 2nd molars at 7 years. The roots of the teeth close in the 2–4 years following these ages (*ibid*). The permanent teeth are all developed by between 17 and 20 years, but the 3rd molar, or wisdom tooth, often does not erupt until later in the 20s, or not at all (Figure 68). Again, as for the bones, the teeth of females develop about 1–2 years earlier than in males.

Various order and timings for the development of each of the teeth are provided in Van Beek (1983), Hillson (1996a), and Scheuer and Black (2000a), but the 'Ubelaker' chart (1989), based originally on Schour and Massler (1941), appears to be the one of the most favoured datasets used, along with data from Moorrees *et al* (1963a, b). However, there have been many sets of data published for different populations around the world and ideally the most appropriate one should be chosen to reflect 'similarity' with the archaeological sample being studied (see table 3.1 in Lewis 2007). Diet, disease, ethnicity, and social status may affect whether teeth develop at the normal rate or not, and each of these factors will vary for the modern datasets. Furthermore, studies indicate that using different methods on the same skeletal material may produce different ages (Saunders *et al* 1993b). A recent paper by Halcrow *et al* (2007) confirms that using modern data for dental development to age archaeological children has its drawbacks. They studied the development of the permanent teeth in Thai prehistoric children using data from North American (Massachusetts and Ohio) and Thai schoolchildren. They found a difference in estimated age for the prehistoric children using the two sets of modern data.

(iv) Adult

The details of what features are recorded to age adult skeletons are described generally in Buikstra and Ubelaker (1994), Cox (2000b), Jackes (2000), O'Connell (2004), and Bass (2005). Adult skeletons usually fall into three categories: young adult (20–35 years), middle adult (36–49 years), and older adult (50 years plus) (Buikstra and Ubelaker 1994). The wider age ranges provided for adult skeletons is in contrast to the narrower ranges obtainable for non-adults, and reflects the lower accuracy that is attainable using the methods of analysis available. There is certainly a tendency to utilise several methods for age estimation (eg see Saunders *et al* 1992; Bedford *et al* 1993), although one could argue that if all the methods have inherent problems then the age range obtained using multiple methods will be even less accurate than that obtained by using just one method.

Certainly, some studies have shown that the methods used tend to underage skeletons known to be over 70 years and overage those less than 40 years (see study by Molleson and Cox 1993).

As indicated, there are many adult ageing methods and generally speaking there is a greater likelihood of obtaining a relatively high accuracy for age in younger adults than older adults. The final development of the teeth (ie eruption of the 3rd molar) can occur as late as the early to late 20s, and some of the epiphyses fuse in the 20s (eg the basilar suture of the base of the skull, the sternal ends of the clavicles, the rims of the vertebral bodies, the iliac crest of the innominate bone, and the heads of the ribs). The wear on the biting or occlusal surfaces of the teeth is also used by many for ageing adults (Figure 69), but it should be remembered that the rate of wear is related to the coarseness or softness of the dietary components and/or whether a person uses their teeth as tools. Therefore, using a particular dental wear method to age a skeleton should be one appropriate for that population. It is not useful to use Brothwell's (1981) wear chart, based on Neolithic to medieval skeletons in Britain, to age skeletons from any other part of the world unless one can be sure that diet, and any other factors affecting tooth wear, are the same or similar. Another method, developed using an Anglo-Saxon sample of skeletons (Miles 2001, originally published in 1962), uses the relative wear rate on the three permanent molar teeth to assess age. Assuming that the 1st permanent molar erupts around six years, by the time the 2nd erupts at twelve years the 1st molar has had around six years of wear; when the 3rd molar erupts at around eighteen years the 1st molar will have had twelve years of wear, while the 2nd molar will have had six years of wear. Thus, it is possible to create a 'clock' against which wear can be calibrated (Mays 1998). Ideally, in order to use this method for any skeletal sample it is necessary to have more than twenty child dentitions with erupted permanent molars within that sample (Nowell 1978, in Mays 1998), although in reality the method may be the only one usable for small assemblages.

Figure 69: Example of no dental wear (a) and heavier dental wear (b); arrows give a basic comparison of one of the teeth in two different mandibles (with permission of Stewart Gardner)

(a)

(b)

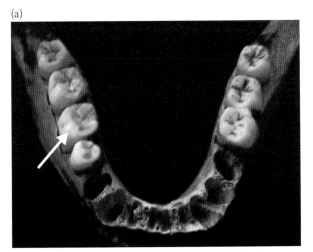
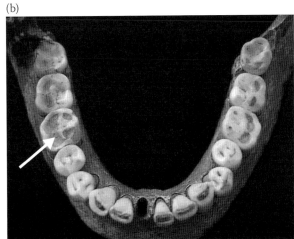

Other methods include the degree of closure of the joints in the skull (outside and inside), or cranial sutures. As a person ages the cranial sutures eventually disappear when viewed on a dry skull. The appearance of sutures is compared with descriptions and figures and photographs. Probably of all the methods used, this one is the least accurate (Meindl and Lovejoy 1985; Masset 1989; Key *et al* 1994). The degeneration of the surfaces of the pubic symphysis at the front of the pelvic girdle (Brooks and Suchey 1990), the auricular surface on the sacroiliac joint on the innominate bones where the sacrum (bottom of the spine) meets with the pelvis (Lovejoy *et al* 1985; Buckberry and Chamberlain 2002; Falys *et al* 2006) and the sternal ends of the 4th ribs (Loth and Iscan 1989; Russell *et al* 1993) are also observed. On the pubic symphysis and the auricular surface, the surfaces degenerate with age from an undulating, and in the former a sort of 'ridge and furrow' pattern, to a smoother surface (Figure 70). The rib ends develop a deeper pit which becomes more 'U' shaped, and the edges of the pit become 'ragged' with age. Both the pubic symphysis and rib end methods require knowledge of the sex of the skeleton to use them (and casts of them are available for comparative use). The auricular surface method has data for both sexes pooled and the method is used by comparing the surfaces with photographs and descriptions. The advantage of using the auricular surface to age a skeleton in an archaeological context is that this area of the skeleton tends to survive burial well, unlike the pubic symphysis or the rib ends. However, for the methods described there are issues of subjectivity in assigning ages, and intra- and inter-observer error in recording.

Figure 70: Example of young (a) and old (b) pubic symphyses (with permission of Stewart Gardner)

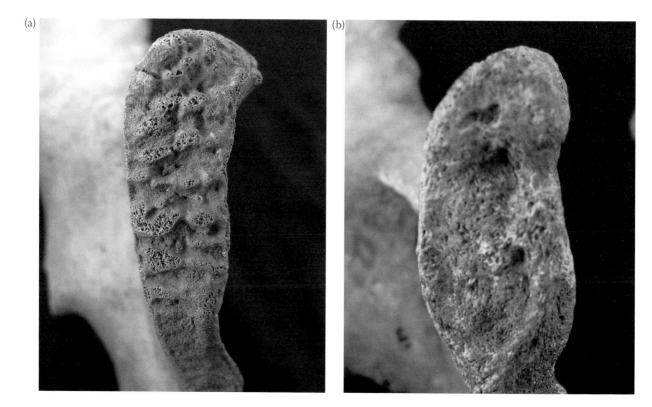

(a)
(b)

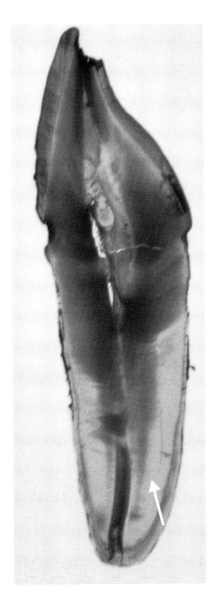

Figure 71: Example of dental root transparency (arrowed) in a known individual of 60 years, and estimated to be 54.8 years old using this method (with permission of Dave Lucy)

The presence of osteoarthritis (synovial joint degeneration) and osteoporosis (loss of bone mass), in addition to ossification of the cartilages of the ribs and neck, may provide a general indication of an older individual, but people can develop all these changes in the skeleton when they are young. For example, if a person works physically hard, they might develop premature osteoarthritis, and a young person with rheumatoid arthritis might have associated osteoporosis as part of the disease. Osteoarthritis and osteoporosis should *never* be used as a sole indication of age at death.

There are also methods of adult age estimation that utilise radiography of specific parts of the skeleton (especially the clavicle, humerus, and femur), and microscopy of sections of bones and teeth. Microscopic ageing of bone involves taking sections of bone, usually from the cortex of the femur, and observing the number of osteons and osteon fragments, and lamellar bone. An increase in osteons and fragments and a decrease of lamellar bone is associated with increased age (Robling and Stout 2000). While microscopic methods of ageing adult skeletons using bone sections have been suggested to be more accurate than macroscopic, the methods are destructive and time consuming, needing expertise as well as good dental and bone preservational states, while diet and disease can affect age indicators observed. In the teeth there are also features, in addition to dental wear, that are age-related. Gustafson (1950) described six age-related features: attrition, periodontosis, secondary dentine formation (as a response to attrition), translucency of dentine in the tooth roots, deposition of cementum around the roots, and resorption of the roots (see Hillson 1996a for more details). The features are recorded on a point scale which is then converted into an age estimate. Research suggests that root transparency is probably the most useful age indicator (Figure 71), producing ages to within ±7 years in forensic situations (Lucy *et al* 1994; Sengupta *et al* 1998; Whittaker 2000), along with incremental lines in cementum (Wittwer-Backofen *et al* 2004; Blondiaux *et al* 2006). Dental microstructural features as an indicator of age are also studied in non-adult skeletons, as described by Fitzgerald and Rose (2000). Finally, radiographic techniques of ageing consider the appearance of the cancellous and cortical bone in radiographs of the femur and humerus head, and also the clavicle (Sorg *et al* 1989). As a person ages, the cancellous bone declines in mass and the cortical bone thins (also with activity), but one must be careful not to record post-mortem changes that have led to these alterations.

In the case of adult cremated remains, the enamel of erupted teeth shatter during the cremation process, and relevant parts of the pelvis and ribs do not usually survive for examination. Ribs in any case are not usually preserved. Therefore, it is often the case that a broad age range is provided based on the closure of the skull sutures. Thus, ageing cremated adults is compromised even more than for unburnt inhumations, although there are possibilities using cement lines on teeth (see above).

It should be noted that the methods described that utilise microscopy and radiography to age adult skeletal remains are usually not accessible to most bioarchaeologists and thus are not commonly used, certainly not in contract archaeology in Britain.

(v) The problems

Clearly, there are problems with ageing both non-adult and adult skeletons, certainly from the point of view of the original data collected to develop the methods used, the main question being: how appropriate and applicable are the data/methods to my skeletal sample? In effect, the methods reflect the age profile of the skeletal samples on which they were developed. It will also never be possible to establish controls for all the variables affecting growth and development in a population in the past; people even within the same population will grow at different rates because their lifestyles and diets will vary. Thus, even if an appropriate dataset/method is used, ages may be inaccurate. There are also issues of intra- and inter-observer error in the recording of age-related features in the skeleton, especially when focusing on subtle changes in particular parts of the body, or recording by the use of measurements. Furthermore, many of the methods used for adult ageing place people into wide age ranges, especially at the upper end of the age spectrum.

Developments in the use of Bayesian statistical methods of analysis of age at death data have allowed bioarchaeologists to attain more realistic ages for both adult and non-adult skeletons (eg Konigsberg and Frankenberg 1992; Buck *et al* 1996; Lucy *et al* 1996; Aykroyd *et al* 1999; Gowland and Chamberlain 2002, 2005; Schmidt *et al* 2002; Hoppa and Vaupel 2002; Chamberlain 2006). For a general survey of Bayesian statistics in archaeology, see Buck (2001).

5.7 Reconstructing a palaeodemographic profile for the cemetery sample

Once data on age at death and sex of the individuals from a 'population' under study have been collected, these data are used to look at the mortality profile of the sample of individuals, ie at what age people were most likely to die, and whether males or females had a greater likelihood of dying at certain ages. It should be remembered, however, that the profile we see is that of a dead, not living, population. The people died because of disease or injury and therefore may not be representative of the living population that contributed (at death) to the burial ground from which the skeletal sample derived. Waldron (1994) and Wood *et al* (1992) have more than adequately documented the problems of studying human skeletal remains in terms of how representative they are. As Waldron (1994) has pointed out, the sample of skeletons being analysed may only be a small sample of the original living population. The total dead of any population will not be all those buried, and those buried will not be all preserved to be discovered, and of those discovered only a proportion may be recovered. How representative are they then of the living? Were all members of the living population buried there? How dense was the population? How fast did it grow or decline through the period of the cemetery use? How fertile was the population? Was immigration or emigration occurring during the population's history? Perhaps victims of violent deaths, such as suicide or infanticide, or those suffering from specific diseases, were buried elsewhere. Likewise, in some communities at specific points in time, non-adult individuals were disposed of in places away from the main cemetery (eg Roman infants, see Chapter 3). Thus, those parts of society that were not buried in the local graveyard will be absent from the mortality profile.

The limitations already discussed with sex estimation of non-adult skeletons, and age at death estimation for adult skeletons means that there will be missing and inaccurate data. The problem of ageing adult skeletons is widely accepted but this has led to the development of new methods of statistical analysis (discussed above and by Chamberlain 2006). As traditional methods have tended to underage older skeletons and overage younger adults, the notion has developed that everybody in the past died young. Clearly, this was not the case if the ages given on coffin plates from the Christ Church, Spitalfields, site are representative (Molleson and Cox 1993), as well as general records on Victorian and earlier period gravestones in churchyards, and from Roman tombstones. Along with problems of preservation of skeletal remains at different archaeological sites, and the general under-representation of non-adult skeletons, these issues have to be considered when looking at palaeodemographic profiles (Bello *et al* 2006).

A palaeodemographic profile does, however, provide a window on mortality for a population and allows us to explore the possible reasons for deaths at specific ages. Palaeodemography allows us to consider the size and structure of a population and its dynamics (Chamberlain 2001), but because of missing/poor data, and perhaps a lack of specific data concerning the archaeological context of the site, it is not an easy study. While skeletons are our primary source of information, there are other features of archaeological sites and contemporaneous information that can help us to explore the size of a population (Bintliff and Sbonias 1999; Chamberlain 2006). These include historical data such as written records, exemplified by the Domesday Book of the 11th century in England, a population census, along with later birth, marriage, and death data from parish records and tombstones; settlement characteristics such as the number and size of houses and storage pits; characteristics of the environment exploited for food or carrying capacity (how many could it support?); and ethnographic data of living people who may have lived in a similar way to our ancestors. An example of a study of mortality using purely historical sources comes from Victorian England and illustrates the detailed information available (Woods and Shelton 1997). Data from 614 districts show the variations and changes in the principal causes of death from the 1860s to 1890s, clearly illustrating that where one lived in Victorian England affected the quality of life and how death might occur. Another set of data on cause of death and the number of people affected are the 'London Bills of Mortality', which describe the number of people baptised and dying, their ages, and cause of death between the mid-17th and mid-19th centuries (see Roberts and Cox 2003 for an analysis of these data). Naturally, such detailed data are not available for most human bioarchaeological samples.

There are, of course, many factors that will influence the palaeodemographic profile appearance such as diet, living environment (Budnik and Liczbińska 2006), social status, climate, immigration and emigration, biological sex, and also occupation – these may all have affected people's longevity and life expectancy. For example, Ocaña-Riola et al (2006) in a study of small areas of southern Spain today found around a 14% reduction in mortality in both men and women who lived in rural areas compared to urban areas. Determining whether migration has affected the observed profile is difficult and many factors determine migration, much of this depending on individual decision making (Chamberlain 2006). Opportunities for a better life in terms of employment, living conditions, and the provision of an escape from war-torn zones today, will be instrumental in determining movement of people and, in turn, their effect on the demographic profile of both the population they leave and the one they enter. Clearly too in the past, as in developing countries today, many infants died very young due to acute diseases such as those affecting the respiratory and gastrointestinal tracts, and the hazards of childbearing and childbirth in the past would have claimed many women's lives, and led to the deaths of foetuses, perinates and neonates (as seen in the archaeological record). These 'events' may be seen in a demographic profile.

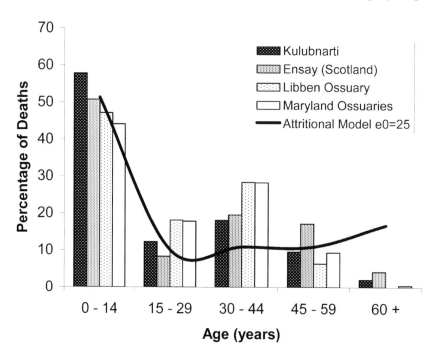

Figure 72: Example of a mortality profile. Age-specific mortality in four archaeological samples of human skeletal remains (data from Ubelaker 1974; Lovejoy et al 1977; Greene et al 1986; Miles 1989; after figure 4.3 in Chamberlain 2006, reproduced with permission of Andrew Chamberlain)

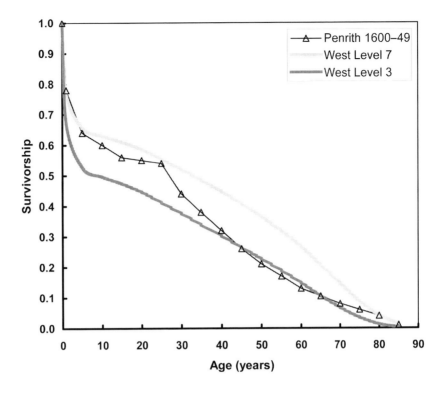

Figure 73: Example of a survivorship curve. A 17th-century population from Penrith, Cumbria, England (Scott and Duncan 1998), compared with a model life table (West); (data from Coale and Demeney 1983; reproduced with permission of Andrew Chamberlain)

Figure 74: Example of life table. Northern Ache females calculated from survivorship data from Hill and Hurtado (1995): x = age at start of 5-year interval; L_x = average years per person lived within age intervals; T_x = sum of average years lived within current and remaining age intervals; l_x = survivorship; d_x =proportion of deaths; q_x = probability of death; e_x = average years of life remaining (average life expectancy) (after table 2.2 from Chamberlain 2006, reproduced with permission of Andrew Chamberlain)

x	l_x	d_x	q_x	L_x	T_x	e_x
0	1.00	0.27	0.27	4.34	37.35	37.35
5	0.73	0.09	0.12	3.45	33.01	44.97
10	0.64	0.04	0.05	3.13	29.57	45.91
15	0.61	0.02	0.03	2.99	26.43	43.40
20	0.59	0.03	0.06	2.86	23.44	39.86
25	0.56	0.01	0.02	2.75	20.58	37.09
30	0.54	0.04	0.07	2.62	17.84	32.78
35	0.50	0.01	0.01	2.50	15.22	30.19
40	0.50	0.03	0.07	2.40	12.71	25.58
45	0.46	0.04	0.10	2.21	10.31	22.27
50	0.42	0.02	0.05	2.04	8.11	19.35
55	0.40	0.05	0.13	1.86	6.07	15.24
60	0.35	0.07	0.19	1.57	4.20	12.11
65	0.28	0.03	0.11	1.32	2.60	9.41
70	0.25	0.11	0.45	0.97	1.31	5.27
75	0.14	0.14	1.00	0.35	0.35	2.50
80	0.00	0.00	-	0.00	0.00	0.00

There are also what are termed times of 'crisis mortality' where extraordinary causes of death such as warfare and famine might lead to changes in the stability of the demographic structure of a population (Chamberlain 2006).

The demographic profile may be reflected in life tables, mortality profiles and curves, and survivorship curves. Mortality is the relative frequency of deaths in relation to population numbers, while the mortality profile shows when people were dying and whether there were differences between males and females, in different age groups, and according to socio-economic status (if data for the latter are available) (see Figure 72). The survivorship curve reflects the proportion of people in each age group, starting at 100% for the youngest age category; it shows the probability that a person will survive to a specified age (Figure 73). Life tables are a 'mathematical device to represent the mortality experience of a population' (Chamberlain 2001, 260) and provide more detailed information about mortality and survivorship in a population, including the probability of dying in a specific age group and life expectancy (Figure 74).

The study of palaeodemography in general is a popular area of bioarchaeology, despite the problems with the data highlighted here and elsewhere. However, recent research suggests that if the problems can be overcome (and methods are being developed to do this) then palaeodemography has a bright future (Milner *et al* 2000; Chamberlain 2006). In particular, biomolecular methods of assessing the sex of non-adult skeletons, Bayesian analysis of adult age data, and stable isotope analysis to look at the migration of populations will enable us to establish more accurate reflections of the demography of past populations. We have seen surges in population numbers through time with the development of tools to allow the hunting and butchery of animals, the development of agriculture to produce more food, and the Industrial Revolution. The alternative view is that population growth has been enabled by cultural change (as discussed by Chamberlain 2006). However, in recent times, agricultural intensification and developments in medicine and surgery (particularly in western society) have allowed people to live much longer although degenerative diseases such as those affecting the heart have more time to take their toll. Females live comparatively longer lives than males, and there is less infant mortality. The data also show that those in the higher social classes, both male and female, have a better life expectancy in general. However, of interest is the fact that women in poorer social classes may live longer than men in the highest social class (Tsuchiya and Williams 2005), and the 'will to live' can affect life expectancy (eg seen in a study in Israel by Carmel *et al* 2007).

5.8 Normal variation within and between human populations

There are two areas we need to consider when trying to document differences in individuals and populations as seen through their remains: the taking of measurements, and the noting of variations from the normal appearance in bones and teeth (metric and non-metric analysis, respectively, or biodistance studies). The differences being assessed are normal variations and are not due to disease or other mechanisms; in effect, measurements and non-metric trait presence are used to assign 'unknown' individuals to specific 'reference' groups, and an unusually high or low frequency of specific traits is generally taken to indicate a close biological relationship.

(i) Taking measurements (metrical analysis)

Taking measurements of bones and teeth has been the pre-occupation of bioarchaeologists since the study of human remains from archaeological sites started. While much early work was devoted to analysing shapes of skulls with a view to 'pigeon holing' people into 'racial' groups, there have been considerable developments in the use of metrical analysis to determine: general variation in size – for example height – within and between populations from archaeological sites both geographically and temporally; evolutionary aspects of human populations; relatedness between populations; and the effect of 'activity' on people's skeletons. Metrical analysis is also used to aid sex estimation of adult skeletons and age estimation of non-adult skeletons, as we have already seen. However, as Robb (2000) points out, how the data are collected and analysed, along with the research tradition people are involved in, and the period of time in which bioarchaeologists are working (eg early 20th century, mid-20th century, or 21st century), are very much related to the ultimate interpretation of the data.

The taking of single measurements, two measurements to produce an index (eg the cranial index, which gives the general shape of the skull), or multivariate analysis (collection of multiple measurements which are then analysed together to look at relationships) are all common in bioarchaeology. The problems encountered with measuring the skeleton are numerous. These have to some extent been overcome by developments in techniques of analysis, particularly 3D geometric morphometric analysis, for those who have access to the technology (eg see O'Higgins 2000; DeLeon 2007; Ivan Perez *et al* 2007). Measuring skeletal remains using conventional techniques and equipment described above is subject to intra-observer and inter-observer error. That is, a measurement can be taken one day by one person, and the same measurement taken the next by the same person, with different readings resulting (intra-observer error). Likewise, a different person could take the same measurement and obtain a different reading (inter-observer error). Testing for this intra- and inter-observer error is essential. While the points on bones and teeth from, and to, which measurements should be taken are described in general texts (eg Brothwell 1981; Buikstra and Ubelaker 1994; Hillson 1996a; Brothwell and Zakrzewski 2004; Bass 2005), there is still room for error if those points are not accurately identified and used. If some metrical data is not as accurate as it could be, it becomes pointless comparing data between samples of skeletons. The other problem to contend with is: how many measurements should and can be taken? Various texts define different numbers but the key guide is to consider what questions you wish to answer using the data (or hypotheses you want to test), allowing also for the fact that an adequate set of measurements must exist that 'describe' the bones and teeth of each skeleton such that, if reburial occurs, there is a good record of the skeleton. It is not the purpose here to describe all the possible measurements that could be taken because there are excellent texts that do this job, as identified above. There are also detailed accounts about the uses of the data (eg Pietrusewsky 2000), and the types of analyses that can be undertaken using the measurements taken. Suffice it to say that analyses are becoming highly sophisticated, to the extent that extremely valuable information about population variation is being generated. A few examples will provide support for this statement.

(a) The skull

The skull has always been a focus for studies using measurements and the analysis of cranial vault shape reflects early physical anthropology's attempts to reconstruct 'racial' history ('typological racial classification' – Pietrusewsky 2000, 376). Those early data, based on assigning people to groups which reflected features of the skull, are now seen to have little value. Certainly, post-war there was a decline in studies of 'race' through the analysis of the skull as a key concept for understanding human variation (Robb 2000), and more recently there has also been a move away from 'habitual collection of traditional data in an interpretive void' (*ibid*, 476). The new emphasis on understanding the underlying processes that influence cranial shape, reflecting adaptation and behaviour, are welcomed in the bioarchaeological community. Nevertheless, in forensic anthropology, one of the features recorded when attempting the identification of victims of crime is 'race', or better termed 'ancestry', as seen, usually, in the skull; it is also one of the features recorded on 'Missing Persons Lists' by the police. Three traditional groups are seen: 'Mongoloid' (associated with Asia including China, Japan, and Native Americans), 'Negroid' (associated with Africa and African Americans), and 'Caucasoid' (associated with Europe, India, America, and North Africa), with many variations; each in their most distinct form possesses specific features in the skull, including the face (eg see Buck and Strand Viddarsdottir 2004). However, over time the distinctive appearances of the three 'types' of skulls are not as clear in some places because of a considerable global admixture of populations, along with environmental effects on the skull's development.

Mathematical approaches to looking at skull shape appeared later, with a particular emphasis on analysis of multiple variables (in this case, measurements). Population differences, inter-relationships between measurements, and the interpretation of groupings in terms of internal or external influences, have dominated studies. Multivariate analyses include discriminant function analysis (to assign sex and 'race'), and cluster analysis, which groups individuals on the basis of the characteristics they possess, producing a tree-like structure or dendrogram (Pietrusewsky 2000). It is assumed that if a sample of skulls shows similar dimensions through multiple measurements then they must have genetic similarity; the more similar two groups are, the more closely related they are assumed to be. The vast majority of studies have been on adult skeletal remains because many of the features used for measurement develop as secondary sexual characteristics. There are, however, a few samples of non-adult skeletons reflecting different ancestries where specific measurements and other observations have been used to help identify forensically derived non-adult skeletons.

A good example of the study of cranial measurements to look at relationships between groups comes from a study of 29 measurements of over 2000 skulls from 53 Japanese groups (*ibid*). It showed that there were two distinct groups. The first was from prehistoric Jomon and modern Ainu groups (supported genetically and through other skeletal analysis), and the second consisted of groups of people dated to since 300 BC. The latter group was seen to be associated with modern Japanese, which suggested that there was immigration and displacement of the indigenous Jomon and their descendants. Furthermore, no relationship was found between the first group and neighbouring Pacific groups, again based on skull measurements. Another study considered sixteen measurements in skulls in ten Egyptian samples from six time periods dating from 4000 to 1900 BC (Zakrzewski 2007). Here the aim was to explore state formation in Egypt by looking at whether this was indigenous to Egypt or affected by immigration. Overall, population continuity was seen, supporting indigenous development, but some migration was noted to have occurred along the Nile Valley.

As many studies have indicated, it is not only genetic influences that affect the skull's shape and size, because environmental influences, ie non-genetic, such as climate, diet, and disease, can also contribute (see Larsen 1997 for a discussion). For example, because the skull has a high degree of plasticity, alterations in chewing mechanisms through a change in diet can lead to a distinctive change in the metrical characteristics of the cranium and face. Through time, as diet has become softer, for example with the introduction of agriculture, and more highly processed foods in recent times, the skull has become less robust and shorter (*ibid*). Thus, it is essential if craniometric analysis is being undertaken in bioarchaeology that contextual data from the site from which the skulls derive is taken into account in interpretation.

So, skull size and shape may be partly reflecting the type of diet, coarse or soft, the person was consuming. Indeed, this was noted by Mays (2000) in his consideration of skull shape reflected in the cranial index (length and breadth of the skull). As he observed, up until the 1960s changes in material culture on a site were explained by immigrant people, and cranial analysis was used to identify those 'invading' people, that is, if a different skull shape to the norm was identified in a skeletal population then 'incomers' or migrants were inferred. This approach was then replaced by a move to explaining change not because of immigration but as a result of continuity of populations, and developments in material culture within the population. In recent years, because of the rise in the recognition of the importance of modern genetic studies in reconstructing population history, there has been a revival in the study of migrations in the past, along with ethnicity, using craniometry (*ibid*). Studies of the Neolithic/ Bronze Age transition in Britain has often focused on the change in skull shape from 'long-headed' to 'round-headed', as seen in the cranial index. The fact that climate and diet/subsistence did not change at that transition, and there were new burial types with characteristic pottery ('Beakers') and metalwork, suggests immigration into the late Neolithic population. The use of stable isotope analysis to track migration, along with ancient DNA studies and the analysis of non-metric traits (see below), have encouraged researchers to revisit craniometry as a way of looking at the movement of people, with the emphasis on taking a multi-method approach to understanding population history and change. As there is a strong correlation between measurements and biochemical genetic markers, this has provided even more encouragement for bioarchaeologists.

(b) Stature

Another area of bioarchaeological study that has seen much attention is estimation of stature, or height, in adult skeletons, based on the measurement of the length of complete long bones or the total length of bones from head to foot. When estimating stature we may be asking questions such as: has height changed through time nationally, regionally, or locally in Britain (Figure 75)? Two methods have been used by bioarchaeologists to approach this, the mathematical and the anatomical. The mathematical method has seen the attention of many researchers, with the work of Trotter and Gleser (1952, 1958) and Trotter (1970) probably being the most cited and used. As we have seen with age and sex estimation methods, it is necessary to utilise data that is most appropriate to the archaeological 'population' being studied. While the stature regression equations produced by Trotter and Gleser are easy to use, because they were developed on American World War Two and Korean War dead, along with the Terry Collection early 20th-century individuals, their appropriateness is questioned when using them for archaeologically derived skeletons. Regression tables provide methods for calculation of stature according to sex and ancestry, although there are relatively large standard errors (Petersen 2005). In Britain, nevertheless, there are no more appropriate data available that can be used to estimate stature and, as it is an estimate anyway, perhaps this does not matter. In recent years, because of the errors introduced by using the mathematical method of stature analysis on long bone lengths, recommendations have been made to record long

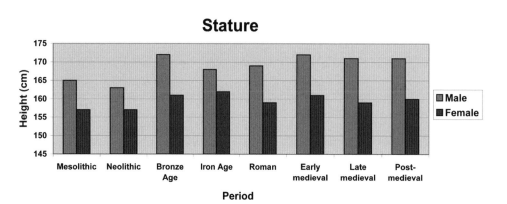

Figure 75: Stature through time in Britain (Charlotte Roberts)

bone lengths as a measure of height rather than use the length measurements to calculate attained stature.

The anatomical method (Fully 1956) relies on measuring the total added heights of all skeletal elements from the top of the skull to the lowest point of the heel bone (calcaneum); unfortunately in archaeological contexts, skeletons are usually too fragmentary to use this method, and some funerary contexts (eg crouched burials in British contexts) would not enable this method to be used at all. Nevertheless, a recent study compared stature reconstructed using skeletal length in the original grave, two stature estimations based on linear regression (sample and sex specific, utilising the Euro-American formulae of Trotter and Gleser 1952), and anatomically reconstructed stature. It found that measuring the skeleton length in the grave to provide anatomically reconstructed stature was the most accurate method to reconstruct stature, and recommends that the mathematical method should be avoided (Petersen 2005). This is because of the inevitable errors introduced with using the mathematical method of stature. A more recent paper has actually developed Fully's original method, finding stature could be estimated for skeletons of known height to within 4.5cm in 95% of individuals (Raxter *et al* 2006).

In non-adult skeletons stature cannot be calculated, although long bone diaphyseal lengths provide an indication of rates of growth between non-adult individuals (Lewis 2007). If cremated remains are being analysed it is difficult to determine stature because the bones shrink to varying degrees during the cremation process and are distorted, although shrinkage factors have been incorporated into calculations (McKinley 1994a). For inhumations, long bone lengths have been calculated from the diameters of the ends of unburnt long bones, assuming there is a constant relationship between diameters and lengths. This method is not suitable for cremated remains due to shrinkage of the bone during cremation; in addition, it is rare to see complete joint surfaces preserved for measurement.

Stature correlates with nutritional status, genetics, and environmental stress (Steckel 1995), although environmental and dietary stress are probably most important, especially during childhood and adolescence. Inequality in access to resources, hard physical work, disease, subsistence change, and living in an urban environment can all be used to explain reduced stature in an archaeological sample. For example, Lewis (2002) found disruptions in growth of some of the urbanised and industrialised non-adult individuals she studied from medieval England, as seen by diaphyseal long bone length. Gunnell *et al* (2001) also found that medieval English populations with shorter long bones died younger.

(c) Pathological lesions

While measurements of tooth crown size have generated information about inheritance in, and relationships between, populations, body size, aspects of hominid evolution, and reduction in dental size as a consequence of evolution (see Hillson, 1996a for more details), measurements have also played their part in the recording and analysis of pathological lesions in human skeletal remains. For example, measurements of the distance between the junction of the cement and enamel of the teeth to defects in the enamel caused by stress in growth (enamel hypoplasia) have allowed some to suggest at what age the stress occurred (Moggi-Cecci 1994; Reid and Dean 2000; King *et al* 2005). King *et al* (2005) studied two 18th- to 19th-century skeletal samples from Christ Church, Spitalfields, and St Bride's, Fleet Street, London. They found that people who died younger had an earlier 'age at first occurrence' of enamel defects than those who lived longer, suggesting they had health problems that shortened their lifespan. Another example involved taking measurements of the angle of deformity on radiographs of healed fractures in a late medieval population from York. Comparison with data from radiographs of modern conservatively (ie not surgically) treated fractures revealed some success for medieval treatment (Grauer and Roberts 1996). Periodontal disease has also received attention through measurement of the amount of bone lost in the jaws (detailed in Hillson 1996a), while basic measurements of pathological lesions as part of the descriptive process in palaeopathology provide an indication of the extent of the pathological process on bones and teeth (for example, the system of recording dental caries outlined by Lukacs 1989).

(ii) Recording non-metric traits

'Non-metric' refers to a feature that is recorded visually as to whether it is present or absent, how much it is developed and in what form (Hillson 1996a). First described in the 17th century (Tyrrell 2000), these features in the bones and teeth of the skeleton have been recorded in archaeological samples for decades. Based on animal experiments, they have been used to infer familial relationships in cemeteries and also 'ethnicity', because of their assumed heritability. Berry and Berry (1967) initiated the study of these traits in archaeologically derived skeletal samples through the publication of a description of cranial traits which they linked directly to the influence of genes (see also Hauser and Stefano 1990). Because the study of traits was low cost, easy to do, and could be applied to fragmentary remains (Tyrrell 2000), bioarchaeologists became increasingly enthusiastic about undertaking population studies in the late 1960s and 1970s, with study being firmly established by the late 1990s (eg see Saunders 1989). Finnegan (1978) also produced a description of postcranial non-metric traits, but these are felt to be less suited to biodistance study because of their susceptibility to remodelling and change through activity (Tyrrell 2000).

In more recent times there appears to be more of an emphasis on recording dental non-metric traits in the permanent teeth of adult skeletons because teeth are less affected by the 'environment' (Turner *et al* 1991; Scott and Turner 1997); there is also a strong genetic link to their presence, based on living populations (see also Lewis 2007; and Scott and Turner 1997 for a survey of dental non-metric trait studies of the deciduous teeth). Arizona State University in the US has produced reference plaques of permanent teeth showing over 30 different non-metric traits (Turner *et al* 1991); this has become the most used system in bioarchaeology, also described in Hillson (1996a). Features are recorded as present or absent along with their level of development. Biodistance analyses of dental non-metric traits concentrate on collections of dental features common to large groups of people, such as the 'Mongoloid' and 'Caucasoid' complexes. For example, 'shovelling' on the incisor teeth is noted in Native American and Asian populations, suggesting that the former's origin lies in north-east Asia (Siberia); immigration across the Bering land bridge to Alaska is implicated (Larsen 1997). A study by Irish (2006) considered 36 dental non-metric traits in Neolithic to Roman period dentitions from Egypt. Overall population continuity was seen with a largely homogenous group of people through time. Another study, by Ullinger *et al* (2005), recorded 30 non-metric traits in around 500 Southern Levant individuals from the late Bronze Age site of Dothan (1500–1100 BC) and the Iron Age II site of Lachish (701 BC). They wanted to test the hypothesis that the transition observed was the result of invading peoples, but found that there was continuity between the two periods based on the trait analysis; this suggested material culture change occurred without the influence of immigrants. As Hillson has stated (1996a, 100), 'It does seem clear that there is a strong genetic component in the distribution of at least some non-metrical features ...', and there is increasing work in bioarchaeology because of this observation. The reader is referred to Scott and Turner (1997) for a detailed account of variations from the norm of dental morphology.

Skeletal non-metric traits (Figure 76) can be classified into five categories according to their association with anatomical structures (see table 1 in Tyrrell 2000): arterial (eg mastoid foramina); venous (eg condylar canal); neural (eg mental foramen); sutural (eg coronal ossicle); and functional (eg mandibular torus). The

Figure 76: Vastus notch, a non-metric trait in the patella (Charlotte Roberts)

latter category is of particular importance because there are also increasing studies of activity/occupationally related skeletal changes in bioarchaeology, and some postcranial non-metric traits are now being recognised as useful in this respect. Unfortunately, we have insufficient knowledge about the nature of skeletal non-metric trait development and the level of trait heritability; there are also age and sex differences in occurrence, asymmetric findings, and inter-trait correlations. Recording of non-metric traits (just as with measurements) has the potential for intra- and inter-observer error, and there is a need for selecting traits according to the questions about the population that require answering. However, there are long lists of non-metric traits in various publications, with over 200 cranial traits alone being available for study (Larsen 1997). In cremated remains, recording of the full list would never be possible because of the fragmentary nature of the remains and incomplete recovery, but McKinley (1994a) does note that wormian bones and retention of the metopic suture, both found in the skull, can be identified in cremated remains. There have been a number of studies of non-metric cranial (Ishida and Dodo 1993) and postcranial traits (eg Oygucu *et al* 1998), and some studies suggest a higher than normal frequency of some traits. For example, Larsen *et al* (1995) found nine of fourteen skulls (64.3%) with a retained suture/joint down the forehead, called metopism; the normal rate is less than 10%, suggesting that there may be a strong genetic component to the retention of this suture. This also matched the archaeological and historical data for the cemetery which indicated that there was a high frequency of closely related individuals. Certainly, non-metric trait studies in bioarchaeology have a clear role in biodistance studies and, when combined with other methods of analysis such as those of biomolecular archaeology (aDNA and stable isotope), they can potentially strengthen arguments about relatedness and migration (eg see Corruccini *et al* 2002).

5.9 Analysing and interpreting data within an archaeological context

(i) What to do with the data

It should always be remembered that the skeletal data collected come from a dead population and therefore one has to consider how representative of the living they are, as we have seen. As both Waldron (1994) and Wood *et al* (1992) have pointed out, and many other authors since the early 1990s, there are several factors that will affect what skeletons or skeletal parts are studied and how much the 'sample' represents the living. Analysis of data can take the form of looking at features (eg disease, or measurements) on parts of bones and teeth, on whole bones and teeth, or in regions of the skeleton. Alternatively this can be done by looking at features across sub-groups of skeletons from a cemetery site, or indeed across the whole sample, or pooled samples. How the skeletal remains are analysed will depend on whether there are discrete graves that contained individual skeletons or whether the assemblage is commingled and disarticulated; in the latter case individual skeletal elements will be analysed for frequency of certain features, while in the former case it is possible to consider frequencies in individual skeletons that preserve the necessary bones or teeth which are of interest.

Basic information produced for a sample of skeletons will include the minimum number of individuals represented by the skeletons observed. Here a basic count of the left and right bones will reveal the most commonly occurring element which will represent the minimum number of individuals. Next, the number of male, female, ?male, ?female, adult, and non-adult (unsexed) skeletons is provided, along with the distribution of age at death, by sex. Finally, data on measurements, non-metric traits, and pathological lesions in the teeth and bones complete the information needed. It is vitally important that it is clear to the reader how many skeletons analysed for a particular piece of information had the requisite parts of the skeleton preserved for observation. Saying 50 skeletons had infection in the spine does not give a true frequency unless we know that all 50 had their total spines preserved to observe. Frequencies of observations should provide data according to total number of bones or teeth, and also by number of individual skeletons affected with the part preserved to observe. However, as archaeological skeletons are usually fragmentary, any frequency data will tend to be lower than the real rate. The reader is referred to Robb (2000, table 2) for a summary of the techniques used in data analysis.

Today, standard relational databases and spreadsheets are utilised to record data, and statistical packages are used to manipulate the data and test it for 'significance', ie verify patterns seen. There are three data analysis techniques (Robb 2000): descriptive and exploratory, which summarise the data and reveal patterns, and inferential, which tests the validity of the patterns in terms of statistical significance. Statistical significance is inferred if there is a less than 5% chance of the result having arisen because of random fluctuation (English Heritage 2004). A summary of the mean (and % frequency), range, standard deviation, and number of observations for specific findings such as a particular measurement, non-metric trait or pathological lesion, provides basic information about the skeletal sample, and the data are represented in tables and figures. Statistical tests are also necessary to validate observations and are described in Robb 2000; English Heritage 2004; and in more general texts such as Fletcher and Lock 1991; Shennan 1997; and Madrigal 1998. Variables such as social status (high or low), subsistence pattern (hunter-gatherer or agricultural), and living environment (urban or rural) can also be linked to the observations in order to explore and explain the data better.

(ii) The importance of context to interpretation

It is vitally important that the archaeological contexts from which skeletal remains derived are considered fully when interpreting data. This 'bioarchaeological' or 'biocultural' approach takes the primary skeletal data and then interprets the patterns seen by consideration of the archaeological and/or historical data. For example, if the focus is on skeletal indicators of dietary deficiency then the bioarchaeologist needs to understand the subsistence economy that the population was practising by looking at written records and/or the remains of plants and animals at the site, along with exploring stable isotope analysis data which will reflect the type of diet the person was (or was not) eating, whether that be marine, terrestrial etc. If a skeleton shows signs of infectious disease then the focus would be on understanding their living environment (eg population density), their hygiene levels, or whether there is evidence for migration of people who might be bringing in infections. Unless we understand the whole picture of the existence of past populations, we cannot understand what their skeletons are telling us.

5.10 Summary

In this chapter the laboratory context has been considered, including the necessary working arrangements and equipment needed. Prior to analysis, the skeletal structure and its function provide a basis from which to start to analyse skeletal remains. Methods for identification of bones and teeth and distinguishing them from non-human remains are discussed. Sex and age at death estimation, palaeodemographic profile reconstruction, and metric and non-metric data recording of the dentition and skeleton are discussed, with relevant examples from the literature, providing an emphasis on contextual information for interpretation. The chapter finishes with a consideration of how the data may be presented and analysed.

5.11 Key learning points

- the laboratory environment, in its broadest sense, if correctly arranged provides the necessary space and facilities for analysis of human remains
- standardisation of recording is essential
- understanding the normal human skeletal and dental structure is essential prior to analysing human remains
- being able to identify bones and teeth, and fragments thereof, along with animal bones is a first step to analysis
- sex estimation of non-adult skeletons is extremely difficult, if not impossible in most circumstances
- sex estimation of adult skeletons is much easier, and relies primarily on the pelvis
- ageing adult skeletons is difficult but non-adult skeletons can be aged relatively easily
- new methods for ageing adults are developing, particularly the use of statistical analysis
- modern reference skeletal collections have been used to develop analytical methods and therefore the methods may be inappropriate for bioarchaeological samples

- age and sex data can be used to create a demographic profile
- many factors affect how a person ages, both intrinsic to the body and extrinsic or within the 'environment' in its broadest sense
- metric and non-metric analyses record normal variation in the skeleton; they are used to examine 'differences' in skeletal remains (eg stature) both geographically and temporally; they may also be used to consider relatedness and evidence of migration of populations
- age, sex, metric, and non-metric data should be analysed in specific and systematic ways in order that populations can be compared
- context is key to interpretation of the data

CHAPTER SIX

Recording and analysis of data II: palaeopathology

The pattern of disease or injury that affects any group of people is never a matter of chance ... it reflects their genetic inheritance ..., the climate in which they lived, the soil that gave them sustenance and the animals and plants that shared their homeland. It is influenced by their daily occupations, their ... diet, their choice of dwellings and clothes, their social structure, even their folklore and mythology.

(Wells 1964)

6.1 Introduction

Chapter 5 provided an overview of collecting initial data to reconstruct the 'biological picture' of the person, as represented by their skeletal remains. To understand what health problems people encountered in the past, a number of areas of evidence are utilised to aid interpretation. In addition to evidence for disease, there is information about sex, age at death, and normal variation. What we do not have access to is information about people's immune systems in the past, whose strength and weakness determined whether a person contracted a disease or not. Today there is much debate about the lack of exposure of children to micro-organisms because they live in too clean an environment – so their immune system cannot develop effectively to defend the body against disease. For example, children brought up on farms are less likely to have allergies than those in cities because those in rural areas are exposed to a range of micro-organisms from an early age (Hamilton 2005). An example from the past also demonstrates the problem but in another way. Larsen (1994) notes the major impact on the health of Native Americans when Christopher Columbus, and others, reached America in the late 15th century AD, exposing a previously unexposed native population to new diseases. They quickly became ill and died because their immune systems were not familiar with European pathogens. Thus, immune strength is a key variable affecting the range of diseases seen in skeletal and mummified remains.

Palaeopathology is the term used to denote the study of disease in the past. As a subdiscipline of bioarchaeology, it was defined by Marc Armand Ruffer in 1910 (Aufderheide and Rodríguez Martín 1998) as the science of diseases whose existence can be demonstrated on the basis of human and animal remains from ancient times. It focuses on 'abnormal variation', attempting to chart the origin and evolution of disease over thousands of years from a global perspective. It is, by its very nature, an holistic study informed by data coming from a multitude of analytical methods.

Today, health is defined by the World Health Organisation as 'a state of complete physical, mental and social well-being, and not merely the absence of disease or infirmity' (http://www.who.int/about/definition/en/print.html). This definition entered into force on 7 April 1948 and has not been amended since that date. However, we should not forget that our ancestors' perceptions of health and disease may have been very different from our own, and we know that treatment of illness was certainly not as we see it in Britain today. We are aware, for example, that people's perceptions of why disease occurred in their community changed through time as medical knowledge advanced. In the Roman period people often thought that disease occurred because of divine displeasure and/or an imbalance of the four humours of the body. If there was an excess or lack of one or more of yellow bile, phlegm, black bile, or blood then disease could occur. These humours were seen as inter-related with elements of the universe (fire, water, earth and air, respectively) and had specific characteristics (hot and dry, cold and wet, cold and dry, and hot and wet, respectively). As an example, treatments in the Roman period were also interesting: 'In an uncertain world there was every good reason to employ every means available to ensure good health' (Jackson 1988, 138). Thus, gods, goddesses, demons, and magic played a part in treatments for medical complaints. Bathing at specific sites was also recommended; for example, tuberculosis benefited from alkaline waters, and if acidic water was drunk then this cured bladder stones (ibid). Herbal remedies were used a lot for wounds, and in anaesthesia for operations, and there is evidence for surgical 'drilling' of the skull (trepanation) in several skulls from the Roman period in Britain (see Roberts and McKinley 2003). Furthermore, fractures were treated in very similar ways to a casualty department today; the 5th-century BC Greek writer Hippocrates, whose writings influenced Roman and later modes of treatment, describes reduction and splinting of fractures using pads and bandages reinforced by clays and starches (Withington 1927).

While concepts of disease occurrence and methods of treatment may have changed through time, it is safe to say that nobody will go through life today anywhere in the world without experiencing some ill health; the same can be said of the past. As we have seen in Chapter 5, a demographic profile represents the dead 'population', the people who died from disease or trauma. As Brown et al say (1996, 183), 'The experience of disease, by individuals and whole populations, is as inescapable as death itself'. Thus, key to understanding the past is assessing the health problems our ancestors suffered from because those very illnesses would have had an impact on their ability to function normally. Ultimately this could have affected the very nature of how their community, society, or state developed. One could, therefore, argue that studying how healthy people were in the past via their skeletal remains is the most important part of any bioarchaeological study because it will allow us to understand how that 'population' developed. For example, in 14th-century England, the Black Death killed a huge proportion of the population – on average a third, but ranging from 20% to 60/70% regionally. This of course ultimately affected social and economic systems and would have compromised the health and well-being of the surviving parts of the population of England (Platt 1996; Ziegler 1991).

However, we should not forget that 'health and disease are measures of the effectiveness with which human groups, combining biological and cultural resources, adapt to their environments' (Lieban 1973, 1031). People have a great capacity to adapt to changes in their environment and to alter how they function in order that they may survive, something that has been described as 'one of the most remarkable aspects of being human' (McElroy and Townsend 1996, 105). Certainly, the resilience of the surviving population after devastating pandemics like the Black Death is striking. Over varying periods of time too there are genetic and physiological adjustments. The former occurs through natural selection at the population level over a long time span, and the latter occurs over the person's lifetime (*ibid*). There may also be psychological and emotional adjustments that make people feel more positive and provide a sense of well-being. Some examples of the mechanisms that people might utilise to adapt to situations and prevent illness might be: keeping waste out of water supplies to prevent disease, cooking foods to kill micro-organisms, wearing warm clothes at high altitudes, and protecting the skin from exposure to the sun. For example, in Peru infants are protected from the cold temperatures by being wrapped tightly in multiple layers of blankets and clothing. Infants are also carried by their mothers within a much warmer internal micro-environment, in a pouch on the mother's back (Tronick *et al* 1994, in McElroy and Townsend 1996): these are cultural adaptive responses. Physiological responses might include developing enhanced lung function to obtain higher levels of oxygen, and increasing the number of red blood cells that carry oxygen (in their haemoglobin) to the body's tissues, as seen with people living at high altitudes. An example of genetic adaptation is seen in people who live at high altitude for their whole life; these people are short legged, grow slowly and have a large lung capacity. We should also remember that disease-causing organisms can mutate and adapt to circumstances in order that they remain successful in inducing disease in a population, as seen for tuberculosis in recent decades (Coninx *et al* 1998).

6.2 Sources of evidence for disease in the past

There are many sources of evidence for disease in the past. Our primary source consists of human remains from archaeological sites (eg see Figure 77) and, for the most part in Britain, these are skeletal remains (for evidence of disease in mummified bodies, see Aufderheide 2000). Thus, we are restricted to what we can say about disease by the very fact that many diseases only affect the soft tissues. Therefore, childhood diseases such as measles, whooping cough, chicken pox, and mumps, along with other conditions that can affect both children and adults alike, such as cholera, malaria, plague, and smallpox, will not be seen as evidence in skeletal remains. However, there are alternative ways for 'finding' these diseases. For example, scientific developments can enable detection of these soft tissue diseases; malaria (Sallares and Gomzi 2001) and the plague (Weichmann and Grupe 2005) have both been detected in skeletal remains through chemical analysis (see Chapter 7). Another way of looking at mortality due to soft tissue disease is to consider the palaeodemographic profile of the 'population'. For example, Margerison and Knüsel (2002), and Gowland and Chamberlain (2005), both considered the profile of the 14th-century Black Death cemetery at the site of the Royal Mint in London (Figure 78). The latter study found the use of Bayesian statistical analysis could help to explain the age profile of people affected by the infection.

Secondary sources of evidence for diseases in the past include written records and artistic (eg painting, drawings, sculpture) representations (Figures 79 and 80). It may be that an archaeological site producing skeletons has contemporaneous written records or other associated evidence about disease but this tends to be rare. If secondary sources exist then it may be possible to integrate the skeletal data for disease with that evidence to provide a fuller picture of past health as no one source of evidence is usually sufficient to explain what health problems people faced when alive. While diagnosis of disease is not always straightforward, written records can be biased and may reflect the author's preferences and opinions. There can also

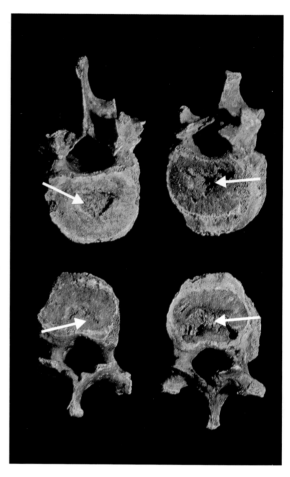

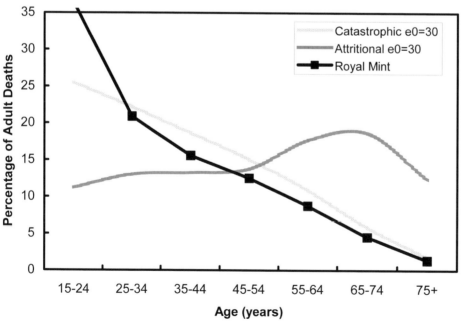

Figure 77: Example of pathological bones: Schmorl's nodes (arrowed) (with permission of Jeff Veitch)

Figure 78: Mortality profile of a plague cemetery (Royal Mint, London) compared to attritional and other catastrophic profiles (with permission of Andrew Chamberlain)

Figure 79 (below left): Example of historical data for disease (title page of Glisson's *A treatise of the rickets*, 1651; with permission of the Wellcome Library, London)

Figure 80 (below right): Example of artistic data for disease – front of 16th-century Job statue showing syphilitic ulcers, from a French church (with permission of the Wellcome Library, London)

be a tendency for people to write about, and illustrate, the more dramatic (and even rarer) diseases: 'Diseases with the greatest impact in terms of mortality, personal disfigurement, or social and economic disruption probably evoked the greatest response from society' (Roberts and Manchester 2005, 2). Additionally, when reading about signs and symptoms of disease in historical records, one must be careful not to interpret the wrong disease. People who cough up blood, for example, could have been suffering from lung cancer, tuberculosis, or chronic bronchitis. With respect to frequency of disease, there is much historical and art evidence for leprosy in medieval Europe, and yet the data from skeletal remains do not bear this out, although, as will be seen, there can be problems with our primary evidence. Of use too for understanding health and disease in the past and how it is related to lifestyles, is the consideration of people who live traditionally or similarly to our ancestors (termed medical anthropology – see McElroy and Townsend 1996; Panter-Brick *et al* 2001). While these people live in marginal environments (eg arctic or desert), and are distanced in space and time from our ancestors, it is believed that they may well lead similar lives.

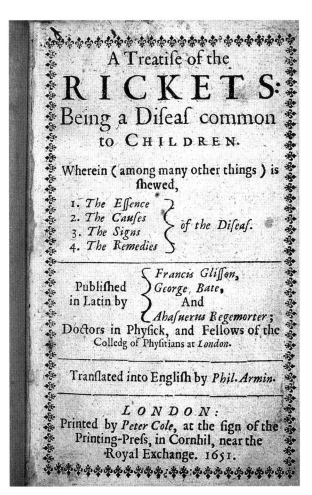

6.3 How do we study disease in skeletal remains?

In order to diagnose and interpret evidence for disease, it is necessary to work from what is termed a 'clinical base'. This means that we need to know how specific diseases affect skeletal remains and what the impact on that person might be in terms of the symptoms they might experience. Take, for example, rheumatoid arthritis. This is a chronic inflammatory disease that affects the joints and associated soft tissues. It involves the synovial joints of the body, especially in the hand, foot, shoulder, elbow, wrist, knee, and neck (cervical) vertebrae. The surfaces and edges of the joints erode or disappear. Ligaments and tendons of the joints are also affected, and some joints can dislocate partially (the bones of the joint are displaced out of normal alignment). If this pattern of bone damage is seen in a skeleton then a diagnosis may be made (with care); one assumes that the bone changes have not altered through time, and that drug therapy has not changed the way bone reacts to the disease as described in clinical texts. We also know from clinical data that rheumatoid arthritis leaves people weak, with anaemia, weight loss, swollen, stiff and painful joints, deformity, reduced function, and osteoporosis. Thus, by using clinical data we can start to build a picture of the impact of the disease on a person and population.

It should be remembered though that skeletal remains only provide us with evidence of chronic disease, disease that was initially acute in nature. In effect, we are seeing the healthy people of a population, even though they are dead! A person who died in the acute stages of a disease that they had not been exposed to before, because of their weaker immune system, may not have lived long enough to develop bone changes (thus, no evidence is present in the skeleton). A person with acute disease is therefore indistinguishable from one who did not have the disease. A person with chronic healed bone lesions on the other hand indicates that their immune system was strong enough to deal with the acute stages of the disease, allowing the person to survive into the chronic stages and develop chronic bone change. This is the 'osteological paradox' (Wood *et al* 1992). Thus,

Figure 81 (below left): Bone formation: osteoid osteoma, a benign bone tumour (Charlotte Roberts)

Figure 82 (below right): Bone destruction: cancer of skull (Charlotte Roberts)

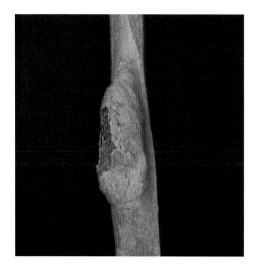

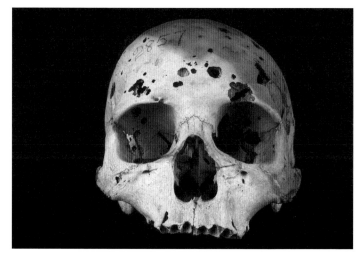

a skeleton with no bone changes may represent a person who died from a soft tissue disease, ie they would never have developed bone changes because the disease does not affect the skeleton, or it may represent a person who died of a disease that *does* affect bone, but did not live long enough for the changes to occur in their skeleton. There are many scenarios that should be considered, all of which will be affected by a person's inherent 'frailty' or susceptibility to disease (essentially unknown for the past). What we are trying to do when we look at evidence for disease in a skeletal sample is to document their health history, ie what they suffered from during life. We can rarely determine what killed people unless there is, for example, an unhealed blade injury; neither can we estimate when the disease first affected them if the lesions are chronic and healed.

To document the evidence for disease in a skeletal sample we have to look for evidence of bone formation or bone destruction and make a full description of the observations made (Figures 81 and 82). This ensures that if the diagnosis is found to be incorrect then other bioarchaeologists can reassess the description (especially if the skeleton has been reburied and is not available for further study). As described in Chapter 5, osteoblast bone cells form bone and osteoclast bone cells destroy bone. Throughout life bone undergoes remodelling with a normal balance between formation and destruction, but if that balance is disrupted by disease, there may be more bone formed or destroyed than normal, which can be seen on the skeleton. For example, as a person ages and develops osteoporosis, bone loss overtakes bone formation. The bone formation seen on skeletal remains is either woven (disorganised deposit formed initially as a response to disease or injury) or lamellar (more organised and denser), which represents healing and chronicity (Figures 83 and 84). The former lesions may indicate that the disease was active at the time of death, or in the case of the latter that the person adapted and coped with the disease and developed healed chronic lesions. These bone changes are distributed on the skeleton according to the disease the person suffered, although the same bones may be affected by several different diseases (for example, bone formation can occur on the lower leg bones in leprosy, syphilis, tuberculosis, scurvy, and through trauma to the shins). Therefore, it is important to have as complete a skeleton as possible and to record the distribution and type of changes (Figure 85). This is difficult for cremated remains, because although pathological lesions can be seen, the incomplete nature of the remains means diagnosis is limited and calculating disease frequency is not feasible (McKinley 1994a). Once the recording is completed then a range of possible (differential) diagnoses are considered, which are then hopefully pared down to just one.

Diagnosis of disease using skeletal remains is not easy. Imagine your doctor who has a 'battery' of diagnostic tests available to him/her which can be carried out on any of the many body systems; despite this wealth of available information from tests, a diagnosis is not always forthcoming and sometimes it is wrong (see Waldron 1994, table 3.2). Imagine if all there is to work with is one system – the skeleton; it is easy to appreciate how difficult it is to make a diagnosis, especially if the skeleton is incomplete and fragmentary, as is often the case from archaeological sites. Again, there are recommendations for the recording

384380

BONES PRESENT   BONE LESIONS

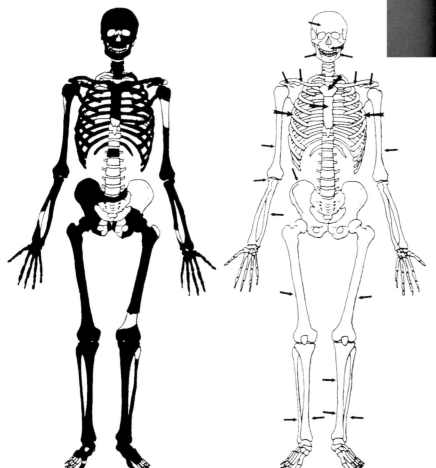

Figure 83 (above left): Active (unhealed) bone formation (Charlotte Roberts)

Figure 84 (above right): Healed (non-active) bone formation (Charlotte Roberts)

Figure 85: Distribution pattern in a disease – treponemal disease in an individual from late medieval Gloucester (Charlotte Roberts)

of palaeopathological data (Buikstra and Ubelaker 1994; Roberts and O'Connell, 2004) so that there may be some possibility of undertaking comparative analysis of 'populations' if the same data have been recorded using the same methods. This is anticipated in the 'Global History of Health' project (see Chapter 1). It is also increasingly the case that more sophisticated methods of analysis are used to help with diagnosis such as radiography, histology, trace element analysis and, more recently, ancient DNA analysis; these methods of analysis are described in more detail, with examples, in Chapter 7.

Cremated bones provide their own problems for recording and diagnosis of disease, as has been noted above, but they are also often distorted by the cremation process; this results in a limited amount of information on disease, not least because some pathological conditions can weaken the bone and predispose it to disintegration on cremation (McKinley 2000b). However, with a keen eye, some useful data can emerge. For example, McKinley (1994a) notes that of 2284 individuals at the Anglo-Saxon cremation cemetery of Spong Hill in Norfolk, nearly one third of the individuals had some evidence of a pathological lesion or a sign of normal variation (non-metric trait). Dental disease – tooth loss, caries (6%), calculus and enamel hypoplasia; joint disease (17% of adults); metabolic disease; infections; gall stones; and calcified lymph nodes were all seen (see Figure 86 for an example of gall stones from a living person).

Once data on disease have been collected we then look at the frequency or prevalence of each condition (Tables 2 and 3) but, as Waldron (1994) has documented, we have to be aware that the frequency of disease recorded may not be representative of the 'truth'. First, any group of skeletons examined from a site usually represents only a sample of the once-living population (Figure 87). It may be an unrepresentative sample and thus may not show the actual disease load in the population. For example, children may have been

Figure 86: Gall stones from a living person (Charlotte Roberts, with permission of the patient)

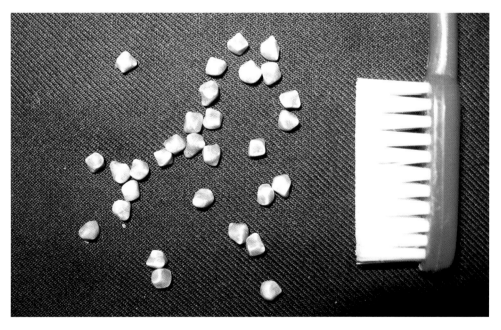

buried in a part of the cemetery that was not excavated, and people with certain diseases may have been buried elsewhere. Common too are burial contexts where the dating of the site provides only a broad time span, for example 12th to 16th centuries AD for the late medieval period in Britain. It is therefore not possible to highlight specific times when certain diseases were more common because the frequency rate obtained is for the whole cemetery over several hundred years (Figure 88).

The study of individual skeletons with specific diseases dominated publications in the early years of palaeopathological study. This is seen in certain parts of the world even today, including Britain (see Mays 1997a). However, there has been a considerable effort on the part of North American bioarchaeologists in particular to emphasise that more insightful information about health can be gained by considering 'population' rather than individual health (see recent commentaries on developments over time in Buikstra and Beck 2006). Important

Table 2: Fracture frequencies for bones observed in six British late medieval urban populations

Site	Fracture number	Total bones	%	Source
Blackfriars, Gloucester	11	1861	0.6	1
Chichester, Sussex	41	1554	2.6	2
St Andrew, Fishergate, York	26	3232	0.8	3
St Helen-on-the-Walls, York	41	4938	0.8	4
St Nicholas Shambles, London	18	296	6.1	5
Whithorn, Scotland	27	9563	0.3	6

Table 3: Fracture prevalence by bone element for six British late medieval urban populations (%)

Bone	1	2	3	4	5	6
Humerus	0.3	4.2	0.4	0.8	5.3	0.0
Radius	1.4	3.2	0.8	1.3	8.8	0.5
Ulna	0.5	2.8	0.8	1.5	8.2	0.1
Femur	0.5	0.4	0.2	0.1	3.8	0.2
Tibia	0.5	2.3	0.5	0.7	6.0	0.4
Fibula	0.3	7.2	1.7	0.8	1.1	0.8

1 = Wiggins *et al* 1993; 2 = Judd and Roberts 1998; 3 = Stroud and Kemp 1993; 4 = Grauer and Roberts 1996; 5 = White 1988; 6 = Cardy 1997

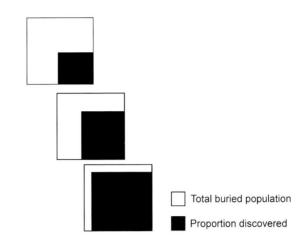

Figure 87: Potential scenarios when a cemetery is excavated showing the possible proportion of individuals buried that might be represented in those skeletons analysed (redrawn by Yvonne Beadnell, after Waldron 1994)

Total buried population

Proportion discovered

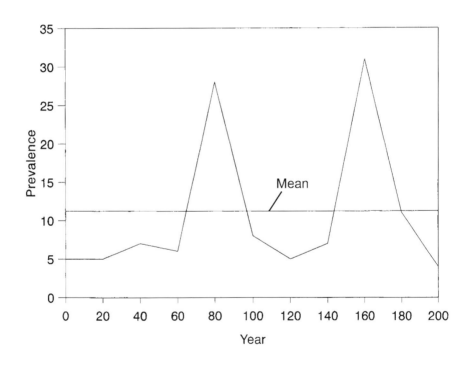

Figure 88: Hypothetical disease frequency in an archaeological skeletal sample where peaks would be undetectable without good dating evidence (redrawn by Yvonne Beadnell, after Waldron 1994)

in this respect is to consider context, and interpret data on disease using available archaeological, historical, and other relevant data. There have been some increases in population-led studies of health in Britain published in recent years. Nevertheless, a relative lack of equivalent developments in Britain probably reflects that there have been, until recently, fewer bioarchaeologists and there is a lack of research funding available for basic palaeopathological studies. Although we have many well-trained bioarchaeologists in Britain, there are simply not enough opportunities to accommodate the number of people with the requisite skills for employment in bioarchaeology, both in academia and in contract archaeology (see Chapter 8).

6.4 Themes in palaeopathology

This chapter will now consider some themes that may be explored in palaeopathology in order to understand specific aspects of people's lives in the past. Their subsistence base and diet (hunter-gatherer – Figure 89, farmer, pastoralist, nomad); where they lived (urban, rural, coastal – Figure 90, inland, island, highland, lowland, or in poorly ventilated housing); their hygiene levels; what the climate was like – determined by seasonality and latitude and longitude (hot and dry or cold and wet); what work they did (potter, farmer, builder, labourer; Figure 91); whether they moved around through trade or migration; and whether they had access to health care – all these variables will influence the diseases any human will ultimately encounter. A multitude of factors in each 'situation' will come together and make a person or population susceptible to certain diseases. The following sections will take a look at the impact on health of the living environment, diet, work, conflict, and access to health care. The emphasis is to consider the skeletal evidence for each of these themes within its context, or utilise other types of data to 'put flesh on the bones'; no one piece of evidence can provide the full story.

Of course, in such a short handbook it is not possible to cover all aspects of palaeopathology, including all possible diseases that might be recognised in skeletal remains, but there are other sources of information that provide much more detailed information (eg Kiple 1993, 1997; Larsen 1997; Aufderheide and Rodríguez Martín 1998; chapters in Cox and Mays 2000; Ortner 2003; Roberts and Cox 2003; Roberts and Manchester 2005), with more synthetic examples from Cohen (1989); Grauer and Stuart-Macadam (1998); Howe (1997); and Steckel and Rose (2002).

(i) Living environment

People live in all sorts of different geographical locations and environments today and each has a particular set of features that could potentially influence their health. Furthermore, people can have basically three different micro-environments

Figure 89: Australian aboriginal hunter-gatherers (with permission of Bob Layton)

Figure 90: External living environment showing rubbish pollution on a beach with nearby houses on Zanzibar, an island off the east coast of Africa (with permission of Catherine Panter-Brick)

Figure 91: Working in mountainous Nepal (Charlotte Roberts)

Figure 92: Internal house environment reconstructed from an Iron Age house at Lejre, Denmark (Charlotte Roberts)

where they will be exposed to factors that may compromise health, but there might be more, depending on their lifestyle. Take, for example the average Londoner today. Most people will have a house or apartment, they will have a workplace (eg office, factory, hospital, fire-station), and they experience the outdoor environment when they travel between the two. They will use public transport (bus, train, underground), their own car or bicycle, or they may walk to work. In their leisure time they may visit a local public house, a restaurant, a night club, the theatre, a gym, or they may simply have a walk in one of the many parks. Now, imagine the potential benefits and hazards to their health that they might experience within all those environments. Added to this, we are experiencing global warming and an increase in environmental pollution, particularly in developing countries where pollution control is not as well developed. Such an individual exposure risk is impossible for bioarchaeologists to reconstruct in the past, but the impact of certain living conditions on a group can be assessed using skeletal remains. How might we explore, for example, the effects of air quality on health through examining the remains of our ancestors? There are a number of examples that can be provided.

If a person experiences poor air quality then they will inhale 'polluted' air and this could set up an inflammatory reaction in the respiratory system, but more particularly in the facial sinuses and lungs; potentially the bone of the sinuses and ribs may be affected. Today, chronic respiratory disease is one of the most common causes of morbidity and mortality (World Health Organisation 2006), and more than 1.5 million deaths each year are caused by respiratory infections due to environmental factors. Respiratory tract diseases can be caused by inorganic or organic gases (eg sulphur dioxide, tobacco smoke), inert substances (eg carbon), and allergenic (eg pollen), or living (eg bacteria) particulates. *Outdoor air pollution* can be traced back to periods when 'industries' developed, for example in the Neolithic of Europe when pottery production began (smoke from kilns), and in the Bronze Age when metals were smelted. *Indoor air pollution* can be traced back to when people started using shelters (eg caves), and open fires for warmth and cooking (Figure 92). Who spent most time indoors in the past – women, children, the sick? Although the perception is that outdoor pollution is worse than indoor pollution, indoor pollutants are 'often higher than those typically encountered outside' (Jones 1999, 4536). Indoor polluting factors include dust mites, cockroaches, and animals, as well as cold and damp houses which encourage mould growth, building materials, lack of ventilation, furnishings, and air-conditioning systems. External pollutants from nearby industries, as well as smoke from cigarettes and fuel used on open fires, may also affect indoor air quality. Half the world's population today (up to 90% of rural households) rely on unprocessed biomass fuels such as wood, dung, and crop residues, which are typically burnt in open fires; women and children are the most vulnerable because they spend more time indoors (Bruce *et al* 2002).

A number of recent studies have explored air quality and health in bioarchaeology using evidence on ribs (eg Capasso 1999; Lambert 2002) and sinuses (eg Boocock *et al* 1995; Lewis *et al* 1995; Merrett and Pfeiffer 2000; Roberts 2007). Lambert (2002) analysed the ribs of individuals from six prehistoric Anasazi sites in south-west Colorado, USA, dated to between AD 1075 and 1280, along with individuals from two contemporary sites in northern Arizona and north-western New Mexico. The results showed that respiratory disease was a serious health problem for Colorado. A more recent study by Roberts (2007) considered maxillary sinusitis (Figure 93) as an indicator of poor air quality in fifteen skeletal samples from archaeological sites in North America, England, the Netherlands, and Nubia – selected to represent different geographic locations, environments, and subsistence economies. Frequency rates varied considerably (Figure 94), with female rates exceeding male at most sites. Urban agricultural sites had a mean frequency of 48.5%, rural agricultural sites had a mean frequency of 45.0%, and hunter-gatherer sites had a mean frequency of 40.0%. In the

Figure 93: Bone formation (arrowed) in a maxillary sinus, indicating a reaction to sinusitis (Charlotte Roberts)

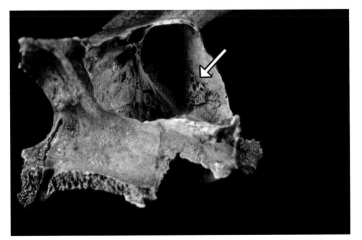

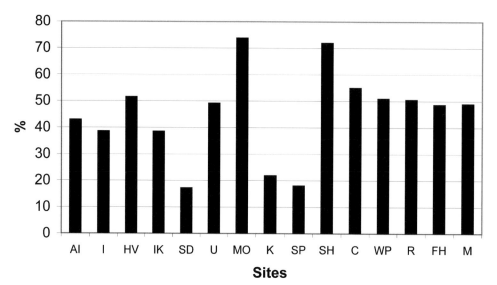

Figure 94: Maxillary sinusitis in fifteen skeletal populations from England, the Netherlands, Nubia, and North America (Charlotte Roberts)

North America (USA)
AI = Aleutian Islanders
I = Illinois sample
HV = Hardin Village, Kentucky
IK - Indian Knoll, Kentucky
SD = South Dakota sample
North America (Canada)
U = Uxbridge
MO = Moatfield
Nubia
K = Kulubnarti

England
SP = Christ Church, Spitalfields, London
SH = St Helen-on-the-Walls, York
C= St James and St Mary Magdalene, Chichester,
   Sussex
WP= Wharram Percy, North Yorkshire
R = Raunds Furnells, Northamptonshire
FH = Fishergate House, York
The Netherlands
M = Maastricht

urban sites, male and female frequencies were near equal, but in the rural agricultural and hunter-gatherer sites, female frequencies exceeded those of males. Of particular interest was the very low frequency seen at Christ Church, Spitalfields, London (18%); it was suggested that these people of higher status were 'protected' from their polluted 18th/19th-century environment in some way, and they generally lived in houses that had chimneys for ventilation purposes.

Other evidence, for example historical documentation, suggests people have been aware of environmental pollution and its effect on health for a long time. As early as the 5th century BC, Hippocrates in his 'Airs, Water, and Places' recognised the relationship between health and the properties of air (Lloyd 1978), and in the 17th and 18th centuries Bernardino Ramazzini described occupations that produced pollution-related illnesses in their workers, for example making pottery, mining, or weaving (Ramazzini 1705). Respiratory disorders have also been noted in mummified remains. Munizaga *et al* (1975) found twelve AD 1600 Chilean mummies with lung tissues affected by pneumoconiosis (silicosis) as a result of working in dusty mines, and Pabst and Hofer (1998) revealed anthracite in the lungs of the late Neolithic 'Iceman', probably the result of being exposed to sooty fires. Pyatt and Grattan (2001) also document ancient mining activities in Jordan and their potential impact on human health, while Oakberg *et al* (2000) analysed arsenic levels in skeletons from a copper smelting site in Israel, finding higher levels in those working in the industry (although see Pike and Richards 2002, on the possible problems of diagenetic uptake of arsenic in this study).

Another result of poor air quality can be explored through looking at the frequency of rickets in the past. Vitamin D is formed in the skin chemically by the action of sunlight. The majority of vitamin D is acquired by the body in this way, with the diet contributing about 10% (via fish oil and animal fat). Vitamin D is necessary for the absorption of calcium and phosphorus and the mineralisation of osteoid, the bone that is first formed (Elia 2002). It is essential for making the bones hard and strong during growth. If vitamin D is not made in the skin then the bones will become deformed when the child starts to crawl and walk. If an infant or child is not exposed to ultraviolet light this can happen and, indeed, was quite common in the past due to polluted environments (smog). Children living in these smog-ridden environments, in crowded housing, and often working from a young age for long hours indoors, were very susceptible to developing rickets, particularly in the post-medieval period in Europe. In England in the 17th and 18th centuries, it was called the 'English Disease' or a 'Disease of Civilisation'. The evidence for rickets is not very common in skeletal samples until this period but this might be because diagnostic criteria have only been detailed relatively recently (Ortner and Mays 1998). In adult skeletons rickets is often identified as originating in childhood in the form of residual bowing deformities of the long bones. However, Ortner and Mays (1998) have identified ten major features that should be considered in combination. Recent studies (Mays *et al* 2006a; Brickley *et al* 2007) have identified 38 adult and non-adult individuals (of a total of 505) with rickets from the 19th-century urban population excavated at the churchyard of St Martin's-in-the-Bull Ring, Birmingham. Frequencies were higher here than at the medieval rural site of Wharram Percy in North Yorkshire (Ortner and Mays 1998). It was suggested that at the latter site, the eight children affected may have been sick and spent their time mostly indoors. At a contemporary site to St Martin's, that of Christ Church, Spitalfields, London, Lewis (2002) found 24 children with rickets, and four with both rickets and scurvy (vitamin C deficiency). Feeding prepared infant foods, swaddling infants in clothing, and keeping them indoors may all have contributed to the disease in this population.

(ii) Diet

'You are what you eat'. This is certainly true and has been for thousands of years. Furthermore, people's intake of food and drink is strongly linked to the strength of their immune system so that, if they are poor and/or are not eating a well-balanced diet, they will be more likely to become ill. Debates abound today about the variety of diet-related health issues that affect the western world and these are clearly much more complex than a straightforward link between poor diet and social deprivation. Increased wealth and urbanisation have brought with them a distinctive set of problems: lack of balance in the diet –'fast foods' with too much salt and sugar and too little fibre, excessive alcohol/drug consumption, or culturally induced anxieties about food and body image. Even in developing countries such as China, modernisation has brought with it a reduction in physical activity that has been noted as contributing to obesity (Monda *et al* 2007). So, in the modern world, lifestyle choices do have a direct link with rising trends in particular diseases – obesity, heart disease, cancers, liver disease, and diabetes. These trends have even led to intervention from governments to improve people's awareness of the dangers of poor diet.

One could argue that in the past, our farming ancestors accessed better-quality foods that were not covered in insecticide to prevent pests; in effect, food was grown organically. That is not to say that there were no food shortages as these are well documented in historical records. However, in general, there is no reason to doubt that in the past people had access to a range of foods, probably ate a more balanced diet compared to today, and were not prone to obesity and anorexia nervosa. In the western world, therefore, we have a rising problem with either being too fat or too thin, but in the developing world, we see different problems of food intake. While in some countries there is an increasing adoption by many of 'fast foods' (see above), there are many areas where a lack of food or poor use of available food can lead to protein-energy malnutrition (PEM). For example, approximately 50 million pre-school children in the world have PEM (Elia 2002).

What do we need to have a healthy diet? Food provides us with energy, and energy balance is the difference between intake and expenditure. In a 55-year-old female an average of 1940 kilocalories are needed daily, while for a male it is 2550 kilocalories. This is made up of about 50% carbohydrate, 35% fat, and 15% protein (Elia 2002); in developing countries carbohydrate may be 75% of the intake and fat less than 15%. Overall, recommendations suggest that we should be eating less fat, while increasing consumption of fish, wholegrain cereals, and fruit and vegetables. However, the quality and quantity of what is or was grown, harvested, stored, processed, bought, cooked and eaten, by choice or not, will have a significant effect on health. Furthermore, age, sex, where you live, and what social status you have will determine what foods you eat. A person living in the Arctic will not have the same foods as somebody living in the tropics, and the rich may have access to a wider diversity of foods, more meat, and perhaps more exotic foods. Of course, markets in the past provided wider access to more exotic foods, while supermarkets today boast of the wide variety of foods they sell and greater choice for the consumer.

Studies of diet through analysing skeletal remains have been frequent. They have focused on periods of time when people hunted and gathered their food, when they domesticated plants and animals, and when food production intensified in later times. Hunting and gathering sustained small groups of people and provided a generally healthy and well-balanced diet, with a wide variety of foods, lots of fibre, a high concentration of minerals and vitamins in wild plants, and lean meat from animals that they hunted (Jenike 2001), as opposed to less lean farmed animals. They were also regularly mobile and therefore probably fitter

Figure 95: Dental caries in a young individual from medieval Whitefriars, Norwich (with permission of Anwen Caffell)

than more sedentary farmers. Farmers ate a less varied and less reliably produced diet than hunter-gatherers, and lived in settled communities; this generated a number of health problems because increased food production sustained an increase in population who lived in close contact with each other in permanent housing. They were also susceptible to diseases contracted from their animals (zoonoses), and generally lived in less hygienic conditions than hunter-gatherers. Industrialisation brought with it more processed foods, more people, and access to foodstuffs which were not necessarily good for health, such as more sugar. While there have been synthetic studies focusing on general subsistence themes (eg Cohen and Armelagos 1984; Cohen 1989; Larsen 2006; Cohen and Krane-Cramer 2007), there are other studies that consider specific dietary deficiencies and excesses in skeletal samples.

Dental caries (Figure 95) is a condition that has plagued humans for hundreds of years and is recognised by cavities in the enamel (and underlying dentine) of the teeth (Hillson 1996a). This infectious disease is the result mainly of the fermentation of carbohydrates (sugars) in the diet by bacteria in dental plaque. This leads to the production of acid which destroys the tooth substance. A lack of fluoride in the water/food eaten and poor oral hygiene are also predisposing factors. Recent pooled data for British populations from the Neolithic to the post-medieval period (as early as 4000 BC to as late as the mid-19th century AD) suggest an association between an increase in caries and sugar and refined flour consumption through time, apart from the early medieval period where

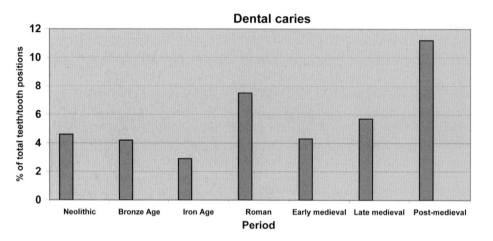

Figure 96: Dental caries data for Britain through time (Charlotte Roberts)

frequencies declined (Roberts and Cox 2003; Figure 96). Attention has also been given to studies of male and female frequencies and differences by social status. For instance, in a study of a Mayan population dated to the Classic period in Mexico (AD 250–900) the frequency of caries related to social status was considered (Cucina and Tiesler 2003). Results showed that elite males had the lowest rate of caries but the highest rate of ante-mortem tooth loss; this correlated with poor oral hygiene and a diet containing relatively soft and refined foods. A study by Pietrusewsky and Douglas (2002) of a north-east Thailand population from Ban Chiang (2100 BC to as late as AD 200) found a caries rate of 7.3% in 60 skeletons (74 of 1016 teeth); males were more affected than females. The data revealed that the low rate of caries was consistent with a mixed economy, and that males may have had differential access to caries-producing foods. The overall frequency was lower than at the Central Thailand site of Khok Phanom Di where the skeletons studied by Tayles (1999) were dated to 2000–1500 BC. Here, a frequency of 11% caries was seen in all intact teeth but females were more affected than males. Tayles (*ibid*, 276) suggests that this frequency may be related to ingestion of high levels of sugar from bananas or from palm sugar made from the coconut palm.

Another condition in which excess in the diet may be one of the predisposing factors is DISH (diffuse idiopathic skeletal hyperostosis). This condition appears to be associated with obesity and late onset diabetes (Julkunen *et al* 1971; Rogers and Waldron 2001), and it may have a genetic component. Recent work has supported the suggestion that multiple factors are at work in its occurrence as a wide variety of populations appear to have been affected in the past (eg Japanese sea mammal hunters and English medieval monks: Oxenham *et al* 2006; Rogers and Waldron 2001). Characteristically this condition affects the spinal ligaments, leading to their fusion (Figure 97), and new bone forms on other bones at the sites of the tendon and ligament insertions (Rogers and Waldron 1995). Older males are most affected today, and it is suggested that, as monastic groups tend to show the highest frequencies in the past, they were predisposed to the condition because of a rich diet and a lack of exercise.

Waldron (1993) found 37 male and 17 female skeletons with DISH at the post-medieval Christ Church, Spitalfields, London; perhaps the higher status of this site, although not monastic, meant that people were susceptible. Stroud and Kemp (1993) also noted seven definite and eight probable individuals with DISH at the late medieval Gilbertine Priory of St Andrew, Fishergate, York. Janssen and Maat (1999) report a 100% frequency of DISH in 27 canons from the Saint Servaas Basilica in Maastricht, the Netherlands, dated to AD 1070–1521. More recently, Jankauskas (2003) documented the frequency of DISH in Iron Age to early modern period skeletons from Lithuania with defined social status, as indicated by grave structure and/or burial location. He found that it increased with age, was associated with males more frequently, and high rates were found in the high social status individuals (27.1%) when compared to average or urban groups (11.9%), and rural or poor groups (7.1%). Clearly, DISH appears to be associated with monastic populations and possibly their diet in late medieval Europe particularly. However, comparisons of frequency between the Wharram Percy non-monastic population in North Yorkshire and monastic groups show similarities! As Mays (2006) intimates, if the people of rural Wharram Percy

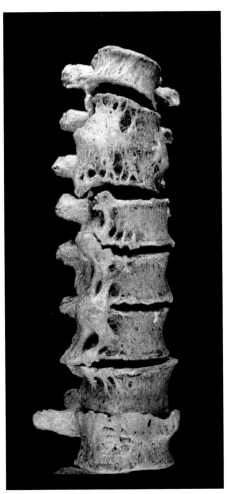

Figure 97: Spine affected by Diffuse Idiopathic Skeletal Hyperostosis, or DISH (Charlotte Roberts)

had a lower calorie intake then we would expect to see lower rates, and this is not the case. Julkunen *et al* (1971) also note that, although living people have a higher weight-height index if they have DISH and may be obese, because there are regional differences in rates, a direct association of DISH and obesity cannot be assumed. Further research may highlight other reasons for DISH such as the relative contribution genetic predisposition makes.

(iii) Work

Today, just as in past periods, our jobs may vary according to our age, sex, where we live, and our status. Most of us need to work to provide essentials such as housing, food, and clothes. However, as people become more financially secure, more consideration is given to earning spare cash for holidays and luxuries. Even so, improvements in living standards in the western world have not necessarily reduced some work-related health problems such as stress or injury. What evidence, then, can we gather from their remains about the work of our ancestors?

Past people initially worked to ensure food was available (hunting and gathering and farming) but, as society developed greater diversity, a wide range of manufactured produce was associated with complex societies who traded with others locally, regionally, nationally, and internationally. As has been noted above, occupationally induced health problems have been recognised for hundreds of years and Ramazzini was called the 'father of industrial medicine'. Although not something we can identify as existing in the more remote past, in recent times in the West, a plethora of rules and regulations regarding health and safety indicates how focused we are on keeping people safe at work. Nevertheless, we regularly hear about work-related injuries and illness, for example 'sick building syndrome', 'repetitive strain injury' and 'wool sorters' disease' (anthrax).

Our ancestors also suffered health problems as a result of the work they did. Although they had a close association with their animals and likely contracted their diseases, there is not space here to consider these potential health hazards (but see Baker and Brothwell 1980; Brothwell 1991; Swabe 1999; Davies *et al* 2005). There are a number of factors that might influence whether the impact of work is visible in the skeleton. The age at which a person started work will influence whether changes will occur in their skeleton, and the longer a person has done a particular task, the more likely it is that changes will be seen, ie if a job was commenced prior to skeletal maturity. The duration of the work will also influence whether we can recognise the 'job' in the skeleton. Did the person do work on a daily, weekly, or annual basis? For example, did they grind grain for flour to make bread every day, and for several hours, did they clean out the animals' stable once a week for two hours, did they harvest the crops in the fields once a year, or did they do all these tasks? Think about the many different tasks you might do during your daily life and throughout your whole life; there will be dozens of tasks and the question is how many of them might we be able to recognise in your skeleton?

There are a number of specific changes in the skeleton that might be present and can be interpreted as the result of an 'activity'. Essentially, bones can adapt to activity, and bone will change shape if it is placed under physical stress because it is 'plastic' in nature (Knüsel 2000). If somebody starts an 'activity' at a young age then the bone response via shape change will be greater. These changes may be work-related, but direct correlations are fraught with problems because the changes observed in the skeleton could be due to more than just 'occupation'. Indeed it is advocated that it would be safer if bioarchaeologists reconstructed body and limb 'movements' and not 'occupations', as is currently the norm. It should also be remembered that increasing age, obesity, and being female can all increase your likelihood of osteoarthritis, one of the main features in the skeleton used to reconstruct 'occupation' in the past (eg see Bridges 1994; but also Waldron 1994; and Jurmain 1999 for a balanced discussion). However, if a person is using a limb for a specific activity and does the activity regularly, this is likely to stress the joints severely in a particular pattern and lead to osteoarthritis (Figure 98).

There is no doubt that some 'activities' lead to osteoarthritis in certain joints today, for example in the elbow in pneumatic drill operators and in the ankles of ballet dancers, but there is not always a direct correlation, ie not all people who use a pneumatic drill get elbow osteoarthritis. Waldron and Cox (1989) found no correlation between hand osteoarthritis and weaving in skeletons from the Christ Church, Spitalfields site. On the other hand, activity-related

Figure 98:
Osteoarthritis of
the shoulder in
an Anglo-Saxon
individual from
Pewsey, Wiltshire
(left) – with the
opposite side
for comparison
(Charlotte Roberts)

disease was suggested by Stirland (2000) and Stirland and Waldron (1997) when they studied spinal osteoarthritis of young adult individuals recovered from the Tudor warship, the *Mary Rose* (see Chapter 3). There were 200 mariners, 185 soldiers and 30 gunners reported to have been on board, so an assessment of activity-related skeletal changes could be correlated with 'occupation'. As similar frequencies of spinal osteoarthritis were found to those in a population of older males from a late medieval site in Norwich, Norfolk, it was suggested that the activities undertaken by the crew of the *Mary Rose*, such as manhandling heavy guns, accelerated age-related changes in the spine. These people were probably a semi-permanent/part-time professional crew who had started their work as adolescents (Stirland and Waldron 1997). Other studies have also used osteoarthritis to study the impact of agriculture on the body (see Cohen and Armelagos 1984, for example).

Other markers in the skeleton that may be considered as representing 'activity' include the presence of enthesophytes (bone formation or destruction at tendon and ligament sites on bones), changes in the shape of bones, asymmetry of bone size and shape, and other features suggesting specific associations with an activity. Here we will consider enthesophytes, asymmetry, and other features. Much attention has been focused on enthesophytes in the reconstruction of activity in the past. These musculo-skeletal markers of stress at tendon and ligament insertions on bones indicate movement using specific muscles or groups of muscles (Figure 99). For example, Eshed *et al* (2004) observed them in the upper limb bones of hunter-gatherer and Neolithic agricultural populations in the Levant, and found that the upper limbs were more heavily used in the Neolithic than in earlier periods. Again, however, there are many predisposing factors to the development of these markers, as described in Jurmain (1999); these include age, hormonal, and genetic factors, dietary variables, disease, and activity. For example, Weiss (2003) in her study of muscle markers at seven sites in the upper limb bones documents that age is the best overall predictor of groups of muscle markers; in other words you get more as you age. Furthermore, before we even consider all those variables affecting development, the detailed anatomical and clinical basis for their occurrence has not even been explored, and new methods of recording need to be developed (Henderson and Gallant 2007). There have been some useful studies, including focusing on the pattern of involvement of major muscle groups to reflect specific movements. After all, we have so many muscles that can be moved in so many ways that lots of activities could replicate the same movements (McKinley pers comm, November 2007). Nevertheless, the main problem to overcome is still the fact that if patterns of enthesophytes cannot be seen to be related to a specific activity then the skeletal data alone are unconvincing (Jurmain 1999, 159).

Studies of the size and shape of limb bones have used metrical analysis of bones and features on radiographs as indicators of the use of one limb more than the other for an activity/movement. For example, professional tennis players develop increased size of the dominant arm, including its bones (Jones *et al* 1977, in Larsen 1997). The upper limb is usually used for analysis because lower limb asymmetry is smaller and more variable, and the arms are used for a multitude of tasks while the lower limbs are mainly used for locomotion (Larsen 1997, 213; Ruff 2000). Steele (2000) describes the subject of handedness and how it may be recognised in the skeleton, and some bioarchaeological studies have studied handedness related to activity. For example, Mays (1999) focused on the upper arm bones (humeri) of female and male lay people and a male monastic group from St Andrew, Fishergate, York. The results showed a difference in 'activity' between the males and females, and the male lay people and male monastic group. The humeral diaphyseal shaft strength values were lower in the monastic males, suggesting that these people did not do heavy work. This type of biomechanical analysis of skeletal remains from archaeological sites does hold potential for more research although it should be remembered that changes in size and shape of bones may be affected by many factors, including diet, biological sex, age,

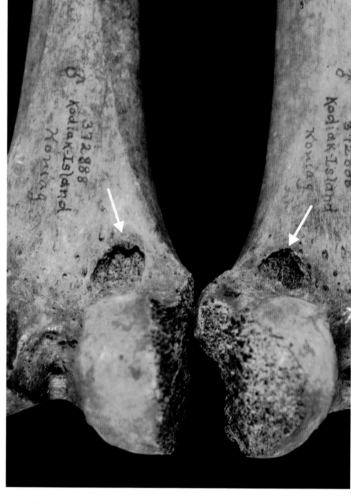

Figure 99: Destruction of bone on the posterior aspect of femurs of an adult male from Alaska as a result of strain of a muscle that helps to flex/bend the knee and foot (Charlotte Roberts)

genetic factors, environment (terrain), and activity (Jurmain 1999, 258). Jurmain adds that the type of loading, duration, amplitude, age at which loading began and stopped, bone element involved, and site within the bone element affected are all relevant for interpreting patterns that might help us to understand past activity.

Another specific variation from the normal provides us with a particular insight into activities in the past. New bone formation (exostosis) within the outer ear hole (external auditory meatus) has been suggested to correlate with immersion regularly in cold water (Figure 100). Kennedy (1986) suggested that lower frequencies might be expected in colder climates as people would not expose themselves to cold water; higher rates were found in people exploiting marine or fresh water resources in warmer climates. More recent studies have upheld these findings, although some do not agree. Standen *et al* (1997) studied ear exostoses in 1149 crania from 43 sites in northern Chile, dated from 7000 BC to AD 1450; a significant association was found between the condition and sex, and the condition and a coastal environment, which might be expected. Another study focused on ear exostoses in two skeletal samples of different social status (1st to 3rd centuries AD, Rome); it revealed no evidence in females but a higher frequency in the higher-status males (Manzi *et al* 1991). It was suggested that as males frequented thermal baths, they would also have experienced cold baths which could have induced the exostoses observed. The most recent study analysed 676 skeletons from 27 coastal and inland sites in Brazil, dating from 5000 years BP to the mid- to late 19th century AD (Okumura *et al* 2007). It found higher frequencies in the coastal groups but a large variation in frequency between sites; no significant differences between the sexes were seen,

Figure 100: Bone formation in the ear (ear exostosis) in an individual from Indian Knoll, Kentucky (Charlotte Roberts)

suggesting they all partook of 'aquatic activities'. This latter finding is supported by ethnographic accounts in other Brazilian regions of both men and women fishing. It was also suggested that the coastal findings reflect a combination of wind chill, lower atmospheric temperatures, and exposure to water via 'above-water' aquatic activities. An absence of exostoses does not necessarily mean no exposure to cold (or warm) water.

(iv) Conflict

In the media age, news about conflict around the world seems to be a constant feature of our lives. We hear and watch more about violence – both fictional and factual – and there are fewer taboos about violent imagery. Undoubtedly, media exposure and heightened awareness through better communication can lead us to think that we live in increasingly dangerous times. The study of human remains demonstrates, however, that conflict has beset populations with varying intensities since prehistory, although technology has contributed to humanity's capacity for more devastating violence.

What might we find out about violence in the past from studying skeletal remains? Was it the young or old, male or female that fought, and in what circumstances. Were settled communities or hunter-gatherers more likely to experience interpersonal aggression? What weapons and armour were used, what was the likelihood of surviving (and being treated)? Investigation of injury that either did or did not lead to death allows us to assess environmental (eg pressure on resources), and socio-cultural-political influences on how people behaved (Larsen 1997; Martin and Frayer 1998; Buzon and Richman 2007). The evidence of fortified settlements, weapons, armour, funerary contexts such as mass graves, historical writings, artistic representations of violence, and ethnographic evidence, means we are in a very good position to learn a lot about conflict in the past; it is something that has been with us from time immemorial. The evidence of interpersonal violence from skeletal remains includes head, facial (including dental fractures), neck and chest injuries, in addition to defence injuries to the hands and arms; there may also be injuries to other parts of the body depending on whether protective 'clothing' was worn. Decapitation, scalping, and cannibalism may also reflect violence, although evidence for these acts in the past are not ubiquitous around the world in the past (see summary in Roberts and Manchester 2005).

Skull injuries are often seen in past populations, and are usually more common in males (eg Walker 1989; Jurmain and Bellifemine 1997), often affecting the left side of the skull, suggesting hand to hand and face to face fighting of right-handed people. Fatal skull injuries tend to be singular. Facial injuries are less common, perhaps because the bones do not survive burial and excavation as well as the cranial vault. Nevertheless, nasal fractures have been noted (Walker 1997). The direction, force, and time taken to produce the injury will determine the type of skull fracture, along with the area of skull involved, and the size, shape, and velocity of the weapon used to produce it. In addition, the individual characteristics of the skull, hair, and scalp can ultimately affect the resulting fracture pattern (Gordon *et al* 1988). Boylston (2000) also notes that whether a person is moving or stationary, on a horse or on foot, or wearing protective armour, will affect the resulting fracture appearance. These are other factors to consider in the interpretation of head injuries, but are often forgotten in bioarchaeological contexts.

Three types of head injury are seen: the sharp, blunt, and projectile injury. Sharp injuries are usually the result of an edged weapon. The blunt injury, caused by a blunt instrument or a fall, usually results in a depressed fracture. The projectile injury is characterised by the velocity with which a weapon comes into contact with the body (Novak 2000, 91); in this latter type there are very obvious entry and exit wounds and extensive fracturing. All these injuries can produce radiating fractures away from the site of impact. Projectile injuries are rare archaeologically (but see Larsen *et al* 1996). Of course, the availability of different materials to produce projectile weapons changed through time from flint arrowheads to metal blades. Bennike (1985) reports weapons embedded in the pelvis, palate of the mouth, cervical vertebrae, and sternum of skeletons of various dates from the Neolithic (4200–1800 BC) to the Viking period (AD 800–1050), all leaving unhealed injuries. At the Battle of Towton, North Yorkshire, in AD 1461, there were many victims of violence but only around 40 individuals were found in the mass grave excavated (Fiorato *et al* 2000). Novak (2000) considered the evidence for trauma in the skeletons (Figure 101). Thirteen of 39 discrete burials had an average of about two postcranial wounds each, mostly in the forearms; defence injuries are suggested as the mechanism behind

Figure 101: Multiple sharp and penetrating force trauma on a male skull (skeleton 18) from Towton, North Yorkshire (with permission of the Biological Anthropology Research Centre, Archaeological Sciences, University of Bradford)

these injuries. Of 28 crania, 9 (32%) had healed trauma, with 27 having evidence of peri-mortem trauma (*c* four wounds per cranium). Sixty-five per cent were sharp weapon injuries, 25% blunt weapon injuries, and 10% puncture wounds. Most of the sharp and blunt injuries were interpreted as being the result of blows from the front in face to face combat. Twelve puncture wounds were seen in eight people, being mostly square shaped; arrowheads, poleaxes, top-spikes, war-hammers, swords, or cross-bow bolts were suggested as likely weapons producing these injuries. It is also evident that these soldiers were professional because of the healed and unhealed nature of their injuries. Bioarchaeologists, as we have seen, try to assess the types of weapon that have caused injuries on skulls, and forensic science research can help with interpretation (eg see Kanz and Grosschmidt 2006 and the head injuries of Roman Ephesus gladiators in Turkey). For example, Humphrey and Hutchinson (2001) and Tucker *et al* (2001) found differences in the characteristic macroscopic and microscopic features of wounds on fresh pig bone using machetes, axes, and cleavers. Of course an injury may be healed or unhealed and it is important to distinguish between the two as the latter may relate to cause of death; detailed guidelines for distinguishing ante-mortem, peri-mortem and post-mortem trauma are given by Lovell (1997).

Particular studies of trauma reveal how useful they are to explore the characteristics of a population. Walker (1989) analysed and compared trauma evident in skulls from the Californian mainland coast and the Northern Channel Islands in Southern California. Dating to between *c* 3500 BC and AD 1782, nearly 20% had one or more fractures, with males more affected than females, but the Island people had more injuries overall, possibly because there was competition for scarce resources. Another study, of five young adult male soldiers from a Crusader garrison in Vadum Iacob Castle, Galilee, Jerusalem dated to the 12th century AD, revealed multiple weapon injuries to the skull and other parts of the skeleton from the use of swords and arrows (Mitchell *et al* 2006). Historical data provided information that the castle was stormed in AD 1179 by invaders; the dead soldiers appeared to have been stripped of their armour and dumped with horses that also died in the battle. Finally, a study of 682 skulls from San Pedro de Atacama in Chile revealed a rise in cranial injuries through time from around 200 BC to a notable decline around AD 1400. This increase, especially in males, was associated with major droughts, fortified settlements, and an increase in population and poverty, all seen in the archaeological record. The decline occurred as environmental conditions improved, demonstrating that 'environmental stress', in its broadest sense, can contribute to interpersonal violence (Torres-Rouff and Costa Junqueira 2006).

Another indicator of interpersonal violence is seen in the form of decapitation, as evidenced by cut marks on cervical vertebrae and other parts of the body such as the mandible. We tend to assume that most decapitations were deliberate and the result of corporal punishment by another person (performed on living or dead people), although self-decapitation has been seen in a modern context (Prichard 1993). There may be other reasons for decapitation; these include interpersonal aggression causing trauma to the neck and leading to decapitation, mismanaged hanging, as a means to trophy or reliquary collection, and as a form of bloodletting (Boylston *et al* 2000). Decapitation also appears to be fairly frequent in Romano-British burials. For example, Boylston *et al* (2000) found twelve of the 92 3rd–4th century AD Romano-British burials at Kempston, Bedfordshire had been decapitated. In all the graves the skull had been placed near the lower legs or feet. Eight had been buried in the main cemetery and four had been buried in a ditched enclosure and classed as 'special'. Five of the twelve burials were made in coffins and five individuals had evidence of cut marks on their cervical vertebrae. It was hypothesised that these people were either already incapacitated or dead when they were beheaded, but some may have been casualties of armed conflict (*ibid*, 250). In a more recent study of an early 3rd-century AD Romano-British site in York (Driffield Terrace), over 40 younger males had been decapitated (Figure 102), such a large concentration in one cemetery being very rare (Hunter-Mann 2006). Most decapitated individuals have been found in Britain in late 4th- and early 5th-century cemeteries; at York most were decapitated from the front, which, along with their early date, is unusual.

Figure 102: Skeleton 45 from Driffield Terrace, York, showing his grave (a) (note head near pelvis) and a cut across a cervical vertebra (b), indicating decapitation (with permission of York Archaeological Trust)

(a)

(b)

(v) Access to health care

In Britain, National Insurance was introduced in the early 20th century. It gave a large part of the population a General Practitioner (GP) service and sickness benefits. In 1948 the National Health Service (NHS) was then founded, following the Beveridge Report (Bartley *et al* 1997).

In modern society in general, we know much more about why health problems occur and how we can prevent them happening. We also have access to detailed health information via the Internet. Furthermore, we are fortunate to be able to access effective drugs (antibiotics from the 1940s, and more recently effective cancer chemotherapy), as well as vaccination. Indeed, it is suggested that vaccination, despite uneven uptake, is one of the few areas of public health in Britain where everybody has access (Wilhelm Hagel 1990); in other countries, for example, boys are more likely to be vaccinated than girls (Borooah 2004). Clearly, where no programmes of such protection are available, poor child health can predispose individuals to health problems in adulthood, as seen in a study of North Americans (Blackwell *et al* 2001). Finally, the Genome Project (http://www.ornl.gov/sci/ techresources/Human_Genome/home.shtml) is also enabling the development of novel therapeutic regimens ('genomic medicine'); this may in the future include 'gene therapy' where disease-causing genes are replaced by 'normal' genes.

Although improved health provision has not been universal, nevertheless we are living longer, on average, than our ancestors – long enough for degenerative diseases such as cancer and heart problems to take their hold (Charlton and Murphy 1997). Infant mortality has declined too, even in recent years (Pearce and Goldblatt 2001; Charlton 1997). Females tend to live longer than males, and a recent survey suggested that by 2021 on average men will be living to 78.8 years and women to 82.9 years in England and Wales (Anonymous 2001), although the figures for Scotland are lower. This does of course vary considerably from region to region (eg see Shaw *et al* 2000), within each region, and between the sexes and social classes. However it is a fair generalisation that many live longer because of improved medical and surgical care and living conditions, as well as a cleaner environment.

There is evidence from prehistoric times onwards for the treatment of ailments, which would have benefited the overall health of that society, but it is clear from modern ethnographic parallels that there are differences in access to care in different groups in traditional developing and non-traditional developed societies. In pastoral communities, for example, health care availability for women may be controlled by men, and seasonal mobility will also affect access (Hampshire 2002). In some studies maternal and child health are indeed very poor, which may reflect access to health care, but other factors such as access to a good water supply should also be considered (Foggin *et al* 2006). Furthermore, in Britain today, those of lower social status and from ethnic minority groups, while accessing primary health care more than those of higher social status, seek secondary health care such as GP consultation and outpatient visits less often (Morris *et al* 2005). Men in Scotland are particularly reluctant to seek routine health care (O'Brien *et al* 2005).

So, how did our ancestors manage their health care? Indeed, did they have any health care at all? What health care was available for different subsistence bases? Did males or females get preference, and were the young and old cared for better than the not so young or old? How did that vary geographically and temporally?

There is extensive evidence from historical sources that medical and surgical care has existed for hundreds of years (eg see Conrad 1995; Porter 1997; Rawcliffe 1997). Physicians and surgeons practised alongside other groups, such as bone setters, who focused on treating specific ailments. While some diagnostic methods and techniques of treatment might seem unfamiliar to us today, and were very much related to society's concepts of disease occurrence (see Cawthorne 2005), there are some that have remained with us for a long time. For example, examination of the urine, blood, and faeces, and taking the pulse all featured strongly as diagnostic tests for the medieval physician (Rawcliffe 1997), diagnostic tests that are still used today by health practitioners.

Different treatments were also widely available at this time and included dietary measures, medication, and laxatives (often herbal remedies – see Zias *et al* 1993; Ilani *et al* 1999; Ciaraldi 2000), letting of blood, cautery (applying hot 'irons' on affected parts of the body), and bathing. These were all aimed at restoring the balance of the humours (see above, Introduction) but the use of treatments was also very much linked to astrology and when it was best to treat health problems of specific parts of the body. Surgical treatments were used in the medieval period and included setting broken bones and performing amputations and trepanations; surgeons were also the ones who let blood and practised cautery. There is a wealth of evidence for the founding of hospitals by rich benefactors (Figure 103), especially in the late medieval period (Orme and Webster 1995). Some were general hospitals while others were specifically for treating people with leprosy (Rawcliffe 2006), with later ones for tuberculosis (see Bryder 1988).

Figure 103: The late medieval leprosy hospital of St Mary Magdalen at Sprowston, Norwich, Norfolk, founded in AD 1119 (with permission of Carole Rawcliffe)

Earlier hospitals have been noted from the Roman period, specifically for the army (eg at Housesteads fort on Hadrian's Wall – Penn 1964; also see Baker 2004). At the start of the late medieval period there were 69 hospitals; by its end there were around 700. Medieval hospitals not only served the poor but also performed a variety of other functions. They served the needs (not always medical) of people such as travellers, elderly priests, children, and people who had 'fallen on hard times' (Rawcliffe 1997, 205); in fact some hospitals refused to admit the very ill. The rich were treated at home. Few hospital sites and their associated cemeteries have been excavated in Britain but examples include: the hospital of St Leonard, Newark,

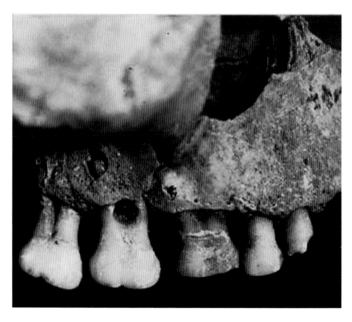

Figure 104: Drilled tooth from a Middle Neolithic individual from Denmark dated to 3200–1800 BC (with permission of Pia Bennike)

Nottinghamshire (Bishop 1983); the leprosy hospital at Chichester, Sussex (Lee and Magilton 1989; Magilton *et al* 2008); the hospital of St Giles, Brough, Yorkshire (Cardwell 1995); the priory and hospital of St Mary Spital, London (Thomas *et al* 1997); and St Bartholomew's Hospital, Bristol, Avon (Price with Ponsford 1998).

The evidence from skeletal remains for the care and treatment of disease and injury is very scarce but includes amputation, trepanation, the use of copper plates for wounds and infections, dentistry (eg see examples from Bennike and Fredebo 1986 and Figure 104; Zias and Numeroff 1987; Whittaker 1993) and (but more subjective in interpretation) the survival of what appear to be disabled people, apparently indicating proactive care (but see Roberts 2000; Lebel and Trinkaus 2002; DeGusta 2002, 2003). For a general review of the evidence for amputation, trepanation, and dental care in Britain, see Roberts and Cox (2003). The surgical treatment of ailments requires some knowledge of human anatomy but anatomical knowledge was gained late in the medieval period in Europe, and developed with the artistic products of Leonardo da Vinci, Vesalius, and Michelangelo during the 15th and 16th centuries. Surgeons further emphasised that human anatomy needed to be understood to become a good surgeon, with a 14th-century surgeon in France stating that, 'the surgeon ignorant of anatomy carves the human body as a blind man carves wood' (MacKinney 1957, 402).

Amputation has been carried out for a long time although it is not seen very commonly in skeletal remains. It was usually done to remove a badly injured appendage following battle or a domestic/industrial accident, but also in the treatment of disease such as severe infection (eg leprosy), and as a punishment for some misdemeanour. A particularly horrific use of amputation is described by Brothwell and Møller-Christensen (1963) where, from the 19th Dynasty (Egypt), or 1295–1186 BC, the hands of prisoners were amputated to allow the number of prisoners to be counted. Amongst the reasons for the rarity of skeletal evidence of amputation are the likelihood that the person died during the operation through haemorrhage, with no healing of the stump; this scenario might be missed by bioarchaeologists if the cut end of the bone is mistaken for a post-mortem break. False limbs and crutches are rare too, but probably because they were made of materials that do not survive burial and excavation; it may also be that they are not recognised as such because other everyday items might have been used for the purpose. However, numerous illustrations show that artificial limbs and crutches were used, most notably in the medieval period (Epstein 1937). Mays (1996) provides a useful review of amputations in the bioarchaeological record from the Old World. In one example, Bloom *et al* (1996) discuss a skeleton of an adult male dated to 3600 years old from Israel with an amputated hand, the amputation showing clear evidence of healing. A unique example comes from evidence for the amputation of the big toe in an adult female mummy from the necropolis of Thebes-West, Egypt (*c* 1550–1300 BC). Here, the toe had been replaced with a wooden false toe (Nerlich *et al* 2000; Figure 105). Evidence from the New World is less but Ortner (2003), Aufderheide and Rodríguez Martín (1998), and Verano *et al* (2000) describe some examples from South America. Verano's evidence consists of three probable foot amputations from Peru dated to AD 100–750; interesting here is the fact that the amputations correlate well with Moche ceramic depictions of people who do not have feet.

Figure 105: Mummy from Thebes-West, Egypt, with amputated toe and artificial wooden toe in its place; 1550–1300 BC (with permission of Andreas Nerlich and Albert Zink)

Trepanation is also a practice that has been known from thousands of years ago, the operation being noted in Europe as early as the Neolithic period. It was first recorded by Hippocrates, the Greek medical writer in the 5th century BC (Mariani-Costantini *et al* 2000). Why was it done? A number of suggestions have been made: for headaches, epilepsy, migraine, head injuries (eg see a recent example of a healed Neolithic trepanation and head injury from Germany – Weber and Wahl 2006), 'to let the spirits out', and to treat certain conditions. For example, Zias and Pomeranz (1992) suggest that 5500 years ago three trepanations were performed on an individual in Israel for sinus infection, while Mogle and Zias (1995) think an attempt to treat scurvy by trepanation is evident in an 8/9-year-old child from 2200 BC, also in Israel. Furthermore, Smrčka *et al* (2003) describe trepanation in a male with a tumour of the meninges of the brain (AD 1298–1550).

The operation involves removing a piece of the skull, which means that the practice is potentially visible in the bioarchaeological record. Once the piece has been removed the outer membrane of the brain is exposed which provides a 'nice' entry for infection, one of the greatest risks. While neurosurgeons today do this operation under controlled conditions, with their patients under anaesthesia, and with the prospect of preventing and treating infections with antibiotics, our ancestors were not so lucky. If infection did not occur and the major blood vessels were avoided, although the person could have developed brain damage (not easy to determine with only a skull to observe), he or she might be expected to have survived the surgery. Indeed, this seems to have been the case because there are a surprising number of people with healed trepanations. Some people even survived more than one operation, for example as seen in the skull of someone who had seven healed holes (Oakley *et al* 1959). Thousands of ancient examples of trepanations exist (see Arnott *et al* 2003 for a recent survey; and Aufderheide and Rodríguez-Martín 1998), and Piggott (1940) suggests that the 'home' of trepanations may have been in central and northern Europe.

There are five types of trepanation that have been observed in the bioarchaeological record and to a certain extent they reflect what materials were available for the surgical implement used to make the hole: scraped, gouged, bored and sawn, square sawn, and drilled. The scraped method appears quite common in Europe and the sawing types in South America (eg see recent work by Verano 2003; Nystrom 2007). A recent study of trepanations in Britain by Roberts and McKinley (2003) documented 62 trepanations dating from the Neolithic (4000–2000 BC) to the post-medieval period (post-16th century AD) – Figure 106. The majority derived from the early medieval/Anglo-Saxon period (5th–11th centuries) and most were found in males (64.5%). In 43 of the skulls there was no evidence for the reason for the operation but in eight examples there was clear evidence of a head injury, with all except one being healed. Nearly two-thirds of the trepanations had healed. Most interesting was the fact that the vast majority of individuals with trepanations had been excavated from funerary contexts 'normal' for that particular period of time, indicating that people who had been trepanned were generally not treated any differently to their peers through time. Only one of the Iron Age examples may have been a ritual deposit, and one early medieval burial was deposited prone in a Roman villa complex.

Like trepanation and amputation, the treatment of long bone fractures is seen in historical and artistic representations; we also see good attempts in some developing societies to treat fractures using traditional methods (Huber and Anderson 1995), again described originally by Hippocrates in 5th-century BC Greece. Reduction of

Figure 106:
Trepanation in a
Roman individual
from Oxborough,
Norfolk (with
permission
of Jacqueline
McKinley)

the broken bones, or pulling the bone ends apart and putting them into the right position, and splinting them (holding them in the right position until they heal) were described and are necessary procedures for treating long bone fractures, as seen today. While traditional groups might use reeds, bamboo, bark or clay to splint limbs that are fractured, plaster of Paris and other substances are recent developments. Open surgical splinting with plates and screws is also common today. Hippocrates recommended maintaining the reduced fracture with pads and bandages reinforced with clay and starch; he also suggested eating a balanced healthy diet. Herbal remedies were used for fractures as well as wounds, and include 'knitbone' (comfrey) and 'bonewort' (violet or pansy), mixed with egg white, which contains protein for healing (Bonser 1963). In the archaeological record, it is likely that splints were made of organic materials and common everyday objects were also used such that they are invisible to us. However, very rare examples of splints have been found (eg Elliot-Smith 1908; Figure 107); here bark splints were held in place with linen bandages on a fractured forearm in a mummy dated to 5000 BC. Assessing how well a fracture has healed also provides a window of opportunity to examine how well people treated fractures in the past (eg see Roberts 1988a and b, 1991; Grauer and Roberts 1996; Neri and Lancellotti 2004; Mitchell 2006). For example, Roberts (1988b) found that fractures from British Roman and early medieval contexts healed better than those from later periods. Mitchell (2006) also found that lower limb spiral fractures had healed well in his sample, suggesting that surgeons had successfully treated these people from Crusader period Caesarea in the Eastern Mediterranean.

Other direct evidence for treatment seen in skeletal remains includes the use of copper-alloy plating on infected wounds and injuries. They have been found in medieval contexts in Sweden, Belgium, and England. In Sweden, Hällback (1976–77) described copper-alloy plates on the humerus of an individual buried in the late medieval period, while Janssens (1987) documents a skeleton of 16th- to 17th-century date from Sweden, again with copper-alloy plates around the humerus. In Britain, there is evidence from a late medieval skeleton from Reading, Berkshire (Wells 1964; Figure 108), recently described as being from the leprosy hospital of St Mary Magdalene (Gilchrist and Sloane 2006). Here, the two copper plates were lined with dock leaves, a herb used to treat skin disease; it is possible that there was some confusion between skin disease per se and the skin lesions of leprosy. Three other examples of copper-alloy plates from English

Figure 107: Bark splints around the bones of a forearm, Egypt (Charlotte Roberts)

Figure 108: Copper plate around a humerus from an individual from the late medieval cemetery of the leprosy hospital of St Mary Magdalene, Reading (Charlotte Roberts)

cemeteries have recently been highlighted (*ibid*): two with males at St Mary, Stratford Langthorne, Essex (*c* 1230–1350; Barber *et al* 2004), another with a male at St Mary Spital, London (Gilchrist and Sloane 2006), and others with two adult skeletons from the Cluniac priory at Pontefract, Yorkshire. The Swedish (Hällback, 1976–77) and English (Wells 1964) examples provide evidence also for ante-mortem disease or trauma. A further case of copper-alloy plate application, but this time to the knee, is described by Knüsel *et al* (1995) in a 13th- to 14th-century AD male individual from the St Andrew, Fishergate, site in York. Here, the plates were perforated around their edges, probably for carrying binding or stitching to hold the plates in place. It appears that our ancestors were well aware, as we are, of the therapeutic effect of copper in combating infections.

Clearly, when in pain, people in the past did not necessarily sit and suffer; there is evidence for care and treatment but little, relatively speaking, from skeletal remains. The quality and quantity of care would, however, have varied from region to region in Britain, as well as between the sexes, ages and those of different social status, thus making for inequality in access, as we see today. We would also expect to see differences in access according to the subsistence economy, whereby agricultural communities would be more likely to have the resources and facilities to care for ill people because they were sedentary, compared to hunter-gatherers who had temporary dwellings and were very mobile.

6.5 Summary

Palaeopathology, or the study of disease in human remains from archaeological sites is, like any area of human remains study, a multidisciplinary holistic exploration which places the evidence from human remains in their archaeological context. While there are limitations to the study of palaeopathology, documented above, it provides a useful window on the health and welfare of our ancestors, and it can be studied thematically to illustrate the impact of people's lifestyles on their health, and in turn how their health might have affected the way society functioned in the past.

Key learning points

- All people in the past, as today, will have suffered ill health at some time
- Ill health affects how you function in life
- The study of palaeopathology is holistic and multidisciplinary using different methods of analysis
- Many diseases do not affect the skeleton
- We only see what people suffered during their lives and rarely what caused their death
- Population-based studies are key to understanding health and welfare in the past
- Concepts of disease occurrence determine treatment today as they did in the past
- Human remains are the primary source of evidence for disease
- Secondary sources include art and documentary evidence, supplemented by observations in medical anthropology
- Bone formation, bone destruction, and lesion distribution in the skeleton are used to attempt to diagnose disease

- Bone changes in disease may be similar in different diseases
- There is an osteological paradox in palaeopathology
- Standardisation of recording of pathological lesions is essential
- Palaeopathology should be studied within an archaeological context, and through themed approaches, eg living conditions, diet, work, conflict, and access to health care

CHAPTER SEVEN

Recording and analysis of data III: the 'hard sciences'

A scientific tool is only as good as the quality of the question to which it is applied

(Pollard 2001, 298)

7.1 Introduction

The study of skeletal remains from archaeological sites more often than not utilises non-invasive, relatively straightforward, and cheap methods of analysis. Preserved bodies, on the other hand, by the very nature of their preservation (soft tissues), have probably had a greater range of more sophisticated methods of analysis applied to them (see Aufderheide 2000 for a survey). Many bioarchaeologists do not have the time, expertise, or money to access these methods, but nevertheless, over the years we have seen an increase in the number and variety of destructive techniques applied generally to human remains in order to generate more detailed and informative data on aspects of people's lives in the past. It is, of course, accepted that the field of bioarchaeological research is ever moving forward, and new techniques of analysis are attractive to funding bodies. We must not 'run before we can walk', however, and we should be very careful about destroying irreplaceable samples of bone, teeth, and other tissues unless we can be certain of the value of doing so. Having questions to answer or hypotheses to test, along with placing the data in an archaeological/social context, are certainly pre-requisites for any destructive analyses.

This chapter covers the use of histological, radiographic, biomolecular, and dating methods for human skeletal remains, providing examples of work, limitations, and future directions. It does not give details of preparation of samples for the methods but rather illustrates the uses of the techniques. The reader is directed to general papers on the subject for those details. It also focuses on the use of the methods for our better understanding of health and disease patterns.

7.2 Histology

Histological methods of analysis allow the study of the microscopic structure of the tissues of the body. They were first used at the end of the 19th century to look at the microstructure of fossil bone (Schultz 2001). To use these methods effectively, an excellent knowledge of the normal microstructural appearance of the body tissues is needed in order that normal and abnormal variation (and

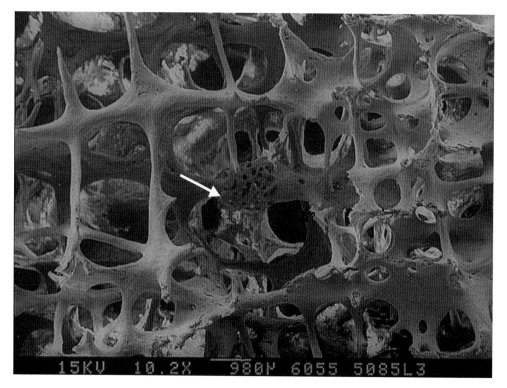

Figure 109: Scanning electron microscope image of a section of a lumbar vertebra in an Anglo-Saxon individual from Raunds, Northamptonshire, showing a microfracture, probably a consequence of osteoporosis (Charlotte Roberts)

post-mortem changes) can be recognised in bioarchaeological samples (eg see scanning electron microscopy study of ribs and vertebrae by Wakeley *et al* 1989; Figure 109).

Histological methods can be applied to skeletal material for a variety of reasons; some examples of use include: to assess post-mortem change (eg Hackett 1981; Garland 1987; Garland *et al* 1988; Bell 1990; Schultz 2001); to assess biomolecular preservation (eg Schultz 2001; Haynes *et al* 2002); to determine age at death using bones or teeth (eg Aiello and Molleson 1993; Hillson 1996a; Robling and Stout 2000; Renz and Radlanski 2006; Chan *et al* 2007); to differentiate between animal and human bone (eg Owsley *et al* 1985; Harsanyi 1993); to diagnose disease (eg Aaron *et al* 1992; Schultz 2001; Strouhal and Němečková 2004); to consider the impact of activity (eg Lazenby and Pfeiffer 1993); to look at diet through analysis of specific materials such as dental calculus (plaque – eg Dobney and Brothwell 1988; Boyadjian *et al* 2007; Figures 110 and 111); or dental microwear (eg Hillson 1996a; Perez-Perez 2003; Mahoney 2006; Figure 112); and to look at details of surgical interventions such as tooth drilling or trepanation (eg Bennike and Fredebo 1986; Stevens and Wakely 1993; Seidel *et al* 2006). Whilst they provide a greater level of detail which can be used for interpretation, there is little training available for bioarchaeologists, and the methods are destructive; before using such methods, a serious reason for pursuing this type of analysis should be identified. In addition, the costs in time and money can be prohibitive for many (see Aufderheide 2000 for an assessment of costs for different methods); the cost

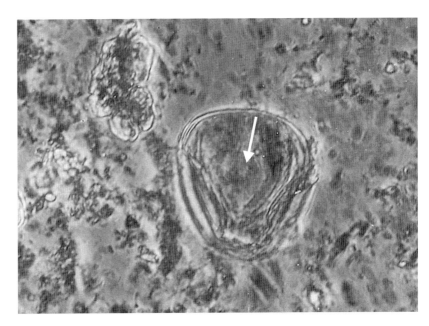

Figure 110 (right): Histological image of a pollen grain preserved in human medieval calculus (with permission of Keith Dobney)

Figure 111 (below left): Histological image of human dental calculus showing the build up of layers (with permission of Keith Dobney)

Figure 112 (below right): Dental microwear on a molar tooth from an adult male skeleton from the Meriotic period cemetery at Semna South, Sudanese Nubia (dated to 100 BC–AD 500): frequent dental scratches and some pits reflect a tough abrasive diet requiring shearing forces for effective mastication (with permission of Patrick Mahoney)

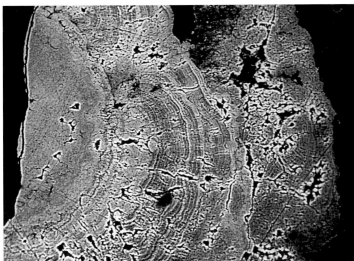

of the 'microscope' itself, the running of it (maintenance, technical support), sample preparation, and the time involved, can discourage many people who may find it useful.

There are a number of methods of histological (or histomorphological) analysis that may be used to analyse samples of bones and teeth, incorporating a range of hardware: transmitted light microscopy (TLM); scanning electron microscopy (SEM); transmission electron microscopy (TEM); and confocal reflecting scanning laser light microscopy (CRSM). Bioarchaeologists also use a traditional magnifying glass when needing to get a closer look at bones and teeth, and often this works very well. Microradiography, another 'histological' method, is covered in the next section (Radiography).

TLM is the most frequent method used and involves creating a thin section from the material (bone or tooth) and visualising it under a light microscope at low power magnification (Bell and Piper 2000; Pfeiffer 2000). SEM provides a 3D surface picture of the sample and involves a much higher magnification of around x1000. The SEM can also be used in 'backscattered' mode where elements in the sample can be analysed and the degree of mineralisation may be examined, for example in disease (Bell and Piper 2000). The TEM provides greater magnification compared to the SEM and can enable the visualisation of internal bone cell structures (*ibid*). The confocal reflecting scanning laser light microscope is the most recent development and can focus on specific areas of a sample, and capture the image digitally, ultimately being able to generate a 3D image. It functions at the micron and submicron levels (*ibid*). Schultz (2001) considers that palaeohistological diagnosis of disease provides a more reliable diagnosis, and many studies have been done to identify the features of specific diseases. Some of those diseases identified histologically in bioarchaeological skeletal samples include Paget's disease, fluorosis, rickets, scurvy, anaemia, osteoporosis, infections, and tumours; essentially, disease changes the microstructure of bone such that identification can aid diagnosis.

For example, Schultz and Roberts (2002) identified structures, albeit poorly developed, called 'polsters' (padding) and 'grenzstreifen' (border stripes) in bone sections from lower leg bones (tibiae) of individuals who suffered leprosy in the late medieval period in England. Whilst polsters and grenzstreifen are usually associated with treponemal disease affecting those bones, it was felt that the changes seen in the histological analyses could equally have been caused by leprosy (a conclusion also reached by Blondiaux *et al* 2002 on their study of two 5th-century French individuals with leprosy). In a more recent study, Von Hunnius *et al* (2006) used histological analysis of bone sections from individuals with venereal syphilis from the late medieval Hull Magistrates Court site, England, to confirm the diagnosis. They suggest that polsters and grenzstreifen are useful as a 'rough guide for identifying syphilis in bone sections' (*ibid*, 564), but that they vary considerably in size and shape. However, many diseases, including leprosy and other treponemal diseases such as yaws and endemic syphilis, can produce these changes and, therefore, they cannot be specifically associated with venereal syphilis.

SEM has seen wide use in palaeopathology. For example, Maat and Baig (1991) found fossilised sickle cells in a rib section from a 2000-year-old skeleton which helped to diagnose the type of anaemia the person had suffered from, along with skeletal changes in the skull (Figure 113). Traumatic lesions have also been a focal point for SEM studies. Hogue (2006) used SEM and light microscopy to determine what tool was used to make cut marks on the skull of a young male from Mississippi, USA, dated to between AD 1640 and 1814. Cut marks were made on a sample skull with a stone flake, a stone knife, two different metal knives and three different cane knives. Casts of the marks were made and also of the cut marks on the skull and then visualised using microscopy. Stone and heat-treated canes appeared to be the causes of the cut marks and the analysis also indicated

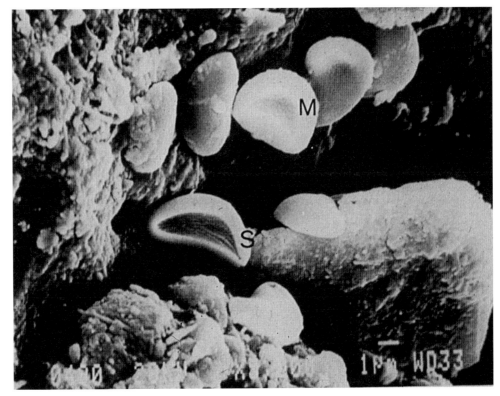

Figure 113: Scanning electron microscope image of a section of rib from a 2000-year-old skeleton showing a sickle cell (S) (with permission of George Maat)

that the person had been scalped. Another experimental SEM study to assess the impact of stone-tipped projectile weapons on bone was undertaken by Smith *et al* (2007). Samples of fresh animal bone were used and the data generated suggested that the use of flint-tipped weapons to inflict traumatic lesions on bone could be identified microscopically (and macroscopically). Furthermore, small fragments of the flint appear to be left embedded in the bone.

The study of metabolic disease has also received attention using microscopic methods. Roberts and Wakely (1992) and Brickley and Howell (1999) found thinning of the vertical and horizontal 'struts' of trabecular bone in vertebrae and microfractures as indicators of osteoporosis, suggesting these features might be used to diagnose osteoporosis in bioarchaeology. A more recent study identified skeletal changes in infants indicative of scurvy in a post-medieval cemetery from Birmingham (Brickley and Ives 2006). The study used SEM to examine more closely the porous changes seen in this condition and was able to differentiate normal porosity seen in growing children's bones from pathological changes resulting from scurvy. Brickley *et al* (2007) also used SEM in backscattered mode to consider bone changes due to osteomalacia in adult skeletons from the same site (Figure 114). They found defective rapidly formed new bone with evidence of poor mineralisation; when compared to bone from a modern clinical hip with a diagnosis of osteomalacia, the appearance was the same.

More indirect histological analyses that have a bearing on health and disease are those recently identified by Blondiaux *et al* (2006). One hundred and twelve

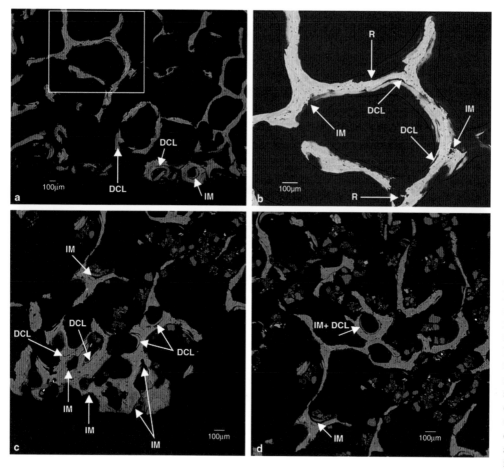

Figure 114: Example of disease shown in a histological image. Backscattered scanning electron microscope images of bone defects of osteomalacia in clinical and archaeological bone: (a) = clinical example of iliac crest biopsy (defective mineralised cement lines visible – DCL and incomplete bone mineralisation – IM); (b) = detail of (a) showing large areas of bone resorption with no replacement of mineralised new bone, inadequate mineralisation of new bone (IM) and stretches of defective cement lines (DCL); (c) = archaeological example of an affected rib: incomplete mineralisation (IM) and defective cement lines (DCL); (d) = archaeological example of an affected rib with poor mineralisation (IM and DCL) (with permission of Alan Boyde, Megan Brickley, and *American Journal of Physical Anthropology*)

teeth from individuals of known age, and 128 bioarchaeological teeth (from 110 people, 16 with evidence of tuberculosis) from eight archaeological sites in northern France were microscopically analysed to assess age at death and the impact of tuberculosis on the appearance of the 'rings' of cement on their roots. It was found that the rings (or annulations) correlated with the occurrence of tuberculosis. Other studies of teeth have used the analysis of the presence of 'Wilson's' bands in enamel to assess health. Fitzgerald *et al* (2006) studied 274 deciduous teeth from 127 non-adult skeletons from a Roman site called Isola Sacra in Rome (2nd–3rd century AD). Wilson's bands are microscopic defects in enamel caused by disruption to development caused by 'stress'. It is possible to attach precise timings to the formation of these bands, and thus was possible to say that there were two periods of high prevalence, at around age two to five months, and another between six and nine months; these appeared to correlate with historical data indicating weaning and the use of supplementary foods.

7.3 Radiography

Radiography is usually the second most common method of analysis used on human remains. Discovered in 1895 by William Conrad Roentgen, X-rays produce radiographic images on film of radiographed 'objects' such as bones; soon after X-rays had been discovered, mummies of both humans and animals from Egypt were being radiographed. Like histology, there are a number of different methods used. Plain film radiography is the most commonly used type of radiographic analysis in bioarchaeology (Figure 115), while microradiography, computed tomography (CT) and, specifically for a diagnosis of osteoporosis, dual-energy X-ray absorptiometry (DEXA) and Energy Dispersive Low Angle X-ray Scattering (EDLAXS) have also been applied to skeletal remains (the latter however has a number of problems, outlined by Brickley 2000 in her review of the diagnosis of osteoporosis in bioarchaeology). Each provides a visualisation analysis of the interior of bones, teeth, and soft tissues, but some can also give details of the mineral content of the tissues. Portable plain film radiographic and CT machines exist that can be taken into the 'field', be it a museum, excavation, or other situation where skeletal material cannot be taken away for analysis.

In plain film radiography a 2D, life-size image of the bone is produced. X-rays pass through the bone or other tissues to differing degrees, depending on their density. This is why the settings on the machine used to produce radiographs vary according to the size and density of the different bones of the body. The disadvantages of plain film radiography are that post-mortem damage of skeletal remains can affect what can be seen, a 3D 'object' is reduced to a 2D image, X-rays can damage DNA and thus prevent bones radiographed from being used for aDNA analysis, and subtle bone formation on bones may not be seen radiographically. The advantages are that it is a relatively cheap method to use, the equipment and facilities often exist in museums and universities, it is non-destructive, and it can be used to visualise internal pathological conditions or other features before they become visible externally. For example, Rothschild and Rothschild (1995) used

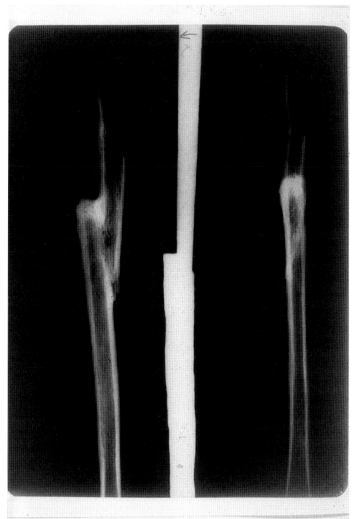

Figure 115: Plain film radiography: two views of a healed fractured fibula with overlapping of the fractured ends (Charlotte Roberts)

radiography and macroscopic analysis to assess the presence of skeletal changes of cancer in 128 known individuals diagnosed with the condition. While 33 were identified radiographically, only 11 were identified macroscopically.

Microradiography also produces a 2D image, and consists of producing contact radiographs on glass plates using sections of bone or teeth; it can show the degree of mineralisation of bones and may be used for disease diagnosis and for assessing post-mortem changes (eg see Garland 1987; Blondiaux *et al* 1994, 2002). CT produces images from thin 'slices' taken through an 'object' which may be a bone, tooth, or even a mummy. These digitally transformed cross-sectional images represent 'slices' 1–10mm thick; by manipulating the images with a computer, a 3D image may ultimately be recreated. CT has become an increasingly useful analytical technique for mummified bodies (Aufderheide 2000). Of course, the cost of creating a CT image compared to a plain film radiograph is very different and, as Aufderheide (2000, 380) says, because of this there is a 'powerful incentive to employ this potentially valuable diagnostic tool in a highly selective manner'.

Radiographic analysis can be used to generate information on a number of subject areas in human bioarchaeology: post-mortem changes and damage, differentiation of human and animal bone (eg Chilvarquer *et al* 1991), age at death in both adults and non-adults (eg Walker and Lovejoy 1985; Sorg *et al* 1989; Beyer Olsen 1994), trauma and disease (eg Roberts 1988; Grauer and Roberts 1996; Boylston and Ogden 2005; Mays 2005a), and the impact of activity/ occupation on bone (eg Wescott and Cunningham 2006).

The range of diseases that has been studied using radiography is wide and includes dental, joint and infectious disease, as well as trauma and metabolic, endocrine, and neoplastic conditions. Very straightforward applications of plain film radiography have been made, for example confirming a diagnosis of rheumatoid arthritis in a medieval skeleton from Abingdon Abbey in Oxfordshire (Hacking *et al* 1994) and of Paget's disease in a late medieval adult female skeleton from Norton Priory in Cheshire (Boylston and Ogden 2005). By comparing the changes seen in the skeletal remains with clinical descriptions and images of radiographic changes, it was possible to propose a disease diagnosis, although allowance had to be made for post-mortem damage, and it was assumed that radiographic changes were the same in the past as they are today. Another example of this process comes from the study of vertebrae from a 16th- to 19th-century ossuary in a Clarist monastery in southern Portugal. Two vertebrae had radiographic and macroscopic changes attributable to brucellosis, a disease of animals transmitted to humans via infected dairy products and close contact with goats and sheep (Curate 2006). Mays *et al* (2006a) also highlight plain film radiographic features of rickets (vitamin D deficiency) in infants and young children from St Martin's churchyard, Birmingham. These included coarse trabeculae, loss of the cortex-medullary cavity distinction, and biomechanical alterations. As noted above, plain film radiography can show lesions of a disease that are not all visible macroscopically but in the case of a 31-year-old female from 18th-century London, multiple destructive lesions in her skeleton indicative of metastases or 'secondaries' were also identified (Melikian 2006).

Osteoporosis, or loss of bone mass with age (usually), has received much attention through analysis of skeletal remains using plain film radiography and DEXA. Plain film radiographs are taken of the 2nd metacarpal and the total width and medullary cavity width are measured at the midpoint of the radiograph; the total amount of cortical bone is then calculated. In their study, Ives and Brickley (2005) found that cortical bone loss correlated well with bone loss elsewhere in the body where trabecular bone dominates. Mays (2005b), using the same method, found that 3rd- to 4th-century AD women from Ancaster, Lincolnshire, had a greater degree of post-menopausal bone loss than modern reference data. DEXA analysis of bone will show, additionally, a pattern of radiation absorption that allows bone mineral content and density to be assessed, and whether osteoporosis can be diagnosed (Ives and Brickley 2005). Mays *et al* (2006b) explored the frequency of osteoporosis using DEXA in medieval Norwegians and compared the data with information from individuals buried at the site of the late medieval Wharram Percy in North Yorkshire. Both modern and bioarchaeological data indicate that osteoporotic fractures are more common in Norway and may be due to the colder climate and harder surfaces on to which people fall (packed with snow and ice).

Another popular radiographic technique that is now being used on skeletal and mummified remains is computed tomography, ranging from the analysis of trepanations (Weber and Wahl 2006), injuries (Pernter *et al* 2007; Ryan and Milner 2006), and age changes (Macho *et al* 2005), to biomechanical interpretations reflecting mobility/activity. For example, Rühli *et al* (2002) applied CT analysis to three skulls with lesions of unclear origin. In two cases it was determined that the lesions were ante-mortem and in the other of post-mortem origin. Probably the most common application of CT in bioarchaeology is for biomechanical study (eg see Ruff 2000), where it has been used to look at the impact on bone of subsistence activities and labour. The body of literature is vast and therefore only a few examples will be presented here. Sládek *et al* (2006a and b, 2007) used CT to try and understand better the absence of settlements in the Late Eneolithic (2900–2300 BC) in Lower Austria, Bohemia, and Moravia when compared to the early Bronze Age. This absence had been explained by archaeologists, rather unsatisfactorily, as a consequence of a pastoral subsistence and a high degree of mobility in the Eneolithic (ie moving seasonally with their herds of animals). CT scanning of femurs (151), tibiae (130), and humeri (67) revealed no differences in cross-sectional shape between the two periods, thus indicating that the transition between the Eneolithic and the early Bronze Age was a continuous process, suggesting that people's 'mobility' was the same. However, there were differences between the males and females in both periods and this was suggested to reflect gender-specific activity. This is a good example of bioarchaeological analysis being used to address a particular archaeological question where other explanations had been found unsatisfactory.

Of course technology moves on and CT provides ever-more detailed information not only for doctors today treating living patients, but also for

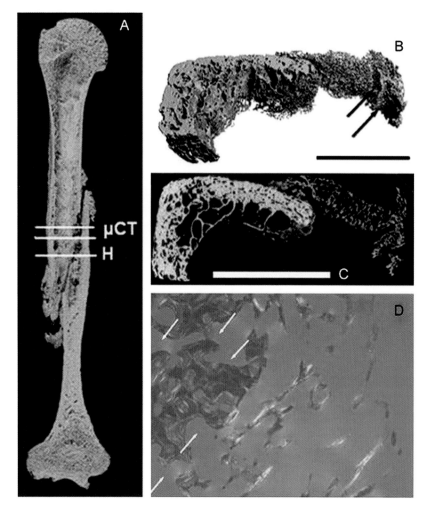

Figure 116: Example of microCT of a humerus fracture (Kuhn *et al* 2007, 105):

(A) = macroscopic appearance – white lines show where samples were taken for µCT and histology (H);

(B) = 3D µCT reconstruction – compact bone on left and fracture callus (woven bone) on right; arrows point to blood vessels in callus; scale is 10mm;

(C) = 2D µCT slice with cortical bone on left and callus on right (grey-value image; scale 10mm);

(D) = polarised light microscopic image; cortical bone on left and callus on right. Arrows show resorption lacunae in compact bone; magnification approximately x25 (reprinted with permission from Elsevier)

bioarchaeologists. For example Ryan and Milner (2006) used high resolution CT to observe a chert arrowhead in a 700-year-old tibia from a site in Illinois, USA. The shape and size of the arrowhead, the body's response at the bone trabecular level, and the possible direction the arrowhead came from were all identified. In fact, the woman had survived the injury and lived with the arrowhead embedded in her lower leg for some time. Increasingly, high resolution microCT is being used to look at details of normal and abnormal changes in bone (Rühli *et al* 2007; Figure 116). Macho *et al* (2005) used microCT to see whether ages determined using conventional age at death techniques, applied to twenty early medieval skeletons from Raunds Furnells, Northamptonshire, matched those obtained from looking at changes in trabecular microstructure. It was found that we should be suspicious of macroscopic techniques, as indicated by other studies (eg see the under-ageing of older adult skeletons and the over-ageing of younger adults at Christ Church, Spitalfields; Molleson and Cox 1993).

7.4 Biomolecular analysis

In this section the focus is on stable isotope (Sealy 2001) and ancient DNA (Brown 2001) analyses, although other biomolecules have been identified in bioarchaeological remains such as mycolic acids of tuberculosis (eg see Gernaey *et al* 2001). Trace element analysis has also seen a lot of work in bioarchaeology over the years, although its use in reconstructing palaeodiet has been overtaken by stable isotope analysis. The issue of uptake of trace elements into the skeleton from the surrounding burial environment, and thus levels not reflecting real levels in the living person and the type of diet, is something that researchers have discussed frequently (eg Waldron 1983; Pate and Hutton 1988), and continue to debate (see Sandford and Weaver 2000; Pike and Richards 2002).

(i) Stable isotope analysis

(a) Reconstructing palaeodiet

In order to consider the actual basic components of the diet, chemical analysis of stable carbon and nitrogen isotope values in teeth and bone can be undertaken. Different types of foods (eg marine, terrestrial, meat, vegetables) can be distinguished through these analyses, and there is less concern for diagenesis affecting results (Katzenberg 2000). There are still problems, however, with understanding the biochemical mechanisms involved with the conversion of food eaten into its representation in the body tissues (Sealy 2001).

First it is necessary to summarise the basis behind carbon and nitrogen stable isotope analysis. Carbon and nitrogen in skeletal materials sampled and analysed are largely derived from protein that comes from the ingested diet; this will reflect an average of ten years of diet prior to death. Tens of milligrams of bone are needed for analysis, preferably from the thick cortex of the femur (Richards 2004). Carbon has two isotopes: ^{12}Carbon and ^{13}Carbon. Most plants are C_3 plants, but some tropical grasses are C_4 plants which use a different method of photosynthesis. Relevant to isotopic analysis, C_4 plants, including maize, have more ^{13}C (heavier isotope) relative to ^{12}C (Katzenberg 2000). Marine plants have ^{13}Carbon values between the values of C_3 and C_4 plants (Larsen 1997, 272), while marine fish and mammals have ^{13}Carbon values 'less negative ... than animals feeding on C_3 based foods and more negative values than animals feeding on C_4 foods' (*ibid*). Nitrogen isotope ratio levels will also vary. There are two isotopes, ^{14}N and ^{15}N, and their ratio is useful for distinguishing marine from terrestrial diets. ^{15}N levels for terrestrial plants are lower than for marine plants (Larsen 1997, 283), and higher levels are seen in hot areas compared to lower values in cooler areas. The ratios of ^{12}Carbon and ^{13}Carbon and ^{14}N and ^{15}N are measured in foods and human skeletal samples, with the ratios being compared to known standards. For those wishing to read in more detail see the monograph by Faure and Mensing (2005). It can therefore be seen that the type of diet people ate in the past can be distinguished using stable isotope analysis (Figure 117), although the detailed components of the diet cannot. While tooth enamel and bone are usually used for analysis, increasingly hair samples, primarily from mummified remains, are being utilised (eg Roy *et al* 2005). Knudson *et al* (2007) analysed hair from two archaeological sites in southern Peru and confirmed that marine products and C_4 plants such as maize had been eaten; the results could also indicate that there was seasonality in consumption.

In the Americas stable isotopic analysis of bone and teeth has been extensively used to explore when, where, and to what extent maize agriculture was adopted (eg Katzenberg *et al* 1995; Hutchinson and Norr 2006). Consideration has focused on the relationship between maize consumption and such factors as geographic differences and social status (see Larsen 1997). Furthermore, sex differences in maize consumption have been identified in the Americas (eg males eating more maize than females at Copán, Central America – see White *et al* 1993).

Whether marine- or terrestrial-based diets were being consumed has been explored using isotope analysis, particularly in Europe. Richards *et al* (2000a) investigated stable isotopes of carbon and nitrogen in Croatian Neanderthal remains. They found that almost all of their protein came from animals, suggesting that Neanderthal groups most probably hunted animals rather than scavenged ones already dead. In Portugal, Lubell *et al* (1994) found more domesticated plants and animals being consumed in the Neolithic compared to the Mesolithic, while Lillie and Richards (2000) found in both the Mesolithic and early Neolithic of the Ukraine that hunting animals, fishing, and gathering plant foods produced the main components of the diet, with an increase in fish consumption into the Neolithic. In a further study in the Ukraine, Lillie

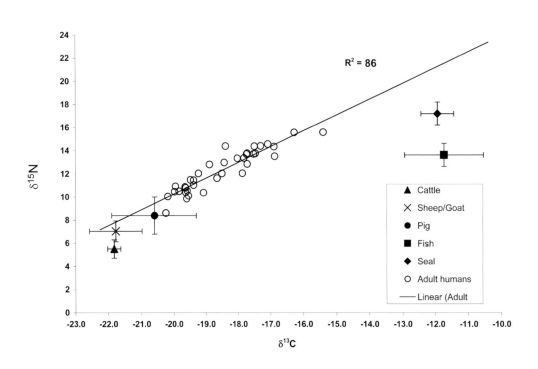

Figure 117: δ ^{13}C and δ ^{15}N values of humans and other animals from Newark Bay, Orkney, showing a range of diets, with different proportions of marine and terrestrial foods; some people acquired up to 50% of their diet from marine sources (with permission of Mike Richards; Richards *et al* 2006)

et al (2003) showed that before the Mesolithic animal protein and freshwater resources such as fish were the main components of the diet.

In Greece, Papathanasiou (2003) considered whether marine resources were more important at coastal versus inland sites in the Neolithic and found in both cases marine resources were a small part of the diet. There have been two recent studies of diet in Bulgaria, one of people from the cemetery of a Greek colony on the Black Sea coast dated to the 5th to 2nd century BC (Keenleyside *et al* 2006), and the other of two Copper Age cemeteries from Neolithic Varna I and Eneolithic Durankulak (Honch *et al* 2006). Keenleyside *et al* found the diet was a mix of terrestrial and marine resources, with little variation between the sexes, ages, or burial type. Given their proximity to the sea it was, however, surprising that the marine component was not higher. Similarly, Honch *et al* found that, despite the populations living close to the Black Sea, a diet of mainly terrestrial sources was eaten.

Turner *et al* (2007) recently showed that age-related differences in diet can also be seen using stable isotope analysis; they found that at medieval Kulubnarti in Nubia (AD 550–800) children ate isotopically depleted protein and plant sources relative to the adults. Prowse *et al* (2005) also found age differences in 1st- to 3rd-century diet at Isola Sacra, Rome, Italy. As people got older the consumption of prestige foods such as marine resources and olive oil increased, while the non-adult part of the population had a diet dominated by plant foods.

In recent years, a number of studies of palaeodiet using stable isotope analysis have also appeared in Britain. Richards *et al* (2000b) analysed human bone from Gough's Cave, Cheddar, Somerset, and saw that a high consumption of meat was practised, mainly consisting of deer and bison. Richards and Mellars (1998) found that on the island of Oronsay, Scotland, a high protein diet very much composed of marine resources was eaten in the Mesolithic. Furthermore, Schulting and Richards (2000) found a mix of terrestrial and marine resources when human remains were isotopically analysed from Caldey Island, Wales, with an abrupt cessation of marine resource consumption in the Neolithic. In the Iron Age of Yorkshire, at Wetwang Slack, Jay and Richards (2006) saw a diet high in animal protein with no significant marine input or differences in diet between higher ('chariot') and lower status burials. Analyses of individuals from the Romano-British site of Poundbury Camp, Dorchester, Dorset, revealed that in the early period people ate a mixed diet and no marine resources, while in the late Roman period they had different diets according to status, the richer people having similar diets to each other including some marine resources (Richards *et al* 1998). At the late Roman site of Queenford Farm, Dorchester-on-Thames, Oxfordshire, Fuller *et al* (2006a) found that females appeared to have reduced consumption of animal and fish protein compared to males, explained by the authors as possibly due to preference, family needs, or societal values. At the Anglo-Saxon cemetery of Berinsfield, Oxfordshire, a study of carbon and nitrogen stable isotope ratios in the people buried found differences in diet between social groups, but none between males and females (Privat *et al* 2002). Mays (1997b) considered the diet of late medieval lay and monastic individuals

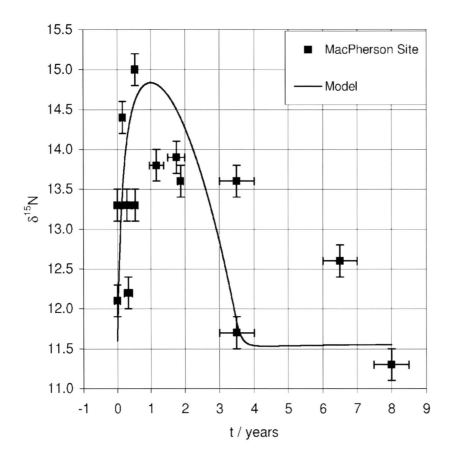

Figure 118: Model of weaning using stable isotope analysis of nitrogen (Millard 2000; using data from the MacPherson site, an Iroquoian village in Ontario, Canada (Katzenberg *et al* 1993); reproduced with permission of Andrew Millard)

from northern England: terrestrial foods dominated, but marine resources were important sources of protein. Monastic diets had a higher marine component than those of lay people and, as expected, coastal diets contained more marine components. In the post-medieval period, in Birmingham, carbon and nitrogen stable isotope analysis of 18 bone and 30 hair samples from the people buried in St Martin's churchyard showed that protein in the diet was mainly terrestrial in origin, and that the high nitrogen values probably reflect freshwater food and omnivore (pig?) consumption (Richards 2006). In a very recent study of diet in York through time (Roman to the early 19th century), Müldner and Richards (2007) found that there was much dietary variation between the periods but that the most important change was the introduction of large amounts of marine fish in the 11th century AD; they suggest that this may be the result of fasting regulations introduced by the church.

Stable isotopes of carbon, oxygen, and nitrogen can also inform us about breastfeeding and the timing and duration of the weaning process in infants in the past (see a model of weaning created from stable isotope data of nitrogen from an archaeological site; Figure 118). Diet changes when a child is weaned, and also when new foods are introduced into the diet. Carbon isotope ratios will be higher in breastfed infants and can be used to show the introduction of solid foods into the diet; oxygen and nitrogen are also higher in breastfed infants, and provide information about the duration of weaning (Fuller *et al* 2006b). For example, children who are weaned off milk protein and onto solid food protein show a decline in nitrogen (Larsen 1997; Schurr 1997). These differences are because the nursing infant is at a different trophic level compared to the mother (the former is higher). There is usually also a general reduction in nitrogen isotope ratios through childhood which indicates that the replacement of breastfeeding with other foods is gradual rather than abrupt. Wright and Schwarcz (1998) studied individuals from Guatemala dating to 700 BC–AD 1500 and, through carbon and oxygen isotope ratios, found that children had begun to eat solid foods before the age of two years but that they also continued to drink breast milk until much later. Herring *et al* (1998) further analysed nitrogen isotopes in 19th-century infant skeletons from Belleville, Ontario, Canada, and noted that weaning started around five months of age and could extend to fourteen months, data that was corroborated by historical demographic analysis. A similar picture was seen by Dupras *et al* (2001) who studied nitrogen and oxygen stable isotope levels in infants from the Roman site of Dakhleh Oasis, Egypt (*c* AD 250). They found that the weaning process started at six months and was completed by three years of age. At Wharram Percy, North Yorkshire, Richards *et al* (2002) found weaning occurred by two years of age or earlier. There was also a decrease in consumption of isotopically enriched breast milk and the introduction of less-enriched weaning foods (Fuller *et al* 2003). Some studies have also shown a correlation between enamel defects of the teeth and age of weaning, as determined by nitrogen isotopic analyses, and others have noted a relationship between a decline in nitrogen isotopes, weaning, loss of passive immunity and mortality (Herring *et al* 1998).

(b) Origin and mobility

In recent years analysis of stable isotope levels of strontium (Bentley 2006; Figure 119), lead (Carlson 1996), and oxygen (White *et al* 1998) in teeth has also been applied to questions of the origin and mobility of past humans. While strontium levels reflect the geology of an area and the consumption of food and water by people, oxygen reflects the climate and geography, as seen in levels in drinking water (Budd *et al* 2004). Both provide a basis for reconstructing place of residence when the teeth of an individual were forming, although there is still much to be learnt about the processes behind the levels of isotopes seen in the bones or teeth and how that reflects levels in soils and water.

Why do we want to look at mobility in the past? Today, people might move to escape danger (war-torn areas), famine or disease, to access health care, or to get work in the hope of a better, safer, and more healthy life. Naturally, longer journeys lead to larger and more significant changes in climate and culture. Often a better life may not be the ultimate outcome; people may experience poverty, poor living conditions and diet, hostility, pollution, and pressure on resources. In many developing countries today people migrate to cities from rural areas to gain

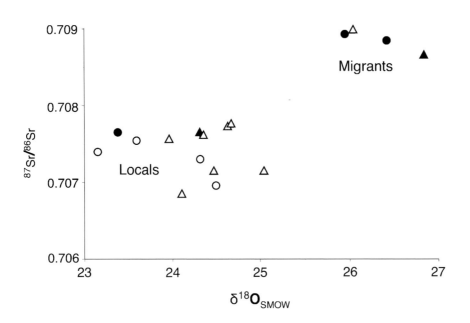

Figure 119: Isotopes of strontium and oxygen in human tooth enamel from Teouma, Vanuatu (dated to the 2nd millennium BC): females shown by circles; males shown by triangles – the lower left cluster are locals and the upper right cluster are probably migrants to the island, one who had three skulls of locals placed over his chest (from Bentley *et al* 2007, reproduced with permission of Alex Bentley)

employment, just as they did in the late and post-medieval period in England, and people may move temporarily or permanently, but the ability to move will depend on economic and social status. Mobility can also influence your health. Today travel and tourism have made it possible for pathogens to be transmitted more rapidly than ever before (Armelagos 1998). Contact between people through markets and trade may lead to the introduction of new diseases to people who have not experienced them before and to which they have little or no immunity (Swedlund and Armelagos 1990; Larsen and Milner 1994; Sellet *et al* 2006); people are also susceptible to contracting the diseases prevalent in the area they have moved to (Mascie-Taylor and Lasker 1988). For example, in a modern study from Australia it was found that mobility was more strongly associated with poor than good health (Larson *et al* 2004). Additionally, it has been found that the migration of people can influence the geographic extent of a disease. A study of the impact of refugee flows on malaria in Pakistan's north-west frontier province between 1972 and 1997 showed that the influx of 2.5 million Afghan refugees, living in tented villages, affected the spatial distribution of malaria (Kazmi and Pandit 2001). Of course, people may move from north to south or south to north in an area, from highland to lowland or lowland to highland, and from a rural to an urban environment.

People who moved from one place to another in the past may be recognised by means other than isotope analysis in archaeological contexts, and using only one indicator to suggest mobility would not be sensible anyway. For example, there might be evidence of diseases that are not indigenous to the area that people have moved to, or possibly high levels of trauma due to interpersonal violence as a result of hostility between the native population and incomers. For example, malaria, sickle cell anaemia, thalassaemia, and fluorosis would not be expected in Britain today unless a person had visited a malaria-ridden country, or originated in Africa or the Mediterranean, or a country with high levels of fluoride in the soil or water. We might also expect to see more immigrants suffering 'stress' through under-nourishment, or obesity and diabetes (consuming a different high fat and calorie diet), mental illness, cancers, and occupation-related diseases because of a different lifestyle. In archaeological contexts we could also look at normal variation in the skeleton such as the presence of non-metric traits in bones and teeth (eg see Coppa *et al* 2007), stature differences, and the presence of imported and/or exotic grave goods, or foreign architecture, which might highlight that there are different groups (locals and incomers) of people buried in a cemetery. Historical documents and depictions of travel might confirm the presence of immigrants. Bioarchaeologists have recognised that the signatures of stable isotopes of the place in which a person was born and raised, as seen in their teeth, may differ from those in the place to which a person may migrate. One has to remember that in any cemetery population sample there may be permanent, temporary, and non-migrant people; there may also be offspring of migrants.

Oxygen and strontium isotopes can be used to help identify first-generation immigrants to a population, and suggest their childhood residence (Budd *et al* 2004). Strontium isotopes are the most commonly analysed isotope to assess mobility (Montgomery and Evans 2006; and see Buzon *et al* 2007; Knudson and Buikstra 2007), and less commonly lead. Strontium in bone reflects the place of residence in the last few years prior to death and the level in the enamel of the teeth reflects it in early childhood (Grupe *et al* 1997). Both strontium and lead enter animals, including humans, via soil, water, and plants. The body holds most of the isotopes in bones and teeth, but how and when the body incorporates these into the skeleton is still not completely understood (*ibid*; Montgomery and Evans 2006). These types of analysis are being used increasingly to address archaeological questions. For example, Montgomery and Evans (2006) found that in their analyses of lead and strontium isotopes in skeletal remains from the Isle of Lewis, Outer Hebrides, Scotland, migrants arrived during the 1st millennium AD, although where exactly they came from is unknown. Montgomery *et al* (2005) also analysed skeletal remains from the early medieval (5th- to 7th-century AD) site at West Heslerton, North Yorkshire, for the same isotopes; a small sample of prehistoric burials was also investigated. They found two distinct groups within the cemetery but they differed according to which data (lead or strontium) were viewed. The strontium data implied a local and non-local group, but the lead data could not be used fully to assess local versus non-local groups because of the impact of 'cultural' (not geological) lead in the post-Roman and later periods. Another study analysed oxygen and strontium levels in late Roman burials from the cemetery of Lankhills, Winchester, Hampshire, to test the hypothesis that there were two groups – local inhabitants and an immigrant population from Hungary. Two groups were identified, but the non-local group was identified as being from several different places in Europe (Evans *et al* 2006).

Elsewhere in Europe, other studies of strontium, and sometimes oxygen and lead isotope levels, have addressed particular archaeological questions. Müller *et al* (2003) analysed lead, strontium, and oxygen in the bones and teeth of the Neolithic 'iceman' found on the border of Austria and Italy. It was suggested that he came originally from an area within a 60km radius to the south-east of where he was found dead but that he migrated to his final resting place in early adulthood. A considerable number of analyses of individuals from cemeteries in Germany have also been undertaken. Grupe *et al* (1997) studied bone and tooth samples from 69 individuals from a Bell Beaker site in southern Bavaria and found that up to 25% were non-local, and that they moved in a south-westerly direction. Bentley *et al* (2002) considered mobility of the earliest farmers in south-west Germany, dated to 7500 years ago (Linearbankeramik – LBK). A high level of migration was found, with non-local females being a common occurrence, and a correlation identified between non-locals, burial orientation, and the lack of a characteristic LBK artefact being found (shoe-last adze); strontium levels in non-locals were higher than their resting place range. It was suggested that the higher rates might indicate that a proportion of the diet of the non-locals came from the uplands, and that they may have been foragers, thus suggesting that foragers persisted into the LBK. Bentley *et al* (2003) also found that at the Neolithic village of Vaihingen, Germany, strontium isotope ratios were non-local in skeletons buried in a ditch surrounding the village when compared to those buried within the settlement. Finally, Schweissing and Grupe (2003) identified that 30% of the dead at a Roman fortress cemetery at Neuberg/Donau in Bavaria were non-local but had come from the north-east areas of Bavaria. Less research has been done in other areas of the world but two further examples are worth citing. Prowse *et al* (2007) analysed oxygen isotopes in people buried at Isola Sacra in Rome (1st–3rd centuries AD) and found that about one third of 61 people analysed were not born in the region. It was suggested that they may have come from around the Apennine Mountain range (100km from Rome). In South America, Knudson *et al* (2004) considered strontium isotope ratios in human remains from the sites of Tiwanaku and Chen Chen in Peru and found both sites had non-local individuals, indicating colonisation.

Clearly, there is still much potential in using stable isotopes to answer questions about diet and mobility in the past, questions that may be generated by bioarchaeologists working alongside archaeologists and historians.

(ii) Ancient DNA (aDNA)

Perhaps the other area of bioarchaeology that has also become very media worthy has been the development in the last 20 years of the ability to extract and amplify ancient DNA (aDNA) fragments from human remains, using polymerase chain reaction (PCR). Techniques from molecular biology have been developed in order that they may be applied to archaeological remains, including those of past humans, ideally to answer archaeological questions.

Body cells are the basic units of life in all living things and an adult human is composed of as many as 1000 billion cells (Turnbaugh *et al* 1996). Within each cell is a nucleus containing a set of chromosomes and inside each chromosome is a single nuclear DNA molecule which contains a genetic code; outside the cell's nucleus is found mitochondrial DNA. The 'genome' of an organism can be used to describe the whole hereditary information encoded in the DNA, or the complete DNA sequence of one set of chromosomes (see http://www.ornl. gov/sci/techresources/Human_Genome/home.shtml). The Genome Project was completed in 2003 and aimed to identify all the genes in human DNA, determine the sequences of the three billion chemical base pairs that make up human DNA, and store the information (analysis of the data continues). The individual units in the DNA are called nucleotides and each has a slightly different structure, depending on whether they are A, C, G, or T (Brown 2001). The nucleotides in each DNA molecule link together to make very long chains. The key feature of a DNA molecule is its nucleotide sequence, and part of the sequence are the genes that contain the biological data that is characteristic of the organism (80,000 genes for human DNA: *ibid*). The structure of DNA was discovered in 1953 by Watson and Crick and 'heralded a new era in biological sciences' (Brown 2000, 455). Both mitochondrial DNA (to explore relationships between people and migration patterns) and nuclear DNA (to determine biological sex and diagnose disease) have been successfully extracted from bioarchaeological remains. There are a number of excellent reviews of the development of aDNA analysis in bioarchaeology and the reader is directed to these for more detailed information (Brown 2000; Stone 2000; Brown 2001; Kaestle and Horsburgh 2002).

In 1985, Pääbo reported the first human aDNA from a 2400-year-old Egyptian mummy. In 1989 Hagelberg *et al* reported the first amplification of mitochondrial DNA from ancient bone from sites dated to between 300 and 5500 years of age in England. Later, and in order to investigate the scope and methods for tracing the history of life (with a particular emphasis on aDNA), between 1993 and 1998 the Natural Environmental Research Council of England and Wales funded eighteen research projects on ancient DNA analysis. These projects focused on animal, human, and plant remains, totalled £1.9 million, and were very much cross-disciplinary. At this stage the survival of aDNA in both different environments and periods of time was essentially unknown, as were the problems that have faced many researchers since regarding contamination of samples with 'foreign' DNA (eg see a study by Gilbert *et al* 2006 on the processes behind DNA contamination). In fact many researchers are now reluctant to utilise curated skeletal collections because of the great potential for contamination with other sources of DNA over the years of their curation; they prefer to excavate and sample the skeletal material themselves to try to limit possibilities of contamination. Another problem in the early work was the almost universal concentration on the analysis of individual skeletons or mummies, often with what seemed to be the sole aim of seeing 'if aDNA survived to be analysed'.

Clearly, from a recent survey of publications on the use of aDNA for diagnosis of disease (Roberts and Ingham 2008, early view), there needs to be some recognition of, and adherence to, set standards in analytical procedures too. As the method of aDNA analysis requires destructive techniques through sampling of a few grams of bone or teeth for analysis, there is now a sense of urgency to rectify problems in analysis before more valuable skeletal and mummified material is destroyed (eg see Cooper and Poinar 2000 on standards to be met in aDNA analysis; and DeGusta and White 1996 on the use of skeletal collections for aDNA analysis). As Stone (2000, 354) has said, 'The questions asked and the probability of actually getting sufficient data to answer the questions should be carefully considered before undertaking a project'. If there is no question to ask or hypothesis to test that might be answered or tested using aDNA analysis then the work should not be done. Neither should inadequate procedures and methods be used for analysis.

We are now seeing research that is assessing the survival of aDNA in different environments. There have been warnings given in the published literature that it is pointless sampling human remains from certain areas of the world for aDNA analysis because research to date suggests that aDNA does not survive well in tropical areas (Kumar *et al* 2000 for tropical India; Reed *et al* 2003 for tropical Sri Lanka), or indeed sampling from some museum skeletal collections (Barnes and Thomas 2006). With respect to ancient pathogen DNA, contamination from environmental micro-organisms is a real risk (Gilbert *et al* 2005). Indeed there have even been arguments in the published literature about whether aDNA data is authentic or not, and whether aDNA would be expected to survive in different parts of the world (eg see *ibid* and Zink and Nerlich 2005). It may be that aDNA survives in one skeleton buried in a cemetery site but not in another skeleton at the same site, and that aDNA survives in a particular bone of a skeleton but not in other bones of the same skeleton. Both these scenarios illustrate that different burial environments within one site and within one grave can affect survival of aDNA. Thus, it is difficut to predict when aDNA will be present to extract and amplify.

Attempts to consider the survival of aDNA in bioarchaeological remains include Waite *et al*'s (1997) study of DNA stability during artificial heating of cattle bone, Banerjee and Brown's (2004) experiments with heat and the survival of DNA, and Haynes *et al*'s (2002) analysis of the survival of aDNA by assessing bone preservation both macroscopically and histologically; they found that if both were good then DNA would survive. Bouwman *et al* (2006) further describe a method of identifying authentic aDNA sequences in human bone contaminated with modern DNA, and Pruvost and Geigl (2004) discuss 'real-time' PCR to recognise real aDNA and also contaminated aDNA. Brown (2000) also recommends improved sampling strategies to minimise contamination; indeed in their paper in 1992 Brown and Brown provided very clear guidance for archaeologists on sampling techniques at the excavation level. For example, the use of sterile gloves should be routine on all excavations when sampling for aDNA analysis to limit contamination of aDNA samples (Brown 2000).

Despite the problems, to date, researchers have analysed aDNA from human remains to determine the following: biological sex in non-adult remains,

Figure 120: Norris Farm cemetery: spatial patterning of mtDNA lineages; arrowed burial contained two individuals with the Hinc II-13259 marker, suggesting they were related (from Stone and Stoneking 1993, reproduced with permission of Anne Stone)

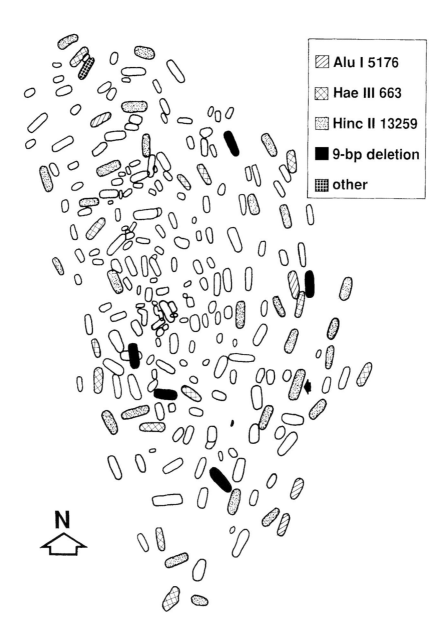

Alu I 5176

Hae III 663

Hinc II 13259

9-bp deletion

other

N

fragmentary adult remains, and cremated remains; relationships between individuals (Figure 120); migration; presence of disease (Figure 121); and patterns of human evolution. Unfortunately DNA does not usually survive in cremated bone because the temperature used to cremate the body would have been too high, ie >300°C, and the protein is lost (McKinley pers comm, November 2007). Increasingly, more population-based studies answering specific archaeological questions are being undertaken. There are also many studies of DNA in living populations to look at relationships and the way people have moved around the globe, and studies of mitochondrial aDNA in past populations are increasingly

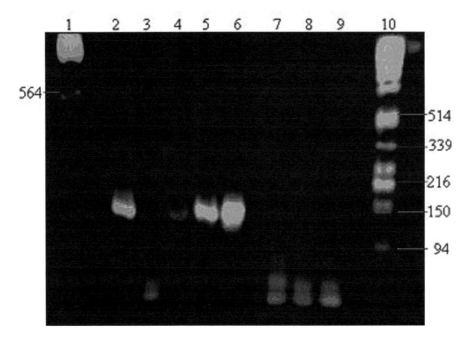

Figure 121: Results of aDNA analysis for tuberculosis; sequences in the samples are compared to known tuberculosis sequences (with permission of Abigail Bouwman)
Lane 1: lambda DNA (this has been cut with the restriction enzyme *Hin*DIII to give a 'ladder' of known-sized DNA fragments), making the image easier to interpret
Lane 2: non-tuberculous ancient DNA (from an individual from the 14th-century plague cemetery at East Smithfield, London)
Lane 3: Opaque mark = a primer dimer (no DNA present to amplify so the primer has replicated itself); sample from a skeleton from the post-medieval cemetery of One Poultry in London
Lanes 4, 5 & 6: ancient DNA of tuberculosis (three individuals from post-medieval Farringdon Street, London)
Lanes 7, 8 & 9: Opaque mark = a primer dimer (no DNA present to amplify so the primer has replicated itself) – a negative control
Lane 10: lambda DNA (this has been cut with the restriction enzyme *Pst*I to give a 'ladder' of known-sized DNA fragments), making the image easier to interpret

NB: The numbers down the two sides of the image are the length of the bands on the 'ladder' in base pairs

being used to track mobility and kinship (eg Alzualde *et al* 2006; Mooder *et al* 2006; Shinoda *et al*, 2006; Gao *et al* 2007; Gilbert *et al* 2007; Kemp *et al* 2007; Wang *et al* 2007). Some studies consider multiple lines of evidence rather than using just one, such as mtDNA, and indeed the study of dental and skeletal non-metric traits, stable isotopes of strontium, lead, and oxygen, and other variables discussed above could all be used in tandem to assess population mobility.

Research using aDNA analysis of pathogens over the past fifteen years or so has concentrated on: diagnosis of diseases only affecting soft tissues (eg Taylor *et al* 1997 on malaria; Fricker *et al* 1997 on *E. coli*; Raoult *et al* 2000, and Weichmann and Grupe 2005 on the plague); identifying infection in individuals with no visible pathological change (eg Jankauskas 1999 on tuberculosis); diagnosis of non-specific pathological lesions (eg Haas *et al* 2000 on tuberculosis); confirming a diagnosis based upon other criteria (Baxarias *et al* 1998; Mays and Taylor 2002, all on tuberculosis); and identification of the specific organism causing a disease (eg Zink *et al* 2004 on tuberculosis). Tuberculosis is obviously the most common disease considered (eg Salo *et al* 1994; Gernaey *et al* 2001; Mays and Taylor 2003).

Ancient DNA of the tuberculosis (TB) organism was first isolated in the early 1990s in both soft tissue and bone (Spigelman and Lemma 1993; Salo *et al* 1994), with many more papers to follow, mainly based on individual skeletons or mummies, but later studies focusing on 'populations' (Faerman *et al* 1997; Mays *et al* 2001; Fletcher *et al* 2003a and b). Research on tuberculosis in a larger number of individuals by Mays *et al* (2001) considered skeletal remains with bone changes of TB at the late medieval rural site of Wharram Percy, Yorkshire. It was expected that in this rural environment, where people were in close contact with their animals, the bovine strain of TB would have caused the disease in these individuals, but it was the human form that was isolated. Zink *et al* (2004) in their study of Egyptian skeletal material found that the Africanum strain of TB was predominant in the past, as it is today. Interestingly, through analysis of the genome of tuberculosis it has also been possible to overturn the theory that humans first got their TB from animals; it seems that the human form existed first (Brosch *et al* 2002), and may explain Mays *et al*'s (2001) data.

Most research to date has concentrated on tuberculosis, as we have seen, but other diseases have also been studied, some more successfully than others: leprosy (Taylor *et al* 2000, 2006; and some papers in Roberts *et al* 2002); treponemal disease (Bouwman and Brown 2005; Von Hunnius *et al* 2007); malaria and plague (see above); and the 1918 Spanish influenza (Reid *et al* 1999). However, it should be remembered that, even if aDNA of a pathogen can be extracted and identified, it does not mean the person suffered (or even died from the disease) as they could merely have been a carrier of it, with no ill effects.

Disregarding the problems of the process, as discussed above, the main advantage of diagnosing disease in this way is that we may be able to identify disease that produces non-specific bone changes. The methods may also help with assessing differential diagnoses for lesions and could potentially provide us with real prevalence rates for disease. Further, they could help to diagnose disease in people who died before any bone changes occurred (although it would be hard to select the individuals to analyse), and additionally could provide information on the evolution of strains of infectious disease organisms. However, there appear to be increasing comments in the literature suggesting that data produced from pathogenic aDNA analysis may be flawed (see Gilbert *et al* 2004; and Bouwman and Brown 2005). Now is the time to ensure that standard methodological procedures are followed and full descriptions of these methods provided in publications; it may well be that journal editors need educating as to how to evaluate such publications.

7.5 Dating human remains

'Dating is the key to organizing all archaeological evidence' (Greene 2000, 101). There are a number of ways that archaeological sites and materials may be dated (see Aitken 1990 for a full overview), but 'no single general method seems remotely possible to register the complete range (of possible dates)' (Hedges 2001, 3). Here, the focus is on radiocarbon (^{14}C) dating of the human skeleton; this is the most common method used in archaeology, and has had a profound effect on the development of the discipline (Taylor 2001). The reader is directed to Bowman (1990) for more details on radiocarbon dating. While Hedges (2001) notes that around 95% of archaeological dates overall have been achieved through radiocarbon dating, it is not free from problems (Greene 2000). The ^{14}C time scale ranges from 40,000–60,000 years to about 300 years ago, but there are some limitations at the younger end of the range (Taylor 2001). There may also be problems with obtaining good dates for bone samples from skeletal remains of people who had a high proportion of marine components in their diet (Bayliss *et al* 2004). This is often seen in late medieval monastic contexts in Britain and has confounded obtaining precise dates for skeletons from sites with evidence of venereal syphilis that have been archaeologically dated as pre-Columbian. Thus, this problem can prevent Britain contributing to a very important area of debate between the Old and New Worlds.

Radiocarbon dating, an absolute method of dating developed in the 1940s by Willliam Libby in the United States, has revolutionised our understanding of prehistory, in particular. The rate of decay of ^{14}C is known; ^{14}C is absorbed by all living organisms but stops entering them when the organism dies (including in humans). Thus, in theory, measuring the amount of radiocarbon in a skeleton can be used to determine how long has elapsed since death (Greene 2000), although it is not that straightforward. Conventional radiocarbon dating is now less used than its more modern version using accelerator mass spectrometry (AMS); for the latter much smaller samples of bone (500mg–5g versus 100–500g: Aitken 1990; and even down to less than 100 mg: Taylor 2001) are needed and therefore the method is less destructive. However, the dating precision is actually similar (Andrew Millard pers comm, November 2007), although AMS dating takes less time. The protein component of the bone, collagen, is extracted and measured to provide a date. However, radiocarbon ages should be considered as ranges of possible ages and not absolute dates. Dates are presented in a standard way: uncalibrated dates in years BP (before present; BP=AD 1950). This also incorporates an 'unavoidable counting error' estimated by the laboratory, expressed as ± a number of years; this provides an indication of the 'chance' of a date lying within that ± number of years (Greene 2000, 119). This raw uncalibrated date is calculated on Libby's 'half-life' of 5568 years, or the speed of decay of carbon 14 in samples analysed. The date is then calibrated by referring to a calibration curve, which has been developed from dated tree ring samples of wood. Essentially, it is assumed that living things are in equilibrium with the atmospheric ^{14}C content.

The reasons for dating human remains (cremated or unburnt) from an archaeological site may be to provide a date for human occupation of a site, or to date a specific burial or group of burials; the latter is often seen for prehistoric sites in Britain where dating may be an assumption based on burial position and associated features (McKinley pers comm, November 2007). It is also used to help with the dating and interpretation of stratigraphy or phases within a cemetery context, or to date a skeleton that has evidence of a specific disease and where a date would help with placing the individual within the context of the history of that disease, for example venereal syphilis. While radiocarbon dating often provides a more precise date it does not automatically replace conventional relative dating methods such as looking at stratigraphic relationships, and typologies of artefacts. For example, grave goods found with burials commonly give an indication of the date (pottery, coins), along with coffin furniture dated by style. Coffin plates in post-medieval burials may provide the date of death, and textiles, again, may be dated on style or by absolute dating. The orientation of burials has also been used to date them; for example at Whithorn Priory in Scotland ten stages of burial in three phases were identified, all between the 13th century and AD 1450 (Hill 1997, in Gilchrist and Sloane 2005). Furthermore, contemporary historical data may be directly associated with a cemetery, such as at the East Smithfield plague cemetery in London where plague victims were buried in AD 1348 (Hawkins 1990). However, historical data may not always be reliable and could be overturned by radiocarbon dating. Of course, there are other catastrophes that occurred at specific dates, such as the sinking of the Tudor warship the *Mary Rose* in AD 1545 off the south coast of England (Stirland 2000); this certainly gives the date of death of the sailors on board (and a certain cause of death in this instance).

Obtaining precise radiocarbon dates can be crucial for dating phases in cemeteries. This allows the progression of the use of the cemetery to be assessed. It may also give an indication of whether certain aged/sexed groups of people were buried at certain times during the cemetery's lifetime. Dating might also help us to understand when people with specific diseases were disposed of and whether they were buried in specific parts of the cemetery. If migrants are identified in the cemetery sample, based on aDNA, stable isotope, metrical and non-metrical analyses or a combination, it may also be possible to assess when they were significant within the population. It is often the case, however, that dates for phases of cemeteries are not available and then it becomes impossible to assess for example the rise and fall of certain diseases through time (Waldron 1994). Finds of 'important' individual burials may also be dated. For example, the 'Iceman' found in the European Alps in 1991 was dated to between 3300 and 3200 years BC using dates calculated from six European dating laboratories (Spindler 1994). It has also been important to obtain precise radiocarbon dates for skeletons with specific diseases in order to establish the first evidence for a disease and/or contribute to debates about the origin and evolution of a disease. For example, radiocarbon dating has established the earliest evidence of skeletal tuberculosis in the world in Italy, at 5800±90 BC (early Neolithic) (Canci *et al* 1996). Furthermore, increasing numbers of skeletons with bone changes of venereal syphilis are now being found in Europe and are contributing to debates about syphilis in the Old and New Worlds. Key to these debates are well-dated skeletons. Recently Mays *et al* (2003) reported two skeletons with probable treponemal disease from Essex that were dated to the pre-Columbian period (ie prior to AD 1492). This confirms that the disease was present in the Old World before Christopher Columbus and his crew sailed to the New World; thus, Columbus and his crew could not have returned in AD 1492 and infected people in the Old World because the Old World already had the disease. In fact, all the well-dated skeletons with bone changes of treponemal disease on both sides of the Atlantic prove that the disease was present before Columbus's voyages in AD 1492/3 (see Dutour *et al* 1994; Powell and Cook 2006 for more extensive discussions).

7.6 Summary

In this chapter we have seen the variety of methods of analysis that can be used and applied to human remains in an effort to understand more about how people lived in the past. Clearly there is an increase in the use of these methods, perhaps driven, firstly, by the fact that bioarchaeologists have come to realise that 'big' questions can be tackled and there are ways of getting the answers that were not possible using more conventional methods of analysis. Secondly, certainly in Britain, many people working in academic institutions are driven by the funding councils in choosing what research they wish do because it is obvious that certain types of research are more likely to be funded (to the detriment of more conventional research that still may need to be done). Currently the type of research in favour in archaeology is biomolecular in focus. It should be noted that bioarchaeologists working in contract archaeology do not usually have the need to access research funding for the purposes of fulfilling their obligations to developers of producing a skeletal report; unfortunately, they are also not eligible to do so. Of course, many of the methods described here are destructive in nature and researchers (and curators of skeletal collections) therefore need to be clear in their minds that this destructive analysis is justified. However, research using the methods described is undoubtedly exciting and is providing us with a view of certain aspects of our past ancestors' world that was not possible before.

7.7 Key learning points

- Histology, radiography, and biomolecular analyses, and radiocarbon dating of human remains have considerably aided our understanding of the past
- There are advantages and limitations to all the methods described
- Destructive methods of analysis must be justified with important archaeological questions to answer, or hypotheses to test
- Some analytical procedures can be expensive and time consuming, and problematic in their process
- Plain film radiography is probably the most common of the 'hard science'

analyses used in bioarchaeology because it is non-destructive and relatively cheap to use

- Stable isotope and ancient DNA analyses are being used increasingly in bioarchaeology, although the former more frequently because of the availability and accessibility of facilities, and lower costs, when compared to aDNA analysis; this trend looks set to continue as funding bodies appear to favour this type of research

- Disease, injury, age at death, sex estimation, post-mortem damage, diet, surgery, mobility, and kinship are some areas of bioarchaeology that have been successfully explored using radiographic, histological, and biomolecular analyses

CHAPTER EIGHT

The future for the study of human remains in archaeology

*The cloud on the horizon, which will probably not go away, is the reburial issue
... there is good cause to review where our studies have got to and which aspects
deserve our special research efforts before it is too late!*

(Brothwell 2000, 5)

8.1 Introduction

This book has taken the reader rapidly through the history of the study of
human remains from archaeological sites, the ethical issues surrounding
their study, how people were disposed of in the past through time,
what factors preserve buried bodies well, and what might affect the quality of
human remains ultimately studied by the bioarchaeologist. We have also seen
how human remains may be excavated, processed, conserved, and curated, as
well as the ultimate effect of these processes on preservation. Additionally, we
have focused upon how basic analysis – including identification, age and sex
estimation, and normal variation through measurements and non-metric traits
– can greatly aid meaningful interpretation of disease in the past. The study
of disease has also been considered via thematic approaches including living
environment, diet, work, conflict, and access to health care, while hard scientific
analysis of human remains has been explored through histology, radiography,
biomolecular analysis, and dating.

Clearly, much excellent work in bioarchaeology has been achieved from a global
perspective and much of that has been in Britain. It is also evident that the study
of human remains has become much more of a central theme in archaeology as
a whole, and that may well reflect the plethora of trained people in the field, ie
more people available to do this sort of work, and more people lobbying for more
integration and involvement in archaeology. The bioarchaeological approach to
the study of human remains – integrating biological with archaeological data
– is essential to the understanding of what is being observed; studying human
remains 'for their own sake' is now no longer accepted in bioarchaeology. The
bioarchaeologist should always be considering the site context data to enable him/
her to make that integration effective. Furthermore, attempting to test a hypothesis
or answer a question (hopefully, population-based) in research-driven work in
bioarchaeology is essential in order that we may learn more about our ancestors'
lives. The big projects in bioarchaeology, such as that of the 'Global History of

Health' are very ambitious, and the results will undoubtedly have an impact on our understanding of people in the past on a large scale and allow comparisons to be made between geographic areas of the world and through time that have never been possible before.

Nevertheless, we do not live in a perfect world and there are still problems to solve and developments that need to be made, even though I believe that we are now in an incredibly good position to make an even greater impact on the study of archaeology.

8.2 The resource

As indicated in Chapter 2, there seems to be an ever-increasing control on the resources (human remains) that provide us with a window on the past. However, improvements have been made to guidelines for dealing with human remains from excavation to curation; these should ensure that our ancestors' remains are treated ethically and with respect. There are many extant skeletal collections, large and small, curated in museums and other institutions in Britain. They provide bioarchaeologists with a large and valuable resource for research and teaching. The collections allow us to teach students at all levels about change and adaptation in our ancestors through long periods of time – providing a temporal and geographical perspective that is essential in enabling us to understand society today. In addition, study of collections allows observation of the great variation in the skeleton's appearance from one person to another and from one population to another. Retaining and curating these skeletal samples with respect and care is vital to generating knowledge about our past; this knowledge is continually evolving as ideas change and analytical methodology develops. However, we desperately need a centralised database of all human remains curated in Britain. This would help considerably in identifying skeletal samples that could be used for answering new questions and testing hypotheses generated about the past. With the advent of the Department of Culture, Media and Sport (2005), museums are certainly now being encouraged to make information about their human remains holdings accessible to all.

Increasingly in Britain we see reburial of remains, often with no discussion with bioarchaeologists about the value of retaining and curating the remains. There thus needs to be a better dialogue between bioarchaeologists and archaeologists and also with curators of collections, particularly in museums where perhaps the value of retention of human remains is not always recognised, although space to curate human remains can be an issue. Improvements in curation conditions and environments are also badly needed for some collections, and more debate about the value of using destructive sampling of curated skeletal remains for research. Additionally, more discussion is needed between *all* interested parties, and not just professionals, with respect to the question of the retention and reburial of human remains from British archaeological contexts. While reburial may be regarded as proper in some circumstances, it does hold problems. Reburial can only take place in a formal place of burial, if done under licence, but these areas are pressed for space dealing with burial of the dead today. Cremation is not a realistic option, and it may have been abhorrent to some populations in the past.

If these issues above can be adequately discussed, debated, and agreements made, then we should be in a better position for further advancement of the discipline of bioarchaeology, particularly in Britain.

8.3 Recording and analysis

There have been efforts to address problems in the recording of data by developing recognised standards, although we still need to persuade all bioarchaeologists to use these (see Chapter 1). Some are still unaware they exist, some feel constrained by using them, and some object to being told what to do! However, it is to the benefit of all bioarchaeologists (and archaeologists) if agreed standards are adhered to so that effective and useful comparisons of data between 'populations' can be made. This, of course, does not prevent additional data being collected by bioarchaeologists who feel more is needed.

In contract archaeology in Britain, it is clear that the quality of work undertaken by bioarchaeologists has improved considerably and funding has increased since 1990 and PPG 16. This ultimately has an impact on the quality of the data available for use by other bioarchaeologists, which may be for research or other contract work. There remains a problem, however, with so much bioarchaeological data being in the 'grey' literature, often inaccessible to most people. Frequently it may be difficult to find out where that grey literature is located (and what it consists of), but all skeletal assessment and full reports should be available on request. Furthermore, copies and records are also deposited in Historic Environment Records (HERs, formerly Sites and Monuments Records) and relevant museums (usually the closest to the site) and are available in their archives (McKinley pers comm, November 2007). Without access to this literature, we are severely compromised in our ability to carry out comparative work and to find gaps in our knowledge of our ancestors (whether that is the time period, funerary context, or geographic region). More also needs to be done to get that grey literature published for the sake of the advancement of bioarchaeology in Britain.

It is very clear from the plethora of publications in the last fifteen years that the 'hard sciences' have made an enormous contribution to our understanding of palaeodiet, mobility of people, relatedness between people and populations, and diagnosis of disease, as seen in Chapter 7. There is no doubt that this will continue, especially as the large grant-giving bodies appear to want this sort of research to be undertaken. Unfortunately, to a certain extent this will be to the detriment of research in basic recording and analysis in bioarchaeology, routinely done by contract bioarchaeologists. It would be nice to think that bioarchaeologists could persuade funding bodies in Britain that both types of research should be done. In the United States and elsewhere, this problem is not so apparent.

8.4 Research agendas

While we have advanced much in our understanding of our ancestors and their lives, there are still a number of areas that we need to concentrate on and develop in bioarchaeology. These include: developing methods for sex estimation of non-adult skeletons and new methods for assessing age at death of adults (see Chapter 5); further research on identifying health differences by sex, age, socio-economic and social status; looking at the impact of climate and different environments on health in the past; and assessing the impact of migration (see Chapter 6). Additionally, some serious work needs to be done on exploring whether skeletal indicators of occupational stress can be reliably recorded and utilised to look at work loads in the past. More concentration on the impact of diseases in animals on their human counterparts is gravely needed. I feel too that medical anthropology can play a much more important role in the interpretation of palaeopathological data in bioarchaeology than has been done in the past.

As indicated above and in Chapter 7, the hard sciences will continue to play a very important role in bioarchaeological research agendas and, therefore, more research is needed to understand the diagenetic aspects of survival of aDNA (and contamination) in bones, teeth, and mummified tissues in different parts of the world and periods of time. Additionally, diagenetic effects on stable isotope levels in bones and teeth and mummified tissues needs more research. This will ultimately prevent unwanton and ill thought-out destruction of valuable and irreplaceable human remains. Clearly, too, methods of analysis must encompass high standards, and be comparable between researchers and laboratories, if data is to be accepted as really meaningful. However, to repeat: of key importance is the development of a database of curated skeletal remains in Britain so that skeletal samples can be identified that will help bioarchaeologists answer the questions they are exploring. Although funding has not yet been forthcoming, time is certainly of the essence to establish this database.

8.5 Higher education and career opportunities

The author was instrumental in developing the study of bioarchaeology at Masters level in the 1990s and into the 21st century in two university departments of Archaeology; this has led to further Masters courses being established around the country. While this has created a large body of graduates 'trained' in the analysis of human remains from archaeological sites, it has led to a situation of far more people than jobs or PhD places available. This is very unfortunate but perhaps reflects the recognition in universities in Britain that the subject of bioarchaeology is popular with graduates, and courses can therefore be financially beneficial to the university. This development has paralleled changes in funding of higher education. Such courses, however, need to be seen to be taught in a cost-effective way.

Career prospects for people trained in bioarchaeology therefore are limited, and it is highly unlikely now that a first degree graduate will be employed to analyse human remains in contract archaeology or start a PhD; having a Masters degree is now usually a requirement, although a typical Masters graduate will usually have little experience of analysing skeletal remains from archaeological sites and producing reports, or working in commercial archaeology. However, working in contract archaeology or progressing to undertake research for a PhD are the most likely careers followed. Funding for PhDs is also limited and most PhD students are self-funded. Having a PhD can provide the necessary training and intellectual development to pursue post-doctoral research, although again this is limited to only the brightest and most motivated students; funding may come via being named as a postdoctoral research assistant on a grant application, or through a personal postdoctoral research fellowship being awarded. This latter prospect could lead to bioarchaeologists gaining more experience working relatively unsupervised, which would make them more employable in the commercial world. The large numbers of PhD students in bioarchaeology means that the opportunities for funding at postdoctoral level are scarce. For the lucky few in Britain, a bioarchaeology post in a higher education establishment may be possible either on a teaching-only contract or, more normally, to do teaching and research. Competition is usually fierce for all career opportunities in bioarchaeology and many are disappointed.

In effect, the rapid development of bioarchaeology in Britain has been admirable but has come at a cost, and that is a lack of job opportunities. It is hoped that archaeology as a whole will embrace the fact that bioarchaeology has made an important contribution to the discipline, especially over the last fifteen or so years in Britain, and that more employment opportunities for bioarchaeologists will be seen in the future. However, on a more sombre note, the author is reminded that most archaeological contractors do few excavations of human remains, probably because of the high cost and time needed to excavate cemeteries (McKinley pers comm, November 2007). There will, therefore, always be a limited number of posts in Britain, although there are far more now than when the author started work in bioarchaeology in 1983. It is unfortunate that the bioarchaeology job market is now more than saturated due to the plethora of taught Masters courses in universities which generate approximately 100 graduates per year.

Bioarchaeology in Britain has a very bright future and is increasingly showing its worth to the discipline of archaeology both nationally and internationally. It has emerged phoenix-like from the ashes over the last twenty years and looks set to remain a major part of both academic and contract archaeology.

Glossary

Accelerator mass spectrometry – an analytical technique that measures mass to charge ratio of charged particles; it is used to determine the concentration of carbon 14, which provides a date for a burial

Acetone – a colourless, mobile and inflammable solvent. It is used to make plastics, chemicals, drugs, and fibres

Adhesive – a compound that adheres or bonds two items together

Adipocere – insoluble residue of fatty acids from fats in decomposing human bodies

Aerosol – fine liquid droplets in a gas

Afterlife – continuation of existence after death

Allergic alveolitis – inflammation of the alveoli of the lungs caused by an immune response to an inhaled aerosol of fine particles; commonly associated with certain occupations (eg 'farmer's lung')

Alveoli – the air sacs or cavities in the lung where the primary gas exchange takes place

Amelogenin – protein found in developing enamel of the teeth

Amputation – removal of a limb or other appendage

Anaemia – reduction below normal of the standard quantity of red blood cells, quantity of haemoglobin (important in carrying oxygen in the blood), or volume of packed cells in the blood

Anaerobic – lack of oxygen

Anaesthesia – local or general loss of bodily sensation, or loss of sensation induced by drugs

Ancestry – lineage from which a person has descended over time

Anorexia nervosa – psychological disorder characterised by the fear of becoming fat and failing to eat

Anthracite – hard jet-black coal

Anthracosis – coal dust in the lungs causing lung disease

Anthrax – infectious disease of animals and humans caused by a spore in the soil

Anthropology – the study of humans

Antibiotic – a chemical that inhibits or stops the growth of micro-organisms (bacteria, fungi and protozoa)

Antibody – a protein produced in the blood as a response to the presence of an antigen

Antigen – a substance that stimulates the production of antibodies as an immune response

Archaeobotany – the study of ancient plant remains

Archaeology – the study of the human past using material remains

Arterial – relating to the arteries (muscular blood vessels that carry blood away from the heart)

Artery – blood vessel carrying blood away from the heart

Asphyxiation – lack of oxygen in the blood due to restricted respiration

Assessment report – an initial report on excavated remains produced in contract archaeology which provides basic data and future potential

Atom – the smallest component of an element having the chemical properties of that element

Atomic mass – the number of protons and neutrons in the nucleus

Atomic number – the number of protons found in the nucleus of an atom

Bases (in nucleotides of DNA) – adenine (A), guanine (G), thymine (T), and cytosine (C); in forming the double helix representing the DNA molecule

Base pair (in DNA) – where two bases bond together. This is essential for the DNA molecule's ability to replicate or make a copy of itself; in forming the DNA molecule base pairs can only form between adenine and thymine and between guanine and cytosine

Bayesian – a method in probability and statistics which aims to estimate parameters based on an underlying distribution grounded in the observed distribution

Bile – a bitter greenish to golden brown alkaline fluid secreted by the liver and stored in the gall bladder; it aids the emulsification and absorption of fats

Bioarchaeology – the study of human remains from archaeological sites, understood and interpreted by considering the context from which they derive

Biomass fuel – a renewable fuel derived originally from a living organism or the by product of a living organism (eg wood, animal dung)

Biomolecular – of a chemical compound which naturally occurs in living organisms; consists primarily of hydrogen and carbon and oxygen, sulphur, phosphorus, and nitrogen

Black Death – a pandemic due to a bacterial infection caused by *Yersinia pestis* transmitted from rats to humans via fleas (bubonic plague, involving swelling of the lymph nodes and forming buboes) or via human to human (pneumonic plague, a rapidly progressive highly contagious pneumonia)

Bloodletting – a very old medical practice which was used to treat disease. Blood was drained away from the body using leeches, cutting into a blood vessel, or by cupping

Bone setter – one who reduces and splints fractures/dislocations

Bovine spongiform encephalopathy (BSE) – a degenerative neurological disease of cattle believed to be caused by infection-causing agents called prions. Brain tissue deteriorates and becomes spongy in appearance; abnormal behaviour and loss of muscle control develops. A variant form, Creutzfeld-Jakob Disease, is transmitted to humans via eating infected meat

Bovine tuberculosis – an infectious disease caused by the bacterium *Mycobacterium bovis*, affecting mainly animals

Brucellosis – an infectious disease transmitted from animals to humans through contaminated milk or via close contact, caused by the genus *Brucella*. The bacteria can penetrate the skin

Cairn – an artificial pile of stones which may mark a burial, a summit of a mountain, or a route

Calcified – a hardening of tissue through the influx of calcium, usually as a result of chronic inflammation

Calcium – an abundant chemical element, essential for living organisms

Calculus – calcified deposits on the teeth (tartar or plaque)

Calibrate – the process of verification that a measuring instrument is within its designated accuracy

Cancellous – a type of bone with low density and strength but large surface area; contains red bone marrow

Cancer – a growth or tumour caused by abnormal and uncontrolled cell division in the body

Canon – a priest who is a member of a cathedral chapter

Capillaries – small blood vessels 5–10 micrometres in diameter that connect the venules (small diameter vessels linking capillaries and veins) and the arterioles (small diameter vessels linking arteries with capillaries)

Carbohydrate – any of a large group of organic compounds, including sugars such as sucrose

Caries (dental) – an infectious disease of the teeth

Cartilage – a dense tough connective tissue

Cartilaginous (joint) – a joint where the apposing bone surfaces are covered in cartilage

Causewayed enclosure – circular or oval-shaped area bounded by one or more lines of banks or ditches; thought to be used variously as settlements or ceremonial sites; found in the Midlands and southern England

Cautery – where an instrument or agent is used to destroy abnormal tissue by burning, searing or scarring

Celt – a person who speaks a Celtic language; a member of an Indo-European people who in the pre-Roman period inhabited Britain, France, and Spain and other parts of west and central Europe

Celtic – referring to a branch of the Indo-European family of languages which includes Gaelic, Welsh, and Breton

Charnel – a vault or building used for the deposition of excavated human bones, often when a graveyard of a church was overcrowded (to make way for new burials) or when parts of a church were being extended

Chemotherapy – treatment of disease by means of chemical agents (eg antibiotics)

Chert – an impure black or grey variety of quartz that resembles flint

Chicken pox – highly contagious disease caused by a virus (*Herpes zoster*) characterised by a rash on the body

Chlorophyll – the green pigment of plants that traps the energy of the sun for photosynthesis

Cholera – an acute infectious disease endemic and epidemic in Asia today caused by the bacteria *Vibrio cholerae*; marked by extreme diarrhoea and vomiting and muscle cramps

Cholesterol – a lipid or fat found in cell membranes of all animal tissues

Chromosome – a structure in the body cells' nucleus containing DNA, the self-replicating genetic structure of cells

Chronic – persisting for a long time

Chronic bronchitis – inflammation of one or more of the bronchi (the larger passages within the lungs that convey air to and from the lungs)

Chumash – a native American group that inhabit (historically and today) the southern coastal regions of California

Coca – the plant, Erythroxylon, from which cocaine is derived

Collagen – a fibrous protein

Colony – the result of a body of people who settle in another country distant to their homeland but maintain ties with it (an overseas territory or dependent state are the preferred terms now)

Computed tomography – an imaging method where cross-sectional images of the structures in a human body are reconstructed by a computer programme from the absorption of X-rays projected through the body

Concepts of disease – causal networks that represent the relationships between symptoms, causes and treatments of disease in specific cultures

Confocal – reflecting scanning laser light microscopy

Connective tissue – one of four tissues of the body; includes bone and cartilage

Consecrated – to make or declare sacred or holy

Conservation – the act of conserving or preventing change, loss, or injury etc

Consolidant – a substance used to make bone stronger or more stable

Contact radiograph – the end result of microradiography

Contract archaeology – archaeological work conducted under legal agreement with a government or private organisation; designed to protect the cultural heritage when modern development is taking place

Copper alloy – a mixture of metals; copper blended with zinc, tin, or lead

Copper smelting – a process of heating and melting metal ores and concentrates and then separating the desirable molten metals such as copper

Cortex (cortical) – external layer of bone, under the periosteal membrane

Cremation – the act of burning a corpse

Creutzfeldt-Jakob disease (CJD) – a brain disease in humans and some animals caused by a prion. There are sporadic (occur for no reason) and acquired forms. The acquired form may develop via medical procedure contamination. Variant CJD has been found in young people and is believed to be contracted through ingestion of beef infected by BSE (see above)

Cross-bow – a weapon consisting of a bow mounted on a stock that shoots projectiles

Cultural patrimony – an object having ongoing historical, traditional or cultural importance central to a group, such as Native Americans, or a culture, that is not owned by any one individual

Cupping – a vacuum is created within a glass vessel by heating air within it and then it is placed on a patient's skin; as the air cools a vacuum is created. Prior to application, the skin is scratched or incised leading to extraction of blood due to pressure differences created by the vacuum

Curate – to care for

Demography – the science of studying population dynamics

Dentine – the chief substance of the teeth which surrounds the central pulp cavity and underlies the outer white enamel and cementum (fixes teeth in their sockets)

Descendant – something that derives from an earlier form

Diabetes – any disorder characterised by excessive urine secretion

Diabetes mellitus – a disorder of carbohydrate metabolism characterised by excessive thirst and excretion of abnormally large amounts of urine containing excessive sugar caused by a deficiency of insulin

Dimer – a chemical or biological entity made up of two sub-units called monomers

DNA – deoxyribonucleic acid (molecules inside the body cells that contain genetic information)

DNA replication – where new strands of DNA develop from the two original DNA strands; each strand serves as a template. When replication is completed there will be two new DNA molecules and each new molecule has one new and one original DNA strand

Double helix – the structure of the DNA molecule, or a two-stranded 'twisted ladder' appearance; sugars and phosphates are the two sides of the ladder and the bases or bonds join them to form the rungs

Dual-energy X-ray absorptiometry (DEXA) – imaging technique that uses a very low dose of radiation to measure bone density and content for the diagnosis of osteoporosis

Ecclesiastical – associated with the Christian church or clergy

E. coli (Escheria coli) – a bacteria that normally resides in the gastrointestinal tract; some strains can cause diarrhoeal diseases

Embalm – to treat a dead body with preservatives to retard putrefaction

Embryo – animal in the early stages of development

Emigration – to move away from a place and settle in another

Enamel – the hard, thin, translucent substance composed almost entirely of calcium salts covering the dentine

Enamel defects (hypoplasia) – a deficiency of enamel thickness occurring when the enamel is developing and caused by dietary deficiencies or childhood diseases

Endemic syphilis – a chronic inflammatory infection caused by a bacteria of the genus Treponema prevalent today in arid zones of the world; it is transmitted non-sexually – it is contracted in childhood via physical contact

Endocrine – relating to the endocrine glands in the body that secrete hormones into the bloodstream

Endoscope – a small flexible tube used for examining the interior of the body

Energy dispersive low angle X-ray scattering (EDLAXS) – an analytical technique that produces a mineral spectrum, and illustrates the type and quantity of the minerals present

Enzyme – any of a group of complex proteins that are produced by living cells and act as catalysts in specific biochemical reactions

Epilepsy – any of a group of syndromes characterised by transient disturbances of brain function

Epiphysis (es) – typically the expanded end of a long bone developed from a secondary ossification centre that eventually fuses with the main part of the bone; also occur in other types of bone

Ethics – the philosophical study of the moral value of human conduct and the rules and principles that ought to govern it; a social, religious or civil code of behaviour considered correct

Ethnicity – relating to or characteristics of a human group having certain other traits in common such as language

Ethnography – a branch of cultural anthropology that deals with the scientific description of human cultures

Eugenics – the social philosophy that advocates improving human hereditary traits through various forms of intervention, especially by selective breeding

Excarnation – to deprive or strip of flesh

Exposure (of body) – expose a body to the elements following death

Extended (burial) – lying flat generally with the arms and legs straight down, parallel to the body

Federal – relating to a form of government

Fertilisation – the union of male and female gametes during sexual reproduction to form a zygote

Fibre optic – the use of flexible fibres to transmit light

Fibrocartilage – cartilage of parallel, thick, compact collagenous bundles

Fibrous – a body tissue containing fibres

Flexed (burial) – semi-foetal position with the knees drawn up against the chest and hands near the chin

Flint – an impure opaque greyish form of quartz that occurs in chalk

Fluorine dating – the use of levels of fluorine to determine the age of an object found buried, based on the absorption of fluorine from groundwater; a relative dating technique

Fluorosis – a condition where excessive amounts of fluorine are ingested through food or water; common in some parts of the world, eg some areas of India

Foetus – the embryo of a mammal in the later stages of development when it shows all the recognisable features of the mature animal; in the case of humans from the end of the second month of pregnancy until birth

Forager – one who relies on searching for food for survival (eg a hunter-gatherer)

Gall bladder – a muscular sac attached to the liver that stores bile and ejects it into the duodenum of the gastrointestinal tract during digestion

Gall stone – a small hard concretion of cholesterol, bile pigments and lime salts formed in the gall bladder or its ducts

Gamete – a reproductive cell that can undergo fertilisation (eg an ovum)

Gastric ulcer – a local defect of the stomach produced by death of tissue

Gene – the biological unit of hereditary, self reproducing and located at a definite position (locus) on a particular chromosome

Gene pool – the collective genetic information contained within a population of sexually reproducing organisms

Genealogy – the direct descent of an individual or group from an ancestor; a chart showing the relationships and descent of an individual or group

Genetic – relating to genes or the origin of something

Gene therapy – treatment that alters a gene; the manipulation of a person's genetic makeup which may help ultimately to treat a disease

Genetic code – the nucleotide sequence of a DNA molecule in which information for the synthesis of proteins is contained

Genome Project – completed in 2003; a study to identify all the genes in human DNA and determine the sequences of the chemical base pairs that make up human DNA

Genus – any of the taxonomic groups into which a family is divided and which contains one or more species

Gypsum – a colourless white or tinted mineral of hydrated calcium sulphate, occurring in sedimentary rocks and clay and used mainly for making plasters and cement

Haem – a complex red organic pigment containing ferrous iron present in haemoglobin

Haemoglobin – a protein consisting of haem and the protein globin that gives red blood cells their colour; it is very important in carrying oxygen in the blood to the body's tissues

Haemorrhage – profuse bleeding from ruptured blood vessels

Handedness – a preference for using one hand rather than the other

Hantavirus – a genus of viruses of the family *Bunyaviridae* that cause epidemic haemorrhagic fever or pneumonia

Hard water – an alkaline water containing a high concentration of dissolved salts, eg calcium or magnesium

Henge – a circular area enclosed by a bank or ditch often containing a circle of stones or sometimes wooden posts dating to the Neolithic and Bronze Ages

Histology – the study of the microscopic (minute) structure, composition and function of tissues of an animal or plant

Histoplasmosis – an infection caused by the fungus *Histoplasma capsulatum* commonly affecting the lungs; the fungal spores are found in bird and bat droppings

Holistic/holism – the idea that the whole is greater than the sum of its parts

Hominid – any primate of the family *Hominidae*, which includes modern humans (*Homo sapiens*) and the extinct precursors of humans

Homininae – a subfamily of *Hominidae*, including *Homo sapiens* and some extinct relatives, as well as chimpanzees and gorillas. It comprises all those, such as *Australopithecus*, that arose after the split from the other great apes (orang utans are the only surviving group)

Homogenous – composed of similar or identical parts or elements; of uniform nature

Hormone – a chemical substance produced in an endocrine gland and transported in the blood to a certain tissue on which it exerts a specific effect

Humic – organic matter of soil that makes it dark brown

Humic acid – one of the major components of humic substances (humus); these are dark brown in colour and a major part of the organic matter in soil called humus

Humidity – the state of being humid, or damp

Hyaline cartilage – a common type of cartilage with a translucent matrix containing little fibrous tissue

Iliac crest – the lateral edge of the hip bone

Immigration – to come to a place or country of which one is not native in order to settle there

Immunity – the ability of an organism to resist disease, for example by producing its own antibodies

Independent replication – producing the same data independently in two or more laboratories, as in ancient DNA analysis

Indigenous – originating or occurring naturally; native

Infanticide – the act of killing an infant

Inhumation – a buried body

Inhume – to bury

Innominate – the hip bone

Insecticide – a substance that kills insects

Insulin – a protein hormone produced in the pancreas and secreted into the blood that controls the level of glucose

Interment – burial

Intersex – an individual with characteristics that are intermediate between male and female

Inventory – a detailed list; to make a list

Isotope – a form of chemical element that has the same atomic number as another element but a different mass

Kinship – a blood relationship; the state of having common characteristics or a common origin

Lambda DNA – double-stranded DNA molecule

Lamella – thin leaf or plate, as of bone

Latitude – an angular distance in degrees north or south of the equator

Leech – a subclass of the annelids (a large phylum or taxonomic rank of animals), some of which, including *Hirudo medicinalis*, suck blood

Leprosy – a chronic bacterial infection caused by *Mycobacterium leprae* affecting the peripheral nerves and skin

Leptospirosis – any infectious disease caused by the bacterial genus *Leptospira*, found in water, food or soil containing urine excreted by infected animals

Ligament – any of the bands of tough fibrous connective tissue that restrict movement in joints; they connect various bones (eg tibia and fibula)

Lineal – being in a direct line of descent from an ancestor

Liver fluke – a parasitic worm that infests the liver and bile ducts

Longitude – distance in degrees east or west of the prime meridian (an imaginary 0° line running north to south through Greenwich, England)

Lyme disease – an acute bacterial inflammatory disease caused by *Borrelia burgdorfei*, transmitted to humans via ticks and affecting the skin, joints, and nervous system

Lymph – almost colourless fluid containing mainly white blood cells collected from the body tissues

Lymphatic system – the extensive network of capillary vessels that transports the interstitial fluid of the body as lymph to the venous blood circulation

Lymph node – bean-shaped masses of tissue along the course of lymphatic vessels in the body that help to protect against infection by killing bacteria and neutralising toxins

Malaria – an infectious disease caused by the protozoa of the genus *Plasmodium* which are parasitic in red blood cells; transmitted by *Anopheles* mosquitoes

Maori – native population of New Zealand

Marrow – the fatty network of connective tissue that fills the cavities of bones

Masking tape – an adhesive tape

Measles – a highly contagious viral infection, usually of childhood, primarily involving the respiratory tract and marked by a skin rash

Membrane – a thin layer of tissue that covers a surface, lines a cavity, or divides a space or organ

Meninges – the three membranes covering the brain and the spinal cord (dura, arachnoid, and pia maters)

Metabolic disease – a disorder of metabolism

Metabolism – the sum total of the chemical processes that occur in living organisms, resulting in growth, production of energy, elimination of waste etc

Metastasis (es) – spreading of disease, especially cancer cells from one part of the body to another

Microcrystalline – composed of microscopic crystals

Micron – unit of length equal to 10^{-6} metre

Micro-organism – any organism such as a bacterium, protozoa or virus, of microscopic size

Microradiography – production of a radiograph of a small or very thin object (eg a bone or tooth section) on fine-grained photographic film which allows subsequent microscopic examination

Microscope – an optical instrument that uses a lens or combination of lenses to produce a magnified image of an object

Microscopy – investigation by use of a microscope

Microwear (teeth) – study of the microscopic scratches and pits that form on a tooth's surface as a result of its use, for example during chewing food or using the teeth as tools

Migraine – a symptom complex of periodic headaches, often with sickness, gastrointestinal upset, and sensitivity of the eyes to light

Mineral – any of a class of naturally occurring solid inorganic substances with a characteristic crystalline form and homogeneous chemical composition

Mineralisation – to impregnate with a mineral substance

Mitochondrial DNA – found in the organelles called mitochondria

Molecular biology – study of biology at the molecular level

Molecule – the smallest part of a compound that has all the chemical properties of that compound

Monomer – a small molecule that may become bonded chemically to other monomers to form a polymer

Morphology – the branch of biology concerned with the form and structure of organisms

Mortality – the condition of being dead

Mumps – an acute contagious viral disease seen mainly in childhood which principally affects the salivary glands in the mouth

Muscle – a body tissue composed of bundles of elongated cells capable of contraction and relaxation to produce movement in an organ or part

Mutant – an animal, organism, or gene that has undergone mutation (change/alteration)

Mycolic acid – saturated fatty acids found in cell walls of some bacteria

Mycosis (es) – any infection or other disease caused by a fungus

Narcotic – any group of drugs such as morphine and opium that produces numbness and stupor; used medicinally today to relieve pain, they are sometimes taken for their pleasant effects but prolonged use may cause addiction

Natron – a whiteish or yellow mineral that consists of hydrated sodium carbonate and occurs in saline deposits and salt lakes

Neanderthal – often seen as a sub species of *Homo sapiens* (*H. sapiens neanderthalensis*); also refers to the cultural period known as the Middle Palaeolithic and is almost always associated with the Mousterian stone tool industry (stone flake tools)

Nematode – any unsegmented worm of the class *Nematoda*

Neoplastic – any abnormal new growth of tissue (or tumour)

Neural – of or relating to a nerve of the nervous system

Neutron – one of the basic particles that make up an atom

Neurosurgery – the branch of surgery concerned with the nervous system

Nomad – a person who moves from place to place to find pasture and food

Nuclear DNA – DNA that is present in the nucleus of a body cell that is inherited from both parents

Nucleotide – basic units of a DNA molecule composed of a sugar, a phosphate, and one of four DNA bases (adenine (A), guanine (G), thymine (T), and cytosine (C))

Ochre – any of various natural earths containing ferric oxide, silica and alumina; used as yellow or red pigments

Oestrogen – any of several steroid hormones secreted primarily by the ovaries and placenta

Ore – a rock that contains minerals from which one or more metals can be extracted

Organelle – specialised subunit within a cell that has a specific function and is enclosed within its own lipid membrane

Organic – relating to, or derived from, or characteristic of, living plants and animals

Ornithosis – a viral disease of birds that is occasionally transmitted to humans

Ossified – to convert or be converted into bone

Osteoarthritis – a non-inflammatory degenerative joint disease marked by initial degeneration of the cartilage

Osteomalacia – vitamin D deficiency in adults characterised by inadequate or delayed mineralisation of bone often leading to deformity in the spine, ribs, and pelvis

Osteon – the basic unit of the structure of compact bone comprising an Haversian canal and concentric lamellae

Osteoporosis – abnormal rarefaction of bone

Pagan – a member of a group professing any religion other than Christianity, Judaism, or Islam

Paget's disease – a chronic disease of bone characterised by inflammation, excessive bone turnover and destruction, and deformity

Palaeolithic – the period characterised by the development of stone tools extending from about 2.5 million years ago

Pancreas – a large elongated organ located behind the stomach that secretes insulin and pancreatic juice that contains digestive enzymes

Palm sugar – a sugar obtained from the sap of certain species of palm trees

Pandemic – an epidemic of infectious disease that spreads through human populations across a large region, for example a continent

Parasite – an animal or plant that lives in or on another (host) from which it obtains nourishment

Parturition – relating to childbirth

Passage grave – a tomb that consists of a chamber that is reached via a corridor made of stone slabs, all usually covered by a mound of earth; common in the Neolithic of Europe

Passive immunity – protection resulting from the transference of antibodies from another person, as from mother to child

Pastoralism – a form of farming involving animal husbandry and a mobile element where herds of animals are moved regularly to access grazing

Peat bog – wet acidic spongy ground of decomposing vegetation (peat)

Perimortem – around the time of death

Periodontium – the tissues that support the teeth

Periodontosis – a degenerative disorder of the periodontal structures marked by destruction

Permeability – capable of being penetrated by liquids

Pesticide – a chemical used for killing pests such as insects or rodents

Philosophy – the rational investigation of being, knowledge and right conduct

Phosphate – any salt of any phosphoric acid

Phosphorus – a non-metallic element in phosphates and living matter

Photosynthesis – the synthesis of organic compounds from carbon dioxide and water using light energy absorbed by chlorophyll

Pigment – substance in plant or animal tissue producing a characteristic colour, such as chlorophyll in plants

Placenta – the vascular organ formed in the uterus of most mammals during pregnancy which provides oxygen and nutrients for the foetus and transfer of waste products to the maternal blood circulation

Plague – a severe acute or chronic infectious disease caused by *Yersinia pestis* with a high fatality rate

Plaque (dental) – a soft thin film of food debris, salivary protein and dead cells on the teeth, providing a medium for bacterial growth

Pneumoconiosis – any lung disease due to permanent deposition of substantial amounts of particulate matter in the lungs (eg anthracosis)

Pneumonia – inflammation of the lungs with exudation and consolidation

Pneumonitis – inflammation of the lungs

Pollen – a fine powdery substance produced by seed-bearing plants

Polymer – a naturally occurring or synthetic compound that has large molecules made up of relatively simple repeated units

Post-mortem – following death

Primer – a strand of nucleic acid that serves as a starting point for DNA replication

Prion – proteinaceous infectious particle; a poorly understood infectious agent

Projectile weapon – a weapon that is designed to be thrown

Prone (burial) – buried face down

Protein – any of a large group of nitrogenous compounds of high molecular weight; essential constituents of all living organisms

Proton – a stable positively charged elementary particle found in the nuclei of atoms

Psittacosis – an ornithosis

Puberty – the period at the beginning of adolescence when the sex glands become functional and the secondary sexual characteristics emerge

Pubic symphysis – the joint that links the two hip bones at the front of the pelvic girdle

Putrefaction – decomposition

Pyre – a heap or pile of combustible material, such as wood

Quaker – a member of the Society of Friends, a Christian sect founded by George Fox in about 1650 whose central belief is the doctrine of the Inner Light

Quartz – a hard glossy mineral present in most rocks, especially sandstone and granite

Race – a group of people who have been placed together into a specific category associated with particular geographic localities, based on various attributes such as skin, eye and hair colour, and the shape of the face and nose

Radiation – energy that is radiated or transmitted in the form of rays, particles or waves

Radiograph – an image produced by radiation on a specially sensitised photographic film or plate

Radiography – production of radiographs

Reburial – to re-inter a body following excavation

Reduction (fractures) – to restore to the normal place (the two fractured bone ends)

Reformation – a religious and political movement of 16th-century Europe that began as an attempt to reform the Roman Catholic Church and resulted in the establishment of the Protestant Churches

Regression – the analysis or measure of the association between one (dependent) variable and one or more other (independent) variables

Relative humidity – the mass of water vapour present in the air expressed as a percentage of the mass that would be present in an equal volume of saturated air at the same temperature

Repatriation (human remains) – to send back to their place of origin

Repetitive strain injury – a group of debilitating disorders characterised by the stress of repeated movements

Resin – any of a group of solid or semi-solid amorphous compounds that are directly obtained from certain plant exudations

Restriction enzyme – an enzyme that cuts double-stranded DNA at specific recognition nucleotide sequences (restriction sites)

Reversibility – capable of returning to an original condition

Rheumatism – inflammatory, degenerative and metabolic derangement of the connective tissue structures, for example rheumatoid arthritis

Rickets – vitamin D deficiency in infants and children characterised by abnormal ossification and deformity of bones

Sap – a solution of mineral salts, sugars etc that circulates in a plant

Scanning electron microscope – a microscope that uses electrons to produce a high resolution image of an object

Scoliosis – lateral cuvature of the vertebral column (caused by a number of conditions)

Scurvy – vitaimin C deficiency characterised by anaemia, spongy gums, and bleeding

Seasonality – relating to or occurring at a certain season or seasons of the year

Secondary (ies) – see metastases

Secular – of or relating to worldly, as opposed to sacred, things

Sesamoid bone – a bone formed in a tendon (eg patella or knee cap)

Sexual dimorphism – a distinct difference between the appearance of males and females of the same species

Shoe-last adze – stone artefact (also termed axe)

Shrunken head – a human head that has been prepared for display

Sick building syndrome – a combination of ailments associated with an individual's place of work or residence often caused by flaws in ventilation, heating and air conditioning

Sickle cell – abnormally shaped red blood cells characteristic of sickle cell anaemia. It is seen in areas of the world where malaria is common, for example sub-Saharan Africa

Silt – a fine deposit of mud, clay etc

Slag – the fused material formed during the smelting or refining of metals

Smallpox – an acute, highly contagious and often fatal infectious disease caused by the viruses *Variola major* or *minor*, characterised by a fever and a skin rash

Soft water – water that contains few or no magnesium or calcium ions

Solvent – a substance capable of dissolving another substance

Spanish influenza – the 1918 influenza pandemic caused by the deadly *influenza A virus*

Sphagnum – any moss of the genus Sphagnum in temperate bogs having leaves capable of holding much water; layers of these mosses decompose to form peat

Splinting (fractures) – a rigid support for restricting movement of an injured part, especially a broken bone

Spore – a reproductive structure adapted for dispersion and survival for long periods of time in unfavourable conditions

Sternum – the breastbone

Steroid – fat-soluble organic compound

Stigma – a distinguishing mark or social disgrace

Stratigraphy – the study of the composition, relative positions etc. of rock/soil strata in order to determine their history

Subsistence – the means by which one maintains life

Suffocate – to kill or be killed by the deprivation of oxygen

Suture (cranial) – the joints in the skull

Swaddling – long strips of linen or other cloth formerly wrapped around a newly born baby

Synovial (joint) – the most common and most freely moveable joint in the body; characterised by a synovial membrane that secretes synovial fluid to keep the joint lubricated and nourished, a fibrous joint capsule surrounding the joint as a whole, supporting and protecting the joint, and hyaline cartilage covering the joint surfaces

Tapeworm – any parasitic ribbon-like flatworm of the class *Cestoda*

Taxonomy – the scientific classification of an organism

Tendon – a cord or band of white inelastic collagenous tissue that attaches muscle to bone or some other part

Testosterone – a steroid hormone secreted mainly by the testes

Tetanus – an acute infectious disease caused by a neurotoxin produced by the bacterium *Clostridium tetani* whose spores enter the body through wounds

Thalassaemia – a group of hereditary anaemias that is characterised by a genetic defect in one of the globin chains that make up haemoglobin; this results in abnormal haemoglobin molecules. It is more common in Mediterranean people

Toluene – a colourless volatile inflammable liquid obtained from petroleum and coal tar and used as a solvent and in the manufacture of many chemicals

Trace element analysis – the use of chemical techniques to determine the incidence of trace elements in rocks, pottery, bones, teeth etc; often used to determine the origin of raw materials

Transexualism – when a person identifies with a biological sex different to the one they were born with

Transmission electron microscopy – a microscopic technique whereby a beam of electrons is transmitted through an ultra thin specimen/section, interacting with the specimen as it passes through it.

Transmitted light microscopy – any type of microscopy where the light is transmitted from a source on the opposite side of the specimen from the objective

Trepanation – the surgical cutting of a hole in the skull using any tool except a trephine

Trephination – the surgical cutting of a hole in the skull using a trephine (or cylindrical saw / 'drill')

Treponemal disease – infectious diseases caused by bacteria of the genus *Treponema*

Trophic level – the position that an organism occupies in a food chain

Tuberculosis – an infectious disease in humans and other animals caused by the bacterium *Mycobacterium tuberculosis* and *bovis*

Tumour – a new growth of tissue where cell multiplication is uncontrolled and progressive

Urn – a vase-like receptacle or vessel, often used for the ashes of the cremated dead

Vaccine – a suspension of dead, attenuated micro-organisms for inoculation to produce immunity to a disease by stimulating the production of antibodies

Venereal syphilis – a chronic inflammatory infection caused by a bacteria of the genus *Treponema*, transmitted through sexual intercourse

Vein – blood vessels carrying blood towards the heart

Venous – relating to veins

Venules – small blood vessels carrying blood from the capillaries to the veins

Velocity – speed of motion, action, or operation; rapidity; swiftness

Vicus (vici) – provincial civilian settlement established near an official Roman site; usually a military garrison

Villa – a Roman country house usually of farm buildings and residential quarters around a courtyard

Virus – a minute infectious agent

Votive – offered, given, undertaken, performed, or dedicated

Wean – to cause to replace mother's milk by other nourishment

Weight-height index – 'body mass index'

Whipworm – any of several parasitic nematode worms of the genus *Trichuris*, having a whiplike body and living in the intestines of animals

Whooping cough (pertussis) – an infectious disease caused by *Bordetella pertussis* characterised by catarrh of the respiratory tract and coughing

Wormian – isolated bones in the sutures (joints) of the skull

X-ray – a type of high energy radiation

Yaws – a chronic inflammatory infection caused by a bacteria of the genus *Treponema*, transmitted non-sexually in childhood via physical contact

Zoonosis – any infectious disease that can be transmitted from any other wild or domesticated animal to humans via a vector (or from humans to animals)

Bibliography

Aaron, J, Rogers, J, & Kanis, J, 1992 Paleohistology of Paget's Disease in two medieval skeletons, *American J Physical Anthropology*, **89**, 325–31

Abrahams, P H, Marsk, S C, & Hutchings, RT, 2002 *McMinn's colour atlas of human anatomy*, 2nd edition. London: Mosby Limited

Abrahams, P H, Logan, B M, Hutchings, R T, & Spratt, J D, 2008 *McMinn's the human skeleton*. London: Mosby Limited

Adams, M, & Reeve, J, 1993 *The Spitalfields Project. Volume 1 – The Archaeology. Across the Styx*, CBA Research Report **85**. York: Council for British Archaeology

Aiello, L C, Molleson, T, 1993 Are microscopic ageing techniques more accurate than macroscopic ageing techniques? *J Archaeological Science,* **20**, 689–704

Aitken, M J, 1990 *Science-based dating in archaeology*. London: Longman

Aldhouse-Green, S, & Pettitt P, 1998 Paviland Cave: contextualizing the 'Red Lady', 72, *Antiquity,* **75**, 6–772

Alfonso, M P, & Powell, J, 2006 Ethics of flesh and bone, or ethics in the practice of paleopathology, osteology, and bioarchaeology, in V Cassman, N Odegaard, & J Powell (eds) 2006a, 5–19

Alzualde, A, Izagirre, N, Alonso, S, Alonso, A, Albarrán, C, Azkarate, A, de la Rúa, C, 2006 Insights into the 'isolation' of the Basques: mtDNA lineages from the historical site of Aldaieta (6th–7th centuries AD), *American J Physical Anthropology*, **130**, 394–404

Anderson, T, 2000 Congenital conditions and neoplastic disease in palaeopathology, in M Cox & S Mays (eds) 2000, 199–225

Andrews, G, 1991 *Management of Archaeological Projects 2.* London: English Heritage

Anonymous, 2001 Population review of 1999, England and Wales, *Health Statistics Quarterly,* **9**(2)

Armelagos, G J, 1998 The viral superhighway, *The Sciences*, **January/February,** 24–9

Arnott, R, Finger, S, & Smith C U M (eds), 2003 *Trepanation: history, discovery, theory.* Lisse: Swets and Zeitlinger

Arriaza, B, & Pfister L-A, 2006 Working with the dead. Health concerns, in V Cassman, N Odegaard, & J Powell (eds) 2006a, 205–21

Atkinson, R J C, 1965 Wayland's Smithy, *Antiquity,* **39**, 126–33

Aufderheide, A C, 2000 *The scientific study of mummies.* Cambridge: University Press

Aufderheide, A, & Rodríguez-Martín, C, 1998 *The Cambridge Encyclopedia of Human Palaeopathology.* Cambridge: Cambridge University Press

Aykroyd, R G, Lucy, D, Pollard, A M, & Roberts, C A, 1999 Nasty, brutish, but not necessarily short: a reconsideration of the statistical methods used to calculate age at death from adult human skeletal age indicators, *American Antiquity*, **64**, 55–70

Bahn, P, 1984 Do not disturb? Archaeology and the rights of the dead, *J Applied Philosophy* **1**, 213–26

Bahn, P, 2002 *Written in bones. How human remains unlock the secrets of the dead.* Newton Abbot: David and Charles

Baker, J, & Brothwell, D, 1980 *Animal diseases in archaeology.* London, Academic Press

Baker, P, 2004 *Medical care for the Roman army on the Rhine, Danube and British frontiers in the 1st, 2nd and early 3rd centuries AD.* Oxford: John and Erica Hedges

Banerjee, M, & Brown T A, 2004 Non-random DNA damage resulting from heat treatment: implications for sequence analysis of ancient DNA, *J Archaeological Science,* **31**, 59–63d

Barber, B, & Bowsher, D, 2000 *The Eastern cemetery of Roman London. Excavations 1983–1990*, Monograph Series **4**. London: Museum of London Archaeological Service

Barber, B, Chew, S, & White, W, 2004 *The Cistercian abbey of St Mary Stratford Langthorne, Essex: archaeological excavations for the London Underground Limited Jubilee Line Extension Project*, Monograph Series **18**. London: Museum of London Archaeological Services

Barber, E W, 1999 *The mummies of Ürümchi.* London: Macmillan

Barley, N, 1995 *Dancing on the grave. Encounters with death.* London: John Murray

Barnes, I & Thomas MG, 2006 Evaluating bacterial pathogen DNA preservation in museum osteological collections, *Proceedings of the Royal Society B*, **273**, 645–53

Bartley, M, Blane, D, & Charlton J, 1997 Socioeconomic and demographic trends 1841–1991, in J Charlton & M Murphy (eds), *The health of adult Britain 1841–1994. Volume 1.* London: The Stationery Office, 74–92

Barton, N, 1999 The late glacial colonisation of Britain, in J Hunter & I Ralston (eds) *The archaeology of Britain. An introduction from the Upper Palaeolithic to the Industrial Revolution.* London: Routledge, 13–24

Bass, W M, 2005 *Human osteology. A laboratory and field manual.* 5th edition. Columbia, Special Publication No 2. Missouri: Missouri Archaeological Society

Bass, W M, & Jefferson, J, 2003 *Death's acre. Inside the legendary 'Body Farm'.* London: Timewarner

Baxarias, J, Garcia, A, Gonzalez, J, Perez-Perez, A, Tudo, B G, Garcia-Bour, C J, Campillo, D D, & Turbon, E D, 1998 A rare case of tuberculosis gonoarthropathy from the middle ages in Spain: an ancient DNA confirmation study, *J Paleopathology*, **10**, 63–72

Baxter, P J, Brazier, A M, & Young, S E J, 1988 Is smallpox a hazard in church crypts? *British J Industrial Medicine*, **45**, 359–60

Bayliss, A, Shepherd Popescu, E, Beavan-Athfield, N, Bronk Ramsey, C, Cook, G T, & Locker, A, 2004 The potential significance of dietary offsets for the interpretation of radiocarbon dates: an archaeological significant example from Medieval Norwich, *J Archaeological Science*, **31**, 563–75

Bedford, M E, Russell, K F, Lovejoy, C O, Meindl, R S, Simpson, S, & Stuart-Macadam P, 1993 Test of the multifactorial aging method using skeletons with known ages-at-death from the Grant Collection, *American J Physical Anthropology*, **91**, 287–97

Bell, L, 1990 Palaeopathology and diagenesis: an SEM evaluation of structural changes using backscattered electron imaging, *J Archaeological Science*, **17**, 85–102

Bell L, & Piper L, 2000 An introduction to palaeohistology, in M Cox & S Mays (eds) 2000, 255–74

Bello, S M, Thomann, A, Signoli, M, Dutour, O, & Andrews, P, 2006 Age and sex biases in the reconstruction of past population structures, *American J Physical Anthropology*, **129**, 24–38

Bennike, P, 1985 *Palaeopathology of Danish skeletons: a comparative study of demography, disease and injury.* Copenhagen: Akademisk Forlag

Bennike, P, 2002 Vilhelm Møller-Christensen: his work and legacy, in C A Roberts, M E Lewis, & K Manchester (eds) 2002, 135–44

Bennike, P, & Fredebo L, 1986 Dental treatment in the Stone Age, *Bulletin History of Dentistry*, **34**, 81–7

Bentley, R A, 2006 Strontium isotopes from the earth to the archaeological skeleton: a review, *J Archaeological Method and Theory*, **13**, 135–87

Bentley, R A, Price, T D, Lüning, J, Gronenborn, D, Wahl, J, & Fullagar, P D, 2002 Prehistoric migration in Europe: strontium isotope analysis of early Neolithic skeletons, *Current Anthropology*, **43**, 799–804

Bentley, R A, Krause, R, Price, T D, & Kaufmann B, 2003 Human mobility at the early Neolithic settlement of Vaihingen, Germany: evidence from strontium isotope analysis, *Archaeometry*, **45**, 471–86

Bentley, R A, Alexander, R, Buckley, H R, Spriggs, M, Bedford, S, Ottley, C J, Nowell, G M, Macpherson, C G, & Pearson, G P, 2007 Lapita migrants in the Pacific's oldest cemetery: isotopic analysis at Teouma, Vauatu, *American Antiquity*, **72**, 645–56

Beresford, M, & Hurst, J G, 1990 *Wharram Percy deserted medieval village.* London: Batsford

Berger, M, Wagner, T H, & Baker L C, 2005 Internet use and stigmatised illness, *Social Science and Medicine*, **61**, 1821–27

Berry, A C, & Berry, R J, 1967 Epigenetic variation in the human cranium, *J Anatomy*, **101**, 361–79

Bethell, P H, & Carver, M O H, 1987 Detection and enhancement of decayed inhumations at Sutton Hoo, in A Boddington, A N Garland, & R C Janaway (eds), *Death, decay and reconstruction. Approaches to archaeology and forensic science.* Manchester: Manchester University Press, 10–21

Beyer-Olsen, E M S, 1994 Radiographic analysis of dental development used in age determination of infant and juvenile skulls from a medieval archaeological site in Norway, *Int J Osteoarchaeology*, **4**, 299–303

Bienkowski, P, 2007 Care assistance, *Museums Journal*, **3**, 18

Bintliff J, & Sbonias, K (eds), 1999 *Reconstructing past population trends in Mediterranean Europe (3000 BC–AD 1800).* Oxford: Oxbow Books

Bishop, M W, 1983 Burials from the cemetery of the hospital of St Leonard, Newark, Nottinghamshire, *Transactions of the Thoroton Society*, **87**, 23–35

Blackwell, D L, Hayward, M D, & Crimmins, E M, 2001 Does childhood health affect chronic morbidity in later life? *Social Science and Medicine*, **52**, 1269–84

Blondiaux, J, Duvette, J-F, Vatteon, S, & Eisenberg, L, 1994 Microradiographs of leprosy from osteoarchaeological contexts, *Int J Osteoarchaeology*, **4**, 13–20

Blondiaux J, Dürr J, Khouchaf L, & Eisenberg, L E, 2002 Microscopic study and X-ray analysis of two 5th-century cases of leprosy, in C A Roberts, M E Lewis, & K Manchester (eds) 2002, 105–10

Blondiaux, J, Alduc-Le Bagousse, A, Niel, C, Gabard, N, & Tyler E, 2006 Relevance of cement annulations to paleopathology, *Paleopathology Association Newsletter*, **135**, 4–13

Bloom, A I, Bloom, R A, Kahila, G, Eisenberg, E, & Smith, P, 1995 Amputation of the hand in the 3600-year-old skeletal remains of an adult male: the first case reported from Israel, *Int J Osteoarchaeology*, **5**, 188–91

Boddington, A, 1996 Raunds Furnells. The Anglo-Saxon church and churchyard. London: English Heritage

Bond, J M, & Worley, F L, 2006 Companions in death: the roles of animals in Anglo-Saxon and Viking cremation rituals in Britain, in R Gowland & C Knüsel (eds) 2006, 89–97

Bonser, W, 1963 *Medical background to Anglo-Saxon England*. London: Wellcome Institute for the History of Medicine

Boocock, P, Roberts, C A, & Manchester, K, 1995 Maxillary sinusitis in medieval Chichester, England, *American J Physical Anthropology*, **98**, 483–95

Borooah, V K, 2004 Gender bias among children in India in their diet and immunisation against disease, *Social Science and Medicine*, **58**, 1719–31

Bouwman, A S, & Brown T, 2005 The limits of biomolecular palaeopathology: ancient DNA cannot be used to study venereal syphilis, *J Archaeological Science*, **32**, 703–13

Bouwman, A S, Chilvers, E R, Brown, K A, & Brown T A, 2006 Brief communication: identification of the authentic ancient DNA sequence in a human bone contaminated with modern DNA, *American J Physical Anthropology*, **131**, 428–31

Bowman, S, 1990 *Radiocarbon dating*. London: British Museum

Bowron, E, 2003 A new approach to the storage of human skeletal remains, *The Conservator*, **27**, 95–106

Boyadjian, C H C, Eggers, S, & Reinhard, K, 2007 Dental wash: a problematic method for extracting microfossils from teeth, *J Archaeological Science*, **34**, 1622–8

Boyle, A, & Keevil, G, 1998 'To the praise of the dead, and anatomie': the analysis of post-medieval burials at St Nicholas, Sevenoaks, Kent, in M Cox (ed) 1998, 85–99

Boylston, A, 2000 Evidence for weapon-related trauma in British archaeological samples, in M Cox & S Mays (eds) 2000, 357–80

Boylston, A, & Ogden, A, 2005 A study of Paget's disease at Norton Priory, Cheshire. A medieval religious house, in S R Zakrzewski & M Clegg (eds), *Proceedings of the 5th Annual conference of the British Association for Biological Anthropology and Osteoarchaeology*. British Archaeological Reports International Series **1383**. Oxford: Archaeopress, 69–76

Boylston, A, Knüsel, C J, & Roberts, C A, 2000, Investigation of a Romano-British rural ritual in Bedford, England, *J Archaeological Science*, **27**, 241–54

Bradley, R, 1992, The excavation of an oval barrow beside the Abingdon causewayed enclosure, Oxfordshire, *Proceedings of the Prehistoric Society*, **58**, 127–42

Bradley, R, 1998 *The passage to arms. An archaeological analysis of prehistoric hoard and votive deposits*. Oxford: Oxbow

Bradley, R, & Gordon, K, 1988 Human skulls from the Thames, their dating and significance. *Antiquity*, **62**, 503–09

Brickley, M, 2000 The diagnosis of metabolic disease in archaeological bone, in M Cox & S Mays (eds) 2000, 183–98

Brickley, M, 2004a Compiling a skeletal inventory, in M Brickley & J I McKinley (eds) 2004, 6–8

Brickley, M, 2004b Determination of sex from archaeological skeletal material and assessment of parturition, in M Brickley & J I McKinley (eds) 2004, 23–5

Brickley, M, & Howell, P G T, 1999 Measurement of changes in trabecular structure with age in an archaeological population, *J Archaeological Science*, **24**, 765–72

Brickley, M, & McKinley, J I (eds), 2004 *Guidelines to the standards for recording human remains*. Reading: Institute of Field Archaeologists, Paper **7** (available on line: http://www.babao.org.uk)

Brickley, M, & Ives, R, 2006 Skeletal manifestations of infantile scurvy, *American J Physical Anthropology*, **129**, 163–72

Brickley, M, Miles, A, & Stainer, H, 1999 *The Cross Bones burial ground, Redcross Way, Southwark, London. Archaeological excavations (1991–1998) for the London Underground Limited Jubilee Line Extension Project*, Monograph **3**. London: Museum of London Archaeological Services

Brickley, M, Buteux, S, Adams, J, & Cherrington, R, 2006, *St Martin's uncovered. Investigations in the churchyard of St. Martin's-in-the-Bull Ring, Birmingham, 2001.* Oxford: Oxbow Books

Brickley, M, Mays, S, & Ives, R, 2007 An investigation of skeletal indicators of vitamin D deficiency in adults: effective markers for interpreting past living conditions and pollution levels in 18th- and 19th-century Birmingham, England, *American J Physical Anthropology*, **132**, 67–79

Bridges, P S, 1994 Vertebral arthritis and physical activities in the prehistoric United States, *American J Physical Anthropology*, **93**, 83–93

Briggs, C S, 1995 Did they fall or were they pushed? Some unresolved questions about bog bodies, in RC Turner & RG Scaife (eds), *Bog bodies. New discoveries and new perspectives*. London: British Museum, 168–82

Broca, P, 1873 The troglodytes, or cave dwellers, of the Valley of the Vézère, *Annual Report of the Smithsonian Institution 1872*. Washington DC: Smithsonian Institution, 310–47

Brooks, M M, & Rumsey, C, 2006 The body in the museum, in V Cassman, N Odegaard, & J Powell (eds) 2006b, 261–89

Brooks, S, & Suchey J M, 1990 Skeletal age determination based on the os pubis: comparison of the Ascadi-Nemeskeri and Suchey-Brooks methods, *Human Evolution*, **5**, 227–38

Brosch, R, Gordon S V, Brodin, P, *et al* 2002 A new evolutionary sequence for the *Mycobacterium tuberculosis* complex. *Proc National Academy of Sciences USA*, **99**, 3684–9

Brothwell, D, 1961 A possible case of mongolism in an Anglo-Saxon population, *Annals of Human Genetics*, **24**, 141–50

Brothwell, D, 1967 Human remains from Gortnacargy, County Cavan, *J Royal Society of Antiquaries of Ireland*, **97**, 75–84

Brothwell, D, 1981 Digging up bones. London: British Museum (Natural History)

Brothwell, D, 1986 *The bog man and the archaeology of people.* London: Natural History Museum

Brothwell, D, 1991 On zoonoses and their relevance to palaeopathology, in D J Ortner & A C Aufderheide (eds), *Human palaeopathology. Current syntheses and future options.* Washington DC: Smithsonian Institution Press, 18–22

Brothwell, D, 2000 Studies on skeletal and dental variation: a view across two centuries, in M Cox & S Mays (eds) 2000, 1–6

Brothwell, D, Møller-Christensen, V, 1963 Medico-historical aspects of a very early case of mutilation, *Danish Medical Bulletin,* **10,** 21–5

Brothwell, D, & Zakrzewski, S, 2004 Metric and non-metric studies of archaeological human bone, in M Brickley & J I McKinley (eds) 2004, 27–33

Brown, K, 1998 Keeping it clean: the collection and storage of ancient DNA samples from the field, *The Archaeologist,* **33,** 16–17

Brown, K, 2000 Ancient DNA applications in human osteoarchaeology: achievements, problems and potential, in M Cox & S Mays (eds) 2004, 455–73

Brown, T A, 2001 Ancient DNA, in D R Brothwell & A M Pollard (eds), *Handbook of archaeological science.* Chichester: John Wiley and Sons Ltd, 301–11

Brown, T A, & Brown, K, 1992. Ancient DNA and the archaeologist, *Antiquity,* **66,** 10–23

Brown, P J, Inhorn, M C, & Smith D J, 1996 Disease, ecology and human behavior, in C F Sargent & T M Johnson (eds), *Medical anthropology. Contemporary theory and method.* London: Praeger, 183–218

Bruce, N, Perez-Padilla, R, & Albalak R, 2002 *The health effects of indoor air pollution exposure in developing countries.* Geneva: World Health Organisation

Bryder, L, 1988 *Below the magic mountain. A social history of tuberculosis in 20th-century Britain.* Oxford: Clarendon Press

Buck, C E, 2001 Applications of the Bayesian statistical paradigm, in D R Brothwell & A M Pollard (eds), *Handbook of archaeological science.* Chichester: John Wiley and Sons Ltd, 695–702

Buck, C E, Cavanagh, W G, & Litton C D, 1996 *Bayesian approach to interpreting archaeological data.* Chichester: John Wiley and Sons Ltd

Buck, T J, & Strand Vitarsdøttir, U, 2004 A proposed method for the identification of race in subadult skeletons: a geomorphometric analysis, *J Forensic Sciences,* **49,** 1159–64

Buckberry, J, & Chamberlain, A, 2002 Age estimation from the auricular surface of the ilium: a revised method, *American J Physical Anthropology,* **119,** 231–9

Buckley, L, Murphy, E, Ó Donnabháin, B, 2004 *Treatment of human remains: technical paper for archaeologists,* 2nd edition. Institute of Archaeologists of Ireland

Budd, P, Millard, A, Chenery, C, Lucy, S, & Roberts, C, 2004 Investigating population movement by stable isotope analysis: a report from Britain, *Antiquity,* **78,** 127–41

Budnik, A, & Liczbińska, G, 2006 Urban and rural differences in mortality and causes of death in Historical Poland, *American J Physical Anthropology,* **129,** 294–304

Buikstra, J E, 1977 Biocultural dimensions of archeological study: a regional perspective, in R L Blakeley (ed), *Biocultural adaptation in prehistoric America. Proceedings of the Southern Anthropological Society,* Number **11.** Athens, Georgia: University of Georgia Press, 67–84

Buikstra, J E, 2006a Introduction, in M L Powell, D C Cook, G Bogdan, J E Buikstra, M M Castro, P D Horne, D R Hunt, R T Koritzer, S F Mendonça de Souza, M K Sandford, L Saunders, G A M Sene, L Sullivan, & J J Swetman, Invisible hands: women in bioarchaeology, 131–3, in J Buikstra & LA Beck (eds), 2006, 131–94

Buikstra, J E, 2006b Repatriation and bioarchaeology: challenges and opportunities, in J Buikstra & L A Beck (eds) 2006, 389–415

Buikstra, J E, & Gordon, C C, 1981 The study and restudy of human skeletal series: the importance of long-term curation, *Annals of the New York Academy of Science*, **376**, 449–65

Buikstra, J E, & Ubelaker, D, 1994 *Standards for data collection from human skeletal remains*, Research Seminar Series 44. Arkansas: Archaeological Survey

Buikstra, J E, & Beck, L A (eds), 2006 *Bioarchaeology. The contextual analysis of human remains.* Oxford: Elsevier

Buzon, M, & Richman, R, 2007 Traumatic injuries and imperialism: the effects of Egyptian colonial strategies at Tombos in Upper Nubia, *American J Physical Anthropology*, **133**, 783–91

Buzon, M, Simonetti, A, & Creaser, R A, 2007 Migration in the Nile Valley during the New Kingdom period: a preliminary strontium isotope study, *J Archaeological Science*, **34**, 1391–1401

Caffell, A C, 2005 Marking skeletons. Unpublished Manuscript. Durham: Department of Archaeology, Durham University

Caffell, A C, Roberts, C A, Janaway, R C, & Wilson A S, 2001 Pressures on osteological collections – the importance of damage limitation, in E Williams (ed), *Human remains. Conservation, retrieval and analysis. Proceedings of a conference held in Williamsburg, VA, Nov 7th-11th,1999.* British Archaeological Reports International Series **934**. Oxford: Archaeopress, 187–97

Canci, A, Minozzi, S, & Borgognini Tarli, S, 1996 New evidence of tuberculous spondylitis from Neolithic Liguria, *Int J Osteoarchaeology*, **6**, 497–501

Capasso, L, 2000 Indoor pollution and respiratory diseases in ancient Rome, *The Lancet*, **356**, 1774

Cardoso, H F V, 2006a Brief communication: The Collection of Identified human skeletons housed at the Bocage Museum (National Museum of Natural History), Lisbon, Portugal, *American J Physical Anthropology*, **129**, 173–6

Cardoso, H F V, 2006b Environmental effects on skeletal versus dental development: using a documented subadult skeletal sample to test basic assumptions in osteological research, *American J Physical Anthopology*, **132**, 223–33

Cardwell, P, 1995 Excavation of the hospital of St Giles by Brompton Bridge, North Yorkshire, *Archaeological J*, **152**, 109–245

Cardy, A, 1997 The environmental material. The human bones, in P Hill (ed) 1997, 519–62

Carlson, A K, 1996 Lead isotope analysis of human bone for addressing cultural affinity: a case study from Rocky Mountain House, Alberta, *J Archaeological Science*, **23**, 557–67

Carmel, S, Baron-Epel, O, & Shemy G, in press. The will-to-live and survival at old age: gender differences, *Social Science and Medicine*, **65**, 518–23

Carmichael, E, & Sayer C, 1991 *The skeleton at the feast. The day of the dead in Mexico*. London: British Museum Press

Carroll, Q, 2005 Who wants to rebury old skeletons? *British Archaeology*, **May/June**. York: Council for British Archaeology, 11–12

Carver, M, 1998 Sutton Hoo. *Burial ground of kings?* London: British Museum Press

Cassman V, & Odegaard N, 2006a Condition assessment of osteological collections, in V Cassman, N Odegaard, & J Powell (eds) 2006b, 29–47

Cassman V, & Odegaard N, 2006b Examination and analysis, in V Cassman, N Odegaard, & J Powell (eds) 2006b, 49–75

Cassman, V, Odegaard, N, & Powell, J, 2006a Dealing with the dead, in V Cassman, N Odegaard, & J Powell (eds) 2006b, 1–3

Cassman, V, Odegaard, N, & Powell, J (eds), 2006b *Human remains: guide for museums and academic institutions*. Lanham, Maryland: Altamira Press

Cassman, V, Odegaard, N, & Powell, J, 2006c Policy, in V Cassman, N Odegaard, & J Powell (eds) 2006b, 21–8

Cave, A J E, 1940 Surgical aspects of the Crichel Down trepanation, *Proc Prehistoric Society*, **6**, 131

Cawthorne, N, 2005 *The curious cures of Old England*. London: Kiatkus Books Limited

Chamberlain, A, 2001 Palaeodemography, in D Brothwell & AM Pollard (eds), *Handbook of archaeological science*. Chichester: John Wiley and Sons Ltd, 259–68

Chamberlain, A, 2006 *Demography in archaeology*. Cambridge: Cambridge University Press

Chamberlain, A T, & Parker Pearson, M, 2001 *Earthly remains. The history and science of preserved human bodies*. London: British Museum Press

Chan, A H W, Crowder, C M, & Rogers, T L, 2007 Variation in cortical bone histology within the human femur and its impact on estimating age at death, *American J Physical Anthropology*, **132**, 80–8

Charlton, J, 1997 Trends in all-cause mortality: 1841–1994, in J Charlton & M Murphy (eds), *The health of adult Britain 1841–1994. Volume 1*. London: The Stationery Office, 17–29

Charlton, J, & Murphy, M, 1997 Trends in causes of mortality, in J Charlton & M Murphy (eds), *The health of adult Britain 1841–1994. Volume 1*. London: The Stationery Office, 30–57

Chilvarquer, I, Katz, J, Glassman, D, Prihoda, T, & Cottone, J, 1991 Comparative radiographic study of human and animal long bone patterns, *J Forensic Sciences*, **32**, 1645–54

Ciaraldi, M, 2000 Drug preparation in evidence? An unusual plant and bone assemblage from the Pompeian countryside, Italy, *Vegetation History and Archaeobotany*, **9**, 91–8

Clarke, G, 1979 *The Roman cemetery at Lankhills*. Oxford: Winchester Studies 3 II

Clark, J G D, 1972 *Starr Carr: a case study in bioarchaeology*. Modular Publications, **10**. London: Addison-Wesley

Coale, A J, Demeny, P, 1983 *Regional model life tables and stable populations*. 2nd edition. Princeton: Princeton University Press

Cohen, A, & Serjeantson, D, 1996 *A manual for the identification of bird bone from archaeological sites*. London: Archetype Publications

Cohen, M N, 1989 *Health and the rise of civilisation.* London: Yale University Press

Cohen, M N, & Armelagos, G J (eds), 1984 *Paleopathology at the origins of agriculture.* London: Academic Press

Cohen, M N, & Crane-Kramer, G (eds), 2007 *Ancient health: skeletal indicators of economic and political intensification.* Gainesville, University Press of Florida

Coninx, R, Pfyffer, G E, Mathieu, C, Savina, D, Debacker, M, Jafarov, F, Jabrailov, I, Ismailov, A, Mirzoev, F, de Haller, P, & Portaels, F, 1998 Drug resistant tuberculosis in prisons in Azerbaijan: case study. *British Medical J*, **316**, 1423–5

Connell, B, 2004 Compiling a dental inventory, in M Brickley & J I McKinley (eds) 2004, 34–9

Connell, B, Gray Jones, A, Redfern, R, & Walker, D, in press *Spitalfields: a bioarchaeological study of health and disease from a medieval London cemetery. Archaeological excavations at Spitalfields Market 1991–2007*, Volume 3. London: Museum of London Archaeological Services Monograph

Conrad, L I, 1995 *The Western medical tradition: 800 BC–AD 1800.* Cambridge: Cambridge University Press

Cook, J, 2007 Let Lucy sparkle. *British Archaeology* **September/October**. York: Council for British Archaeology, 15

Cook, J, Stringer C B, Currant, A P, Schwarcz, H P, & Wintle, A G, 1982 A review of the chronology of the European Middle Pleistocene hominid record, *Yearbook of Physical Anthropology*, **25**, 19–65

Cool, H E M, 2004 *The Roman cemetery at Brougham, Cumbria. Excavations 1966–67.* Britannia Monograph Series, **21**. London: Society for the Promotion of Roman Studies

Cooper, A, & Poinar, H N, 2000 Ancient DNA: do it right or not at all, *Science*, **289**, 1139

Coppa, A, Cucina, A, Lucci, M, Mancinelli, D, & Vargiu, R, 2007 Origins and spread of agriculture in Italy: a nonmetric dental analysis, *American J Physical Anthropology*, **133**, 918–30

Corruccini, R, Shimada, I, & Shinoda, K, 2002 Dental and mtDNA relatedness among 1000 year old remains from Huaca Loro, Peru, *Dental Anthropology*, **16**, 9–13

Courtenay, W H, 2000 Constructions of masculinity and their influence on men's well-being: a theory of gender and health, *Social Science and Medicine*, **50**, 1385–1401

Cox, M, 1996 *Life and death at Spitalfields 1700–1850.* York: Council for British Archaeology

Cox, M (ed), 1998 *Grave concerns. Death and burial in England 1700–1850*, CBA Research Report **113**. York: Council for British Archaeology

Cox, M, 2000a Assessment of parturition, in M Cox & S Mays (eds) 2000, 131–42

Cox, M, 2000b Ageing adults from the skeleton, in M Cox & S Mays (eds) 2000, 61–81

Cox, M, 2001 *Crypt archaeology.* Institute of Field Archaeologists, Paper **3**. Reading: Institute of Field Archaeologists

Cox, M, & Mays S (eds), 2000 *Human osteology in archaeology and forensic science.* London: Greenwich Medical Media

Crummy, N, & Crummy, P, & Crossan, C, 1993 *Excavations of Roman and later cemeteries, churches and monastic sites in Colchester, 1971–1988*, Colchester Archaeological Report **9**. Colchester: Colchester Archaeological Trust

Cucina, A, & Tiesler, V, 2003 Dental caries and antemortem tooth loss in the Northern Peten area, Mexico: a biocultural perspective on social status differences among the Classic Maya, *American J Physical Anthropology*, **122**, 1–10

Cunha, E, Fily, M-L, Clisson, I, Santos, A L, Silva, A M, Umbelino, C, César, P, Corte-Real, A, Crubézy, & E, Ludes, B, 2000 Children at the convent: comparing historical data, morphology and DNA extracted from ancient tissues for sex diagnosis at Santa Clara-a-Velha (Coumbra, Portugal), *J Archaeological Science*, **27**, 949–52

Cunliffe, B, 2005 *Iron Age communities in Britain. An account of England, Scotland and Wales from the 7th century until the Roman Conquest*, 4th edition. London: Routledge

Curate, F, 2006 Two possible cases of brucellosis from a Clarist monastery in Alcácer do Sal, Southern Portugal, *Int J Osteoarchaeology*, **16**, 453–8

Currant, A P, Jacobi R M, & Stringer, C B, 1989 Excavations at Gough's Cave, Somerset 1986–87, *Antiquity*, **63**, 131–6

Daniell, C, 1997 *Death and burial in Medieval England 1066–1550*. London: Routledge

Daniell, C, & Thompson, V, 1999 Pagans and Christians: 400-1150, in P C Jupp & C Gittings (eds), *Death in England. An illustrated history*. Manchester: Manchester University Press, 65–89

Darvill, T, 1987 *Prehistoric Britain*. London: Batsford

Davies, D, 1995 *British crematoria in public profile*. Maidstone, Kent: Cremation Society of Great Britain

Davies, D, 2005 *Encyclopedia of cremation*. Aldershot: Ashgate

Davies J, Fabiš M, Mainland I, Richards M, Thomas R (eds) 2005 Diet and health in past animal populations: current research and future directions. Oxford: Oxbow Books

Davies, S F, 1993 Histoplasmosis, in K F Kiple (ed) 1993, 779–83

Davis, J B, & Thurman, J, 1865 *Crania Britannica. Delineation and descriptions of the skulls of the aboriginal and early inhabitants of the British Isles. 2 volumes*. London: printed privately

Dawes, J D, & Magilton, J R, 1980 *The cemetery of St. Helen-on-the-Walls, Aldwark. The archaeology of York. The Medieval cemeteries* **12/1**. London: Council for British Archaeology for York Archaeological Trust

Dawson, W R, 1927 On two Egyptian mummies preserved in the Museums of Edinburgh, *Proceedings of the Society of Antiquaries of Scotland*, **61**, 290

DeGusta, D, 2002 Comparative skeletal pathology and the case for conspecific care in Middle Pleistocene hominids, *J Archaeological Science*, **29**, 1435–8

DeGusta, D, 2003 Aubesier 11 is not evidence of Neanderthal conspecific care, *J Human Evolution*, **45**, 821–30

DeGusta, D, & White, T D, 1996 On the use of skeletal collections for DNA analysis, *Ancient Biomolecules*, **1**, 89–92

Delaney, M, and Ó Floinn, R, 1995 A bog body from Meenybraddan bog, County Donegal, Ireland, in R C Turner and R G Scaife 1995, 123–32

DeLeon, V B, 2007 Fluctuating asymmetry and stress in a Medieval Nubian population, *American J Physical Anthropology*, **132**, 520–34

Department for Culture, Media and Sport, 2005 *Guidance for the care of human remains in museums.* London: Department for Culture, Media and Sport

Department of the Environment, 1990 *Planning Policy Guidance Note 16. Archaeology and planning.* London: HMSO

Department of Health, 2000 *Report of a census of organs and tissues retained by pathology services in England.* London: The Stationery Office

De Vito, C, & Saunders, S R, 1990 A discriminant function analysis of deciduous teeth to determine sex, *J Forensic Sciences*, **35**, 845–58

Discover the mysteries under your skin, 2002 *Prof. Gunther von Hagen's Body Worlds. The anatomical exhibition of real human bodies. Catalogue of the exhibition.* Heidelberg, Germany: Institut für Plastination

Dobney, K, & Brothwell, D, 1988 A scanning electron microscope study of archaeological dental calculus, in S Olsen (ed), *Scanning Electron Microscopy in Archaeology.* British Archaeological Reports International Series, **452**. Oxford: Tempus Reparatum, 372–85

Dobney, K, & O'Connor, T (eds), 2002 *Bones and the man. Studies in honour of Don Brothwell.* Oxford: Oxbow Books

Doran, G, Dickel, D N, Basllinger, W E Jr, Agee, O F, Laipis, P J, & Hauswirth, W W, 1986 Anatomic, cellular, and molecular analysis of 8000-year-old human brain tissue from the Windover site, *Nature*, **323**, 803–06

Drinkhall, G, & Foreman, M, 1998 *The Anglo-Saxon cemetery at Castledyke South, Bartonn-on-Humber,* Sheffield Excavation Reports **6**. Sheffield: Academic Press

Duday, H, 2006 Archaeothanatology of the archaeology of death, in R Gowland & C Knüsel (eds) 2006, 30–56

Dufour, D L, Staten, L K, Reina, J C, & Spurr, G B, 1997 Living on the edge: dietary strategies of economically impoverished women in Cali, Colombia, *American J Physical Anthropology*, **102**, 5–15

Dupras, T L, Schwarcz, H P, & Fairgrieve, S I, 2001 Infant feeding and weaning practices in Roman Egypt, *American J Physical Anthropology*, **115**, 204–12

Dutour, O, Palfi, G, Berato, J, & Brun, J-P, 1994 *L'origine de la syphilis en Europe: avant ou apres 1493?* Centre Archeologique du Var, Toulon, France: Editions Errance

Effros, B, 2000 Skeletal sex and gender in Merovingian mortuary archaeology, *Antiquity*, **74**, 632–39

Elia M, 2002 Nutrition, in P Kumar & M Clark (eds), *Clinical medicine, 5th edition.* Edinburgh: W B Saunders, 221–51

Elliott-Smith, G, 1908 The most ancient splints, *British Medical J*, **1**, 732

Elliott-Smith, G, & Wood-Jones, F, 1910 *The archaeological survey of Nubia 1907–8. Volume 2. Report on the human remains.* Cairo: National Printing Department

English Heritage, 2004 *Human bones from archaeological sites. Guidelines for producing assessment documents and analytical reports.* Swindon: English Heritage in association with the British Association of Biological Anthropology and Osteoarchaeology

English Heritage and Church of England, 2005 *Guidance for best practice for treatment of human remains excavated from Christian burial grounds in England.* London: English Heritage

Epstein, S, 1937 Art, history and the crutch, *Annals of Medical History,* **9**, 304–13

Eshed, V, Gopher, A, Galili, E & Hershkovitz, I 2004 Musculoskeletal stress markers in Natufian hunter-gatherers and Neolithic farmers in the Levant: the upper limb, *American J Physical Anthropology* **123**, 303–15

Esmonde Cleary, S, 2000 Putting the dead in their place – burial location in Roman Britain, in J Pearce, M Millett, & M Struck (eds), *Burial, society and context in the Roman world.* Oxford: Oxbow, 127–42

Esper, JF, 1774 *Ausfürliche Nachrichten von Neuentdeckten Zoolithen Unbekannter Vierfüssiger Thiere.* Üremberg: Erben

Evans, J, Stoodley, N, & Chenery, C, 2006 A strontium and oxygen isotope assessment of a possible fourth-century immigrant population in a Hampshire cemetery, southern England, *J Archaeological Science,* **33**, 265–72

Fabrizi, E, & Ley, S (eds), 2006 *Spencer Tunick in Newcastle–Gateshead 17 July 2005.* Gateshead: Baltic

Faerman, M, Jankauskas, R, Gorski, A, Bercovier, H, Greenblatt, ChL, 1997 Prevalence of human tuberculosis in a medieval population of Lithuania studied by ancient DNA analysis, *Ancient Biomolecules,* **1**, 205–14

Faerman, M, Bar-Gal, G K, Filon, D, Greenblatt, C L, Stager, L, Oppenheim, A, & Smith P, 1998 Determining the sex of infanticide victims from the late Roman era through ancient DNA analysis, *J Archaeological Science* **25**, 861–5

Falys, C G, Schutkowski, H, & Weston, D A, 2006 Auricular surface aging: Worse than expected? A test of the revised method on a documented historic skeletal assemblage, *American J Physical Anthropology,* **130**, 508–13

Farwell, D E, & Molleson, T I, 1993 *Excavations at Poundbury 1966-80. Volume 2: The Cemeteries.* Dorchester, England: Dorset Natural History and Archaeological Society

Faure, G, & Mensing, T M, 2005 *Isotopes. Principles and applications, 3rd edition.* Hoboken, New Jersey: Wiley

Fforde, C, Hubert J, & Turnbull, J, 2002 *The dead and their possessions. Repatriation in principle, policy and practice.* London: Routledge

Finnegan, M, 1978 Non-metrical variation of the infracranial skeleton, *J Anatomy,* **125**, 23–37

Fiorato, V, Boylston, A, & Knüsel, C (eds), 2000 *Blood red roses. The archaeology of a mass grave from the battle of Towton AD 1461.* Oxford: Oxbow Books

Fiorato, V, Boylston, A & Knüsel, C (eds), 2007 *Blood red roses. The archaeology of a mass grave from the battle of Towton AD 1461,* 2nd edition. Oxford: Oxbow Books

Fitzgerald, C M, & Rose, J C, 2000 Reading between the lines: dental development and subadult age assessment using the microstructural growth markers of teeth, in M A Katzenberg & S R Saunders (eds), *Biological anthropology of the human skeleton.* New York: Wiley-Liss, 163–86

Fitzgerald, C M, Saunders, S, Bondioli, L, & Macchiarelli, R, 2006 Health of infants in an imperial Roman skeletal sample: perspective from dental microstructure, *American J Physical Anthropology,* **130**, 179–89

Fletcher, H A, Donoghue, H D, Holton, J, Pap, I, & Spigelman, M, 2003a Widespread occurrence of *Mycobacterium tuberculosis* DNA from 18th–19th-century Hungarians, *American J Physical Anthropology*, **120**, 144–52

Fletcher, H A, Donoghue, H D, Taylor, G M, Van der Zanden, A G M, & Spigelman, M, 2003b Molecular analysis of *Mycobacterium tuberculosis* DNA from a family of 18th-century Hungarians, *Microbiology*, **149**, 143–51

Fletcher, M, & Lock, G R, 1991 *Digging numbers. Elementary statistics for archaeologists.* Oxford University Committee Archaeology Monograph **33**. Oxford: Oxbow

Foggin, P M, Torrance, M E, Dorje, D, Xuri, W, Foggin, J M, & Torrance, J, 2006 Assessment of the health status and risk factors of Kham Tibetan pastoralists in the alpine grasslands of the Tibetan plateau, *Social Science and Medicine*, **63**, 2512–32

Foley, R, 1990 The Duckworth Osteological Collection at the University of Cambridge, *World Archaeological Bulletin*, **6**, 53–62

Fornaciari, G, & Marchetti, A, 1986 Intact smallpox virus particles in an Italian mummy, *The Lancet*, **2**, 625

Francalacci, P, 1995 DNA analysis of ancient dessicated corpses from Xinjiang, *J Indo-European Studies*, **23**, 385–97

Fricker, E J, Spigelman, M, & Fricker, C R, 1997 The detection of *Escherichia coli* DNA in the ancient remains of Lindow Man using polymerase chain reaction, *Letters in Applied Microbiology*, **24**, 351–4

Fuller, B T, Richards, M P, & Mays, S, 2003 Stable carbon and nitrogen isotope variations in tooth dentine and serial sections from Wharram Percy, *J Archaeological Science*, **30**, 673–1684

Fuller, B T, Molleson, T I, Harris, D A, Gilmour, L T, & Hedges, R E M, 2006a Isotopic evidence for breastfeeding and possible adult dietary differences from Late/Sub-Roman Britain, *American J Physical Anthropology*, **129**, 45–54

Fuller, B T, Fuller, J L, Harris, D A, & Hedges, R E M, 2006b Detection of breastfeeding and weaning in modern human infants with carbon and nitrogen stable isotope ratios, *American J Physical Anthropology*, **129**, 279–93

Fuller, C (ed), 1998 *The old radical: representations of Jeremy Bentham.* London: University College, The Jeremy Bentham Project

Fully, G, 1956 Une nouvelle méthode de détermination de la taille, *Annales de Médicine Légale*, **36**, 266–73

Ganiaris, H, 2001 London Bodies: an exhibition at the Museum of London, in E Williams (ed) *Human remains. Conservation, retrieval and analysis. Proceedings of a conference held in Williamsburg, VA, Nov 7–11, 1999.* British Archaeological Reports International Series, **934**. Oxford: Archaeopress, 267–74

Gao, S-Z, Yang, Y-D, Xu, Y, Zhang, Q-C, Zhu, H & Zhou, H, 2007 Tracing the genetic history of the Chinese people: mitochondrial DNA analysis of a Neolithic population from the Lajia site, *American J Physical Anthropology*, **133**, 1128–36

Garland, A N, 1987 A histological study of archaeological bone decomposition, in A Boddington, A N Garland, & R C Janaway (eds), *Death, decay and reconstruction. Approaches to archaeology and forensic science.* Manchester: Manchester University Press, 109–26

Garland, A N, & Janaway, R C, 1989 The taphonomy of inhumation burials, in C A Roberts, F Lee, & J Bintliff (eds), *Burial archaeology. Current research, methods and developments*, British Archaeological Reports British Series, **211**. Oxford: British Archaeological Reports, 15–37

Garland, A N, Janaway, R, & Roberts, C A, 1988 A study of the decay processes of human skeletal remains from the Parish Church of the Holy Trinity, Rothwell, Northamptonshire, *Oxford J Archaeology*, **7**, 235–25

Garratt-Frost, S, 1992 *The law and burial archaeology*, Institute of Field Archaeologists Technical Paper **11**. Birmingham: Institute of Field Archaeologists

Gejvall, N-G, 1960 *Westerhus, Medieval population and church in light of their skeletal remains*. Lund: Hakak Ohlssons Boktryckeri

Gernaey, A M, Minnikin, D E, Copley, M, Dixon, R, Middleton, J C, & Roberts, C A, 2001 Mycolic acids and ancient DNA confirm an osteological diagnosis of tuberculosis, *Tuberculosis*, **81**, 259–65

Gilbert, M T P, Cuccui, J, White, W, Lynnerup, N, Titball, R W, Cooper, A, & Prentice, M B, 2004 Absence of *Yersinia pestis*-specific DNA in human teeth from five European excavations of putative plague victims, *Microbiology*, **150**, 341–54

Gilbert, M T P, Barnes, I, Collins, M J, Smith, C, Eklund, J, Goudsmit, J, Poinar, H, & Cooper, A, 2005 Notes and comments. Long-term survival of ancient DNA in Egypt: response to Zink and Nerlich (2003), *American J Physical Anthropology*, **128**, 110–14

Gilbert, M T P, Hansen, A J, Willerslev, E, Turner-Walker, G, & Collins, M, 2006 Insights into the process behind the contamination of degraded human teeth and bone samples with exogenous sources of DNA, *Int J Osteoarchaeology*, **16**, 156–64

Gilbert, M T P, Djurhuus, D, Melchior, L, Lynnerup, N, Worobey, M, Wilson, A S, Andreasen, C, & Dissing, J, 2007 mtDNA from hair and nail clarifies the genetic relationship of the 15th-century Qilakitsoq Inuit mummies, *American J Physical Anthropology*, **133**, 847–53

Gilchrist, R, & Sloane, B, 2005 *Requiem. The Medieval monastic cemetery in Britain*. London: Museum of London Archaeology Service

Giles, E, 1963 Sex determination by discriminant function analysis of the mandible, *American J Physical Anthropology*, **22**, 129–35

Glob, P V, 1969 *The bog people*. London: Faber and Faber

Goodman, C M, & Morant, G M, 1940 The human remains of the Iron Age and other periods from Maiden Castle, Dorset, *Biometrika*, **31**, 295–319

Gordon, I, Shapiro, H, & Berson, S, 1988 *Forensic medicine. A guide to principles*. Edinburgh: W B Saunders

Gowland, R L, 2006 Ageing the past: examining age identity from funerary evidence, in R Gowland & C Knüsel (eds) 2006, 143–54

Gowland, R L, & Chamberlain, A, 2002 A Bayesian approach to ageing perinatal skeletal material from archaeological sites: implications for the evidence for infanticide in Roman Britain, *J Archaeological Science*, **29**, 677–85

Gowland, R L, & Chamberlain, A, 2005 Detecting plague: palaeodemographic characterization of a catastrophic death assemblage, *Antiquity*, **79**, 146–57

Gowland, R, & Knüsel, C (eds), 2006 *The social archaeology of human remains*. Oxford: Oxbow

Grauer, A (ed), 1995 *Bodies of evidence: reconstructing history through skeletal analysis.* New York: Wiley-Liss

Grauer, A, & Roberts, C A, 1996 Palaeoepidemiology, healing and possible treatment of trauma in the medieval cemetery population of St Helen-on-the-Walls, York, England, *American J Physical Anthropology*, **100**, 531–44

Grauer, A, & Stuart-Macadam, P (eds), 1998 *Sex and gender in paleopathological perspective.* Cambridge: University Press

Green, J, & Green, M, 1992 *Dealing with death. Practices and procedures.* London: Chapman and Hall

Greene, D L, van Gerven, D P, Armelagos, G J, 1986 Life and death in ancient populations: bones of contention in paleodemography, *Human Evolution*, **1**, 193–206

Greene, K, 2000 *Archaeology. An Introduction. 3rd edition.* London: Routledge

Grupe, G, Price, T D, Scröter, P, Sállner, F, Johnson, C M, & Beard, B L, 1997 Mobility of Bell Beaker people revealed by strontium isotope ratios of tooth and bone: a study of southern Bavarian skeletal remains, *Applied Geochemistry*, **12**, 517–25

Gunnell, D, Rogers, J, & Dieppe, P, 2001 Height and health: predicting longevity from bone length in archaeological remains, *J Epidemiology and Community Health*, **55**, 505–07

Gustafson, G, 1950 Age determination on teeth, *J American Dental Association*, **41**, 45–54

Guy, H, Masset, C, & Baud, C-A, 1997 Infant taphonomy, *Int J Osteoarchaeology*, 7, 221–9

Haas, C J, Zink, A, Molnar, E, Szeimies, U, Reischl, U, Marcsik, A, Ardagna, Y, Dutour, O, Pálfi, G, & Nerlich, A G, 2000 Molecular evidence for different stages of tuberculosis in ancient bone samples from Hungary, *American J Physical Anthropology*, **113**, 293–304

Hackett, C J, 1981 Microscopical focal destruction (tunnels) in exhumed human bones. *Medicine Science and the Law*, **21**, 243–65

Hacking, P, Allen, T, & Rogers, J, 1994 Rheumatoid arthritis in a Medieval skeleton, *Int J Osteoarchaeology*, **4**, 251–5

Hagelberg, E, Sykes, B, & Hedges, R, 1989 Ancient bone DNA amplified. *Nature*, **342**, 485

Haglund, W C, & Sorg, M H, 2002 Human remains in water environments, in W D Haglund & M H Sorg (eds), *Advances in forensic taphonomy. Method, theory and archaeological perspectives.* London: CRC Press, 201–18

Haglund, W D, Connor, M, & Scott, D D, 2002 The effect of cultivation on buried human remains, in W D Haglund & M H Sorg (eds), *Advances in forensic taphonomy. Method, theory and archaeological perspectives.* London: CRC Press, 133–50

Halcrow, S E, Tayles, N, & Buckley, H R, 2007 Age estimation of children from prehistoric Southeast Asia: are the dental formation methods used appropriate? *J Archaeological Science*, **34**, 1158–68

Hällback, H, 1976–77 A medieval bone with a copper plate support indicating open surgical treatment, *Ossa* **3**/4, 63–82

Hamilton, G, 2005 Filthy friends. *New Scientist*, **16th April**, 34–9

Hampshire, K, 2002 Network of nomads: negotiating access to health resources among pastoralist women in Chad, *Social Science and Medicine*, **54**, 1025–37

Hanks, P (ed), 1979 *Collins Dictionary of the English Language.* London: Collins

Harsányi, L, 1993 Differential diagnosis of human and animal bone, in G Grupe & A N Garland (eds), *Histology of ancient human bone: methods and diagnosis.* London: Springer Verlag, 79–94

Hart, G D (ed), 1983 *Disease in ancient man. An international symposium.* Toronto, Canada: Clarke Irwin

Hart Hansen, J P, Meldgaard, J, & Nordqvist, J (eds), 1991 *The Greenland mummies.* London: British Museum Publications for the Trustees of the British Museum

Haselgrove, C, 1999 The Iron Age, in J Hunter & I Ralston (eds), *The archaeology of Britain. An introduction from the Upper Palaeolithic to the Industrial Revolution.* London: Routledge, 113–34

Hauser, G, & De Stefano, G, 1990 *Epigenetic variants of the human skull.* Stuttgart: Schweizerbart'sche Verlagbuchhandlung

Hawkins, D, 1990 The Black Death and new London cemeteries of 1348, *Antiquity*, **64**, 637–42

Haynes, S, Searle, J B, Bretman, A, & Dobney, K M, 2002 Bone preservation and ancient DNA: the application of screening methods for predicting DNA survival, *J Archaeological Science*, **29**, 585–92

Hedges, R E M, 2001 Overview – dating in archaeology; past, present and future, in D R Brothwell & A M Pollard (eds), *Handbook of archaeological science.* Chichester: John Wiley and Sons Ltd, 3–8

Henderson, C, & Gallant, A J, 2007 Quantitative recording of entheses, *Paleopathology Association Newsletter*, **137**, 7–12

Henderson, J, 1987 Factors determining the state of preservation of human remains, in A Boddington, A N Garland, & R C Janaway (eds), *Death, decay and reconstruction. Approaches to archaeology and forensic science.* Manchester: Manchester University Press, 43–54

Henshall, A S, 1963 *The Chambered Tombs of Scotland*, volume 1. Edinburgh: Edinburgh University Press.

Henshall, A S, 1972 *The Chambered Tombs of Scotland*, volume 2. Edinburgh: Edinburgh University Press

Herring, D A, Saunders, S R, & Katzenberg, M A, 1998 Investigating the weaning process in past populations, *American J Physical Anthropology*, **105**, 425–39

Hill, J D, 1995 *Ritual and rubbish in the Iron Age of Wessex*, British Archaeological Reports British Series, **242**. Oxford

Hill, K, Hurtado, A M, 1995 *Ache life history. The ecology and demography of a forgaing people.* New York: Aldine de Gruyter

Hill, P (ed), 1997 *Whithorn and St Ninian: the excavation of a monastic town 1984–1991.* Stroud: Sutton Publishing

Hillier, M L, & Bell, L S, 2007 Differentiating human bone from animal bone: a review of histological methods, *J Forensic Sciences*, **52**, 249–63

Hills, C, 1999 Early historic Britain, in J Hunter & I Ralston (eds), *The archaeology of Britain. An introduction from the Upper Palaeolithic to the Industrial Revolution.* London: Routledge, 176–93

Hillson, S, 1986 *Teeth*. Cambridge: Cambridge University Press

Hillson, S, 1996a *Dental anthropology*. Cambridge: Cambridge University Press

Hillson, S, 1996b *Mammal bones and teeth: an introductory guide*. London: Institute of Archaeology

Historic Scotland, 1997 *The treatment of human remains in archaeology*. Historic Scotland Operational Policy Paper **5**. Edinburgh: Historic Scotland

Hogue, S H, 2006 Determination of warfare and interpersonal conflict in the Protohistoric period: a case study from Mississippi, *Int J Osteoarchaeology*, **16**, 236–48

Holcomb, S M C, & Konigsberg, L W, 1995 Statistical study of sexual dimorphism in the human fetal sciatic notch, *American J Physical Anthropology*, **97**, 113–25

Holden, T G, 1995 The last meals of the Lindow bog men, in R C Turner & R G Scaife (eds), *Bog bodies. New discoveries and new perspectives*. London: British Museum, 76–82

Honch, N V, Higham, T F G, Chapman, J, Gaydarska, B, & Hedges, R E M, 2006 A palaeodietary investigation of carbon ($^{13}C/^{12}$) and nitrogen ($^{15}N/^{14}N$) in human and faunal bones from the Copper Age cemeteries of Varna I and Durankulak, Bulgaria, *J Archaeological Science*, **33**, 1493–1504

Hoppa, R D, 1992 Evaluating human skeletal growth: an Anglo-Saxon example, *Int J Osteoarchaeology*, **2**, 275–88

Hoppa, R D, & Vaupel, J W (eds), 2002 *Palaeodemography. Age distributions from skeletal samples*. Cambridge: Cambridge University Press

Howe, G M, 1997 *People, environment, disease and death*. Cardiff: University of Wales Press

Huber, B R, & Anderson, R, 1996 Bonesetters and curers in a Mexican community: conceptual models, status and gender, *Social Science and Medicine*, **17**, 23–38

Hubert, J, 1989 A proper place for the dead; a critical review of the 'reburial' issue, in R Layton (ed), *Conflict in the archaeology of living traditions*. London: Unwin Hyman, 131–84

Hubert, J, & Fforde, C, 2002 Introduction: the reburial issue in the twenty-first century, in C Fforde, J Hubert, & P Turnbull (eds) 2002, 1–16

Humphrey J H, & Hutchinson, D L, 2001 Macroscopic characteristics of hacking trauma, *J Forensic Sciences*, **46**, 228–33

Humphrey, L, 2000 Growth studies of past populations: an overview and an example, in M Cox & S Mays (eds) 2000, 23–38

Hunt, D R, & Albanese, J, 2005 History and demographic composition of the Robert J Terry Anatomical Collection, *American J Physical Anthropology*, **127**, 406–17

Hunter, K, 1984 *Storage of archaeological finds*. London: United Kingdom Institute for Conservation. Archaeology Section. Guideline 2

Hunter-Mann, K, 2006 Romans lose their heads. *Annual Newsletter of the CBA Yorkshire*, 11–12

Hutchinson, D L, & Norr, L, 2006 Nutrition and health at Contact in late prehistoric Central Gulf Coast Florida, *American J Physical Anthropology*, **129**, 375–86

Ilani, S, Rosenfeld, A, & Dvorachek, M, 1999 Mineralogy and chemistry of a Roman remedy from Judea, *J Archaeological Science*, **26**, 1323–6

Institute of Archaeologists of Ireland, 2006 *Code of conduct for the treatment of human remains in the context of an archaeological excavation.* Dublin: Institute of Archaeologists of Ireland

Irish, J D, 2006 Who were the ancient Egyptians? Dental affinities among Neolithic through Postdynastic peoples, *American J Physical Anthropology*, **129**, 529–43

Iserson, K V, 1994 *Death to dust. What happens to dead bodies?* Tucson, Arizona: Galen Press Ltd

Ishida, H, & Dodo, Y, 1993 Non-metric cranial variation and the population affinities of the Pacific people, *American J Physical Anthropology*, **90**, 49–57

Ivan Perez, S, Barnal, V, & Gonzalez, N, 2007 Morphological differentiation of aboriginal human populations from Tierra del Fuego (Patagonia): implications for South American peopling, *American J Physical Anthropology*, **133**, 1067–79

Ives, R, & Brickley, M, 2005 Metacarpal radiogrammetry: a useful indicator of bone loss throughout the skeleton? *J Archaeological Science*, **32**, 1552–9

Jackes, M, 2000 Building the bases for palaeodemographic analysis, in M A Katzenberg & S R Saunders (eds), *Biological anthropology of the human skeleton.* New York: Wiley-Liss, 417–66

Jackson, R, 1988 *Doctors and diseases in the Roman Empire.* London: British Museum Publications

Jacobi, R M, 1987 Misanthropic miscellany musings on British Early Flandrian archaeology and other flights of fancy, in PA Rowley-Conwy, M Zvelebil, & H P Blankholm (eds), *Mesolithic north-west Europe: recent trends.* Sheffield: Sheffield Academic Press, 163–8

Janaway, R C, Wilson, A S, Caffell, A C, & Roberts, CA, 2001 Human skeletal collections: the responsibilities of project managers, physical anthropologists, conservators and the need for standardised condition assessments, in E Williams (ed), *Human remains. Conservation, retrieval and analysis. Proceedings of a conference held in Williamsburg, VA, 7–11 Nov, 1999*, British Archaeological Reports International Series, **934**. Oxford: Archaeopress, 199–208

Jankauskas, R, 1999 Tuberculosis in Lithuania: palaeopathological and historical correlations, in G Pálfi, O Dutour, J Deák, & I Hutás (eds), *Tuberculosis: past and present.* Budapest and Szeged: Golden Book Publishers and Tuberculosis Foundation, 551–8

Jankauskas, R, 2003 The incidence of diffuse idiopathic skeletal hyperostosis and social status correlations in Lithuanian skeletal materials, *Int J Osteoarchaeology*, **13**, 289–93

Jans, M M F, Nielsen-Marsh, C M, Smith, C I, Collins, M J, & Kars, H, 2004 Characterisation of microbial attack on archaeological bone, *J Archaeological Science*, **31**, 87–95

Janssen, H A M, & Maat, G J R, 1999 *Canons buried in the 'Stiftskapel' of the Saint Servaas Basilica at Maastricht AD 1070-1521. A paleopathological study.* Leiden: Barge's Anthropologica Number 5

Janssens, P, 1987 A copper plate on the upper arm in a burial at the church in Vrasene, Belgium, *J Palaeopathology*, **1**, 15–18

Jay, M, & Richards, M P, 2006 Diet in the Iron Age cemetery population at Wetwang Slack, East Yorkshire, UK: carbon and nitrogen isotope evidence, *J Archaeological Science*, **33**, 653–62

Jenike, M R, 2001 Nutritional ecology: diet, physical activity and body size, in C Panter-Brick, R H Layton, & P A Rowley-Conwy (eds) 2001, 205–38

Johnson, J S, 2001 A long-term look at polymers use to preserve bone, in E Williams (ed), *Human remains. Conservation, retrieval and analysis. Proceedings of a conference held in Williamsburg, VA, 7–11 Nov, 1999.* British Archaeological Reports International Series, **934**. Oxford: Archaeopress, 99–102

Jones, A P, 1999 Indoor air quality and health, *Atmospheric Environment*, **33**, 4535–64

Jones, D G, & Harris, R J, 1998 Archeological human remains. Scientific, cultural and ethical considerations, *Current Anthropology*, **39**, 253–64

Jones, H N, Priest, J D, Hayes, W C, Tichenor, C C, & Nagel, D A, 1977 Humeral hypertrophy in response to exercise, *J Bone and Joint Surgery*, **59A**, 204–08

Jones, J, 2001 A Bronze Age burial from north-east England: lifting and excavation, in E Williams (ed), *Human remains. Conservation, retrieval and analysis. Proceedings of a conference held in Williamsburg, VA, 7–11 Nov, 1999.* British Archaeological Reports International Series, **934**. Oxford: Archaeopress, 33–7

Joyce, R A, 2002 Academic freedom, stewardship and cultural heritage: weighing the interests of stakeholders in crafting repatriation approaches, in C Fforde, J Hubert, & P Turnbull (eds), *The dead and their possessions. Repatriation in principle, policy and practice.* London: Routledge, 99–107

Judd, M A, & Roberts, C A, 1998 Fracture patterns at the medieval leper hospital in Chichester. *American Journal of Physical Anthropology*, **105**, 43–55

Julkunen, H, Heinonen, O P, & Pyörälä, K, 1971 Hyperostosis of the spine in an adult population, *Annals of Rheumatic Diseases*, **30**, 605–12

Jurmain, R D, 1999 *Stories from the skeleton. Behavioral reconstruction in human osteology.* Amsterdam: Gordon and Breach

Jurmain, R, & Bellifemine, V I, 1997 Patterns of cranial trauma in a prehistoric population from Central California, *Int J Osteoarchaeology*, 7, 43–50

Kaestle, F A, & Horsbaugh, K M, 2002 Ancient DNA in anthropology: methods, applications and ethics, *Yearbook of Physical Anthropology*, **45**, 92–130

Kamberi, D, 1994 The three-thousand-year-old Charchan Man preserved at Zaghunuq, *Silo-Platonic Papers*, **44**, 1–15

Kanz, F, & Grosschmidt, K, 2006 Head injuries of Roman gladiators, *Forensic Science Int*, **160**, 207–16

Katzenberg, M A, 2000 Stable isotope analysis: a tool for studying past diet, demography and life history, in M A Katzenberg & S R Saunders (eds), *Biological anthropology of the human skeleton.* New York: Wiley-Liss, 305–26

Katzenberg, M A, Saunders, S A, & Fitzgerald, W R, 1993 Age differences in stable carbon and nitrogen isotope ratios in a population of prehistoric maize horticulturists, *American J Physical Anthropology*, **90**, 267–81

Katzenberg, M A, Schwarcz, H P, Knyf, M, & Melbye, F J, 1995 Stable isotope evidence for maize horticulture and paleodiet in southern Ontario, Canada, *American Antiquity*, **60**, 335–50

Kazmi, J H, & Pandit, K, 2001 Disease and dislocation: the impact of refugee movements on the geography of malaria in NWFP, Pakistan, *Social Science and Medicine*, **52**, 1043–55

Keenleyside, A, Schwarcz, H, & Panayotova, K, 2006 Stable isotopic evidence of diet in a Greek colonial population from the Black Sea, *J Archaeological Science*, **33**, 1205–15

Keith, A, 1924 Description of three crania from Aveline's Hole, *Proc Bristol Speleological Society*, **2**, 16

Kemp, B M, Malhi, R S, McDonough, J, Bolnick, D A, Eshleman, J A, Rickards, O, Martinez-Labarga, C, Johnson, J R, Lorenz, J G, Dixon, E J, Fifield, T E, Heaton, T H, Worl, R, & Smith, D G, 2007 Genetic analysis of early Holocene skeletal remains from Alaska and its implications for the settlement of the Americas, *American J Physical Anthropology*, **130**, 605–21

Kennedy, G E, 1986 The relationship between auditory exostoses and cold water: a latitudinal analysis, *American J Physical Anthropology*, **71**, 401–15

Key, C A, Aiello, L C, & Molleson, T, 1994 Cranial suture closure and its implications for age estimation, *Int J Osteoarchaeology*, **4**, 193–207

King, T, Humphrey, L T, & Hillson, S, 2005 Linear enamel hypoplasias as indicators of systemic physiological stress: Evidence from two known age-at-death and sex populations from postmedieval London, *American J Physical Anthropology*, **128**, 547–59

Kiple, K F (ed), 1993 *The Cambridge world history of human disease*. Cambridge: Cambridge University Press

Kiple, K F (ed), 1997 *Plague, pox and pestilence. Disease in history*. London: Weidenfeld and Nicholson

Kneller, P, 1998 Health and safety in church and funerary archaeology, in M Cox (ed) 1998, 181–9

Knudson, K J, Price, T D, Buikstra, J E, & Blom, D E, 2004 The use of strontium isotope analysis to investigate migration and mortuary ritual in Bolivia and Peru, *Archaeometry*, **46**, 5–18

Knudson, K J, & Buikstra, J E, 2007 Residential mobility and resource use in the Chiribaya polity of southern Peru: strontium isotope analysis of archaeological tooth enamel and bone, *International J Osteoarchaeology*, **17**, 563–80

Knudson, K J, Aufderheide, A C, & Buikstra, J E, 2007 Seasonality and paleodiet in the Chiribaya polity of southern Peru, *J Archaeological Science*, **34**, 451–62

Knüsel, C, 2000 Bone adaptation and its relationship to physical activity in the past, in M Cox & S Mays (eds) 2000, 381–401

Knüsel, C, Kemp, R, & Budd, P, 1995 Evidence for remedial medical treatment of a severe knee injury from the Fishergate Gilbertine monastery in the City of York, *J Archaeological Science*, **22**, 369–84

Konigsberg, L, & Frankenberg, S R, 1992 Estimation of age structure in anthropological demography, *American J Physical Anthropology*, **89**, 235–56

Kuhn G, Schultz M, Müller R, & Rühli F J, 2007, Diagnostic value of micro-CT in comparison with histology in the qualitative assessment of historical human postcranial bone pathologies, *Homo*, **58**, 97–115

Kumar, S S, Nasidze, I, Walimbe, S, & Stoneking, M, 2000 Brief communication: discouraging prospects for ancient DNA from India, *American J Physical Anthropology*, **113**, 129–33

Kustár, A, 1999 Facial reconstruction of an artificially distorted skull of the 4th to the 5th century from the site of Mözs, *Int J Osteoarchaeology*, **9**, 325–32

Lackey, D P, 2006 Ethics and Native American reburials: a philosopher's view of two decades of NAGPRA, in C Scarre & G Scarre (eds), *The ethics of archaeology. Philosophical perspectives on archaeological practice.* Cambridge: Cambridge University Press, 146–62

Lambert, P M, 2002 Rib lesions in a prehistoric Puebloan sample from southwest Colorado, *American J Physical Anthropology*, **117**, 281–92

Lane, S D, & Cibula, D A, 2000 Gender and health, in G L Albright, R Fitzpatrick, & S C Scrimshaw (eds), *Handbook of social studies in health and medicine.* London: Sage Publications, 136–53

Larsen, C S, 1994 In the wake of Columbus: native population biology in Postcontact Americas, *Yearbook of Physical Anthropology*, **37**, 109–54

Larsen, C S, 1997 *Bioarchaeology. Interpreting behavior from the human skeleton.* Cambridge: Cambridge University Press

Larsen, C S, 1998 Gender, health and activity in foragers and farmers in the American southeast: implications for social organisation in the Georgia Bight, in A Grauer & P Stuart-Macadam (eds) 1998, 165–87

Larsen, C S, 2006 The agricultural revolution as environmental catastrophe. Implications for health and lifestyle in the Holocene, *Quaternary International*, **150**, 12–20

Larsen, C S, & Milner, G (eds), 1994 *In the wake of contact: biological responses to contact.* New York: Wiley-Liss

Larsen, C S, Craig, J, Sering, L E, Schoeninger, M J, Russell, K F, Hutchinson, D L, & Williamson, M A, 1995 Cross Homestead: life and death on the Midwestern frontier in A L Grauer (ed), *Bodies of evidence: Reconstructing history through skeletal analysis.* New York: Wiley-Liss, 139–59

Larsen, C S, Huynh, H P, & McEwan, B G, 1996 Death by gunshot: biocultural implications of trauma at Mission San Luis, *Int J Osteoarchaeology*, **6**, 42–50

Larson, A, Bell, M, & Young, A F, 2004 Clarifying relationships between health and residential mobility, *Social Science and Medicine*, **59**, 2149–60

Lazenby, R A, & Pfeiffer, S, 1993 Effects of a 19th-century below-knee amputation and prosthesis on femoral morphology, *Int J Osteoarchaeology*, **3**, 19–28

Leader, D, 2003 *Domain Field. Anthony Gormley.* Gateshead: Baltic

Lebel, S, & Trinkaus, E, 2002 Middle Pleistocene remains from the Bau de l'Aubesier, *J Human Evolution*, **43**, 659–85

Lee, F, & Magilton, J, 1989 The cemetery of the hospital of St James and St Mary Magdalene, Chichester – a case study, *World Archaeology*, **21**, 273–82

Leff, R D, 1993 Lyme borreliosis (Lyme disease), in K F Kiple (ed), *The Cambridge world history of human disease.* Cambridge: Cambridge University Press, 852–54

Leroi-Gourhan, A, 1975 The flowers found with Shanidar IV, a Neanderthal burial in Iraq, *Science*, **190**, 562–4

Lewis, M E, nd. How to pack a skeleton. Unpublished. Department of Archaeological Sciences: University of Bradford

Lewis, M E, 2002 Impact of industrialisation: comparative study of child health in four sites from Medieval and Postmedieval England (AD 850–1859), *American J Physical Anthropology*, **119**, 211–23

Lewis, M E, 2007 *The bioarchaeology of children. Perspectives from biological and forensic anthropology*. Cambridge: Cambridge University Press

Lewis, M E, Roberts, C A, & Manchester, K, 1995 Comparative study of the prevalence of maxillary sinusitis in Later Medieval urban and rural populations in Northern England, *American J Physical Anthropology*, **98**, 497–506

Lieban, R W, 1973 Medical anthropology, in JJ Honigmann (ed) *Handbook of Social and Cultural Anthropology*. New York: Rand McNally, 1031–72

Lieverse, A R, Weber, A W, & Goriunova, O I, 2006 Human taphonomy at Khuzhir-Nuge XIV, Siberia: a new method for documenting skeletal condition, *J Archaeological Science*, **33**, 1141–51

Lillie, M, & Richards, M P, 2000 Stable isotope analysis and dental evidence of diet at the Mesolithic transition in Ukraine, *J Archaeological Science* **27**, 965–72

Lillie, M, Richards, M P, & Jacob, K, 2003 Stable isotope analysis of 21 individuals from the Epipalaeolithic cemetery of Vasilyevka III, Dnieper Raids region, Ukraine, *J Archaeological Science*, **30**, 743–52

Lloyd, G E R (ed),1978 *Hippocratic writings*. London: Penguin Books

Locock, M, 1998 Dignity for the dead, *The Archaeologist*, **33**, 13

Logie, J, 1992 Scots law, in S Garratt-Frost 1992, 11–15

Lohman, J, & Goodnow, K, 2006 *Human remains and museum practices*. London: United Nations Educational, Scientific and Cultural Organization and the Musuem of London

Loth, S R, & Henneberg, M, 2001 Sexually dimorphic mandibular morphology in the fist few years of life, *American J Physical Anthropology*, **115**, 179–86

Loth, S R, & Iscan, M Y, 1989 Morphological assessment of age in the adult: the thoracic region, in M Y Iscan (ed), *Age markers in the human skeleton*. Springfield, Illinois: Charles Thomas, 105–35

Lovejoy, C O, Meindl, R S, Pryzbeck, T R, Barton, T S, Heiple, K G, Kotting, D, 1977 Paleodemography of the the Libben site, Ottawa, Ohio, *Science*, **198**, 291–3

Lovejoy, C O, Meindl, R S, Pryzbeck, T R, & Mensforth, R P, 1985 Chronological metamorphosis of the auricular surface of the ilium: a new method for the determination of adult skeletal age at death, *American J Physical Anthropology*, **68**, 15–28

Lovell, N C, 1997 Trauma analysis in paleopathology, *Yearbook of Physical Anthropology*, **40**, 139–70

Lubell, D, Jackes, M, Schwarcz, H P, Knyf, M, & Mieklejohn, C, 1994 The Mesolithic-Neolithic transition in Portugal: isotopic and dental evidence of diet, *J Archaeological Science*, **21**, 201–16

Lucy, D, Pollard, A M, & Roberts, C A, 1994 A comparison of three dental techniques for estimating age at death in humans, *J Archaeological Science*, **22**, 151–6

Lucy, D, Aykroyd, R G, Pollard, A M, & Solheim, T, 1996 A Bayesian approach to adult human age estimation from dental observations by Johanson's age changes, *J Forensic Sciences*, **41**, 5–10

Lucy, S, 2000 *The Anglo-Saxon way of death.* Stroud, Gloucestershire: Sutton Publishing

Lucy, S, & Reynolds, A, 2002 Burial in early medieval England and Wales: past, present and future, in S Lucy & A Reynolds (eds), *Burial in early Medieval England and Wales*, Society for Medieval Archaeology Monograph **17**. London: Society for Medieval Archaeology, 1–23

Lukacs, J R, 1989 Dental palaeopathology: methods for reconstructing dietary patterns, in M Y İşcan & K A R Kennedy (eds), *Reconstruction of life from the skeleton*. New York: Alan Liss, 261–86

Lukacs, J R, & Walimbe, S R,1998 Physiological stress in prehistoric India: new data on localized hypolasia of primary canines linked to climate and subsistence change, *J Archaeological Science*, **25**, 571–85

Lunt, D A, 1974 The prevalence of dental caries in the permanent dentition of Scottish prehistoric and mediaeval populations, *Archives of Oral Biology*, **19**, 431–7

Lynnerup, N, 2007 Mummies, *American J Physical Anthropology*, **50**, 162–90

Maat, G J R, 2005 Two millennia of male stature development and population health and wealth in the low countries, *Int J Osteoarchaeology*, **15**, 276–90

Maat, G, & Baig, M, 1991 Scanning electron microscopy of fossilised sickle cells, *Int J Osteoarchaeology*, **5**, 271–6

MacDonald, C, 2000 *Guidance for writing a Code of ethics.* http://www.ethicsweb.ca/codes/coe3.htm

Macho, G A, Abel, R L, & Schutkowski, H, 2005 Age changes in bone microstructure: do they occur uniformly? *Int J Osteoarchaeology*, **15**, 421–30

MacKinney, L, 1957 Medieval surgery, *J Int Coll Surgeons*, **27**, 393–404

Madrigal, L, 1998 *Statistics for anthropology.* Cambridge: Cambridge University Press

Magilton, J R, Lee, F, & Boylston, A, 2008 *'Lepers oustside the gate'. Excavations at the cemetery of the Hospital of St James and St Mary Magdalene, Chichester, 1986–87 and 1993*, CBA Research Report **158** York: Council for British Archaeology

Mahoney, P, 2006 Dental microwear from Natufian hunter-gatherers and early Neolithic farmers: comparisons within and between samples, *American J Physical Anthropology*, **130**, 308–19

Malim, T, & Hines, J, 1998 *The Anglo-Saxon cemetery at Edix Hill (Barrington A), Cambridgeshire*, CBA Research Report **112**. York: Council for British Archaeology

Mallory, J P, & Mair, V H, 2000, *The Tarim mummies.* London: Thames and Hudson

Manchester, K, 1978 Palaeopathology of a royalist garrison, *Ossa*, **5**, 25–33

Manchester, K, 1980 Hydrocephalus in an Anglo-Saxon child from Eccles, *Archaeologia Cantiana*, **96**, 77–82

Manchester, K, 1983 *The archaeology of disease.* Bradford: University Press

Manchester, K, 1984 Tuberculosis and leprosy in antiquity, *Medical History*, **28**, 162–73

Mann, R W, Bass W M, & Meadows, L, 1990 Time since death and decomposition of the human body: variables and observations in case and experimental field studies, *J Forensic Sciences*, **35**, 103–11

Mant, A K, 1987 Knowledge acquired from post-War exhumations, in A Boddington, A N Garland, & R C Janaway (eds), *Death, decay and reconstruction. Approaches to archaeology and forensic science.* Manchester: Manchester University Press, 65–78

Manzi G, Sperduit A, Passarello, P, 1991 Behavior-induced auditory exostoses in Imperial Roman society: evidence from coeval urban and rural communities near Roma, *American J Physical Anthropology*, **85**, 253–260

Marennikova, S S, Shelukhina, E M, Zhukova, O A, Yanova, N N, & Loparev, V N, 1990 Smallpox diagnosed 400 years later: results of skin lesions examination of 16th-century Italian mummy, *J Hygiene, Epidemiology, Microbiology, and Immunology*, **34**, 227–31

Margerison, B, & Knüsel, C, 2002 Paleodemographic comparison of a catastrophic and an attritional death assemblage, *American J Physical Anthropology*, **119**, 134–43

Mariani-Costantini, R, Catalano, P, di Gennaro, F, di Tota, G, & Angeletti, L R, 2000 New light on cranial surgery in ancient Rome, *The Lancet*, **355**, 305–07

Martin, D, & Frayer, D (eds), 1998 *Troubled times. Violence and warfare in the past.* New York: Gordon and Breach Publishers

Mascie-Taylor, C G N, & Lasker, G W (eds), 1988 *Biological aspects of human migration.* Cambridge: Cambridge University Press

Masset, C, 1989 Age estimation on the basis of cranial sutures, in M Y İşcan (ed), *Age markers in the human skeleton.* Springfield, Illinois: Charles C Thomas, 71–104

Mays, S, 1996 Healed limb amputations in human osteoarchaeology and their causes, *Int J Osteoarchaeology*, **6**, 101–13

Mays, S, 1997a A perspective on human osteoarchaeology in Britain, *Int J Osteoarchaeology*, 7, 600–04

Mays, S, 1997b Carbon stable isotope ratios in medieval and later human skeletons from northern England, *J Archaeological Science*, **24**, 561–7

Mays, S, 1998 *The archaeology of human bones.* London: Routledge

Mays, S, 1999 A biomechanical study of activity patterns in a medieval human skeletal assemblage, *Int J Osteoarchaeology*, **9**, 68–73

Mays, S, 2000 Biodistance studies using craniometric variation in British archaeological skeletal material, in M Cox & S Mays (eds) 2000, 277–88

Mays, S, 2005a Supra-acetabular cysts in a medieval skeletal population, *Int J Osteoarchaeology*, **15**, 233–46

Mays, S, 2005b Age-related cortical bone loss in women from a 3rd- to 4th-century population from England, *American J Physical Anthropology*, **129**, 518–28

Mays, S, 2006 The osteology of monasticism, in R Gowland & C Knüsel (eds), *Social archaeology of human remains.* Oxford: Oxbow, 179–89

Mays, S, 2007 United in church. *British Archaeology*, **September/October**. York: Council for British Archaeology, 40–1

Mays, S, & Cox, M, 2000 Sex determination in skeletal remains, in M Cox & S A Mays (eds) 2000, 117–29

Mays S, Faerman, M, 2001 Sex identification in some putative infanticide remains from Roman Britain using ancient DNA, *J Archaeological Science*, **28**, 555–9

Mays, S, & Taylor, G M, 2002 Osteological and biomolecular study of two possible cases of hypertrophic osteoarthropathy from medieval England, *J Archaeological Science*, **29**, 1267–76

Mays, S, & Taylor, G M, 2003 A prehistoric case of tuberculosis from Britain, *Int J Osteoarchaeology*, **13**,189–96

Mays, S, Taylor, G M, Legge, A J, Young, D B, & Turner-Walker, G, 2001 Palaeopathological and biomolecular study of tuberculosis in a medieval skeletal collection from England, *American J Physical Anthropology*, **114**, 298–311

Mays, S, Crane-Kramer, G, & Bayliss, A, 2003 Two probable cases of treponemal disease of Medieval date from England, *American J Physical Anthropology*, **120**, 133–43

Mays, S, Brickley, M, & Ives, R, 2006a Skeletal manifestations of rickets in infants and young children in a historic population from England, *American J Physical Anthropology*, **129**, 362–74

Mays, S, Turner-Walker, G, & Syversen, U, 2006b Osteoporosis in a population from Medieval Norway, *American J Physical Anthropology*, **131**, 343–51

Mays, S, Harding, C, & Heighway, C, 2007 *The churchyard. Wharram. A study of settlement on the Yorkshire Wolds XI*, York University Archaeological Publications **13**. York: University of York

McElroy, A, & Townsend, P K, 1996 *Medical Anthropology in Ecological Perspective*. Boulder, Colorado: Westview Press

McKinley, J I, 1991 Results of the questionnaire on the excavation of human remains in Britain, *The Field Archaeologist*, **15**, 278–9

McKinley, J I, 1994a *Spong Hill. Part Viii. The cremations*, East Anglian Archaeology Report **69**. Norwich, Norfolk: Field Archaeology Division, Norfolk Museums Service

McKinley, J I, 1994b Bone fragment size in British cremation burials and its implications for pyre technology and ritual, *J Archaeological Science*, **21**, 339–42

McKinley, J I, 1994c A pyre and grave goods in British cremation burials: have we missed something? *Antiquity*, **68**, 132–4

McKinley, J I, 1997 Bronze Age 'barrows' and funerary rites and rituals of cremation, *Proc Prehistoric Society*, **63**, 129–45

McKinley, J I, 1998 Archaeological manifestations of cremation, *The Field Archaeologist*, **33**,18–20

McKinley, J I, 2000a Phoenix rising: aspects of cremation in Roman Britain, in J Pearce, M Millett, & M Struck (eds), *Burial, society and context in the Roman world*. Oxford: Oxbow, 38–44

McKinley, J I, 2000b The analysis of cremated bone, in M Cox & S Mays (eds) 2000, 403–21

McKinley, J I, 2000c Putting cremated human remains in context, in S Roskams (ed), *Interpreting stratigraphy. Site evaluation, recording procedures and stratigraphic analysis. Papers presented to the Interpreting Stratigraphy Conferences 1993–97*, British Archaeological Reports International Series, **910**. Oxford: Archaeopress, 135–9

McKinley, J I, 2004a The human remains and aspect of pyre technology and cremation rituals, in H E M Cool (ed), *The Roman cemetery at Brougham, Cumbria. Excavations 1966–67*, Britannia Monograph Series **21**. London: Society for the Promotion of Roman Studies, 283–309

McKinley, J I, 2004b Compiling a skeletal inventory: cremated bone, in M Brickley & J I McKinley (eds) 2004, 9–13

McKinley, J I, 2004c Compiling a skeletal inventory: disarticulated and co-mingled remains, in M Brickley & J I McKinley (eds) 2004, 14–17

McKinley, J I, 2006 Cremation ... the cheap option?, in R Gowland & C Knüsel (eds) 2006, 81–8

McKinley, J I & Roberts, C A, 1993 *Excavation and post-excavation treatment of cremated and inhumed remains*, Technical Paper Number **13**. Birmingham: Institute of Archaeologists

McWhirr, A, Viner, L, & Wells, C, 1982 *Romano-British cemeteries at Cirencester.* Cirencester: Excavations Committee

Meates, G W, 1979 *The Lullingstone Roman villa. Volume I. The site.* Chichester: Phillimore and Kent Archaeology Society

Megaw, J V S, & Simpson, D D A, 1979 *Introduction to British prehistory.* Leicester: Leicester University Press

Meindl, R S, & Lovejoy, C O, 1985 Ectocranial suture closure. A revised method for the determination of skeletal age and death and blind tests of its accuracy, *American J Physical Anthropology*, **68**, 57–66

Mekota, A-M, Grupe, G, Zimmerman, M R, & Vermehren, M, 2005 First identification of an Egyptian mummified human placenta, *Int J Osteoarchaeology*, **15**, 51–60

Melikian, M, 2006 A case of metastatic carcinoma from 18th-century London, *Int J Osteoarchaeology*, **16**, 138–44

Mellars, P A, 1987 *Excavations on Oronsay: prehistoric human ecology on a small island.* Edinburgh: Edinburgh University Press

Merbs, C F, 1997 Eskimo skeleton taphonomy with identification of possible polar bear victims, in W D Haglund & M H Sorg (eds) 1997, 249–62

Merrett, D, & Pfeiffer, S, 2000 Maxillary sinusitis as an indicator of respiratory health in past populations, *American J Physical Anthropology*, **111**, 301–18

Micozzi, M S, 1997 Frozen environments and soft tissue preservation, in W D Haglund & M H Sorg (eds) 1997, 171–80

Miles, A E W, 1962 Assessment of the ages of a population of Anglo-Saxons from their dentitions, *Proc Royal Society of Medicine*, **55**, 881–6

Miles, A E W, 1989 *An early Christian chapel and burial ground on the Isle of Ensay, Outer Hebrides, Scotland with a study of the skeletal remains*, British Archaeological Reports British Series, **212**. Oxford

Miles, A E W, 2001 The Miles method of assessing age from tooth wear, *J Archaeological Science*, **28**, 973–82

Millard, A, 2000 A model for the effect of weaning on N isotope ratios in humans, in G A Goodfriend, M J Collins, M L Fogel, S A Macko, & J F Wehmiller (eds), *Perspectives in amino acide and protein geochemistry.* New York: Oxford University Press, 51–9

Millard, A, 2001 Deterioration of bone, in D R Brothwell & A M Pollard (eds), *Handbook of archaeological science.* Chichester: John Wiley and Sons Ltd, 637–47

Milner, G R, Wood, J W, & Boldsen, J L, 2000 Paleodemography, in M A Katzenberg & S R Saunders (eds), *Biological anthropology of the human skeleton.* New York: Wiley-Liss, 467–97

Ministry of Justice 2008 *Burial law and archaeology*. London: Coroner's Unit, Steel House, Ministry of Justice

Mitchell, P D, 2006 Trauma in the Crusader period city of Caesarea: a major port in the Medieval Eastren Mediterranean, *Int J Osteoarchaeology*, **16**, 493–505

Mitchell, P D, Nagar, Y, & Ellenblum, R, 2006 Weapon injuries in the 12th-century Crusader garrison of Vadum Iacob Castle, Galilee, *Int J Osteoarcheology*, **16**, 145–55

Mithen, S, 1999 Hunter-gatherers of the Mesolithic, in J Hunter & I Ralston (eds), *The archaeology of Britain. An introduction from the Upper Palaeolithic to the Industrial Revolution*. London: Routledge, 35–57

Moggi-Cecchi, J, Pacciani, E, & Pinto-Cisternas, J, 1994 Enamel hypoplasia and age at weaning in 19th-century Florence, *American J Physical Anthropology*, **93**, 299–306

Mogle, P, & Zias, J, 1995 Trephination as a possible treatment for scurvy in a Middle Bronze Age (*ca* 2200 BC) skeleton, *Int J Osteoarchaeology*, **5**, 77–81

Møller-Christensen, V, 1958 *Bogen om Abelholt Kloster*. Copenhagen: Danish Science Press

Molleson, T I, & Cohen, P, 1990 The progression of dental attrition stages used for age assessment, *J Archaeological Science*, **17**, 363–71

Molleson, T I, & Cox, M, 1993 *The Spitalfields Project. Volume 2. The Anthropology. The Middling Sort*, CBA Research Report **86**. York: Council for British Archaeology

Molleson, T I, & Cruse, K, 1998 Some sexually dimorphic features of the human juvenile skull and their value in sex determination in immature skeletal remains, *J Archaeological Science*, **25**, 719–28

Monda, K L, Gordon-Larsen, P, Stevens, J, & Popkin, B M, 2007 China's transition: the effect of rapid urbanization on adult physical activity, *Social Science and Medicine*, **64**, 858–70

Montgomery, J, & Evans, J, 2006 Immigrants on the Isle of Lewis – combining funerary and modern isotopic evidence to investigate social differentiation, migration and dietary change in the Outer Hebrides of Scotland, in R Gowland, & C Knüsel (eds) 2006, 122–42

Montgomery, J, Evans, J, Powesland, D, & Roberts, C A, 2005 British continuity or immigrant replacement at West Heslerton Anglian settlement: lead and strontium isotope evidence for mobility, subsistence practice and status, *American J Physical Anthropology*, **126**, 123–38

Mooder, K P, Schurr, T G, Bamforth, F J, Bazaliiski, V I, & Savel'ev, N A, 2006 Population affinities of Neolithic Siberians: a snapshot from prehistoric Lake Baikal, *American J Physical Anthropology*, **129**, 349–61

Moore, K M, Murray, M L, & Schoeninger, M J, 1989 Dietary reconstruction from bones treated with preservatives, *J Archaeological Science*, **16**, 437–46

Moorrees, C F A, Fanning, E A, & Hunt, E E, 1963a Formation and resorption of three deciduous teeth in children, *American J Physical Anthropology*, **21**, 205–13

Moorrees, C F A, Fanning, E A, & Hunt, E E, 1963b Age variation of formation stages for ten permanent teeth, *J Dental Research*, **42**, 1490–1502

Morris, S, Sutton, M, & Gravelle, H, 2005 Inequity and inequality in the use of health care in England: an empirical investigation, *Social Science and Medicine*, **60**, 1251–66

Morton, R J, & Lord, W D, 2002 Detection and recovery of abducted and murdered children: behavioural and taphonomic influences, in W D Haglund & M H Sorg (eds), *Advances in forensic taphonomy. Method, theory and archaeological perspectives.* London: CRC Press, 151–71

Müldner, G, & Richards, M P, 2007 Stable isotope evidence for 1500 years of human diet at the city of York, *American J Physical Anthropology*, **133**, 682–97

Müller, W, Fricke, H, Halliday, A N, McCulloch, M T, & Wartho, J-A, 2003 Origin and migration of the Alpine Iceman, *Science*, **302**, 862–66

Munizaga, J, Allison, M J, Gerstzen, E, & Klurfeld, D M, 1975 Pneumoconiosis in Chilean miners of the 16th century, *Bulletin New York Academy Medicine*, **51**, 1281–93

Museum Ethnographers Group, 1994 Professional guidelines concerning the storage, display, interpretation and return of human remains in ethnographical collections in UK museums, *J Museum Ethnography*, **6**, 22

Museum of London, 1997 *London Bodies:* Ethics Statement. London: Museum of London Internal Report. Unpublished

Museum of London, 1998 *London Bodies. The changing shape of Londoners from prehistoric times to the present day.* London: Museum of London

Needleman, H, 2004 Lead poisoning, *Annual Review of Medicine*, **55**, 209–22

Neri, R, & Lancelloti, L, 2004 Fractures of the lower limbs and their skeletal adaptations: a 20th-century example of pre-modern healing, *Int J Osteoarchaeology*, **14**, 60–6

Nerlich, A G, Zink, A, Szeimies, U, & Haagedorn, H G, 2000 Ancient Egyptian prosthesis of the big toe, *The Lancet*, **356**, 2176–9

Newell, T S, Westermann, C, & Meiklejohn, C, 1979 The skeletal remains of Mesolithic man in western Europe, *J Human Evolution*, **8**, 1–228

Nicholson, G J, Tomiuk, J, Czarnetzki, A, Bachmann, L, & Pusch, C M, 2002 Detection of bone glue treatment as a major source of contamination in ancient DNA analyses, *American J Physical Anthropology*, **118**, 117–20.

Novak, P D, 1995 *Dorland's Pocket Medical Dictionary, 25th edition.* London: WB Saunders Company

Novak, S, 2000 Battle-related trauma, in V Fiorato, A Boylston, & C Knüsel (eds) 2000, 90–102

Nowell, G W, 1978 An evaluation of the Miles method of ageing using the Tepe Hissar dental sample, *American J Physical Anthropology*, **49**, 271–367

Nyati, L H, Norris, S A, Cameron, N, & Pettifor, J M, 2006 Effect of ethnicity and sex on the growth of the axial and appendicular skeleton of children living in a developing country, *American J Physical Anthropology*, **130**, 135–41

Nystrom, K C, 2007 Trepanation in the Cahchapoya region of Northern Peru, *Int J Osteoarchaeology*, **17**, 39–51

Oakberg, K, Levy, T, & Smith, P, 2000 A method for skeletal arsenic analysis applied to the Chalcolithic copper smelting site of Shiqmim, Israel, *J Archaeological Science*, **27**, 895–901

Oakley, K P, Winnifred, M A, Brooke, A, Akester, R, & Brothwell, D R, 1959 Contributions on trepanning or trephination in ancient and modern times, *Man (London)*, **59**, 93–6

O'Brien, R, Hunt, K, & Hart, G, 2005 'It's caveman stuff, but that is to a certain extent how guys operate': men's accounts of masculinity and help seeking, *Social Science and Medicine*, **61**, 503–15

Ocaňa-Riola, R, Sánchez-Cantalejo, C, & Fernández-Ajuria, A, 2006 Rural habitat and risk of death in small areas of southern Spain, *Social Science and Medicine*, **63**, 1352–62

O'Cathain, A, Goode, J, Luff, D, Strangelman, T, Hanlon, G, & Greatbatch, D, 2005 Does NHS Direct empower patients? *Social Science and Medicine*, **61**, 1761–71

O'Connell, L, 2004 Guidance on recording age at death in adults, in M Brickley & J I McKinley (eds) 2004, 18–20

Odegaard, N, & Cassman, V, 2006 Treatment and invasive actions, in V Cassman, N Odegaard, & J Powell (eds), *Human remains: guide for museums and academic institutions*. Lanham, Maryland: Altamira Press, 77–95

O'Higgins, P, 2000 The study of morphological variation in the hominid fossil record: biology, landmarks and geometry, *J Anatomy*, **197**, 120

O'Kelly, M J, 1973 Current excavations at Newgrange, Ireland, in G E Daniel & P Kjaerum (eds), *Megalithic graves and ritual*, Jutland Archaeological Society Publication **11**, 137–46

Okumura, M M M, Boyadjian, C H C, & Eggers, S, 2007 Auditory exostoses as an aquatic activity marker: a comparison of coastal and inland skeletal remains from tropical and subtropical regions of Brazil, *American J Physical Anthropology*, **132**, 558–67

Orme, N, & Webster, M, 1995 *The English hospital 1070–1570*. New Haven: Yale University Press

Ortner, D J, 1998 Male-female immune reactivity and its implications for interpreting evidence in human skeletal palaeopathology, in A Grauer & P Stuart-Macadam (eds) 1998, 79–92

Ortner, D J, 2003 *Identification of pathological conditions in human skeletal remains*. London: Academic Press

Ortner, D J, & Mays, S, 1998 Dry-bone manifestations of rickets in infancy and early childhood, *Int J Osteoarchaeology*, **8**, 45–55

O'Sullivan, J, & Killgore, J, 2003 *Human remains in Irish archaeology*. Dublin: The Heritage Council

O'Sullivan, J, Hallisey, M, &Roberts, J, 2002 *Human remains in Irish archaeology: legal, scientific, planning and ethical implications*. Dublin: The Heritage Council

Ousley, S D, Billeck, W T, & Hollinger, R E, 2005 Federal repatriation legislation and the role of the physical anthropologist in repatriation, *Yearbook of Physical Anthropology*, **48**, 2–32

Owsley, D W, Mires, A M, & Keith, M S, 1985 Case involving differentiation of deer and human bone fragments, *J Forensic Science*, **30**, 572–8

Oxenham, M F, Matsumura, H, & Nishimoto, T, 2006 Diffuse idiopathic skeletal hyperostosis in Late Jomon Hokkaido, Japan, *Int J Osteoarchaeology*, **16**, 34–46

Oygucu, I H, Kurt, M A, Ikiz, I, Erem, T, & Davies, C, 1998 Squatting facets on the neck of the talus and extensions of the trochlear surface of the talus in late Byzantine males, *J Anatomy*, **192**, 287–91

Pääbo, S, 1985 Molecular cloning of ancient Egyptian mummy DNA, *Nature*, **314**, 644–5

Pabst, M A, & Hofer, F, 1998 Deposits of different origin in the lungs of the 5300-year-old Tyrolean iceman, *American J Physical Anthropology*, **107**, 1–12

Panagiaris, G, 2001 The influence of conservation treatments on physical anthropology research, in E Williams (ed), *Human remains. Conservation, retrieval and analysis. Proceedings of a conference held in Williamsburg, VA, 7–11 Nov, 1999*, British Archaeological Reports International Series **934**. Oxford: Archaeopress, 95–8

Panter-Brick, C, Layton R H, & Rowley-Conwy, P (eds), 2001 *Hunter-gatherers. An interdisciplinary perspective.* Cambridge: Cambridge University Press

Papathanasiou, A, 2003 Stable isotope analysis in Neolithic Greece and possible implications on human health, *Int J Osteoarchaeology*, **13**, 314–24

Parker Pearson, M, 1995 Ethics and the dead in British archaeology, *The Field Archaeologist*, **23**, 17–18

Parker Pearson, M, 1999a *The archaeology of death and burial.* Stroud, Gloucestershire: Sutton Publishing

Parker Pearson, M, 1999b The earlier Bronze Age, in J Hunter & I Ralston (eds), *The archaeology of Britain. An introduction from the Upper Palaeolithic to the Industrial Revolution.* London: Routledge, 77–94

Parker Pearson, M, Chamberlain, A, Craig, O, Marshall, P, Mulville, J, Smith, H, Chenery, C, Collins, M, Cook, G, Craig, G, Evans, J, Hiller, J, Montgomery, J, Schwenninger, J-L, Taylor, G, & Wess T, 2005 Evidence for mummification in Bronze Age Britain, *Antiquity*, **79**, 529–46

Parsons, F G, & Box, C R, 1905 The relationship of the cranial sutures to age, *J Royal Archaeological Institute*, **35**, 30–8

Pate, F D, & Hutton, J T, 1988 Use of soil chemistry data to address post-mortem diagenesis in bone mineral, *J Archaeological Science*, **15**, 729–39

Pauwels, R A, & Rabel, K F, 2004 Burden and clinical features of chronic obstructive pulmonary disease (COPD), *The Lancet*, **364**, 613–20

Pearce, D, & Goldblatt, P (eds), 2001 *United Kingdom Health Statistics, 2001 Edition.* London: The Stationery Office

Pearson, K, 1899 On the reconstruction of prehistoric races, *Philosophical Transactions of the Royal Society of London Series A*, **192**, 169–244

Pearson, K, & Bell, J A, 1919 *A study of the long bones of the English skeleton.* Cambridge: Cambridge University Press

Penn, R G, 1964 Medical services of the Roman army, *J Royal Army Medical Corps*, **110**, 253–8

Perez-Perez, A, Espurz, V, Bermudez de Castro, J M, de Lumley, M A, & Turbon, D, 2003 Non-occlusal dental microwear variability in a sample of Middle and Late Pleistocene human populations from Europe and the Near East, *J Human Evolution*, **44**, 497–513

Pernter, P, Gostner, P, Vigl, E E, & Ruhli, F J, 2007 Radiological proof for the cause of the Iceman's cause of death (*ca* 5300 BP), *J Archaeological Science*, **34**, 1784–6

Petersen, H C, 2005 On the accuracy of estimating living stature from skeletal length in the grave and by linear regression, *Int J Osteoarchaeology*, **15**, 106–14

Pfeiffer, S, 2000 Palaeohistology: health and disease, in M A Katzenberg & S R Saunders (eds), *Biological anthropology of the human skeleton*. New York: Wiley-Liss, 287–305

Philpott, R, 1991 *Burial practices in Roman Britain. A survey of grave treatment and furnishing AD 43–410*, British Archaeological Reports British Series, **219**. Oxford: Tempus Reparatum

Pietrusewsky, M, 2000 Metric analysis of skeletal remains: methods and applications, in M A Katzenberg & S R Saunders (eds), Biological anthropology of the human skeleton. New York: Wiley-Liss, 375–415

Pietrusewsky, M, & Douglas, M T, 2002 *Ban Chiang, a prehistoric village site in northeast Thailand 1: the human skeletal remains.* Philadelphia, University of Pennsylvania, University Museum Monograph **11**

Piggott, S, 1940 A trepanned skull of the Beaker period from Dorset and the practise of trepanning in prehistoric Europe, *Proc Prehistoric Society*, **6**, 112–33

Piggott, S, 1962 *The West Kennet long barrow.* London: Her Majesty's Stationery Office

Pike, A W G, & Richards, M P, 2002 Diagenetic arsenic uptake in archaeological bone. Can we really identify copper smelters? *J Archaeological Science*, **29**, 607–11

Platt, C, 1996 *King Death. The Black Death and its aftermath in late-medieval England.* London: University College Press

Pollard, A M, 2001 Overview – archaeological science in the biomolecular century, in D R Brothwell & A M Pollard (eds), *Handbook of archaeological science.* Chichester: John Wiley and Sons Ltd, 295–9

Pollard, T M, & Hyatt, S B (eds), 1999a *Sex, gender and health.* Cambridge: Cambridge University Press

Pollard, T M, & Hyatt, S B, 1999b Sex, gender and health: integrating biological and social perspectives, in T M Pollard & S B Hyatt (eds) 1999a, 1–17

Porter, R, 1997 *The greatest benefit to mankind: a medical history of humanity from antiquity to the present.* London: Harper Collins

Powell, F, 1996 The human remains, in A Boddington (ed), *Raunds Furnells. The Anglo-Saxon church and churchyard.* London: English Heritage, 113–24

Powell, M L, & Cook, D C (eds), 2005 *The myth of syphilis: the natural history of treponematosis in North America.* Gainesville, Florida: University Press of Florida

Prag, J, & Neave, R, 1997 *Making faces. Using forensic and archaeological evidence.* London: British Museum Press

Price, R, & Ponsford, M, 1998 *St Bartholomew's Hospital, Bristol. The excavation of a medieval hospital, 1976–8*, CBA Research Report **110**. York: Council for British Archaeology

Prichard, P D, 1993 A suicide by self-decapitation, *J Forensic Science Society*, **38**, 981–4

Privat, K L, O'Connell, T C, & Richards, M P, 2002 Stable isotope analysis of human and faunal remains from the Anglo-Saxon cemetery at Berinsfield, Oxfordshire: dietary and social implications, *J Archaeological Science*, **29**, 779–90

Prowse, T L, Schwarcz, H P, Saunders, S R, Macchiarelli, R, & Bondioli L, 2005 Isotopic evidence for age-related variation in diet from Isola Sacra, Italy, *American J Physical Anthropology*, **128**, 2–13

Prowse, T L, Schwarcz, H P, Garnsey, P, Knyf, M, Macchiarelli, R, & Bondioli, L, 2007 Isotopic evidence for age-related immigration to Imperial Rome, *American J Physical Anthropology*, **132**, 510–19

Pruvost, M, & Geigl, E-M, 2004 Real-time quantitative PCR to assess the authenticity of ancient DNA amplification, *J Archaeological Science*, **31**, 1191–7

Pyatt, F B, & Grattan, J P, 2001 Some consequences of ancient mining activities on the health of ancient and modern human populations, *J Public Health Medicine*, **23**, 235–6

Ramazzini, B, 1705 *A treatise on the diseases of tradesmen*. London

Raoult, D, Aboudharam, G, Crubezy, E, Larrouy, G, Ludes, B, & Drancourt, M, 2000 Molecular identification by 'suicide PCR' of *Yersinia pestis* as the agent of medieval Black Death, *Proc of the National Academy of Sciences USA*, **97**, 12800–03

Rawcliffe, C, 1997 *Medicine and society in later medieval England*. Stroud: Sutton Publishing

Rawcliffe, C, 2006 *Leprosy in Medieval England*. Woodbridge, Suffolk: Boydell Press

Raxter, M H, Auerbach, B M, & Ruff, C B, 2006 Revision of the Fully technique for estimating statures, *American J Physical Anthropology*, **130**, 374–84

Ray, K, 1999 From remote times to the Bronze Age:c 500,000 BC to c 600 BC, in PC Jupp & C Gittings (eds), *Death in England. An illustrated history*. Manchester: Manchester University Press, 11–40

Reed, F A, Kontanis, E J, Kennedy, K A R, & Aquadro, C F, 2003 Brief communication: ancient DNA prospects from Sri Lankan highland dry caves support an emerging global pattern, *American J Physical Anthropology*, **121**, 112–16

Reeve, J, 1998 Do we need a policy on the treatment of human remains? *The Archaeologist*, **33**, 11–12

Reid, A H, Fanning, T G, Hultin, J V, & Taubenberger, J K, 1999 Origin and evolution of the 1918 'Spanish' influenza virus hemagglutinin gene, *Proc National Academy of Sciences USA*, **96**, 1651–6

Reid, D J, & Dean, M C, 2000 Brief communication: the timing of linear hypoplasia on human anterior teeth, *American J Physical Anthropology*, **113**, 185–9

Renz, H, & Radlanski, R J, 2006 Incremental lines in root cementum of human teeth – a reliable age marker? *Homo*, **57**, 29–50

Ribot, I, & Roberts, C A, 1996 A study of non-specific skeletal stress indicators and skeletal growth in two mediaeval subadult populations, *J Archaeological Science*, **23**, 67–79

Richards, J, 1999 *Meet the Ancestors*. London: BBC

Richards, J D, 1999 The Scandinavian presence, in J Hunter & I Ralston (eds), *The archaeology of Britain. An introduction from the Upper Palaeolithic to the Industrial Revolution*. London: Routledge, 194–209

Richards, M P, 2004 Sampling procedures for bone chemistry, in M Brickley & J I McKinley (eds) 2004, 43–5 (available on line: www.babaotemp.bham.ac.uk/)

Richards, M P, 2006 Palaeodietary reconstruction, in M Brickley, S Buteux, J Adams, & R Cherrington 2006, 147–51

Richards, M P, & Mellars, P, 1998 Stable isotopes and the seasonality of the Oronsay middens, *Antiquity*, **72**, 178–84

Richards, M P, Hedges, R E M, Molleson, T I, & Vogel, J C, 1998 Stable isotope analysis reveals variations in human diet at Poundbury Camp cemetery site, *J Archaeological Science*, **25**, 1247–52

Richards, M P, Pettitt, P B, Trinkaus, E, Smith, F, Paunović, M, & Karavanić, I, 2000a Neanderthal diet at Vindija and Neanderthal predation: the evidence from stable isotopes, *Proc National Academy of Sciences*, **97**, 7663–6

Richards, M P, Hedges, R E M, Jacobi, R, Currant, A, & Stringer, C, 2000b FOCUS: Gough's Cave and Sun Hole Cave human stable isotope values indicate a high animal protein diet in the British Upper Palaeolithic, *J Archaeological Science*, **27**, 1–3

Richards, M P, Mays, S, & Fuller, B T, 2002 Stable carbon and nitrogen isotope values of bone and teeth reflect weaning age at the Medieval Wharram Percy site, Yorkshire, UK, *American J Physical Anthropology*, **118**, 205–10

Richards, M P, Fuller, BT, & Molleson, T I, 2006 Stable isotope palaeodietary study of humans and fauna from the multi-period (Iron Age, Viking and Late Medieval) site of Newark Bay, Orkney, *J Archaeological Science*, **33**, 122–31

Robb, J, 2000 Analysing human skeletal data, in M Cox & S Mays (eds) 2000, 475–90

Robb, J, Bigazzi, R, Lazzarini, L, Scarsini, C, & Sonego, F, 2001 A comparison of grave goods and skeletal indicators from Pontecagnano, *American J Physical Anthropology*, **115**, 213–22

Roberts, C A, 1984 Analysis of some human femora from a Medieval charnel house at Rothwell Parish Church, Northamptonshire, England, *Ossa*, **9–11**, 137–47

Roberts, C A, 1988a Trauma and its treatment in British antiquity: a radiographic study, in E Slater & J Tate (eds), *Science and archaeology, Glasgow*, British Archaeological Reports British Series, **196**(ii). Oxford, 339–59

Roberts, C A, 1988b Trauma and Treatment in British Antiquity: a multidisciplinary study. PhD thesis, University of Bradford

Roberts, C A, 1991 Trauma and treatment in the British Isles in the historical period. A design for multidisciplinary approach, in D J Ortner & A C Aufderheide (eds), *Human palaeopathology. Current syntheses and future options*. Washington DC: Smithsonian Institution Press, 225–40

Roberts, C A, 2000 Did they take sugar? The use of skeletal evidence in the study of disability in past populations, in J Hubert (ed), *Madness, disability and social exclusion. The archaeology and anthropology of 'difference'*. London: Routledge, 46–59

Roberts, C A, 2006 A view from afar: bioarchaeology in Britain, in J Buikstra & L A Beck (eds) 2006, 417–39

Roberts, C A, 2007 A bioarchaeological study of maxillary sinusitis, *American J Physical Anthropology*, **133**, 792–807

Roberts, C A, & Wakely, J, 1992 Microscopical findings associated with the diagnosis of osteoporosis, *Int J Osteoarchaeology*, **2**, 23–30

Roberts, C A, & Buikstra, J E, 2003 *The bioarchaeology of tuberculosis. A global perspective on a reemerging disease*. Gainesville, Florida: University Press of Florida

Roberts, C A, & Cox, M, 2003 *Health and disease in Britain. Prehistory to the present day*. Gloucester: Sutton Publishing

Roberts, C A, & McKinley, J, 2003 A review of trepanations in British antiquity focusing on funerary context to explain their occurrence, in R Arnott, S Finger, & C U M Smith (eds) 2003, 55–78

Roberts, C A, & Connell, B, 2004 Palaeopathology, in M Brickley & J McKinley (eds) 2004, 34–9

Roberts, C A, & Manchester, K, 2005 *The archaeology of disease. 3rd edition.* Stroud: Sutton Publishing

Roberts, C A, Lewis, M E, & Manchester, K (eds), 2002 *The past and present of leprosy. Archaeological, historical, palaeopathological and clinical approaches. Proceedings of the International Congress on the Evolution and palaeoepidemiology of the infectious diseases 3 (ICEPID), University of Bradford, 26–31 July 1999,* British Archaeological Reports, International Series, **1054**. Oxford: Archaeopress

Roberts, C A, & Ingham, S, 2008 (early view) Using ancient DNA analysis in palaeopathology: a critical analysis of published papers, with recommendations for future work, *Int J Osteoarchaeology*

Roberts, M B, & Parfitt, S A, 1999 *Boxgrove: a Middle Palaeolithic Pleistocene hominid site at Eartham Quarry, Boxgrove, West Sussex.* London: English Heritage

Robling, A G, & Stout, S D, 2000 Histomorphometry of human cortical bone: applications to age estimation, in M A Katzenberg & S R Saunders (eds), *Biological anthropology of the human skeleton.* New York: Wiley-Liss, 187–213

Rogers, J, & Waldron, T, 1995 *A field guide to joint disease in archaeology.* Chichester: Wiley

Rogers, J, & Waldron, T, 2001 DISH and the monastic way of life, *Int J Osteoarchaeology*, **11**, 357–65

Rose, J C, Green, T J, & Green, V D, 1996 NAGPRA is forever: osteology and the repatriation of skeletons, *Annual Review of Anthropology*, **25**, 81–103

Rothschild, B M, & Rothschild, C, 1995 Comparison of radiologic and gross examination for detection of cancer in defleshed skeletons, *American J Physical Anthropology*, **96**, 357–63

Roy, D M, Hall, R, Mix, A C, & Bonnischen, R, 2005 Using stable isotope analysis to obtain dietary profiles from old hair: a case study from Plains Indians, *American J Physical Anthropology*, **128**, 444–52

Ruff, C B, 2000 Biomechanical analyses of archeological skeletons, in M A Katzenberg & S R Saunders (eds), *Biological anthropology of the human skeleton.* New York: Wiley-Liss, 71–102

Ruffer, M A, 1921 *Studies in the paleopathology of Egypt by Sir Marc Armand Ruffer Kt, CMG, MD, edited by R L Moodie.* Chicago: Chicago University Press

Ruhli, F, Lanz, C, Ulrich-Bochsler, S, & Alt, K, 2002 State-of-the-art imaging in palaeopathology: the value of multislice computed tomography in visualising doubtful cranial lesions, *Int J Osteoarchaeology*, **12**, 372–9

Ruhli, F, Kuhn, G, Evison, R, Müller, R, & Schultz, M, 2007 Diagnostic value of micro-CT in comparison with histology in the qualitative assessment of historical human skull bone pathologies, *American J Physical Anthropology*, **133**, 1099–1111

Rumsey, C, 2001 Human remains: are the existing ethical guidelines for excavation, museum storage, research and display adequate. Unpublished Master's thesis, University of Southampton, UK

Russell, K F, Simpson, S W, Genovese, J, Kinkel, M D, Meindl, R S, & Lovejoy, C O, 1993 Independent test of the 4th rib ageing technique, *American J Physical Anthropology*, **92**, 53–62

Rutala, W A, & Weber, D J, 2001 Creutzfeldt-Jakob disease: recommendations for disinfection and sterilization, *Clinical Infectious Diseases*, **32**, 1348–56

Ryan, T M, & Milner, G R, 2006 Osteological applications of high-resolution computed tomography: a prehistoric arrow injury, *J Archaeological Science*, **33**, 871–9

Sallares, R, & Gomzi, S, 2001 Biomolecular archaeology of malaria, *Ancient Biomolecules*, **3**, 195–212

Salo, W L, Aufderheide, A C, Buikstra, J E, & Holcomb, T A, 1994 Identification of *Mycobacterium tuberculosis* DNA in a pre-Columbian Peruvian mummy, *Proc National Academy of Sciences USA*, **91**, 2091–4

Sandford, M K, & Weaver, D S, 2000 Trace element research in anthropology: new perspectives and challenges, in M A Katzenberg & S R Saunders (eds), *Biological anthropology of the human skeleton*. New York: Wiley-Liss, 329–50

Saunders, S R, 1989 Non-metric skeletal variation, in M Y Iscan & K A R Kennedy (eds), *Reconstruction of life from the skeleton*. New York: Wiley Liss, 95–108

Saunders, S R, 2000 Non-adult skeletons and growth-related studies, in M A Katzenberg & S R Saunders (eds), *Biological anthropology of the human skeleton*. New York: Wiley-Liss, 135–61

Saunders, S R, Herring, A (eds), 1995 *Grave reflections. Portraying the past through cemetery studies*. Toronto: Canadian Scholars Press

Saunders, S R, Fitzgerald, C, Rogers, T, Dudar, C, & McKillop, H, 1992 A test of several methods of skeletal age estimation using a documented archaeological sample, *Canadian Society of Forensic Science*, **25**, 97–118

Saunders, S R, Hoppa, R D, & Southern, R, 1993a, Diaphyseal growth in a 19th-century skeletal sample of subadults from St Thomas' Church, Belleville, Ontario, *Int J Osteoarchaeology*, **3**, 265–81

Saunders, S R, DeVito, C, Herring, A, Southern, R, & Hoppa, R D, 1993b Accuracy tests of tooth formation age estimations for human skeletal remains, *American J Physical Anthropology*, **92**, 173–88

Saunders, S R, Chan, A H W, Kahlon, B, Kluge, H F, & Fitzgerald, C M, 2007 Sexual dimorphism of the dental hard tissues in human permanent mandibular canines and third premolars, *American J Physical Anthropology*, **133**, 735–40

Scarre, C, 2005 Preface in C Scarre (ed), *The human past. World prehistory and the development of human societies.* London: Thames and Hudson, 19–23

Scarre, G, 2006 Can archaeology harm the dead?, in C Scarre & G Scarre (eds), *The ethics of archaeology. Philosophical perspectives on archaeological practice.* Cambridge: Cambridge University Press, 181–98

Scheuer, L, 1998 Age at death and cause of death of the people buried in St Bride's Church, Fleet Street, London, in M Cox (ed) 1998, 100–11

Scheuer L, & Black, S, 2000a. Developmental juvenile osteology. London: Academic Press

Scheuer, L, & Black, S, 2000b Development and ageing of the juvenile skeleton, in M Cox & S Mays (eds) 2000, 9–21

Schmid, E, 1972 *Atlas of animal bones*. New York: Elsevier

Schmidt, A, Murail, P, Cunha, E, & Rougé, D, 2002 Variability of the pattern of aging on the human skeleton: evidence from bone indicators and implications on age at death estimation, *J Forensic Sciences*, **47**, 1203–09

Schour, I, & Massler, M, 1941 The development of the human dentition, *J American Dental Association*, **28**, 1153–60

Schulter-Ellis, F P, Hayek, L C, & Schmidt, D J, 1985 Determination of sex with a discriminate analysis of new pelvic bone measurements: part II, *J Forensic Sciences*, **30**, 178–85

Schulting, R J, 2005 Pursuing a rabbit in Burrington Combe: new research on the early Mesolithic burial cave of Aveline's Hole, *Proc University of Bristol Spelaeological Society*, **23**, 171–265

Schulting, R J, & Richards, M P, 2000 The use of stable isotopes in studies of subsistence and seasonality in the British Mesolithic, in R Young (ed), *Mesolithic lifeways. Current research in Britain and Ireland.* Leicester: Archaeology Monographs **7**, 55–65

Schulting, R J, & Richards, M P, 2002 Finding the coastal Mesolithic in southwest Britain: AMS dates and stable isotope results on human remains from Caldey Island, south Wales, *Antiquity*, **76**, 1011–25

Schulting, R J, & Wysocki, W, 2002 The Mesolithic human skeletal collections from Aveline's Hole: a preliminary report, *Proc University of Bristol Spelaeological Society*, **22**, 255–68

Schulting, R J, Trinkaus, E, Higham, T, Hedges, R, Richards, M, & Cardy, B, 2005 A Mid-Upper Palaeolithic human humerus from Eel Point, South Wales, UK, *J Human Evolution*, **48**, 493–505

Schultz, M, 2001 Paleohistology of bone: a new approach to the study of ancient diseases, *Yearbook of Physical Anthropology*, **44**, 106–47

Schultz, M, & Roberts, C A, 2002 Diagnosis of leprosy in skeletons from an English later medieval hospital using histological analysis, in C A Roberts, M E Lewis, & K Manchester (eds) 2002, 89–104

Schurr, M R, 1997 Stable nitrogen istotopes as evidence for the age of weaning at the Angel site: a comparison of isotopic and demographic measures of weaning age, *J Archaeological Science*, **24**, 919–27

Schweissing, M M, & Grupe, G, 2003 Stable strontium isotopes in human teeth and bone: a key to migration events of the late Roman period in Bavaria, *J Archaeological Science*, **30**, 1373–83

Scott, G R, & Turner, C G, 1997 *The anthropology of modern human teeth.* Cambridge: Cambridge University Press

Scott, S, Duncan, C J, 1998 *Human demography and disease.* Cambridge: Cambridge University Press

Sealy, J, 2001 Body tissue chemistry and palaeodiet, in D R Brothwell & A M Pollard (eds), *Handbook of archaeological sciences.* Chichester: John Wiley and Sons Ltd, 269–79

Seidel, J C, Colten, R H, Thibodeau, E A, & Aghajanian, J G, 2005 Iatrogenic molar borings in 18th- and early 19th-century native American dentitions, *American J Physical Anthropology*, **127**, 7–12

Sellet, F, Greaves, R, & Yu, P-L, 2006 *The archaeology and ethnoarchaeology of mobility*. Gainesville, Florida: University Press of Florida

Sengupta, A, Shellis, P, & Whittaker, D, 1998 Measuring root dentine translucency in human teeth of varying antiquity, *J Archaeological Science*, **25**, 1221–9

Shapiro, H L, 1959 The history and development of physical anthropology, *American Anthropologist*, **61**, 371–9

Shaw, M, Orford, S, Brimblecombe, N, & Dorling, D, 2000 Widening inequality between 160 regions of 15 European countries in the early 1990s, *Social Science and Medicine*, **50**, 1047–58

Shennan, S J, 1997 *Quantifying archaeology, 2nd edition*. Edinburgh: Edinburgh University Press

Shinoda, K, Adachi, N, Guillen, S, & Shimada, I, 2006 Mitochondrial DNA analysis of ancient Peruvian highlanders, *American J Physical Anthropology*, **131**, 98–107

Sillence, E, Briggs, P, Harris, P R, & Fishwick, L, 2007 How do patients evaluate and make use of online health information? *Social Science and Medicine*, **64**, 1853–62

Simpson, M, 1994 Burying the past, *Museums Journal*, **July**, 28–32

Simpson, M, 2002 The plundered past: Britain's challenge for the future, in C Fforde, J Hubert, & P Turnbull (eds) 2002, 199–217

Sládek, V, Berner, M, & Sailer, R, 2006a Mobility in Central European late Eneolithic and early Bronze Age: femoral cross-sectional geometry, *American J Physical Anthropology*, **130**, 320–32

Sládek, V, Berner, M, & Sailer, R, 2006b Mobility in Central European late Eneolithic and early Bronze Age: tibial cross-sectional geometry, *J Archaeological Science*, **33**, 470–82

Sládek, V, Berner, M, Sosna, D, & Sailer, R, 2007 Human manipulative behaviour in the Central European late Eneolithic and early Bronze Age: humeral bilateral asymmetry, *American J Physical Anthropology*, **133**, 669–81

Smith, I F, & Simpson, D D A, 1966 Excavation of a round barrow on Overton Down, N Wilts, *Proc Prehistoric Society*, **32**, 122–55

Smith, M J, Brickley, M B, & Leach, S L, 2007 Experimental evidence for lithic projectile injuries: improving identification of an under-recognised phenomenon, *J Archaeological Science*, **34**, 540–53

Smrčka, V, Kuželka, V, & Melková, J, 2003 Meningioma probable reason for trephination, *Int J Osteoarchaeology*, **13**, 325–30

Snape, S, 1996 Making mummies, in P Bahn (ed), *Tombs, Graves and mummies. 50 discoveries in world archaeology*. London: Weidenfeld and Nicholson, 182–5

Sofaer, J R, 2006 Gender, bioarchaeology and human ontogeny, in R Gowland & C Knüsel (eds) 2006, 155–67

Sorg, M H, Andrews, R P, & İşcan M Y, 1989 Radiographic ageing in the adult, in M Y İşcan (ed), *Age markers in the human skeleton*. Springfield, Illinois: Charles C Thomas, 169–93

Sorg, M H, Dearborn, J H, Monahan, E I, Ryan, H F, Sweeney, K G, & David, E, 1997 Forensic taphonomy in marine contexts, in W D Haglund & M H Sorg (eds) 1997, 567–604

Spigelman, M, & Lemma, E, 1993 The use of polymerase chain reaction to detect *Mycobacterium tuberculosis* in ancient skeletons, *International J Osteoarchaeology*, **3**, 137–43

Spindler, K, 1994 *The man in the ice*. London: Weidenfeld and Nicolson

Spriggs, J A, 1989 On and off-site conservation of bone, in C A Roberts, F Lee, & J Bintliff (eds), *Burial archaeology: current research, methods and developments*, British Archaeological Reports British Series 211. Oxford, 39–45

Standen, V G, Arriaza, B T, & Santoro, C M, 1997 External auditory exostosis in prehistoric Chilean populations: a test of the cold water hypothesis, *American J Physical Anthropology*, **103**, 119–29

Stead, I M, 1979 *The Arras culture*. York: Yorkshire Philosophical Society

Stead, I M, 1980 *Rudston Roman villa*. York: Yorkshire Archaeological Society

Stead, I M, 1986 Summary and conclusions, in IM Stead, JB Bourke & D Brothwell (eds), *Lindow Man. The body in the bog*. London: Guild Publishing, 177–80

Steckel, R H, 1995 Stature and the standard of living, *J Economic Literature*, **33**, 1903–40

Steckel, R H, & Rose, J C (eds), 2002 *The backbone of history: health and nutrition in the Western Hemisphere*. Cambridge: Cambridge University Press

Steele, J, 2000 Skeletal indicators of handedness, in M Cox & S Mays (eds) 2000, 307–23

Steinbock, R T, 1989a Studies in ancient calcified tissues and organic concretions I: a review of structures, disease and conditions, *J Paleopathology*, **3**, 35–8

Steinbock R T, 1989b Studies in ancient calcified tissues and organic concretions II: urolithiasis (renal and urinary bladder stone disease, *J Paleopathology*, **3**, 9–59

Steinbock R T, 1990 Studies in ancient calcified tissues and organic concretions III: gallstones (cholelithiasis), *J Paleopathology*, **3**, 95–106

Stepan, N L, 1982 *The idea of race in science. Great Britain 1800–1960*. Hamden, Connecticut: Archon Books

Stevens, G C, & Wakely, J, 1993 Diagnostic criteria for identification of seashell as a trephination implement, *Int J Osteoarchaeology*, **3**, 167–76

Steyn, M, & Henneberg, M, 1996 Skeletal growth of children from the Iron Age site at K2 (South Africa), *American J Physical Anthropology* **100**, 389–96

Stinson, S, 1985 Sex differences in environmental sensitivity during growth and development, *Yearbook of Physical Anthropology*, **28**, 123–47

Stirland, A, 1991 The politics of the excavation of human remains: towards a policy, *Int J Osteoarchaeology*, **1**, 157–8

Stirland, A, 2000 *Raising the dead: the skeleton crew of Henry VIII's great ship, the Mary Rose*. Chichester: John Wiley

Stirland, A, & Waldron, T, 1997 Evidence for activity-related markers in the vertebrae of the crew of the Mary Rose, *J Archaeological Science*, **24**, 329–35

Stock, G, 1998 The 18th and early 19th-century Quaker burial ground at Bathford, Bath and North-East Somerset, in M Cox (ed) 1998, 144–53

Stojanowski, C M, & Buikstra, J E, 2005 Research trends in human osteology: a content analysis of papers published in the American Journal of Physical Anthropology, *American J Physical Anthropology*, **128**, 98–109

Stone, A C, 2000 Ancient DNA from skeletal remains, in M A Katzenberg & S R Saunders (eds), *Biological anthropology of the human skeleton.* New York: Wiley-Liss, 351–71

Stone, A C, & Stoneking, M, 1993 Ancient DNA from a pre-Columbian Amerindian population, *American J Physical Anthropology,* **92**, 463–71

Stone, A C, Milner, G R, Paabo, S, & Stoneking, M, 1996 Sex determination of ancient human skeletons using DNA, *American J Phyiscal Anthropology,* **99**, 231–8

Stone, R J, & Stone, J A, 1990 *Atlas of skeletal muscles.* Dubuque, Iowa: Wm C Brown Publishers

Stringer, C B, & Hublin, J-J, 1999 New age estimates for the Swanscombe hominid, and their significance for human evolution, *J Human Evolution,* **37**, 873–7

Stroud, G, 1989 The processing of human bone from archaeological sites, in C A Roberts, F Lee, & J Bintliff (eds), *Burial archaeology: current research, methods and developments,* British Archaeological Reports British Series, **211**. Oxford, 47–9

Stroud, G, & Kemp, R L, 1993 *Cemeteries of the church and priory of St Andrew's, Fishergate. The archaeology of York. The Medieval cemeteries* **12/2**. York: Council for British Archaeology for York Archaeological Trust

Strouhal, E, & Němečková, A, 2004 Paleopathological find of a sacral neurilemmoma from ancient Egypt, *American J Physical Anthropology,* **125**, 320–8

Sutherland, T, 2000 Recording the grave, in V Fiorato, A Boylston, & C Knüsel (eds), *Blood red roses. The archaeology of a mass grave from the battle of Towton.* Oxford: Oxbow, 36–44

Swabe, J, 1999 *Animals, disease and human society.* New York: Routledge

Swain, H, 1998 Displaying the ancestors, *The Archaeologist,* **33**, 14–15

Swedlund, A C, & Armelagos, G J (eds), 1990 *Disease in transition. Anthropological and epidemiological approaches.* London: Bergin and Garvey

Tanner, J M, 1981 Catch-up growth in man, *British Medical Bulletin,* **37**, 233–8

Tarlow, S, 1999 *Bereavement and commemoration. An archaeology of mortality.* Oxford: Blackwell Publishers

Tarlow, S, 2006 Archaeological ethics and the people of the past, in C Scarre & G Scarre (eds), *The ethics of archaeology. Philosophical perspectives on archaeological practice.* Camridge: Cambridge University Press, 199–216

Tayles, N, 1999 *The excavation of Khok Phanom Di. A prehistoric site in Central Thailand. Volume 5: The People.* London: Society of Antiquaries

Taylor, G M, Rutland, R, & Molleson, T, 1997 A sensitive polymerase chain reaction method for the detection of *Plasmodium* species DNA in ancient human remains, *Ancient Biomolecules,* **1**, 193–203

Taylor, G M, Widdison, S, Brown, I N, & Young, D, 2000 A mediaeval case of lepromatous leprosy from 13th–14th-century Orkney, Scotland, *J Archaeological Science,* **27**, 1133–2113

Taylor, G M, Watson, C L, Bouwman, A S, Lockwood, D N J, & Mays, S A, 2006 Variable nucleotide tandem repeat (VNTR) typing of two palaeopathological cases of lepromatous leprosy from Medieval Britain, *J Archaeological Science,* **33**, 1569–79

Taylor, R E, 2001 Radiocarbon dating, in D R Brothwell & A M Pollard (eds), *Handbook of archaeological science.* Chichester: John Wiley and Sons Ltd, 23–34

Thomas, C, Sloane, B, & Phillpotts, C, 1997 *Excavations at the priory and hospital of St Mary Spital.* London: Museum of London

Thompson, J, 1998 Bodies, minds, and human remains, in M Cox (ed) 1998, 197–201

Torres-Rouff, C, & Costa Junqueira, M A, 2006 Interpersonal violence in prehistoric San Pedro de Atacama, Chile: Behavioral implications of environmental stress, *American J Physical Anthropology*, **130**, 60–70

Toynbee, J M C, 1971 *Death and burial in the Roman world.* Ithaca, New York: Cornell University Press

Tronick, E Z, Brooke Thomas, R, & Daltabuit, M, 1994 The Quechua Manta pouch. A caretaking practice for buffering the Peruvian infant against the multiple stressors of high altitude, *Child Development*, **65**, 1005–13

Trotter, M, 1970 Estimation of stature from intact long limb bones, in T D Stewart (ed), *Personal identification in mass disasters.* Washington DC: National Museum of Natural History, Smithsonian Institution, 71–83

Trotter, M, & Gleser, G C, 1952 Estimation of stature from the long bones of American Whites and Negroes, *American J Physical Anthropology*, **10**, 463–514

Trotter, M, & Gleser, G C, 1958 A re-evaluation of estimation of stature based on measurements of stature taken during life and of long bones after death, *American J Physical Anthropology*, **16**, 79–124

Tsuchiya, A, & Williams, A, 2005 A 'fair innings' between the sexes: are men being treated equitably? *Social Science and Medicine*, **60**, 277–86

Tucker, B K, Hutchinson, D L, Gilliland, M F G, Charles, T M, Daniel, H J, & Wolfe, L D, 2001 Microscopic characteristics of hacking trauma, *J Forensic Sciences*, **46**, 234–40

Turnbaugh, WA, Jurmain, R, Nelson, H, & Kilgore, L, 1996 *Understanding physical anthropology and archaeology, 6th edition.* Los Angeles: West Publishing Company

Turner, B L, Edwards, J L, Quinn, E A, Kingston, J D, & Van Gerven, D P, 2007 Age-related variation in isotopic indicators of diet at medieval Kulubnarti, Sudanese Nubia, *Int J Osteoarchaeology*, **17**, 1–25

Turner, C G, Nichol, C R, & Scott, G R, 1991 Scoring procedures for key morphological traits of the permanent dentition: The Arizona State University dental system, in M Kelley & C S Larsen (eds), *Advances in dental anthropology.* Chichester: Wiley-Liss, 13–21

Turner, R C, & Scaife, RG, 1995 *Bog bodies. New discoveries and new perspectives.* London: British Museum Press

Tyrrell, A, 2000 Skeletal non-metric traits and the assessment of inter- and intra-population diversity: past problems and future potential, in M Cox & S Mays (eds) 2000, 289–306

Tyson, R A, 1995 Mummies at the San Diego Museum of Man: considerations for the future, in *Proceedings of the 1st World Congress on Mummy Studies. Volume 1.* Santa Cruz, Tenerife, Canary islands: Archaeological and Ethnographical Museum of Tenerife, 221–3

Ubelaker, D, 1974 Reconstruction of demographic profiles from ossuary skeletal samples. A case study from the Tidewater Potomac, *Smithsonian Contributions to Anthropology*, **18**, 1–79

Ubelaker, D, 1989 *Human skeletal remains. Excavation, analysis and interpretation.* Washington DC: Taraxacum

Ubelaker, D, 2002 Approaches to the study of commingling in human skeletal biology, in W D Haglund & M H Sorg (eds), 2002, 331–51

Ubelaker, D, & Guttenplan Grant, L, 1989 Human skeletal remains: preservation or reburial? *Yearbook of Physical Anthropology*, **32**, 249–87

Ucko, P J, 1969 Ethnography and archaeological interpretation of funerary remains, *World Archaeology*, **1**, 262–80

Ullinger, J M, Sheridan, S G, Hawkey, D E, Turner, I I CG, & Cooley, R, 2005 Bioarchaeological analysis of cultural transition in the Southern Levant using dental nonmetric traits, *American J Physical Anthropology*, **128**, 466–76

Van Beek, G C, 1983 *Dental morphology. An illustrated guide.* Bristol: Wright PSG

Verano, J W, 2003 Trepanation in prehistoric South America: geographic and temporal trends over 2,000 years, in R Arnott, S Finger, & C U M Smith (eds) 2003, 223–36

Verano, J W, Anderson, L S, Franco, R, 2000 Foot amputation by the Moche of ancient Peru: osteological evidence and archaeological context, *Int J Osteoarchaeology*, **10**, 177–88

Virchow, R, 1872 Untersuchung des Neanderthal-Schädels, *Zeitschrift fuer Ethnologie (Berlin)*, **4**, 157–65

Von Hunnius, T E, Roberts, C A, Saunders, S, & Boylston, A, 2006 Histological identification of syphilis in pre-Columbian England, *American J Physical Anthropology*, **129**, 559–66

Von Hunnius, T E, Yang, D, Eng, B, Waye, J S, & Saunders, S R, 2007 Digging deeper into the limits of ancient DNA research on syphilis, *J Archaeological Science*, **34**, 2091–2100

Wacher, J, 1980 *Roman Britain.* London: JM Dent and Sons Ltd

Waite, E R, Child, A M, Craig, O E, Collins, M J, Gelsthorpe, K, & Brown, T A, 1997 A preliminary investigation of DNA stability in bone during artificial diagnesis, *Bulletin Soc Geol France*, **168**, 547–54

Wakely, J, Manchester, K, & Roberts, C A, 1989 Scanning electron microscope study of normal vertebrae and ribs from early Medieval human skeletons, *Int J Osteoarchaeology*, **16**, 627–42

Waldron, T, 1983 On the post-mortem accumulation of lead by skeletal tissues, *J Archaeological Science*, **10**, 35–40

Waldron, T, 1987 The relative survival of the human skeleton: implications for palaeopathology in A Boddington, A N Garland, & R C Janaway (eds), *Death, decay and reconstruction. Approaches to archaeology and forensic science.* Manchester: Manchester University Press, 55–64

Waldron, T, 1993 The health of the adults, in T Molleson & M Cox 1993, 67–89

Waldron, T, 1994 *Counting the dead. The epidemiology of skeletal populations.* Chichester: Wiley

Waldron, T, 2001 *Shadows in the soil. Human bones and archaeology.* Stroud, Gloucestershire: Tempus Publishing Ltd

Waldron, T, & Cox, M, 1989 Occupational arthropathy: evidence from the past, *J Industrial Medicine*, **46**, 420–42

Walker, P L, 1989 Cranial injuries as evidence of violence in southern California, *American J Physical Anthropology*, **80**, 313–23

Walker, P L, 1995 Problems of preservation and sexism in sexing: some lessons from historical collections for palaeodemographers, in S R Saunders & A Herring (eds) 1995, 31–47

Walker, P L, 1997 Wife beating, boxing and broken noses: skeletal evidence for the cultural patterning of violence, in D L Martin & D W Frayer (eds) 1997, 145–79

Walker, P L, 2000 Bioarchaeological ethics: a historical perspective on the value of human remains, in M A Katzenberg & S R Saunders (eds), *Biological anthropology of the human skeleton*. New York: Wiley-Liss, 3–39

Walker, P L, & Cook, D C, 1998 Brief communication. Gender and sex: vive la difference, *American J Physical Anthropology*, **106**, 255–9

Walker, R A, & Lovejoy, C O, 1985 Radiographic changes in the clavicle and proximal femur and their use in the determination of skeletal age at death, *American J Physical Anthropology*, **68**, 67–78

Wang, H, Ge, B, Mair, V H, Cai, D, Xie, C, Zhang, Q, Zhou, H, & Zhu, H, 2007 Molecular genetic analysis of remains from Lamadong cemetery, Liaoning, China, *American J Physical Anthropology*, **134**, 404–11

Watkins, J, Goldstein, L, Vitelli, K, & Jenkins, L, 1995 Accountability: responsibilities of archeologists to other interest groups, in M Lynott & A Wylie (eds), *Ethics in American archaeology. Challenges for the 1990s.* Washington DC: Society of American Archaeology, 33–7

Watkinson, D, & Neal, V, 1998 *1st aid for finds. 3rd edition.* London: United Kingdom Institute for Conservation. Archaeology Section

Watson, J B, & Crick, F H C, 1953 A structure for deoxyribonucleic acid, *Nature*, **171**, 737–8

Weber, J, & Wahl, J, 2006 Neurosurgical aspects of trepanations from Neolithic times, *Int J Osteoarchaeology*, **16**, 536–45

Weichmann, I, & Grupe, G, 2005 Detection of *Yersinia pestis* DNA in two early medieval skeletal finds from Aschheim (upper Bavaria, 6th century AD), *American J Physical Anthropology*, **126**, 48–55

Weiss, E, 2003 Understanding muscle markers: aggregation and construct validity, *American J Physical Anthropology*, **121**, 230–40

Wells, C, 1964 The study of ancient disease, *Surgo*, **32**, 3–7

Wells, C, 1965 A pathological Anglo-Saxon femur, *British J Radiology*, **38**, 393–4

Wells, C, 1982 The human burials, in A McWhirr, L Viner, & C Wells (eds) 1982, 135–202

Wescott, D J, & Cunningham, D L, 2006 Temporal changes in Arikara humeral and femoral cross-sectional geometry associated with horticultural intensification, *J Archaeological Science*, **33**, 1022–36

Whimster, R, 1981 *Burial practices in Iron Age Britain*, British Archaeological Reports British Series, **90**. Oxford

White, C D, Healy, P F, & Schwarcz, H P, 1993 Intensive agriculture, social status, and Maya diet at Pacbitun, Belize, *J Anthropological Research*, **49**, 347–75

White, C D, Spence, M W, Le Q Stuart-Williams, H, & Schwartcz, H P, 1998 Oxygen isotopes and the identification of geographical origins: the valley of Oaxaca versus the Valley of Mexico, *J Archaeological Science*, **25**, 643–55

White, T D, & Folkens, P A, 2000 *Human osteology*. London: Academic Press

White, T D, & Folkens, P A, 2005 *The human bone manual*. London: Academic Press

White, W, 1988 *The cemetery of St Nicholas Shambles*. London: London and Middlesex Archaeology Society

White, W, & Ganiaris, H, 1998 Excavating bodies. Excavating and analysing human skeletons, in A Werner (ed), *London Bodies. The changing shape of Londoners from prehistoric times to the present day*. London: Museum of London, 14–21

Whittaker, D, 1993 Oral health, in T Molleson & M Cox (eds) 1993, 49–65

Whittaker, D, 2000 Ageing from the dentition, in M Cox & S Mays (eds) 2000, 83–99

Whittle, A, 1999 The Neolithic period *c* 4000–2500/2200 BC, in J Hunter & I Ralston (eds), *The archaeology of Britain. An introduction from the Upper Palaeolithic to the Industrial Revolution*. London: Routledge, 58–76

Wiggins, R, Boylston, A, & Roberts, C A, 1993 Report on the human skeletal remains from Blackfriars, Gloucester. Bradford: University of Bradford, Calvin Wells Laboratory. Unpublished

Wilhelm Hagel, G, 1991 Summary: lessons from a decade of public health, in B Jacobsen, A Smith & M Whitehead (eds) *The nation's health. A strategy for the late 1990s*. London: King Edward's Fund for London, 9–21

Wilkinson, C, & Neave, R, 2003 The reconstruction of a face showing a healed wound, *J Archaeological Science*, **30**, 1343–8

Willey, P, Galloway, A, & Snyder, L, 1997 Bone mineral density and survival of elements and element portions in the bones of the Crow Creek Massacre victims, *American J Physical Anthropology*, **104**, 513–28

Wilson, K J W, 1995 *Ross and Wilson. Anatomy and physiology in health and illness, 7th edition*. London: Churchill Livingstone

Wilson, A S, 2001 Survival of human hair – the impact of the burial environment, in E Williams (ed), *Human remains. Conservation, retrieval and analysis. Proceedings of a conference held in Williamsburg, VA, 7th–11 Nov 1999*, British Archaeological Reports International Series, **934**. Oxford: Archaeopress, 119–27

Withington, E T (ed), 1927 *Hippocrates. Three volumes*. London: William Heinemann Ltd

Wittwer-Backofen, U, Gampe, J, & Vaupel, J W, 2004 Tooth cementum annulation for age estimation: Results from a large known-age validation study, *American J Physical Anthropology*, **123**, 119–29

Wood, J W, Milner, G R, Harpending, H C, & Weiss, K M, 1992 The osteological paradox. Problems of inferring health from the skeleton, *Current Anthropology*, **33**, 343–70

Woods, R, & Shelton, N, 1997 *An atlas of Victorian mortality*. Liverpool: Liverpool University Press

World Health Organisation, 2006. *Preventing disease through healthy environments*. Geneva: World Health Organisation

Wright, L E, & Schwarcz, H P, 1998 Stable carbon and oxygen isotopes in human tooth enamel: identifying breastfeeding and weaning in prehistory, *American J Physical Anthropology*, **106**, 1–18

Young, S E J, 1998 Archaeology and smallpox, in M Cox (ed) 1998, 190–6

Zakrzewski, S R, 2007 Population continuity or population change: formation of the ancient Egyptian shape, *American J Physical Anthropology*, **132**, 501–09

Zias, J, & Numeroff, K, 1987 Operative dentistry in the 2nd century BC, *J American Dental Association*, **114**, 665–6

Zias, J, & Pomeranz, S, 1992 Serial craniectomies for intracranial infection 5.5 millennia ago, *Int J Osteoarchaeology*, **2**, 183–6

Zias, J, Stark, H, Seligman, J, Levy, R, Werker, E, Breuer, A, & Mechoulam, R, 1993 Early medical use of cannabis (Letter), *Nature*, **363**, 215

Ziegler, P, 1991 *The Black Death*. Bath: Alan Sutton Publishing Ltd

Zimmerman, L J, Vitelli, K D, & Hollow-ell-Zimmer, J (eds), 2003 *Ethical issues in archaeology*. Walnut Creek, California: Altamira Press

Zink, A R, & Nerlich, A G, 2005 Notes and Comments. Long-term survival of ancient DNA in Egypt: reply to Gilbert *et al*, *American J Physical Anthropology*, **128**, 115–18

Zink, A R, Sola, C, Reischel, U, Grabner, W, Rastogi, N, Wolf, H, & Nerlich, A G, 2004 Molecular identification and characterization of *Mycobacterium tuberculosis* complex in ancient Egyptian mummies, *Int J Osteoarchaeology*, **14**, 404–13

Zuckerman, A J, 1984 Palaeontology of smallpox, *The Lancet*, **2**, 1454

Index

Entries in bold refer to the illustrations

conservation of 73, 90, 92–4, 97, 101, 102, 229
contamination of 80, 97, 104, 124, 209, 210, 222
cremated 10, 47, 48, 52, 53, 55, 60, 71, 73, 86, 89, 91, 97, 117, **118**, **119**, 120, 124, 126, 127–8, 135–6, 145, 148, 159, 161, 211, 214
curation of 2, 5, 11, 14, 18, 19, 21, 22, 24, 28–9, 36, 37, 43, 73, 79, 89, 94, 101, 102, 220
damage to 61, 74, 75, 85, 87–9, 94, 97–8, 101, 102, 104, 105, 125
databases of 4, 11, 15, 97, 107, 220, 222
disarticulated 43, 45, 68, 86, 120, 148
display of 3, **13**, 14, 19, 22, 30–4, 73, 95
foetal 31, 32, 77, 120, 129, 138
fragmentary 31, 41, 42, 53, 54, 55, 58, 60, 79, 81, 85, 86, 94–5, 105, 115, 117, **119**, 120, 124, 125, 128, 135, 145, 146, 148, 149, 150, 159, 211
frozen 64–5, 168, 208, 215
geographic origin of 10, 107, 130, 141, 151, 167, 202, 206, 220, 221, 238
handling of 104–5
history of the study of 6–8, 14
identification of 2, 115–20, 150
of infants 46, 58–9, 65, 128, 137, 195, 198, 204–5
interdisciplinary study of 3, 6, 15
measuring of 2, 7, 87, 94–5, 105, 106, 107, 115, 123, 124, 125–6, 136, 140–6, 148, 149, 199, 219
mummified 14, 30, 31, 57, 60, 62, 63–4, 71, 82, 83, 126, 128, 153, 155, 168, 185, 187, 197, 198, 199, 201, 209, 210, 213, 222
neonatal **91**, 92, 138
of non-adults 2, 10, 41, 57–9, 65, 70, 74, 77, 79, 115, 122, 123–4, 127–30, 132, 133, 135, 137, 140, 143, 145, 150, 169, 198, 198, 210, 222
normal variation in 8, 13, 29, 115, 140–1, 144, 151, 153, 161, 191, 207, 212, 220

ossified 77, 79, 135, 236
pathological 8, 13, 31, 59, 77, 85, 86, 98, 106, 145–6, 149, **156**, 159, 161, 190, 195, 197, 213, 222
post-excavation processing of 2, 3, 73, 79, 84–6, 101, 102
post-mortem damage to 61, 79, 94, 101, 106, 117, 135, 180, 185, 192, 197, 198, 199, 217
preservation of 2, 5, 41, 55–72, 135, 137, 210, 230, *see also* preservation environments
public interest in 1, 21, 30, 31–3, 37
reburial of 2, 12, 17, 18, 19, 20, 21, 22, 23, 24, 25, 26, 27, 28, 34, 36, 37, 50, 96, 142, 220–1, 238
reconstruction of 94–5, 102
recording of 12, 14, 15, 36, 75, 77, 79, 81, 82, 102, 106–7, 221
redeposited 45, 48
repatriation of 2, 12, 18, 22, 28, 29, 34, 35–6, 37, 239
representative nature of 136–7, 148, 161–2
respect for 17, 19, 20, 22, 23, 25, 27, 32, 34, 36, 37, 40, 74, 100, 220
re-study of 22, 29, 30, 36, 96
retention of 21–2, 24, 25, 35, 37, 96, 220
social implications of 11
storage of 25, 29, 34, 73, 80, 83, 86–9, 90, 94, 96–8
from urban sites 4, 96, 145, 162, 168, 169, 173, 198
human rights 21, 25
hunter-gatherers 42, 63, 149, 164, 167–8, 170–1, 173, 175, 178, 189, 231

immune system/immunity 121, 153, 158, 169, 205, 206, 225, 226, 233, 237, 241
India 52, 142, 210, 231
indigenous peoples 19, 29, 36, 100, 143, 233
    Aboriginal groups 19, 31, **164**
    Inuit 65
    Maori 31, 234
    Native Americans 12, 19, 31,

34–7, 147, 153, 228
infanticide 59, 124, 137, 233
inheritance (genetic) 8, 145, 146, 148, 209, 231, 236
injuries 136, 159, 178–80, 187, 199, 217, 239
    decapitation 178, 180–1
    defence 178, 179
    fractures 66, 111, 146, 154, 162, 178–9, 186–7, 227, 238, 240
    to the skull 178–9
Ireland 23, 43, 66
Iron Age, the 44–5, 46, 54, 67, 70, 130, 147, 186, 203
Israel 18, 124, 140, 169, 185, 186
Italy 45, 64, 68, 203, 208, 215

Japan 142, 143, 172

kinship *see* relatedness

laboratories 2, 28, 29, 73, 80, 115, 103–6, 150, 222
legislation 22–7, 34–6, 37
    Burial Act 1857 24, 25, 26
    Disused Burial Grounds (Amendment) Act 1981 24, 26
    exhumation licences 23, 24, 25
    Human Rights Act 1988 25
    Human Tissues Act 2004 25, 29
    The National Museum of the American Indian Act 1989 (NMAIA) 34–6
    Native American Graves Protection and Repatriation Act 1990 (NAGPRA) 34–5
life expectancy 138, 140, 182
lifestyle 4, 122, 126, 130, 136, 157, 166, 170, 172–3, 189, 207
ligaments 66, 108, 113, 114, 158, 172, 175, 234
living conditions 138, 166, 182, 190, 205

Mary Rose, the 10, 68, 175, 215
mass graves 50, 56, **76**, 77, 82, 178, 179
material culture 29, 35–6, 71, 126, 143, 147, 229
media, the 2, 9, 21, 33, 95, 178
medical theory 154, 183

medical treatments 15, 154, 182, 183–9, 227, 228, 229
    surgery 183, 184, 192, 217, 236
medieval period, the 4, 8, 17, 50–1, 54, 55, 124, 130, 133, 145, 146, 154, 156, 157, 162, 183, 184, 185, 187, 189, 194, 198, 204, 206, 214, 216
    early (Anglo-Saxon) 48, 51, 52, 54, 59, 186, 187, 200, 207
Mediterranean, the 187, 207, 240
Mesolithic, the 42, 54, 202–3
migration patterns 11, 14, 79, 137, 138, 143, 144, 148, 150, 151, 164, 205–8, 211–12, 217, 222, 230, 233
minimum number of individuals (MNI) 120, 149
Møller-Christensen, Vilhelm 8, **9**
mortality 140, 156, 205, 235
    infant 58, 138, 140, 182
mortuary practices *see* funerary rituals
mummification 60, 62–4, 70
muscles 62, 68, 69, 108, 110, 113, 116, 125, 175–6, 227, 228, 235, 240
museum curators 21, 31, 82, 101, 216, 220
museums 2, 3, 4, 5, 12–13, 14, 15, 17, 21, 23, 24, 25, 28, 29, 30–2, 34, 35, 97, 100, 121, 197, 220, 221

Neanderthals 41, 202, 236
Neolithic period, the 43, 54, 133, 143, 144, 147, 167, 168, 175, 185, 186, 202–3, 208
Nepal 52, **165**
Netherlands, the 66, 127, 167, 173
New Zealand 18, 34
nomads 164, 236
Nubia 167, 203
nutrition 124, 145, 170, *see also* diet

occupations 10, 15, 121, 138, 148, 164, 168, 173–8, 190, 198, 207, 225
ossification 128–9, 135, 230
ossuaries 36, 120, 198

palaeodemography 10, 121, 136–40, 150, 151, 154, 156

Palaeolithic, the 12, 24, 28, 39, 41, 42, 236
palaeopathology 2, 7, 9, 146, 153–64, 189–90, 194
parasites 79, 237, 240, 242
pathogens 22, 30, 83, 153, 206, 210, 212, 213
Peru 63, 155, 185, 202, 208
Piltdown Man 8
plagues 50, 83, 155, 215, 237, *see also* disease
    Black Death, the 154–6, 226
Planning Policy Guidance Note 16 (PPG 16) 11, 221
police, the 24, 27, 57, 142
policies for the treatment of human remains 17, 18, 19
    BABAO's Code of Ethics 18, 100
politics 7, 14, 127, 178, 238
pollution **165**, 166–9, 205
polygenism 7, 142
Pompeii, Italy 68–9
population 7, 15, 22, 41, 140, 142, 143, 144, 147, 150, 155, 162, 167, 171, 180, 229
population-based studies 8, 9, 15, 146, 163, 189, 211, 219
populations 2, 5, 7, 10, 19, 55, 64, 71, 79, 121, 122, 125, 128, 130, 132, 133, 136–7, 138, 140, 141, 143, 144, 145, 146, 148, 150, 153, 154–5, 156, 158, 161, 164, 169, 172–3, 175, 180, 182, 203, 206, 207, 211–12, 213, 215, 220, 231
Portugal 4, 5, 130, 198, 202
post-medieval period, the 17, 18, 54, 60, 62, 82, 84, 121, 137–8, 146, 168, 169, 173, 186, 195, 198, 204, 206, 215
pottery 22, 46, 47, 91, 144, 167, 215
pregnancy 124, 138
prehistoric period, the 41, 54, 178, 214
preservation environments 2, 41, 56–7, 58, 59, 60, 61–70, 72, 79, 94, 201, 210
professional bodies 15, 36, 96
    American Anthropological Association 36
    American Association of Physical

Anthropologists 3, 6, 14, 36
Association of Environmental Archaeologists 6
British Association for Biological Anthropology and Osteoarchaeology (BABAO) 3, 6, 14, 18
Dental Anthropology Association 14
European Anthropological Association 3, 14
Institute of Field Archaeologists 17
Paleopathology Association 3, 6, 14
Society of American Archaeology 36
puberty 58, 123, 124, 127, 238
public consultation 21, 30–1
public health 23, 25, 60

radiocarbon dating *see* analytical techniques, dating
relatedness 141, 142, 148, 151, 211–12, 217, 221, 233, *see also* ancestry
relatives of the dead 18, 19, 20, 25, 26
religion 19, 21, 30, 31, 47, 48, 50, 51, 126, 230, 236, 238
religious attitudes to human remains 2, 17, 19, 33, 40, 51, 67
research projects using human remains 4, 12, 15, 107, 161, 219–20
Roman period, the 4, 39, 45–8, 52, 54, 58, 59, 67, 124, 137, 147, 154, 181, 184, 186, 187, 196, 203, 205, 207, 208, 241
    Driffield Terrace, York 46, 47, 181

sample sizes 4, 7, 8, 11, 54, 55, 122
Scandinavia 42, 48
settlement 22, 44, 45, 48, 70, 137
    fortified 178, 180
sex 4, 15, 35, 43, 45, 47, 59, 68, 77, 120, 121–3, 129, 134, 136, 138, 144, 149, 153, 167, 168, 170, 172, 174, 176, 177, 180, 182, 189, 199, 202, 203, 215, 233, 241
    transexualism/intersexuality 122, 233, 241
sex estimation 2, 105, 115, 121–6, 137,

140, 141, 144, 150, 210, 217, 222

Siberia 59, 60, 147

skeleton, the
  appendicular **108**, 109
  axial **108**, 109
  bones of the ear 79, 85
  bones of the extremities 58, 77,
    78, 79, 87, 101, 105, 111, 120,
    158
  bones of the limbs 58, 78, 87,
    109–10, 113, 159, 176
    femur 58, **119**, 129, 135, 176,
      199
    humerus 41, 135, 176, 187,
      199
    tibia 194, 199, 200
    ulna 58
  bones of the pelvis 77, 78, 85, 110,
    113, 123, 124, 125, 126, 134,
    135, 233
    pubic symphysis 77, 105, 113,
      134, 238
  bones of the shoulder girdle
    clavicle 78, 86, 128, 133, 135
    scapula 85, 87, 109
  bones of the thoracic cage 78, 87
    ribs 77, 85, 105, 108, 110, 134,
      135, 167, 192
    sternum 74, 77, 108, 179, 240
  joints 111, **112**, 113, 134, 158,
    227, 240
  skull, the 8, 41, **56**, 58, 66, 78, 85,
    86, 87, 95, 104, 108, 109, 110,
    113, 123, 124–6, 128, 134,
    141, 142–4, 148, **158**, 178–81,
    186, 194, 241
    cranial sutures 8, 134, 136,
      148, 240, 242
    jaws 58, 68, 78, 86, 87, 113,
      114, 128, 130, 131–2, **133**,
      146, 180
  teeth 2, 10, 42, 58, 77, 78, 79, 85,
    94–5, 101, 113, 114–15, 117,
    120, 123, 124, 128, 130, 135,
    136, 145, 146–7, 148–9, 196,
    197, 205, 207, 222, 225, 227,
    229, 237
    canines 114, 115, 123, **131**,
      132

development of 130–2, 133,
  230
incisors 114, 115, 117, **131**,
  132, 147
milk (deciduous) 114, 117,
  124, 131, 132, 146, 196
molars 114, 115, 117, **131**, 132,
  133
premolars 114, 115, 117, **131**,
  132
structure of 114–15
wear of 133, 135, 192
vertebrae 58, 77, 78, 85, 87, 110,
  113, 134, 180, 181, 192, 195,
  198

skeleton record sheets/forms 77, **78**,
  120

skeletons
  archaeological 121, 124, 126, 149
  modern 4, 13, 15, 125, 128, 130,
    150

skin 31, 63, 66, 69, 80, 83, 155, 169,
  187, 227, 229, 234, 238, 240

skulls 7, 45, 46, 67, 68, 85, 105, 141,
  142–3, 148, 154, 180, 186, 199

social identity 10, 123

social status 15, 132, 138, 140, 149,
  168, 170, 172–3, 177, 182, 189,
  202, 203, 206, 220

socio-economic status 21, 140, 206,
  222, *see also* social status

soft tissue 55, 63, 71, 83, 113, 126,
  128, 155–6, 158, 159, 197, 212–13
  preservation of 62, 64, 65,
    66, 67–8, 69, 71, 191,
    see also human remains,
    mummified

Spain 138, 228

'special interest' groups 19–20

spiritual concerns 22, 35, *see also*
  religious attitudes to human
  remains

Spong Hill, Norfolk 48, 118, 126, 128,
  161

stature 7, 15, 35, 121, 130, 144–5, 207

stones
  bladder 77, 79, 154

gall 77, 79, 161, 231
  kidney 77, 79
Sutton Hoo, Suffolk 48, 61
Sweden 8, 187, 188

taphonomy 56
tendons 66, 108, 110, 113, 128, 158,
  172, 175, 239, 240
trauma 154, 159, 179, 180, 188, 194–
  5, 198, 206
trepanation 8, 154, 184, 185–6, 192,
  199, 241

Ukraine, the 202–3
United Kingdom, the
  England 23–5, 26, 29, 41, 45, 145,
    165, 169, 182, 194, 203–4, 206
  Northern Ireland 23–4, 27, 29
  Scotland 23–4, 26–7, 29, 41, 42,
    43, 70, 182, 203, 207
  Wales 23–5, 26, 29, 41, 42, 182,
    203
United States of America, the 3, 6,
  18, 30, 34–7, 67, 83, 167, 200, 221,
  see also Americas, the, North
universities 2, 3, 11, 15, 17, 24, 28, 29,
  96, 97, 222, 223

variations/similarities in human
  remains, factors influencing
  136, 151, *see also* diet; disease;
  occupations
  childhood stress 42, 130, 145, 146
  genetics 8, 127, 130, 142–4, 145,
    146–8, 155, 173, 175, 177, 232
  physical activity 8, 121, 135, 145,
    148, 174–5, 177, 198, 199

Waldron, Tony 9, 10
weaning 58, 196, 204–5, 241
weapons 45, 47, 123, 178, 179, 180,
  195, 200, 229, 238
Wells, Calvin 8, 9

zoology 8